BEYOND SUSTAINABLE

Beyond Sustainable discusses the relationship between human-beings and the constructed environments of habitation we create living in the Anthropocene, an increasingly volatile and unpredictable landscape of certain change.

This volume accepts that human-beings have reached a moment beyond climatological and ecological crisis. It asks not how we resolve the crisis but, rather, how we can cope with, or adapt to, the irreversible changes in the earth-system by rethinking how we choose to inhabit the world-ecology. Through an examination of numerous historical and contemporary projects of architecture and art, as well as observations in philosophy, ecology, evolutionary biology, genetics, neurobiology and psychology, this book reimagines architecture capable of influencing and impacting who we are, how we live, what we feel and even how we evolve.

Beyond Sustainable provides students and academics with a single comprehensive overview of this architectural reconceptualization, which is grounded in an ecologically inclusive and co-productive understanding of architecture.

Ryan Ludwig is an architect and educator teaching at the University of Cincinnati as an Assistant Professor in the School of Architecture and Interior Design, in the college of Design Architecture Art and Planning. He is the founding principal of Ludwig-ArchOffice (L-AO), a design and research studio focused on inclusive and adaptable approaches to architectural design. He is a recipient of a Fall 2018 MacDowell Fellowship and Centrum Artist Residency; is a co-editor of the book *The Function of Form*; and has previously published essays in numerous online and print journals.

BEYOND SUSTAINABLE

Architecture's Evolving
Environments of Habitation

Ryan Ludwig

NEW YORK AND LONDON

First published 2021
by Routledge
52 Vanderbilt Avenue, New York, NY 10017

and by Routledge
2 Park Square, Milton Park, Abingdon, Oxon, OX14 4RN

Routledge is an imprint of the Taylor & Francis Group, an informa business

© 2021 Taylor & Francis

The right of Ryan Ludwig to be identified as author of this work has
been asserted by him in accordance with sections 77 and 78 of the
Copyright, Designs and Patents Act 1988.

All rights reserved. No part of this book may be reprinted or
reproduced or utilised in any form or by any electronic, mechanical,
or other means, now known or hereafter invented, including
photocopying and recording, or in any information storage or retrieval
system, without permission in writing from the publishers.

Trademark notice: Product or corporate names may be trademarks
or registered trademarks, and are used only for identification and
explanation without intent to infringe.

Library of Congress Cataloging-in-Publication Data
Names: Ludwig, Ryan, author.
Title: Beyond sustainable: architecture's evolving environments of
habitation / Ryan Ludwig.
Description: New York, NY: Routledge, 2021. | Includes
bibliographical references and index.
Identifiers: LCCN 2020028920 (print) | LCCN 2020028921 (ebook) |
ISBN 9780367232702 (hardback) | ISBN 9780367232696 (paperback) |
ISBN 9780429279058 (ebook)
Subjects: LCSH: Architecture and anthropology. | Architecture—Philosophy.
Classification: LCC NA2543.A58 L835 2021 (print) | LCC NA2543.A58 (ebook) |
DDC 720.1—dc23
LC record available at https://lccn.loc.gov/2020028920
LC ebook record available at https://lccn.loc.gov/2020028921

ISBN: 978-0-367-23270-2 (hbk)
ISBN: 978-0-367-23269-6 (pbk)
ISBN: 978-0-429-27905-8 (ebk)

Typeset in Bembo
by codeMantra

To Amanda,
   with much love, respect and gratitude.

Decomposers
in each other's arms
warp and weft
closely woven from
earth's elders
Glacial erratics, the oldest
carriers of prophecy
I sit among them.
Mutualism, from graceful longevity
It is changing now.
You're breathing
atmospheric ecosystems
our eyes in climate chaos.
The rise, at the edge
emerging raw and bare.
Another era, say —
Pay attention
They're bringing you an eye-blink of
time.

—by Amanda Zackem

CONTENTS

List of Figures	*ix*
Foreword by Joyce Hwang	*xv*
Acknowledgments	*xviii*

Introduction: Architecture Living in the New World-Ecology   1

PART I
Technological Mediation   **27**

1   In Pursuit of Comfort: From Campfire to Smart Home   29

2   Wall Performance: Two Views of Nature, the Visual
and the Visceral   59

3   Of Life and Death: The Interior Atmosphere-Environments
of the Greenhouse and the Gas Chamber   85

PART II
Environmental Identification   **113**

4   Back Home from the Frontier: Considering an
Eco-Effective Approach to Design   115

viii Contents

5 Dwelling Deep: Toward a Transpersonal Architecture
of Self-Realization!   146

PART III
Bio-Physical Inter-Action   **181**

6 Invisible Worlds: Constructing an Architecture of the
Sensorium   183

7 Beyond the Prosthesis: Architectural Augmentation and
Human Evolution   218

8 The Bio-Physical Dwelling: Shūsaku Arakawa and
Madeline Gins's Bioscleave House (Lifespan Extending Villa)   250

Afterword   *279*
Index   *285*

FIGURES

I.1 Waterhouse Hawkins, comparative skeletal anatomy of various primates, 1863 2

I.2 (a) CO_2 in the atmosphere and annual emissions (1750–2019); (b) Influence of all major human-produced greenhouse gases (1979–2018); (c) CO_2 during ices ages and warm periods for the past 80,000 years 9

I.3 Global temperature anomalies in annual land temperature from 1880 to 2020. Anomalies are with respect to the twentieth-century average 11

I.4 Raging forest fire, Los Padres, CA, December 2017 12

I.5 Niche partitioning of insectivorous wood Warblers 16

I.6 Spatial aspects of different types of speciation 18

I.7 Arakawa and Madeline Gins, *Museum of Living Bodies*, digital rendering, 2003 21

I.8 Philippe Rahm architectes, *Central Park, The Meteorological Garden*, 2012–2020 22

1.1 Inside of a Bushman's hut, 1861 32

1.2 Eugene-Emmanuel Viollet-le-Duc, the first shelter, 1876 34

1.3 Eugene-Emmanuel Viollet-le-Duc, the first hut, 1876 35

1.4 Marc-Antonie Laugier, frontispiece to second edition of *Essai sur l'architecture*, 1755 37

1.5 OMG! (O'Donnell Miller Group), *Primitive Hut*, concept rendering, 2017 39

1.6 OMG! (O'Donnell Miller Group), *Primitive Hut*, photo of completed pavilion, 2017 39

1.7 Ice age shelter composed of Mammoth bones, Mezhirich, Ukraine, ca. 13,000 BC 40

x Figures

1.8 Filarete, Adam covering his head with his hands from the first rain, ca. 1464 — 43

1.9 Le Corbusier, a primitive temple, [1923] 1986 — 44

1.10 Le Corbusier, sketches of early structures grouped according to the primary forms of box, tent, flat roof and vaulted building types, 1928/1998 — 46

1.11 Le Corbusier, huttes des crannoges d'Irlande, 1928 — 47

1.12 Cesare Cesariano, the discovery of fire, 1521 — 49

1.13 Early schematic drawing of early air-conditioning system installed at Sackett & Wilhelms, 1902 — 52

1.14 Environmental spatial conditions produced around the campfire — 54

2.1 Le Corbusier, four functions of architecture – standing, carrying, covering, enveloping, 1948 — 63

2.2 Le Corbusier, rectangular prism sketches, October 5, 1929 — 67

2.3 Le Corbusier and Pierre Jeanneret, *Centrosoyus,* facade study, beginning of 1929 — 68

2.4 Le Corbusier and Pierre Jeanneret, *Centrosoyus,* study model, beginning of 1929 — 69

2.5 Le Corbusier, the window wall, the ribbon window, the mixed wall, nonbearing masonry or masonry cladding — 70

2.6 Le Corbusier, Pierre Jeanneret and Gustave Lyon, principles of *mur neutralisants* and of *aeration punctuelle,* 1928 — 71

2.7 Le Corbusier, sketches of the machines for air exacte, October 5, 1929 — 75

2.8 Le Corbusier and Pierre Jeanneret, *Centrosoyus,* as per wall section at the *pan de verre,* January 1930 — 78

2.9 Le Corbusier and Pierre Jeanneret, *Centrosoyus,* office interior perspective drawing, October 20, 1928 — 79

3.1 Salomon de Caus, portable wooden orangery — 86

3.2 Plant-house heated by Musgrave's iron slow combustion stove — 88

3.3 Dutch forcing-frame with brick back wall flue proportioned for proper draw and maximum length of smoke path — 88

3.4 Charles McIntosh, section through vinery and pine-pit at Dalkeith Palace — 90

3.5 J. C. Loudon, Comparison of 12 historical hothouse sections from 1699 to 1817 — 91

3.6 J. C. Loudon, Section drawing of a campanulated hothouse — 96

3.7 J. C. Loudon, ridge and furrow roof section — 94

3.8 Joseph Paxton, *Victoria Regia House* at Chatsworth, interior, engraving — 97

3.9 Joseph Paxton, *Victoria Regia House* at Chatsworth, section and elevation — 98

3.10 J. C. Loudon, section through proposed mechanical tropical aquatic house — 99

Figures **xi**

3.11 World War I French soldiers making a gas and flame attack on German trenches in Flanders, Belgium 102
3.12 United States, Army, Signal Corps., "The gas attack," ca.1918/1919 102
3.13 Rawlings state prison in Wyoming lethal gas chamber, shown on November 17, 1936 104
3.14 Longitudinal section drawing of a delousing chamber 107
3.15 Auschwitz, Poland, construction of greenhouses, south of Camp I, 1941 108
3.16 Auschwitz, Poland, a prisoner working in a greenhouse, south of Camp I, 1941 109
4.1 Council worker dusting DDT (Dichloro-Diphenyl-Trichloroethane) on mosquito breeding water by using a hand operated machine, Brisbane, Australia, 1949 117
4.2 Ford tri-motor spraying DDT (Dichloro-Diphenyl-Trichloroethane). Western spruce budworm control project. Powder River control unit, Oregon, 1955 117
4.3 Rachel Carson speaking before Senate Government Operations subcommittee studying pesticide spraying, 1963 120
4.4 (a) Global cement and fossil energy production from 1900 to 2016; (b) Global process CO_2 emissions from cement production, with 95% confidence level reflecting data availability and reliability 121
4.5 Total anthropogenic GHG emissions ($GtCO_2eq/yr$) by economic sectors 122
4.6 William McDonough + Partners, *Method manufacturing facility*, photo of exterior, 2015 130
4.7 Energy circuit diagrams of a house 134
4.8 Systems diagram of a pulsing ecosystem and mechanisms 136
4.9 Pulsing paradigm graph showing the cycle of growth, diversification, succession, climax and collapse 137
4.10 Anna Heringer and Eike Roswag, *METI School*, photo west elevation, 2006 138
4.11 Anna Heringer and Eike Roswag, *METI School*, photo upper floor classroom spaces combined into a multifunctional hall, 2006 139
4.12 Anna Heringer and Eike Roswag, *METI School*, photo exterior detail, 2006 139
4.13 Anna Heringer and Stegano Mori, *Ways of Life: Fachwerk Capriccio*, concept drawings and sketches, 2017 141
5.1 Energy transformation diagrams 149
5.2 US energy consumption by energy source for 2018 150
5.3 *The Limits to Growth* study World model diagram, 1972 version 154

xii Figures

5.4 *The Limits to Growth* study feedback loops of population, capital, services and resources diagram 156

5.5 *The Limits to Growth* study World model "Standard" run diagram, 1972 version 157

5.6 *The Limits to Growth* study World model II "Stabilized" run diagram, 1972 version 158

5.7 *The Limits to Growth* study World model "Stabilized" run diagram, 2004 version 159

5.8 Joyce Hwang, *Bat Tower*, concept sketch, 2010 172

5.9 Joyce Hwang, *Bat Tower*, photos completed structure, 2010 173

5.10 Joyce Hwang, *Habitat Wall: Chicago*, photo of installation, 2015 174

5.11 Joyce Hwang and Nerea Feliz, *Hidden in plain sight*, axon drawing, 2019 175

5.12 Joyce Hwang and Nerea Feliz, *Hidden in plain sight*, rendering, 2019 176

6.1 Frederick Kiesler, Man = Heredity + Environment, diagram, September 1939 184

6.2 Frederick Kiesler, Study on perception, New York, ink on paper, ca. 1937–1941 186

6.3 Frederick Kiesler, Study on perception, New York, ink on paper, ca. 1937–1941 186

6.4 Frederick Kiesler, Study on human perception, New York, ink on paper, ca. 1937–1941 189

6.5 Frederick Kiesler, Correlation chart of book-storing, drawing, September 1939 192

6.6 Jakob von Uexküll and G. Kriszat, functional cycle of perception diagram, 1934 193

6.7 Jakob von Uexküll and G. Kriszat, Environment and Umwelt of the Paramecium, diagram, 1934 194

6.8 Sean Lally (Weathers), *SIM House*, simulative thermal studies, 2006 197

6.9 Sean Lally (Weathers), *SIM House*, physical model study, 2006 197

6.10 Philippe Rahm architectes, *Central Park*, human physiological diagrams 202

6.11 Philippe Rahm architectes, *Interior Weather*, drawing, 2006 203

6.12 Philippe Rahm architectes, *Interior Weather*, image of installation, 2006 204

6.13 Philippe Rahm architectes, *Mollier Houses*, section drawing, 2005 206

6.14 Philippe Rahm architectes, *Domestic Astronomy*, thermal section diagram, 2009 207

6.15	Philippe Rahm architectes, *Domestic Astronomy*, photo of installation, 2009	207
6.16	Philippe Rahm architectes, *Central Park, The Meteorological Garden*, diagrams of masterplan composition, 2012–2020	210
6.17	Philippe Rahm architectes, *Central Park, The Meteorological Garden*, diagrams of Anticyclone cooling device, 2012–2020	211
6.18	Philippe Rahm architectes, *Central Park, The Meteorological Garden*, photo Cold Light radiation cooling device, 2012–2020	212
6.19	Philippe Rahm architectes, *Central Park, The Meteorological Garden*, photo Stratus Cloud evaporative cooling device, 2012–2020	212
7.1	Reaction norms examples, phenotype (P) is drawn as a function of environment (E) reflective of different genotypes (G_1 and G_2)	220
7.2	Example of an actual reaction norms for viability of fourth chromosome homozygotes of *Drosophila pseudoobscura*	221
7.3	Douglas Darden, *Oxygen House*, concept sketches	225
7.4	Douglas Darden, *Oxygen House*, composite ideogram, 1993	226
7.5	Douglas Darden, *Oxygen House*, section drawing, 1993	228
7.6	Philippe Rahm and Jean-Gilles Décosterd, *Hormonorium*, plan drawing of installation, 2002	229
7.7	Philippe Rahm and Jean-Gilles Décosterd, *Hormonorium*, photo, 2002	230
7.8	Philippe Rahm and Jean-Gilles Décosterd, *Hormonorium*, diagram of the neuro-physiological impact, 2002	232
7.9	Conrad H. Waddington, part of an epigenetic landscape, 1957	241
7.10	Conrad H. Waddington, the complex system of interactions underlying the epigenetic landscape, 1957	242
7.11	Conrad H. Waddington rganic selection (the Baldwin effect) and genetic assimilation, 1957	243
8.1	Arakawa and Madeline Gins, *Landing Site Study*, digital rendering, 1994	251
8.2	Arakawa and Madeline Gins, *Body Proper + Architectural Surround = ARCHITECTURAL BODY*, digital rendering, 1997	253
8.3	Arakawa and Madeline Gins, *Bioscleave House (Lifespan Extending Villa)*, photo of exterior, completed 2008	255
8.4	Arakawa and Madeline Gins, *Bioscleave House (Lifespan Extending Villa)*, view to the south, digital rendering, 2004	256
8.5	Arakawa and Madeline Gins, *Bioscleave House (Lifespan Extending Villa)*, photo of interior window wall, completed 2008	257
8.6	Arakawa and Madeline Gins, *Bioscleave House (Lifespan Extending Villa)*, photo of interior, completed 2008	257

xiv Figures

8.7 Arakawa and Madeline Gins, *Bioscleave House (Lifespan Extending Villa)*, photos of variations of the interior floor surface, completed 2008   258

8.8 Arakawa and Madeline Gins, *Reversible Destiny Lofts – Mitaka (In Memory of Helen Keller)*, digital rendering, 2001   259

8.9 Arakawa and Madeline Gins, *External Genome House – Shidami*, photo of exterior, 2005   260

8.10 Arakawa and Madeline Gins, *External Genome House – Shidami*, photo of interior, 2005   261

8.11 Inge Bruggeman, *A Crisis Ethicists' Directions for Use – or How to be at Home in a Residence-cum-Laboratory*, 2003   262

8.12 Arakawa and Madeline Gins, *Bioscleave House (Lifespan Extending Villa)*, digital rendering study, 2002   264

8.13 Arakawa and Madeline Gins, *Site of Reversible Destiny IV*, architectural model, 1981–1993   265

8.14 Arakawa and Madeline Gins, *Bioscleave House (Lifespan Extending Villa)*, digital rendering plan, 2006   268

8.15 Arakawa and Madeline Gins, *Isle of Reversible Destiny – Fukuoka*, digital rendering, 2003   271

8.16 Arakawa and Madeline Gins, *Bioscleave House (Lifespan Extending Villa)*, photo of wall detail, completed 2008   273

8.17 Arakawa and Madeline Gins, *Bioscleave House (Lifespan Extending Villa)*, photo of interior, completed 2008   273

9.1 Comparative maps showing the concentrations of nitrogen dioxide and other pollutive emissions over China before and then during the quarantine, January and February of 2020   281

FOREWORD

Joyce Hwang

In *Our Common Future*, the 1987 publication also known as the Brundtland Report, the United Nations articulated what would become one of the most frequently cited definitions of sustainability: "Sustainable development is development that meets the needs of the present without compromising the ability of future generations to meet their own needs." The clarity and urgency of the report ushered in a new set of global priorities and set new progressive initiatives into motion. Environmental protection and social equity emerged as factors to coordinate along with aims for economic growth. Now, over 30 years later, we are familiar with mantras and touchstones of sustainability: conservation of natural resources, renewable and green energy, lowering greenhouse gas emissions – the list goes on. Yet, despite our seeming familiarity with the principles of sustainable thinking, one could argue that their characterizations and implications continue to transform and evolve. What does it mean to be sustainable now, in the age of the Anthropocene? And what will it look like in the future? These are the fundamental questions that Ryan Ludwig posits in provoking us to look beyond familiar tropes.

This book is an invitation to examine the gaps in our common conceptions of sustainability and to explore within and beyond them. While environmental urgencies irrefutably require attention from the sciences, it is also critical to acknowledge that our environments have the capacity to "foster co-productive physiological, psychological and affective responses," as noted by Ludwig, and that these responses bear consequences in shaping substantial decisions. Consider, for example, the role of flora and fauna in broader ecological discussions. At one level, they are "valued" as forms of ecosystem services. Efforts to "save" species – such as the campaign to address Colony Collapse Disorder in bee populations – are driven by the rationale of animals-as-service. Foreshadowing

xvi Foreword

the decline of bee populations which pollinate gardens and farms, thus limiting food production, poses a threat that drives us into action. At another level, however, are the ever-complex debates about species conservation. While animal extinction is an important issue that has ecological impacts around the planet, how do we as a society negotiate the territory of species conservation when ecosystem services are not at the forefront of the conversation? How does one decide to save rhinos and tigers as opposed to moths and spiders? Conservation biologists already use the term "charisma" to describe traits in flagship species, defining "charismatic species" as those that "serve as symbols and rallying points to stimulate conservation awareness and action."[1] While many subjective factors and debates swirl around how – or even whether – to use charismatic species in conservation agendas,[2] it is clear that affective resonances of "nonhuman charisma" have significant impacts on the cultural perceptions of organisms, thus contributing to the politics of animal conservation.[3] At times, the use of affective charisma even runs in contrast to environmental initiatives. For example, "kangaroo culling," the Australian government's ongoing plan to kill a quota of kangaroos, is presented as a means to protect grasslands and wildlife. However, during the catastrophic Australian wildfires in 2019, when massive numbers of wildlife were perishing in the flames, fundraising campaigns around the world used the figure of the kangaroo as an icon for saving animals and restoring habitats.[4]

Indeed, the power of affective resonance in species conservation is far from trivial. While the tasks of confronting grand challenges today necessarily dwell in realms of scientific inquiry, it is also critical to recognize the instrumentality of producing affect and deploying it in tandem with techno-scientific pursuits. Powers of persuasion are becoming increasingly essential as the world grapples with ever more pressing ecological and socio-economic situations. Climate Change is perhaps the planet's most imperative challenge at this time, yet – despite the overwhelming scientific evidence to support its projections – environmental activists are still breathlessly developing campaigns to educate the public and bring awareness to critical data. Given the necessity for activism in our current social and political climate, it is crucial to embrace the capacity of resonance-production to motivate a shift in perception. The question, therefore, is how to translate our focus from "solving the world's problems" to "living together collectively in this world." In other words, how do we move beyond viewing environmental and social challenges as a detached observer toward understanding them through a more immersive, empathetic lens?

Perhaps this shift in perception is the secret weapon to motivating change. At the time of this writing, the world has been engulfed by the COVID-19 pandemic and has pivoted into modes of living that were not previously imaginable, except in times of war. Does it take an acute emergency to force the world's populations to reconsider how we live? If so, why has the world not reacted to Climate Change with the same level of urgency? Do we require the perception of an acute crisis rather than a chronic condition for society to respond quickly to environmental warnings? It is abundantly clear that we live in a world of unpredictable change and that we need to adapt in dynamic ways, not only in terms of managing life's logistics but also in terms of re-considering our subjective, affective sensibilities. Along with these fluctuating changes is the ever-pressing question: how much are we willing to challenge our sense of normalcy? Ludwig asks poignant questions that resonate in the face of COVID-19 – as well as the Climate Crisis – as we reconsider our physical, spatial environments in the collective world:

> How might architecture begin to provide some light from within the darkness of the tunnel we now find ourselves? How might it help us avert "madness" derived from our "profound mutation in our relation to the world" and instead help us adapt to "Our" new "world"?

Beyond Sustainable begins to explore these questions by shifting away from the notion that the environment is a problem to "neutralize" toward strategies to intensify our experiences in the environment instead. A time could not be better than now to launch into these discussions.

April 2020

Notes

1 V. H. Heywood and R. T. Watson (ed.). *Global biodiversity assessment. United Nations Environment Programme* (Cambridge, UK: Cambridge University Press, 1995).
2 Frédéric Ducarme, Gloria Luque, and Franck Courchamp. "What are "charismatic species" for conservation biologists?" *BioSciences Master Reviews* 1 (2013): 1–8.
3 Jamie Lorimer. *Wildlife in the anthropocene: Conservation after nature* (Minneapolis: University of Minnesota Press, 2015).
4 WWF-Australia (World Wildlife Fund): https://donate.wwf.org.au/make-a-donation/monthly-donation?gclid=EAIaIQobChMIrMv95fv06AIVQP7jBx085wVdEAAYASAAEgLBRPD_BwE#gs.3w2tnj (accessed April 15, 2020).

ACKNOWLEDGMENTS

The evolution of this book has taken shape over a number of years, from seeds planted a while ago directly exploring and experiencing the natural world, its more recent trajectory having been shaped through numerous interactions and conversations with many for whom I maintain immense gratitude. The architectural germination of these seeds was most directly fostered through participation in graduate seminars taught by Sanford Kwinter, whose fearless and provocative writing expanded architecture for me into a dynamic field of potentials previously unseen, and Catherine Ingraham, whose intense consideration of the human condition laid bare an architecture previously unfelt. Though the possibility of this book resided under the surface for quite some time, the courage to take it on in a serious way would not have materialized without the encouragement of Caroline O'Donnell, to whom I extend much respect and appreciation. Though she probably did not know it when we first discussed the ideas explored within, her advice and words of support were heard at just the right moment, helping me believe such a project was possible.

This book has been impacted and motivated by many friends, colleagues and teachers, whose support, encouragement, input, advice and generosity have also made its publication possible: Joyce Hwang, Andrea Simitch, Omar Kahn, Mark Shepard, Curt Gambetta, Martin Miller, Richard Rosa, Michael Meredith, Will Provine, Jean-Gabriel Neukomm, Christopher Ketcham ST Luk, Miwako Tezuka, Joke Post and Andrew MacNair. Others along the way have provided both their time and energy, for which I am extremely grateful. Many thanks to Sarosh Anklesaria, who provided sharp constructive feedback when I needed it most. To Marianne Okal, thank you for your generosity and diligent translation work in a field undoubtedly not your own. Much respect and gratitude to Alex Witteman: your early dedication to the project and great efforts researching the many images included within have contributed greatly to its fruition. And thank you to my parents, Jane and Robert, who helped instill in me the necessary confidence and focus without which this book would not have been possible, and Sharon and Ron: thank you for your gracious enthusiasm, interest and ceaseless encouragement.

This project has also been supported by numerous institutions and organizations; my great appreciation to: the MacDowell fellowship program; Centrum Artist Residency; the Reversible Destiny Foundation; Cornell Department of Architecture and the College of Architecture Art and Planning; University of Cincinnati, School of Architecture and Interior Design; and Jill Meissner-Wolfbeisser at the Austrian Frederick and Lillian Kiesler Private Foundation. And to those people and institutions who graciously granted the use of images in this publication, thank you: Philippe Rahm, Sean Lally, Anna Heringer, Kurt Hoerbst, Allison (Darden) Collins, Dennis Meadows, Inge Bruggeman, the Carrier Corporation, the Walter Havighurst Special Collections & University Archives at Miami University, the Avery Architectural & Fine Arts Library at Columbia University and the Yad Vashem Archives.

Though the seeds of this book may have been planted long ago by a deep desire to understand the magic embodied in the living world – a curiosity engendered by my grandfather Dr. Donald Brundage, who helped to open up this new world and lay it at my feet – its coming to fruition would not have been possible without the unending support of Amanda Zackem; with much love, gratitude and respect, thank you.

INTRODUCTION

Architecture Living in the New World-Ecology

> Design is the cardinal means by which human beings have long tried to modify their natural environment, piecemeal and wholesale. The physical surroundings had to be made more habitable and more in keeping with raising aspirations.
>
> (Neutra 1954, 5)

> That entire concept of *environment* versus the *organism* now seems to experts an abstraction, perhaps altogether offkey and certainly often impractical to operate with. Neither physically nor biochemically nor sociologically can the individual really be segregated or isolated as a separate entity.
>
> (Neutra 1954, 12)

> It has become imperative that in designing our physical environment we should consciously raise the fundamental question of survival, in the broadest sense of the term.
>
> (Neutra 1954, 86)

Whether as a Bedouin tent in the desert, a primitive hut in the woods or a ranch house on a suburban cul-de-sac, architecture is, and has been, the immediate form of resistance to the various natures humans have inhabited. The words of the modernist architect Richard Neutra, quoted above from his remarkable 1954 book *Survival through Design*, describe several observations of humanity's long-standing ambition to create more suitable environments of habitation, both by want and by need. In this way our subsistence can be tied not only to our biology and social relations, but also directly to the modifications we make to our surrounding environment – toward the "production of nature"[1] byway of the architectural constructions we create and call "home." Architectural

2 Introduction

environmental habitation understood in this way, as a tool or technology human-beings have deployed to modify and survive "in-the-world," amounts to a kind of revolt against nature, what the Austro-German philosopher Peter Sloterdijk has called an "insurrection against nature...which harks back to the very early stages of evolution" (Sloterdijk 2011, 25). The cultural historian Lewis Mumford writing in his book *Technics and Civilization* describes all of humanity's technological efforts in the following way:

> In back of the development of tools and machines lies the attempt to modify the environment in such a way as to fortify and sustain the human organism: the effort is either to extend the powers of the otherwise unarmed organism, or to *manufacture outside the body* a set of conditions more favorable toward maintaining its equilibrium and ensuring its survival. Instead of a physiological adaptation to the cold, like the growth of hair or the habit of hibernation, there is an *environmental adaptation*, such as that made possible by the use of clothes and the erection of shelters.[2]
>
> *(Mumford 1963, 10)*

Like the first stone deliberately fashioned by hand into useful implement, architecture has implicitly shaped our evolution "from Ape to Man"[3] (Figure I.1) and by extension, the natural world around us. Though, despite this essentialized contribution to humanity's survival, architecture's creative environmental potential and the possibility of it taking on a more *explicit* adaptive responsibility has largely been overlooked by architects beyond the implicit demands

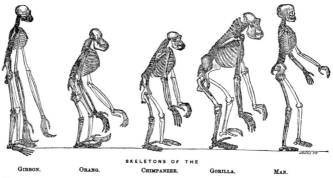

FIGURE I.1 Waterhouse Hawkins, comparative skeletal anatomy of various primates: Gibbon, Orangutan, Chimpanzee, Gorilla and Man. The skeleton of the Gibbon has been drawn at twice its natural size for comparison. Drawn from specimens in the Museum of the Royal College of Surgeons, 1863. Drawing by Warehouse Hawkins. Reprinted from Thomas H. Huxley. *Evidence as to Man's Place in Nature* (New York: D. Appleton and Company, 1863) 3.

of environmental neutralization, thermal equilibrium and the ultimate benefactor of both, human comfort. Simultaneously, the modifications humans have made to the world in the pursuit of maintaining equilibrium and advancing their survival, dominated by the sweeping advancements of modern technics and the current system of global capital production, accumulation and exchange, have not come without extraordinary consequences – immediately advantageous to some, but over time deleterious to "All." *Beyond Sustainable* recognizes that humanity's global ascent since the "long" sixteenth century[4] has, in the twentieth century, been propelled predominantly by its total embrace of fossil fuels as a cheap form of highly concentrated energy, transforming humanity into a dominant global force and prompting an increasingly volatile landscape of ecological but also political, economic and social change.[5] This impact on the planet was formally articulated in 2000 by Nobel Prize-winning atmospheric chemist Paul Cruzten and biologist Eugene F. Stoermer when they proposed that human actions have created a definitive geological epoch they called the Anthropocene.[6] Now, 20 years later, the term has been expansively used outside of the geological community becoming part of the popular lexicon. Its use has helped to activate a further awareness of the destabilizing and deleterious effects humanity's cumulative actions have had on the earth-system, helping to also initiate the realization of a burgeoning *climatological* and *ecological* "crisis."[7]

As part of the Gifford Lectures on natural theology delivered in Edinburgh in February of 2013 and later published in an English translation as *Facing Gaia*, the French social theorist Bruno Latour pushes this realization a step further when he describes how our relationship to the environment, to the earth-system, has already been radically altered, "shifted from a mere ecological crisis into what should instead be called a *profound mutation in our relation to the world*" (Latour 2017, 8). Additionally, he states that an alternation to one's "relation to the world" is in fact the "scholarly" term for madness (Latour 2017, 10) – a pathology brought about by the radical transformation of the planet's climates and the ecologies it supports already underway. Latour describes how this madness has manifested in at least four distinct ways: (1) those who have heard the threats, but are intent on staying calm. At the end of this avenue there are two types of people: either those who are outright "climate deniers" or those who have unconditional faith that God will maintain their salvation through prayer[8] (Latour 2017, 11); (2) those who have heard the threats, interpreting them as a call for even greater mechanization and domination over nature through what they call "climate" or "geo" engineering as a total solution to our climate problems[9] (Latour 2017, 12); (3) those who have heard the threats and come to the conclusion that the situation cannot be ignored, but that it's also impossible to remedy; stirring anger, but ultimately overwhelming them resulting in sadness and depression; and (4) those who have heard the threats and believe that it's not too late, and that if we act rationally and face the situation head-on, the threat can be mitigated and crisis averted (Latour 2017, 12).

4 Introduction

And so, Latour provides the following assessment of this madness from which *Beyond Sustainable* will set forth as it relates to a reconsideration of the design and construction of the architectural environments we inhabit and their potential role in *coping with* and/or *adapting to* this *"profound mutation in our relation to the world."*

> No doubt about it, ecology drives people crazy; this has to be our point of departure – not with the goal of finding a cure, just so we can learn to survive without getting carried away by denial, or hubris, or depression, or hope for a reasonable solution, or retreat into the desert. There is no cure for the condition of belonging to the world. But, by taking care, we can cure ourselves of believing that we do not belong to it, that the essential question lies elsewhere, that what happens to the world does not concern us. The time is past for hoping to "get through it." We are indeed, as they say, "in a tunnel," except that we won't see light at the end. In these matters, hope is a bad counselor, since we are not in a crisis. We can no longer say "this, too, will pass." We're going to have to get used to it. *It's definitive.*
>
> *(Latour 2017, 13)*

The "it" here is twofold; "it" is both the unrelenting fact of anthropogenic climatological and ecological instability, currently referred to as a "crisis" by news headlines, action groups, politicians and even the current Pope Francis in his astonishing Encyclical Letter "On Care for Our Common House."[10] But the "it" is also the changing world itself, to which we "belong" and are integrally bound, unable to separate ourselves from its changing conditions. If, as Latour argues, defining the current moment as "crisis" no longer accurately reflects the reality on the ground – or in the air, in the sea or in the soil – because to be in "crisis" implies that there will be a time in the future when the "crisis" will be neutralized, returning things back to "normal," then, he argues, our only sane option is to *cope*, to *adapt*, toward a more co-productive relation to "Our" changing world.[11] Accepting this fundamental reframing, *Beyond Sustainable* considers how the design of the constructed architectural environment, reimagined as an active creator of evolving "environmental potentials" of habitation, may be capable of influencing and impacting who we are, how we live, what we feel and even how we evolve in "Our" changing world. It considers how architecture might radically leverage these potentials further toward the *explicit* adaptive benefit of human-beings as well as the collective "network" of community actors with which human-beings inter-act and ultimately depend.

To more easily explore this architectural possibility, *Beyond Sustainable* is organized into three parts: (1) *Technological Mediation*, (2) *Environmental Identification* and (3) *Biophysical Inter-Action*. Each part starts from the same set of observations and understandings outlined in this introduction, but can be read independently, offering a different architectural conceptualization for confronting, *coping* and *adapting* to the current moment beyond climatological-ecological "crisis." At a time after "crisis," in the midst of catastrophic changes in the earth-system, how might these three conceptualizations offer alternative trajectories to how we choose to live-in-the-world? How might architects move beyond the design of individual spaces, buildings and cities toward the goal of a "sustainable," unilateral equilibrium with the surrounding environment to instead develop multivalent organizations of evolving "environmental potentials" capable of co-productive human-architecture-environment habitations?

Part 1, "Technological Mediation," considers how the architectural constructs we design provide a means for creating more habitable, more livable, interior milieus through the neutralization of detrimental external circumstances and the amplification of co-productive interior conditions. Chapter 1 begins with an examination of different narratives concerning the origin of architecture as a form of environmental technological mediation. It articulates the concept of the *architectural* "dwelling place" defined as the set of specific elements, strategies, technologies and materials humans recognize and implement toward the mediation of their surroundings and the production of more habitable interior conditions. It considers architectural origin narratives from Bernard Rudofsky, Viollet Le-Duc, Marc-Antoine Laugier, André Leroi-Gourhan, Leon Batista Alberti, Filarete, Le Corbusier, Vitruvius, Gottfried Semper and Reyner Banham. The chapter concludes with an examination of the more recent personal technological advancements taking place in many wealthy countries embodied by the "smart" home, leading toward a yearning for *radical stability* and the reinforcement of a sedentary environmental habitation. Chapter 2 examines in detail Le Corbusier's Centrosoyus building in Moscow as an extreme instance of early twentieth-century environmental technological mediation between exterior climate and the construction of a habitable interior atmosphere. It examines the use of the *pan de verre* and the proposed mechanical systems of *aération ponctuelle* and the *mur neutralisant*, revealing how an extreme separation between exterior and interior was principally motivated by Le Corbusier's desire for an aesthetic purity of form. Chapter 3 considers Reyner Banham's concept of an "environmentalist" architectural project and the twentieth-century *explication* of the atmosphere-environment as proposed by philosopher Peter Sloterdijk. These ideas are defined by architecture's capacity to create intentioned interior atmosphere-environments capable of cultivating spaces conducive to maintaining or even amplifying life as demonstrated in the greenhouse, and in contrast, the possibility of articulating its atmospheric potential toward the construction of spaces intent on occasioning death as demonstrated in the gas chamber.

Part 2, "Environmental Identification," questions broadly the implications of the current disciplinary model of sustainability as an effective strategy toward our radically changing world, suggesting the need for an alternative model capable of helping us better *cope* and *adapt* to the current and future history of the earth-system. Chapter 4 explicitly questions the sustainable architectural project as currently practiced, noting that its approach is largely founded upon ongoing technological advancements rather than challenging how we choose

6 Introduction

to "live-in-the-world." It examines William McDonough and Michael Braungart's Cradle to Cradle, eco-effective and upcycling approaches, acknowledging the benefits of these strategies, but also their limitations by maintaining a grounding within the current system of global capital production, accumulation and exchange – a system dependent on continuous growth, despite the limitations of our finite planet. The work of Howard Odum and his systems-based energetic understanding of the world is considered as it relates to the approaches proposed by McDonough and Braungart. Chapter 5 expands on this premise, further calling into question a model of sustainability dependent on perpetual growth, and addresses concerns raised by overpopulation and the finite closed earth-system voiced by Thomas Malthus, Paul and Anne Ehrlich, *The Limits to Growth* study and economists Herman Daly and Kenneth Boulding. It concludes by considering the non-anthropocentric ideas of the Deep Ecology movement as defined by Arne Naess. His approach is a radical reorientation toward a more expansive identification of the self to include all living-beings – the ecological self – necessitating a psychological transformation toward the creation of "beautiful acts." These acts set the foundation for a profound alternative to how we might choose to "live-in-the-world" not founded on technological advancement and/or perpetual growth, but solidarity and "self"-respect.

Part 3, "Bio-physical Inter-Action," explores architecture's potential to sensorially stimulate, inter-act and even manifest co-productive physiological responses with, and within, inhabitants toward their ability to *cope* and *adapt* to the changing world. The intent of such an approach is not to produce an architecture of control but rather to facilitate an ongoing process of collective liberation through the fulfillment of greater freedoms, explorations and variability of experiences with, and within, the changing world and within our physiological, psychological and even spiritual constitutions. Chapter 6 examines the Austrian-born architect Frederick Kielser's idea of *correalism* and his method of "biotechnique" as a means for reconceptualizing the human-being as the intersection of numerous sensorial correspondences with environment. This sensual approach is further explored through Estonian zoologist Jakob von Uexküll's concept of "Umwelt", and through Sean Lally's concept of "material energies" capable of creating more flexible, adaptable and evolving definitions of space. The chapter concludes with a brief examination of the work of Swiss architect Philippe Rahm who approaches architectural design as the explicit and implicit construction of interior climates of habitation. Chapter 7 explores how the strategic design and incorporation of sensorial stimuli within the *architectural* "dwelling-place" has the potential to foster co-productive bio-physical interactions. It considers the possibility for these responses to be sustained as lasting adaptations through a brief examination of evolutionary mechanisms proposed by Richard Woltereck (Norms of Reaction / *reaktionsnorm*), James Mark Baldwin (Baldwin effect) and Conrad H. Waddington (Organic selection and the epigenetic landscape). Chapter 8 examines in detail a single project of bio-physical architecture, the Bioscleave House, designed by the artists Shūsaku Arakawa and

Madeline Gins. It considers broadly their concept of "procedural architecture" which regards the architectural environment as one of inter-action facilitating a "tentative" relationship with inhabitants, capable of instigating a more active and stimulating architectural experience. This approach aims to cultivate a greater alignment between people and the "architectural surround," toward the achievement of "reversible destiny" and sustaining life "indefinitely."

★ ★ ★

Though there are many who still cling to more heartening data projections, the promise of technological innovation or dogmas, aiming to refute Latour's beyond "crisis" assessment, evidence in support of his view seems to be piling up rapidly from within the scientific community, where alarm bells have been ringing for years, but also more generally within the cultural milieu, not to mention in the conditions just outside our windows – increased heat waves, droughts, rising sea levels, acidification of the ocean, toxic algal blooms, species loss, extreme weather events, massive fires – the list goes on and on.[12] In a recent interview with *The Harvard Gazette*, John Holdren, who ran the White House Office of Science and Technology Policy in the Obama administration and current Harvard Professor of Environmental Policy and Environmental Science, commented on a recent special report issued by the Intergovernmental Panel on Climate Change (IPCC) warning of the intensifying effects of global warming on the earth's oceans and cryosphere,[13] saying: "We're going to have 100-year storms every year. This will happen in spite of a relatively modest change in the globally and annually average surface temperature of the Earth" (Powell 2019). While he recognized that increased awareness brought about by such reports and by global climate activism, more generally, did provide some good news, he also made clear that the report made claim to little positivity on the actual climate numbers – the numbers were "focused only on the science." Relative to global warming, climate change and the most recent data presented in the report, Holdren provides the following insights:

> The difficulty in a problem like climate change is the time lag. By the time there are dead bodies in the street, you're already way down the road. At any given time, we're not experiencing everything that we're already committed to. That causes policymakers and publics to underestimate how bad it is. If we could somehow freeze the atmospheric concentrations of heat-trapping gases and reflecting particles where they are today, the temperature would still rise to close to 1.5 degrees C above preindustrial times. If we actually want to stay below 1.5 — and the IPCC report from last fall [issued October 8th, 2018] argued that doing so would bring big benefits compared to going to 2 degrees or more — we really have to start reducing our emissions very rapidly. We'll eventually have to be actually pulling more carbon dioxide out of the atmosphere than we're adding in order to meet that extremely challenging goal.

> The good news is it's still up to us how bad the impacts of climate change get. It's going to get worse, but it'll get a lot less bad if we take action than if we don't. If we do a lot, we can end up with a temperature increase of 2 or 2.5 degrees. If there are major breakthroughs, maybe we can get back to 1.5. And that will be a vastly better world than business as usual, where, by the turn of this century, you get to 4 or 4.5 degrees C.
>
> *(Powell 2019)*

Holdren also noted that the IPCC is generally considered to be conservative in its assessments and predictions, they typically establish the floor on what's known and predicted, "they are almost never on the cutting edge" (Powell 2019). However, despite this conservative reputation, both the 2019 IPCC special report and its 2018 predecessor suggest that globally destabilizing catastrophic events might be much more likely than previously thought because the possibility of exceeding a "tipping point" in the climate, triggering irreversible catastrophic changes in the environment, could be met at warming levels of between only 1°C and 2°C. Writing in 2008, the outspoken NASA climate scientist James Hansen and his team, in an article titled "Target Atmospheric CO_2: Where Should Humanity Aim?," stated that the current global mean of CO_2 in the atmosphere "is already in the dangerous zone" (Hansen et al. 2008, 218) and that "Paleoclimate evidence and ongoing global changes imply that today's CO_2, about 385 ppm, is already too high to maintain the climate to which humanity, wildlife and the rest of the biosphere are adapted" (Hansen et al. 2008, 228). Ten years later for the year 2018 the average global CO_2 reached 407.4 ppm, according to the National Oceanic and Atmospheric Administration (NOAA),[14] which is a higher level than any reached in the last 800,000 years (Lindsey 2020) (Figure I.2). In trying to determine a necessary goal for humanity's CO_2 levels in order to avoid unstoppable climate catastrophe, Hansen and his team's deep historical analysis, aiming to take into account the still unknowns of climate equilibrium sensitivity, whether slow, fast or variable, called for a CO_2 goal of 350 ppm (Hansen et al. 2008, 229). They also took note of another reality related to the response time of global systems relative to the atmospheric level of CO_2:

> Human-made climate change is delayed by ocean and ice sheet response times. Warming "in the pipeline," mostly attributable to slow feedbacks, is now about 2 °C. No additional forcing is required to raise global temperatures to at least the level of the Pliocene, 2–3 million years ago, a degree of warming that would surely yield "dangerous" climate impacts.
>
> Realization that today's climate is far out of equilibrium with current climate forcings raises the specter of "tipping points," the concept that climate can reach a point where, without additional forcing, rapid changes proceed practically out of our control.
>
> *(Hansen et al. 2008, 225)*

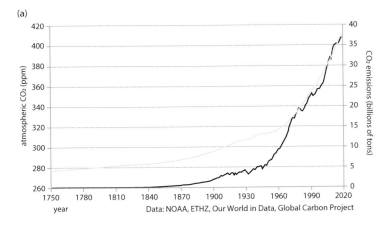
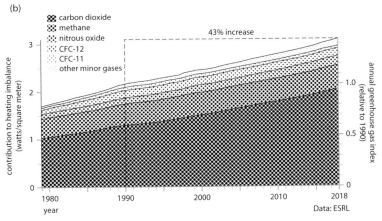
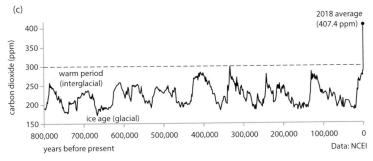

FIGURE I.2 (a) CO_2 in the atmosphere and annual emissions (1750–2019); (b) Influence of all major human-produced greenhouse gases (1979–2018); (c) CO_2 during ices ages and warm periods for the past 80,000 years. Redrawn by author from Rebecca Lindsey. "Climate Change: Atmospheric Carbon Dioxide," February 20, 2020, https://climate.gov/news-features/understanding-climate/climate-change-atmospheric-carbon-dioxide.

10 Introduction

The recognition of how significant tipping points are in order to understand both our environmental future, but also our present, was reflected by a group of prominent international climate researchers who, in the wake of the 2019 IPCC special report referenced by Holdren, published a commentary titled "Climate Tipping Points – Too Risky to Bet Against" in the journal *Nature*. They provided voice to the disturbing reality the world is now facing, regardless of current or future human (in)action.

> We argue that the intervention time left to prevent tipping could already have shrunk towards zero, whereas the reaction time to achieve net zero emissions is 30 years at best. Hence we might already have lost control of whether tipping happens. A saving grace is that the rate at which damage accumulates from tipping — and hence the risk posed — could still be under our control to some extent.
>
> The stability and resilience of our planet is in peril. International action – not just words – must reflect this.
>
> *(Lenton et al. 2019)*

Unfortunately, if recent history is any indication, "our" *actions* – of governments, corporations, institutions, people – have largely not met the reality of increasing global emissions and climate destabilization with an urgency necessary to limit further warming to below 2°C. Speaking to the necessity for action, journalist David Wallace-Wells describes the intent of his book *The Uninhabitable Earth: Life After Warming* as not "about the science of warming" but rather "about what warming means to the way we live on this planet" (Wallace-Wells 2019b, 11). The question of how we choose to live "now" is most relevant to shaping our future, especially as the impact of warming and climate change are already being felt and as our timeframe for mitigating its most drastic effects quickly dwindles to zero. Like Holdren, Wallace-Wells recounts how the current levels of global carbon emissions must be drastically and immediately reduced, even reversed, if we are to combat further substantial warming of the planet.

> It was as recent as 2016 that the celebrated Paris Climate accords were adopted – defining two degrees of global warming as a must-meet target and rallying all the world's nations to meet it – and the returns are already dispiritingly grim. In 2017, carbon emissions grew by 1.4 percent, according to the International Energy Agency, after an ambiguous couple of years optimists had hoped represented a leveling-off, or peak; instead, we're climbing again. Even before the new spike, not a single major industrial nation was on track to fulfill the commitments it made in the Paris treaty. Of course, those commitments only get us down to 3.2 degrees; to keep the planet under 2 degrees of warming, all signatory nations have to significantly better their pledges.[15]
>
> *(Wallace-Wells 2019b, 44)*

It's important to note that projections, scenarios and simulations are just that, *possible* outcomes given the data and information we know, or think we know, at any one moment in time. They are not certainties; they are best guesses and are fundamentally dependent on current and future human (in)actions. For instance, the energy use and emissions data contained in the most recent International Energy Agency (IEA) World Energy Outlook report issued at the end of 2019[16] forecasted lower carbon emissions by 2040 than previously projected by most previous IPCC scenarios, suggesting the often referenced "RCP8.5" scenario may actually be an outlier projection closer to a "worst case" possibility as it relates to energy consumption than to "business as usual" (Wallace-Wells 2019a). In an article following the release of the 2019 IEA report, Wallace-Wells describes the energy use analysis provided by climate scientist Zeke Hausfather and researcher Justin Ritchie suggesting that if current "business as usual" trends in the global energy system continue it would likely lead to the planet warming only 3°C by the end of the current century as actual increase in coal use has been less than previously expected. Or if existing pledges to decrease emissions are implemented, then that level could be lowered to 2.7°C (Wallace-Wells 2019a). This is good news in that it likely lowers the ceiling on the amount of warming that seems possible; though it may also simultaneously raise our floors (Wallace-Wells 2019a) making it much less likely we stay below 2°C of warming (Figure I.3). With definitive changes in global climate patterns already underway, alongside the increased likelihood of reaching 3°C of warming, and notwithstanding the still unknown consequences of feedback loops and global climate sensitivity, we have undoubtedly already created a "new" world for ourselves and all beings who inhabit its spaces.

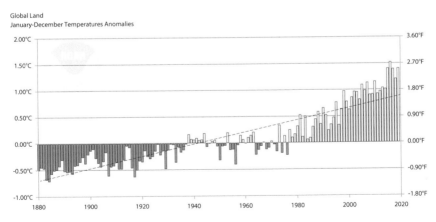

FIGURE I.3 Global temperature anomalies in annual land temperature from 1880 to 2020. Anomalies are with respect to the twentieth-century average. Redrawn by author from chart courtesy of NOAA National Centers for Environmental information, Climate at a Glance: Global Time Series, published April 2020.

Reaching *only* 3°C increase in global temperatures would surely cause untold suffering to humans as well as instigating many catastrophic effects to the ecosphere.

> At just two degrees, the U.N. estimates, damages from storms and sea-level rise could grow 100-fold. Cities in South Asia and the Middle East that are today home to many millions of people would be so hot during summer heat waves, scientists have projected, even going outside during the day could mean risking heatstroke or heat death. The number of climate refugees could pass 200 million, according to the U.N., and more than 150 million would die from the impacts of air pollution alone. North of two degrees, of course, the strain accumulates and intensifies, and while some amount of human adaptation to these forces is inevitable, the scale of adaptation required at even two degrees begins to seem close to impossible.
>
> (Wallace-Wells 2019a)

The world at 3°C of warming above pre-industrial levels is not the same world in which humans, and many other living-beings, biologically evolved, and it is not the same world in which human society and culture developed either. Already today we can point to many adverse social consequences – both observed and felt – that are a resultant of anthropogenic global warming and changes in global climatological patterns (Figure I.4). In many areas of the globe, increased temperatures alongside direct human actions of destruction like deforestation, pollution, resource extraction and sprawling development have greatly accelerated habitat loss, furthering the increase in temperatures, in turn, hastening the transformation of vast areas of the planet to be too hot for humans to live, reducing access to food and clean water, prompting mass climate refugee migrations, political destabilization, conflict and war. These events are taking place *now* and, as the earth's temperature continues to climb, will certainly become further amplified and more widespread.

FIGURE I.4 Raging forest fire, Los Padres, CA, December 2017. Photographs by 272447. Courtesy of Pixabay.

Survival, let alone sustained abundance, in this "new" world will require a vastly different approach in how human-beings choose to inhabit its spaces.

> Annihilation is only the very thin tail of warming's very long bell curve, and there is nothing stopping us from steering clear of it. But what lies between us and extinction is horrifying enough, and we have not yet begun to contemplate what it means to live under those conditions…We may yet see a climate deus ex machina – or, rather, we may build one, in the form of carbon capture technology or geoengineering, or in the form of a revolution in the way we generate power, electric or political. But that solution, if it comes at all, will emerge against a bleak horizon, darkened by our emissions as if by glaucoma.
>
> *(Wallace-Wells 2019b, 34)*

In a piece published as "cultural comment" in *The New Yorker* magazine titled "What if We Stopped Pretending?", the National Book Award-winning American novelist and essayist Jonathan Franzen makes the outright plea that we need to shift our attention away from unrealistic attempts to avert radical and uncontrollable climate change, to instead focus our efforts toward preparation and adaption to "the radical destabilization of life on earth" (Franzen 2019). Franzen's assessment of the situation relies on not only science but also his understanding of human psychology and the current political reality, drawing him to conclude that the best course of action is the acceptance that radical anthropogenic climate change is an impending reality. His position is not blind fait accompli toward death and destruction, but rather a reframing of where we choose to put our energy and how we might choose to "live-in-the-world," to live in this "new" world that is becoming more and more climatically, ecologically, socially, culturally and biologically unfamiliar.

> All-out war on climate change made sense only as long as it was winnable. Once you accept that we've lost it, other kinds of action take on greater meaning. Preparing for fires and floods and refugees is a directly pertinent example. But the impending catastrophe heightens the urgency of almost any world-improving action. In times of increasing chaos, people seek protection in tribalism and armed force, rather than in the rule of law, and our best defense against this kind of dystopia is to maintain functioning democracies, functioning legal systems, functioning communities. In this respect, any movement toward a more just and civil society can now be considered a meaningful climate action. Securing fair elections is a climate action. Combatting extreme wealth inequality is a climate action. Shutting down the hate machines on social media is a climate action. Instituting humane immigration policy, advocating for racial and gender equality, promoting respect for laws and their

14 Introduction

> enforcement, supporting a free and independent press, ridding the country of assault weapons – these are all meaningful climate actions. To survive rising temperatures, every system, whether of the natural world or of the human world, will need to be as strong and healthy as we can make it.
>
> *(Franzen 2019)*

While technological ingenuity and increased "clean" energy production is inevitable, so too are the current limitations of "our" collective will power and the democratic institutions identified by Franzen. As it relates to the current conditions of climate and ecology, *Beyond Sustainable* accepts that human-beings have effectively reached a moment beyond climatological-ecological "crisis," on a path almost certainly reaching upwards of 3°C of warming, a level that will radically remake the world from which most life-forms currently living on earth have evolved. Like Franzen, this acceptance is not intended to propagate a nihilistic positioning toward unending despair, or a stoic retreat to the foothills of a Dark Mountain[17]; rather, *Beyond Sustainable* maintains that there is still much "we" can do to limit the greatest effects of global warming and radical climate change before reaching such devastation or despair. It accepts that the earth-system is already in a period of radical transformation, not asking how do we resolve "the crisis," but instead, how might we rethink our energy demands, dependence on fossil fuels and ultimately how we *choose* to inhabit this "new" world? How can a reconsideration of the design and construction of the built environments we inhabit help to (re)calibrate this relationship? And how might their design ultimately help "Us" *cope* and *adapt* to these ongoing changes within the earth-system and the global climate? The intent of *Beyond Sustainable* is not to propose technical solutions, but to instead consider observations from philosophy, ecology, evolutionary biology, genetics and psychology, alongside specific architectural histories, to construct an alternative theoretical foundation from which to reconceptualize architecture as the implicit collaborative product of environment-inhabitant inter-action. In this sense, architecture is reconceived as the setting that sustains, but also shapes "our" lives – an essential part of *being* human and *being* ecological, now and in the future.

Architecture has always provided human-beings a means for better "surviving-in-the-world," maintaining throughout our biological history a vital adaptive role, through external mediation, inter-action, reciprocity and in its most intensive form, bio-physical stimulation. Within this beyond climatological-ecological "crisis" moment, if architecture intends to help us continue to effectively *cope* and *adapt*, it requires a radical rethinking of its priorities, a reconceptualization of its intentions and a reworking of its relationship to both the larger climatological and ecological environmental constructs, and its inhabitants. How might architecture begin to provide some light from within the darkness of the tunnel we now find ourselves? How might it help us avert "madness" derived from our "profound mutation in our relation to the world"? and instead help us adapt to "Our" new "world"?

Once we've accepted the reality that we are no longer "in" crisis – that there is no going back – it's immediately clear that the current dominant architectural disciplinary concept of sustainability (or "green design") simply no longer holds relevance as a "solution" to our current moment. Its intended invocations of positive reform against environmentally destructive anthropogenic forces provide little in the way of coping in the face of such radical transformation of the earth-system now initiated. Latour describes succinctly the stark simplicity of the situation with which humans must now deal when he says: "it is a matter not of progressive reforms but of catastrophic changes" (Latour 2017, 39) in how human-beings must *choose* to "live-in-the-world," of which the constructed environments we design and inhabit play an integral part. Human-beings must take care, we must adapt, we must alter our "being" to effectively deal with this radical transformation taking place around us, yet the disciplinary model of sustainability, aimed principally at reducing our energy and carbon footprints, reducing pollution and limiting environmental degradation through greater efficiencies of design, fabrication and construction, is largely reliant on technological innovations set within the current systems of power and global commerce that have gotten us to this point, rarely challenging the underlying approach toward how we might choose to "live-in-the-world."

★ ★ ★

Rather than regard "Nature" as something distinct from "Society," the environmental historian and political economist Jason W. Moore sees them as inextricably connected through the interrelated web of living and non-living actors – the "web of life" (Moore 2015, 3). As he explains, this is "Nature" with a lowercase "n," not "out there," not reducible or controllable, but existing within and through society. "This is nature as us, as inside us, as around us. It is nature as a flow of flows. Put simply, humans make environments and environments make humans – and human organization" (Moore 2015, 3). From this position, architecture reconceived in the time of necessary catastrophic changes, beyond climatological-ecological "crisis," cannot be understood simply as a description of the definitive physical settings we occupy, but rather, it must be regarded as the total set of dynamic and overlapping material, biological, ecological, climatic, social and economic systems with which human-beings endlessly engage, and which shape "Us" in this "new" world.

Broadly speaking the critique of a Nature-Society dualism has been voiced by many in numerous disciplinary origins, all of which challenge the concept of *environment* and its relationship to inhabitants. One such relevant challenge pertains to the ecological idea of a niche that presupposes different population groups becoming more or less "fit" relative to these independently occurring

16   Introduction

environmental conditions. For evolutionary biologist Richard Lewontin, a process of organismal adaptive change characterized through better and better "fitness" within the metaphor of a predefined ecological niche "implies a kind of ecological space with holes in it that are filled by organisms, organisms whose properties give them the right 'shape' to fit into the holes" (Lewontin 2000, 44). In this ideation, the space of the niche is predetermined, shaped only by the external physical forces like geological movements, meteor impacts, global cycles of heating and cooling, tidal shifts and changing weather patterns (Lewontin 2000, 42). In this sense, the niche is fundamentally separate from the organisms that have come to inhabit an environment's many nooks and crannies (Figure I.5). The idea that an environment contains such predetermined spaces waiting to be filled by individuals radically distorts and dilutes the effective ecological role organisms play within the places and spaces they inhabit and, by extension, the creative actions they undertake from "within" its bounds. Lewontin calls the metaphor of an autonomous predetermined space waiting to be filled "bad biology." In his view, environments only exist in relationship to those organisms who occupy them and are not causally independent (Lewontin 2000, 48). As he describes:

> An *environment* is something that surrounds or encircles, but for there to be a surrounding there must be something at the center to be surrounded. The environment of an organism is the penumbra of external conditions that are relevant to it because it has effective interactions with those aspects of the outer world.
>
> *(Lewontin 2000, 48–49)*

Over the last four centuries as human-beings developed a system of global commerce and countless technological "advancements," both propelled by increased access and use of fossil fuels, they have become the dominant force

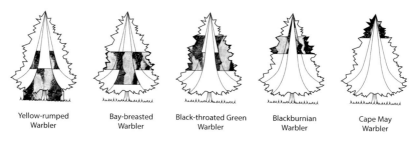

FIGURE I.5   Niche partitioning of insectivorous wood Warblers showing areas of feeding concentration in conifers, based upon Robert H. MacArthur's study of the ecological niches of Warblers. Drawing by Alex Witteman.

within the web of life – distorting, disturbing and degrading the environment and other living-beings for their personal benefit. It is precisely because we are not separate from nature – from the world we inhabit – that makes our impact wide ranging and now, through anthropogenic climate change, total.[18]

The philosopher of literature and the environment Timothy Morton in his book *Ecology Without Nature* provides a further critique related to our conception of the environment and how its current state must be reconsidered if we are to effectively confront, cope and adapt to this "new" world. As Morton describes:

> The environment was born at exactly the moment when it became a problem. The word *environment* still haunts us, because in a society that took care of its surroundings in a more comprehensive sense, our idea of environment would have withered away. The very word *environmentalism* is evidence of wishful thinking. Society would be so involved with taking care of "it" that it would no longer be a case of some "thing" that surrounds us, that environs us and differs from us. Humans may yet return the idea of the "thing" to its older sense of *meeting place*. In a society that fully acknowledged that we were always already involved in our world, there would be no need to point it out.
>
> (Morton 2007, 141)

These words get right to the point; our relationship to environment, and indeed our very concept of it, is fundamentally problematic because contemporary society has yet to understand or perhaps accept that it is itself an integral piece of this collective – an ecological dialectic – comprised of all living and non-living beings with which we inter-act and depend. The "modern" post-enlightenment society we've invented and now inhabit has remained purposefully separate, raising itself above the ecological world down below.[19] However, the implications of Morton's critique are clear: in order to effectively accept "our place" within the world, we must understand it not as a space to inhabit, but instead as a fundamental aspect of *ourselves*, an integral part of the human-*being*. This more cooperative approach provides the possibility of an alternative model, of how "we" might more empathetically choose to "live-in-the-world", especially now amid the ongoing processes of change in the earth-system.

These assertions offer two significant ideas for further articulating a concept of environment: first, that the environment of any organism may be understood through those elements, characters, factors with which it interacts by way of its physiological and cultural systems, and, second, that these external "conditions of life"[20] have the capacity to readily effect the individual toward adaptive change (i.e., speciation) (Figure I.6). According to Lewontin, all organisms choose, as well as help to construct, "a world" in which to live: "organisms not only determine what aspects of the outside world are relevant to them by

18 Introduction

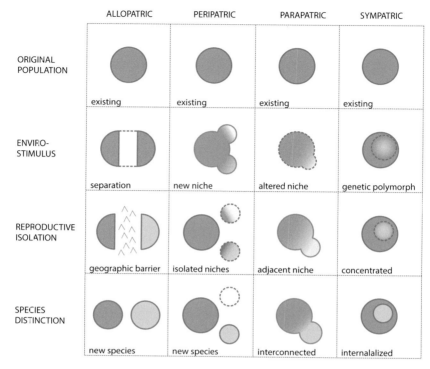

FIGURE I.6 Spatial aspects of different types of speciation. Redrawn by author from wikimedia commons https://commons.wikimedia.org/wiki/File:Speciation_modes_edit.svg.

peculiarities of their shape and metabolism, but they actively construct, in the literal sense of the word, a world around themselves"[21] (Lewontin 2000, 54). It is in this sense that architecture may play a critical role. In this way, a conception of environment must also be predicated upon a description of the relevant activities an individual undertakes (Lewontin 2000, 52; Levins and Lewontin 1985, 57–58).

In discussing the scientist James Lovelock's Gaia hypothesis, Bruno Latour reflects on this potential in the following way:

> If, as a geophysicist, Lovelock was fighting against the geochemists, he was fighting just as much against the Darwinians, for whom organisms settle for "adapting themselves to" their *own* environments. For Lovelock, organisms, taken as the point of departure for a biochemical reaction, do not develop "in" an environment; rather, each one *bends* the environment around itself, as it were, the better to develop. In this sense, every organism intentionally manipulates what surrounds it "in its own interest" – the whole problem, of course, lies in defining that interest.
>
> *(Latour 2017, 98)*

Through *actions*, all organisms are in a constant dialogue with their environment as well as the environments of other organisms – a dynamic process of consumption and production, a form of ecology; "all organisms alter not only their own environments but also the environments of other species in ways that may be essential to the life of those other organisms"[22] (Lewontin 2000, 55). Individuals intake and transform raw materials, synthesizing various forms of matter and energy into other forms, altering aspects of the "conditions of life" around themselves, providing resources for consumption by other adjacent species forming interconnected feedback loops. Human-beings are perhaps the most intentioned and wide-ranging in their abilities to affect their environment through design:

> Man constructs tools, and with these tools more tools to change increasingly natural surroundings, and each product has its own incidental cluster of by-products. It is through this comprehensive activity that houses, road networks, cities – an entirely new environment – are created. The manmade setting reacts through an infinite number of stimuli upon the nervous system of every member of the community. More than that, today design may exert a far-reaching influence on the nervous make-up of generations.
>
> *(Neutra 1954, 83)*

The potential is for this "entirely new environment," described above by Richard Neutra, to extend to the "nervous make-up" of all members of the community, which includes all types of "beings," eliciting co-productive effects and as Neutra portends, these nervous system "stimuli" might even have long-lasting effects on individuals. In keeping with this sentiment, ecologist and population geneticist Richard Levins and Richard Lewontin state, "'Environment' cannot be understood merely as surroundings, no matter how dynamically. It is also a way of life; the activity of the organism sets the stage for its own evolution" (Levins and Lewontin 1985, 58). Or, as Moore states while commenting on hominid evolution, "evolutionary processes were powerfully co-produced: humanity is a species-environment relation" (Moore 2015, 11). In this sense, while architecture is not literally composed of biological material related to information transmission (i.e., genes), it is also not simply an inert envelope within which life occurs. It is a participatory actor helping to contribute to who "we" are, who "we" may become and also by extension many other non-human beings with which we inter-act.

The capacity for design is at a foundational level a primary aspect of how human-beings have inhabited the world, whether explicitly through architecture or more generally through the technics implemented in all aspects of how we live. In their book *Are We Human?*, Beatriz Colomina and Mark Wigley attribute the ability to modify our abilities through "design" and by extension our environment as the defining characteristic of the human condition, ultimately suggesting a radical human–artifact collaboration:

> Designed artifacts have as much agency as the animal that seemingly produced them. They transform the animal just as much as they are transformed by the animal. Or, to say it the other way around, the body and brain become artifacts. What is human is the radicality of this mutual exchange. The human is inseparable from the artifacts that it produces, with the human body having the extended shape of all the artifacts it has made and each artifact being an intimate part of its biology and brain.
>
> *(Colomina and Wigley 2017, 23–24)*

Architecture is not only a unique type of designed artifact capable of extending the abilities of human-beings; through its capacity as a creator of "environmental potentials" of habitation in which and with which many beings inter-act, it may also foster co-productive physiological, psychological and affective responses. Through this reconceptualization, designing architectural constructs in the changing dynamics of the Anthropocene with the sole aspiration of environmental neutralization, sustainability or even homeostasis doesn't go nearly far enough. The potential collaborative activities of the designed human-architecture-environment collaboration amount to a profoundly inter-active and evolving relationship between actors, living and non-living alike, capable of fostering co-productive and beneficial effects for both (Figure I.7). Timothy Morton, partly by way of Bruno Latour, has described this collaboration in the following way:

> The idea of the environment is more or less a way of considering groups and collectives – humans surrounded by nature, or in continuity with other beings such as animals and plants. It is about *being-with*. As Latour has recently pointed out, however, the actual situation is far more drastically collective than that. All kinds of beings, from toxic waste to sea snails, are clamoring for our scientific, political, and artistic attention, and have become part of political life – to the detriment of monolithic conceptions of Nature.[23]
>
> *(Morton 2007, 17)*

The relationship between individual and environment is understood as neither totalizing and hierarchical, nor fragmented and equal, but rather, in the broadest sense possible, it is conceived of as an inter-active collective of engagements between living and non-living "beings." This alternative environmental understanding, what Morton calls "ecocritique," provides the possibility of moving beyond the anthropocentric conception of achieving a "sustainable" or

Introduction **21**

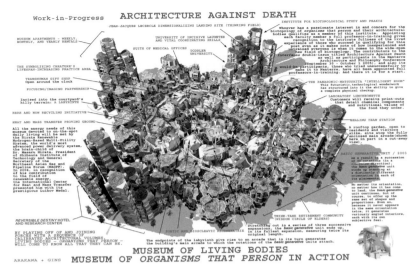

FIGURE I.7 Arakawa and Madeline Gins, *Museum of Living Bodies*, digital rendering, 2003. © 2010 Estate of Madeline Gins. Reproduced with permission of the Estate of Madeline Gins. Image courtesy of Reversible Destiny Foundation.

even a "regenerative" presence of "living-in-the-world" to one that is mutually responsive and empathetic. "Ecocritique could establish collective forms of identity that included other species and their worlds, real and possible. It would subvert fixating images of 'world' that inhibits humans from grasping their place in an already historical nature" (Morton 2007, 141). This is a movement away from "the," "an" or "its" environment to "Our" shared environment,[24] a total collective "being-with."

While the fundamental dissolution of the Nature-Society dualism aims to situate our lives within-the-world rather than removed from it, implying a more collective, inter-active and synthesized understanding of being, humanity's desire to modify and control "Nature" toward shortsighted anthropocentric capital gains has continued to uphold this long-standing oppositional arrangement. Despite its progressive intentions, the dominant architectural disciplinary concept of sustainability has also largely subscribed to this Nature-Society separation, through the dominant role provided to greater technological innovation and perceived "control." To help resolve this dualism and better understand the modernist project's conception of the world including the destabilizing effects it has produced in the earth-system, Moore uses the term "world-ecology." This term reflects a paradigm shift in environmental thinking which describes how "the relationality of nature implies a new method that grasps humanity-in-nature as a world-historical process"; understanding it as an "organic whole" made up of "power, production and

22 Introduction

perception" whereby modernity is realized as a "capitalist world-ecology" (Moore 2015, 3–4). Resolving this Nature-Society dualism through the web of life recognizes that the world-ecology is composed of many different constituent beings, of which human-beings are only one, whose actions are not separate but wholly integral to the total collective of living and non-living inhabitants. This is the first step toward "Our" *coping*, toward "Our" *adapting*, living in the time of necessary catastrophic changes in how we choose to live within the world-ecology (Figure I.8).

Through its reconceptualization as a creator of evolving "environmental potentials" of habitation, architecture presents one significant path, one mode of design that may help human-beings to *cope* and *adapt*, through co-productive inter-active collaboration in the world-ecology. In this sense, our architectural constructs could be understood as an essential synthesizing development of our technical, social and cultural knowledge, providing us the ability to both "survive" and "evolve" in "Our" collective "new" world. Latour describes our fate as such: "In practice, we are all counter-revolutionaries, trying to minimize the consequences of a revolution that has taken place without us, against us, and, at the same time, through us" (Latour 2017, 40). As we have now moved beyond the razors edge, what's on the other side has yet to be fully understood and fully determined, and where we're headed is not clear, but one thing remains certain: radical change is paramount to "Our" future "living-in-the-world-ecology," whether respected by way of strategic recalibration of the evolving environments of habitation we create or whether it continues to be thrust upon us, unpredictably and violently.

FIGURE I.8 Philippe Rahm architectes, *Central Park, The Meteorological Garden*, 3D image, Taichung, Taiwan, 2012–2020. Reproduced by permission from Philippe Rahm architectes, Mosbach paysagistes, Ricky Liu & Associates. Image courtesy Philippe Rahm architectes.

Notes

1 See David Gissen, "The architectural production of nature, Dendur/ New York," *Grey Room* 34 (Winter 2009): 58–79, and David Gissen, "APE," in *Design ecologies: Essays on the nature of design*, ed. Lisa Tilder and Beth Blostein (New York: Princeton Architectural Press, 2010) 62–75.

2 Italics added here for emphasis. Of this same passage the architectural historian Luis Fernández-Galiano has described these types of "environmental adaptations" as working through a sociocultural channel of information transmission, as opposed to the biological channel which utilizes genetic material. In Galiano's assessment this sociocultural transmission has the potential to be "highly variable and dynamic, of exosomatic energy consumption" providing a greater degree of freedom for humans living-in-the-world. "As we see, the genetic channel has the capacity to store and transmit a very small amount of information compared to that which can be channeled through such sociocultural means as language and architecture." Luis Fernández-Galiano, translated by Gina Cariño, *Fire and memory: On architecture and energy* (Cambridge, MA: The MIT Press, 2000) 71,72.

3 This phrase is in reference to the title of Frederick Engels' ca.1876 unfinished essay "The Role of Labour in the Transition from Ape to Man"; see Frederick Engels, "The role of labour in the transition from ape to man," in *Dialectics of nature*, trans. and ed. Clemens Dutt (New York: International Publishers, 1940), 279–296.

4 This concept of the "long" sixteenth century (1451–1648) is an immediate reference from the introduction of Jason W. Moore's book *Capitalism in the Web of Life*, p. 12, as he uses the phrase in reference to the period of time when the current global capitalist system developed the capacity to turn all individual daily activities of life into aspects of a total "world-historical" system. According to Moore this phrase and concept originate with the French historian Fernand Braudel in his 1949 book *La Méditerranée et le monde méditerranéen à l'époque de Philippe II.*

5 The historian George Basalla makes the point that many new forms of energy when first introduced are perceived as both abundant and capable of bringing long-lasting productive social change, before their shortcomings are fully realized, see George Basalla, "Some persistent energy myths," in George H. Daniels and Mark H. Rose, eds., *Energy and transport* (Beverly Hills, CA: 1982), 27–38.

6 See Paul Cruzten and Eugene F. Stoermer, "The anthropocene," IGPB (International Geosphere-Biosphere Programme) Newsletter 41 (2000): 17–18. Jason W. Moore argues that a more pertinent term to define our epoch would be the "Capitalocene," as it more accurately describes humanity's relationship to the world as a reflection of how the global capitalist system engages with the environment, with nature. "'*The economy*' and '*the environment*' are not independent of each other. Capitalism is not an economic system; it is not a social system; it is *a way of organizing nature*." See Moore (2015, 2). For more general overview of alternative terms see Jason W. Moore, ed. *Anthropocene or capitalocene: Nature, history, and the crisis of capitalism* (Oakland, CA: PM Press, 2016).

7 It is now readily accepted by scientists that we are currently undergoing a sixth mass extinction event on Earth, largely derived from human actions like habitat destruction, overhunting, pollution, invasive species and manmade climate change, see Elizabeth Kolbert's Pulitzer Prize winning book *The sixth extinction: An unnatural history* (New York: Henry Holt and Company, 2015). Or for a brief overview see the article in *The Guardian* from July 10th 2017, "Earth's sixth mass extinction event under way, scientists warn" by Damian Carrington, environment editor, https://www.theguardian.com/environment/2017/jul/10/earths-sixth-mass-extinction-event-already-underway-scientists-warn.

24 Introduction

8 Latour refers to them as "quietists."

9 For a more extensive overview on this subject see Clive Hamilton, *Earthmasters: The dawn of the age of climate engineering* (New Haven, CT: Yale University Press, 2013), and Holly Jean Buck, *After geoengineering: Climate tragedy, repair, and restoration* (London: Verso, 2019).

10 See Pope Francis' Encyclical Letter "On Care for Our Common House" first published on July 15th, 2015, in which he explicitly refers to the "environmental crisis" or "ecological crisis," currently underway. The title of his third chapter reads: "The Human Roots of the Ecological Crisis," http://w2.vatican.va/content/dam/francesco/pdf/encyclicals/documents/papa-francesco_20150524_enciclica-laudato-si_en.pdf.

11 On this point also see Bill McKibben, *Eaarth: Making a life on a tough new planet* (New York: Times Books, 2010).

12 As it relates to the potential of an apocalyptic future of collapse see such texts as: Bill McKibben's seminal 1989 book *The end of nature*; or Jared Diamond's 2005 bestseller *Collapse: how societies choose to fail or succeed;* or Elisabeth Kolbert's 2006 book *Field notes from a catastrophe: Man, nature and climate change*; or Naomi Oreskes and Erik M. Conway's 2014 science fictional critique *The collapse of western civilization: A view from the future.*

13 The report referenced, titled "IPCC special report on the ocean and cryosphere in a changing climate," was approved by the IPCC on September 24th 2019. Later that same year on December 10th the National Oceanic and Atmospheric Administration's annual Arctic Report Card was released documenting that 2019 had seen the second warmest temperatures on record, near-record levels of melting Arctic sea ice and melting of glaciers on Greenland. Perhaps most dangerous it also stated their belief that melting permafrost is now contributing to increased CO_2 and methane in the atmosphere, both considered amplifiers to an already warming global climate.

14 At the moment of writing this note, the monthly mean level of CO_2 was measured as 417.07 ppm at the Mauna Loa Observatory, Hawaii, altitude of 3400 MAMSL; see the NOAA website for ongoing monitoring of CO_2 levels in the atmosphere, https://www.esrl.noaa.gov/gmd/ccgg/trends/ (accessed June 07, 2020).

15 As of 2019, out of the 195 signatories only 7 are considered "within range" of targets – Morocco, Gambia, Bhutan, Costa Rica, Ethiopia, India and the Philippines, see Wallace-Wells (2019b, 44) and for the current status of each country see Climate Action Tracker, https://climateactiontracker.org.

16 Released on November 13th 2019, https://www.iea.org/reports/world-energy-outlook-2019.

17 The Dark Mountain Project was initiated in 2009 with the publishing of a manifesto titled "Uncivilization" written by British writers Paul Kingsworth and Dougald Hine. It was a critique of the myth of progress of human civilization, the current system of global capitalism and humanity's aspiration of dominance over nature. They argued for a fundamental shift toward the idea of "uncivilization" and the removal of oneself from the current anthropocentric construction of the world – a kind of retreat or pilgrimage to climb the Dark Mountain. In 2012 Kingsworth published another manifesto called "Dark Ecology" expanding on these ideas.

18 Writing in his 1964 essay "Ecology and Revolutionary Thought", the social theorist and political philosopher, Murray Bookchin makes a distinction between "modern man's" expansive toxic impact on the globe (what he calls "human parasitism"), and the more limited abilities of preindustrial civilizations to spread environmental degradation totally because of their more limited technics.

> Ancient examples of human parasitism were essentially local in scope; they were precisely *examples* of man's potential for destruction, and nothing more...
>
> Modern Man's despoliation of the environment is global in scope, like his imperialisms. It is even extraterrestrial, as witness the disturbances of the Van Allen Belt a few years ago. Today human parasitism disrupts more than the atmosphere, climate, water resources, soil, flora and fauna of a region: it upsets virtually all the basic cycles of nature and threatens to undermine the stability of the environment on a worldwide scale.

See Murray Bookchin, "Ecology and revolutionary thought," in *Post-scarcity anarchism*, 2nd ed. (Montreal/Buffalo: Black Rose Books, [1965] 1986) 81–82.

19 In an essay titled "Thinking Ecologically: A Dialectical Approach" Murray Bookchin describes further how the specific development of our modern society having "unfolded in the direction of hierarchal, class-oriented, and statist institutions, giving rise to the nation-state and ultimately...to a capitalist economy" was only one possible trajectory for its development, now responsible for much of the current ecological and planetary degradation. He proposes a dialectical understanding of the conception of Nature and Society – what he refers to as "first" and "second" nature – into a "free nature" that "would willfully and thinkingly cope with conflict, contingency, waste, and consumption...[a] new synthesis, where first and second nature are melded into a free, rational, and ethical nature, neither first nor second would lose its specificity and integrity." See Murray Bookchin, "Thinking Ecologically: A Dialectical Approach," in *The Philosophy of Social Ecology: Essays on Dialectical Naturalism*, 2nd ed. (Montreal/Buffalo: Black Rose Books, 1996) 132–133 and 136.

20 Interestingly when describing the occurrence of "indefinite variability" – what he defined as "endless slight" and nonuniform variations distinguishing individuals of the same species group caused by changing environmental circumstances – Darwin considered these "changes of structure...as the indefinite effects of the conditions of life on each individual organism." His view however was that they were most often simply "slight peculiarities which distinguish individuals of the same species" but were not of great consequence as they cannot be accounted for by inheritance, it was the "nature of the organism" that he deemed "much more important," see Charles Darwin, 1859. *The origin of species: By means of natural selection or the preservation of favoured races in the struggle for life*. The New American Library ed., with introd. by Sir Julian Huxley (New York: Mentor, 1958) 32.

21 Also see Levins and Lewontin, 1985, 53, 55–56.

22 Also see Levins and Lewontin, 1985, 54–55.

23 Italics added here for emphasis, also see Bruno Latour, *We have never been modern*, trans. Catherine Porter (Cambridge, MA: Harvard University Press, 1993).

24 The use here and throughout of the capitalized possessive adjective "our" in relationship to the concept of *environment* must be distinguished from the same use "our" by Reinhold Martin is his essay "Environment, c. 1973" in which he uses the phrasing in reference to Richard Nixon's signing of the National Environmental Policy Act (NEPA) with its language and decree providing an implied human subject as the inhabitant of "environment" that was "ours," the object of government regulation. As Martin describes: "In the details of the legislation that environment is converted into an object of techno-scientific knowledge associated with what sociologist Ulrich Beck has described as the logico-mathematical regime of *risk*." See Reinhold Martin, "Environment, c. 1973," *Grey Room* 14 (Winter 2004): 79–80. The intent of the capitalized "Our" in this text is to emphasize the collaboration we share among and with other beings *together*.

26 Introduction

References

Colomina, Beatriz and Mark Wigley. 2017. *Are we human? Notes on an archaeology of design*. Zürich: Lars Müller Publishers.

Franzen, Jonathan. 2019. What if we stopped pretending? The climate apocalypse is coming. To prepare for it, we need to admit that we can't prevent it. *The New Yorker*, September 8, https://www.newyorker.com/culture/cultural-comment/what-if-we-stopped-pretending.

Hansen, James, Makiko Sato, Pushker Kharecha, David Beerling, Robert Berner, Valerie Masson-Delmotte, Mark Pagani, Maureen Raymo, Dana L. Royer and James C. Zachos. 2008. Target atmospheric CO_2: Where should humanity aim? *The Open Atmospheric Science Journal* 2: 217–231.

International Energy Agency. 2019. *World energy outlook 2019*. IEA, Paris. https://www.iea.org/reports/world-energy-outlook-2019.

Latour, Bruno. 2017. *Facing Gaia: Eight lectures on the new climatic regime*. Cambridge, UK: Polity Press.

Lenton, Timothy M., Johan Rockström, Owne Gaffney, Katherine Richardson, Will Steffen and Hans Joachim Schellnhuber. 2019. Climate tipping points – too risky to bet against. *Nature*, November 27, https://www.nature.com/articles/d41586-019-03595-0#ref-CR2

Levins, Richard and Richard Lewontin. 1985. *The dialectical biologist*. Cambridge, MA: Harvard University Press.

Lewontin, Richard. 2000. *The triple helix: Gene, organism and environment*. Cambridge, MA: Harvard University Press.

Lindsey, Rebecca. 2020. Climate change: Atmospheric carbon dioxide. *NOAA Climate*, February 20, https://www.climate.gov/news-features/understanding-climate/climate-change-atmospheric-carbon-dioxide.

Moore, Jason W. 2015. *Capitalism in the web of life: Ecology and the accumulation of capital*. London: Verso.

Morton, Timothy. 2007. *Ecology without nature: Rethinking environmental aesthetics*. Cambridge, MA: Harvard University Press.

Mumford, Lewis. 1963. *Technics and civilization*. New York: Harcourt Brace Jovanovich.

Neutra, Richard. 1954. *Survival through Design*. New York: Oxford University Press.

Powell, Alvin. 2019. Red flags on global warming and the seas (includes interview with John Holdren). *The Harvard Gazette*, October 2. https://news.harvard.edu/gazette/story/2019/10/urgency-of-climate-change-may-be-understated-in-intergovernmental-panel-report/.

Sloterdijk, Peter. 2011. *Neither sun nor death*. With Hans-Jürgen Heinrichs. Trans Steve Corcoran. Los Angeles, CA: Semiotext(e).

Wallace-Wells, David. 2019a. We're getting a clearer picture of the climate future – and it's not as bad as it once looked. *New York Magazine*, December 19. https://nymag.com/intelligencer/2019/12/climate-change-worst-case-scenario-now-looks-unrealistic.html

———. 2019b. *The uninhabitable Earth: Life after warming*. New York: Tim Duggan Books.

PART I
Technological Mediation

Technological systems, strategies and elements have been regularly utilized through-out human history for mediating and mitigating undesirable environmental conditions toward the production of more livable interior environments of habitation. Part I, "Technological Mediation," charts out a history that supports the ideation of the architectural surround not simply as a technological device but aims to extend its definition further, understanding it more deeply as an adaptive technological me-diator, profoundly effecting our ability "survive" and "live" in-the-world-ecology. As modern construction technologies rapidly developed during the second half of the nineteenth century, these changes directly impacted the potential for architecture to more radically mediate the external conditions, leading to the conception of an iso-lated interior environment of habitation, fully regulated through the advancement of air heating, cooling and conditioning mechanical systems. These developments, while dramatically increasing inhabitant expectations of comfortability, also separated human-beings from the external ecological world. Today, this level of isolation and sophistication in the technological mediation of the environment has moved beyond simply providing "covering" to help human-beings "survive-in-the-world," as it's done throughout our history, to instead become intentionally capable of amplifying or suppressing the "conditions for life." This active approach articulates an explicit reconsideration of an interior atmosphere-environment construction intent on affect-ing inhabitants. Architecture conceived with this more holistic awareness requires a rethinking of parameters, moving beyond the visual modalities of geometry, compo-sition, icon or style, to instead utilize various qualitative materials like temperature, light intensity, relative humidity, air composition, air pressure, auditory and olfactory stimuli. It maintains what the British architectural historian Reyner Banham, writ-ing about Joseph Paxton's mid-nineteenth-century greenhouse designs, has referred to as an "environmentalist" approach to architectural design.

1
IN PURSUIT OF COMFORT
From Campfire to Smart Home

> The machinery of Society, profoundly *out of gear,* oscillates between amelioration, of historical importance, and a catastrophe.
>
> The primordial instinct of every human being is to assure himself of a shelter. The various classes of workers in society to-day *no longer have dwellings adapted to their needs; neither the artizan nor the intellectual.*
>
> It is a question of building which is at the root of the social unrest of to-day: architecture or revolution.
>
> (Le Corbusier 1986, 8 and 269)

If we do not alter our approach to living-in-the-world-ecology, the potential for violent transformation today, brought about by "*a profound mutation in our relation to the world*" (Latour 2017, 8), will no doubt express itself through social unrest as similarly warned against by Le Corbusier in his 1923 manifesto *Vers Une Architecture* (*Towards a New Architecture*), published in the aftermath of destruction brought by the first great war when access to a modern standard of living had yet to be achieved for the masses. He recites this passage both in the book's introduction and again at the start of the final chapter titled: "Architecture or Revolution," as if to remind the reader of the seriousness of the situation – there are *real* lives at stake, *real* consequences to inaction. Today there also exists a very *real* threat of violence and unrest arising from radical global climate instability. These potentials are a translation of the violence perpetrated by human-beings upon the earth-system,[1] upon the ecological world, fostering the need to recognize what the French social theorist Bruno Latour has called the New Climatic Regime, and in his book *Down to Earth*, he names as a new political actor the "Terrestrial." This burgeoning reality, like Timothy Morton's total collective "being-with," requires a redistribution of agency to non-human *and* non-living beings, recognizing their ability to act, and most importantly react to human (in)actions. Latour posits that to mitigate the current and future potential for violence and social unrest caused by anthropogenic climate destabilization within the New Climatic Regime, human-beings must move away from both modernity's project of globalization and the counter response of retracting into the local, to instead move toward the "Terrestrial." "The attractor designated as Terrestrial – which is clearly distinct from 'nature' and which is not the entire planet but only the thin biofilm of the Critical Zone – brings together the opposing figures of the soil and the world" (Latour 2018, 92). It provides a vantage point "from up close, as *internal* to the collectivities and *sensitive* to human actions..." (Latour 2018, 67). Conceiving a "Terrestrial" approach to living-in-the-world-ecology demands that human-beings consider all "beings," all "actors," with which they inter-act as part of their "dwelling place" – an alternative to the limited idea of territory or even ecology.[2] Latour conceives of a terrestrial being's "dwelling place" as *"that which a terrestrial depends for its survival*, while asking *what other terrestrials also depend on it?"* It reflects a list of what the terrestrial being "needs for its subsistence, and, consequently, what it is *ready to defend,* with its own life if need be" (Latour 2018, 95). Through this lens, the design and conception of the constructed environments we inhabit in the Anthropocene may be redefined as our *architectural* "dwelling places." This describes the specific architectural elements, strategies, organizations, technologies and materials implemented by human-beings toward the mediation of the surrounding environment necessary for survival and to produce a more habitable interior condition(ing). However, in the current context beyond ecological-climatological "crisis", a conceptualization of the *architectural* "dwelling-place" must also not be singularly specific to humans alone, but rather it must reflect a mutually conscious and mutually beneficial "being-with" the "Terrestrial" collective. This suggests an architecture borne out of mutual respect and collaboration with these beings, not as an endeavor external to them.

Beyond Sustainable aims to explore the concept and articulation of the *architectural* "dwelling place" more fully; in order to better understand how we've arrived at our current location so far removed from the ground, this first chapter focuses on a brief history of architecture as an adaptive *technological mediator* as described through numerous architectural origin stories put forth by a variety of architects throughout history. Sometimes mythical, anecdotal or polemical, architectural discourse has been punctuated with numerous stories describing its "origins" as an essential form of environmental mediation. Many of these origin narratives employ the ideation of a "primitive hut" as the source for all future architectural endeavors. The connotation of the word "primitive" in many of these stories was not necessarily intended as a pejorative; rather, the primitive's vantage point, with his/her unconscious and innate responses to dealing with the world, was positively valued. In his 1964 exhibition at the Museum of Modern Art, *Architecture without Architects*, Bernard Rudofsky critiqued the destruction of vernacular architecture by the advancement of twentieth-century development, aiming to elevate the "primitive" to a legitimate status in the eyes of architects, and in particular architectural historians, referring to the many examples included in the exhibition as "non-pedigreed architecture." Ada Louise Huxtable in her *New York Times* review of the show noted that Rudofsky was not the first to invent the subject, referencing Sibyl Moholy Nagy's 1957 publication *Native Genius in Anonymous Architecture*. However, her words were clear in her assessment of the exhibition's "beauty and significance," but also cutting in her view of its immaterial "romanticism."

> These are examples of indigenous, regional architecture before "progress" has brought the materials salesman and his plastic substitutes. This is the self-contained community as it was until the automobile cracked it open and desolated the tightly knit architectural entity of another era.
> More than an exhibition, then, this is a protest – a pointed, bitter, desperate broadside from a cultivated, rebellious heart and mind against the sacrifice of the well-built landscape to the urgencies of the industrial, nuclear age. And later on:
> How valid is the exhibition's thesis? There can be no argument, certainly, with the beauty and significance of the examples shown, nor with the satisfactory solutions of the unknown builders of the anonymous architectural world for their particular needs...
> No one can fail to share the author's despair over vandalism with which this century is treating its handsome vernacular heritage. The lesson, of course, is that radical and necessary changes in the contemporary environment are not being anticipated or planned for. Their force is permitted to be destructive beyond the bounds of sense or sensibility...
> But add this extremely specialized visual appreciation to the love of primitive utopia peculiar to a highly sophisticated man (utopia may turn out to be complete with open sewers and the stench of pigs) and we have a romanticism that complex modern cultures can ill afford. There are few simple, picturesque solutions to contemporary problems.
>
> *(Huxtable 1964)*

In the introductory essay to the exhibition, Rudofsky makes plain his genuine admiration for these "anonymous builders" who developed many "primitive" architectural solutions that "anticipate our cumbersome technology; that many a feature invented in recent years is old hat in vernacular architecture – prefabrication, standardization of building components, flexible and movable structures, and, more especially, floor-heating, air-conditioning, light control, even elevators" (Rudofsky 1964, para. 15). In Rudofsky's view, the "non-pedigreed" architectural approach provided an unbiased and unmediated predilection

FIGURE 1.1 Inside of a Bushman's hut, 1861. Photograph courtesy of Schomburg Center for Research in Black Culture, Manuscripts, Archives and Rare Books Division, The New York Public Library. "Inside of a Bushman's Hut" The New York Public Library Digital Collections. 1861. http://digitalcollections.nypl.org/items/510d47da-6ecc-a3d9-e040-e00a18064a99

for mitigating the discomforts of environment by constructing architecture intrinsically in tune with, and within, its natural context. On display were the numerous latent architectural *instincts* of the "primitive," uncluttered by conscious motivations of advancement related to society, culture or even history (Figure 1.1). Historian Joseph Rykwert articulates this perception of the "primitive" human-being's natural abilities as a series of "heroic archetypal figures."

> 'In the beginning' these figures gave immediate expression to their inner nature, which, uncontaminated, was in unison with the fundamental laws of all creation. They were therefore able to devise the essential skills, and the constant imitation of these first actions led to all the basic human accomplishments.
>
> *(Rykwert 1981, 16)*

This instinctual approach to the design of the dwelling, inherently compatible with its surrounding environment through the use of local materials, forms and construction techniques, was also validated by the early twentieth-century Viennese architect Adolf Loos, in his 1910 essay titled simply "Architecture." In the essay Loos describes the experience of visiting a lakeside village observing the humble houses of farmers, looking as though they came "from God's own workshop." In contrast, he calls out the disturbing effect that a villa designed by "the architect" has had on the beauty and peace of the lakeside.

> [The farmer] wanted to build a house for himself, his relatives and his livestock, and in that he succeeded. Just as successful as his neighbours or his ancestors were. Just as any animal succeeds that allows itself to be guided by its instincts…The architect, like almost every urban dweller,

has no culture. He lacks the certainty of the farmer, who possesses culture. The Urban dweller is an uprooted person. By culture I mean that balance of man's inner and outer being which alone guarantees rational thought and action.

(Loos 1985, 104)

This conception of "culture" is born out of *place*, out of a symbiotic relationship with the surroundings, with environment. The peasant farmer, unlike the architect, may tap into an unconscious sagacity to construct his/her dwelling, what Rykwert refers to as a kind of "hidden, secular, telluric wisdom that is concealed from the 'civilized,' the 'privileged,' and accessible only to the 'primitive.'" (Rykwert 1981, 28) Rudofsky articulates it as a "communal enterprise" (Rudofsky 1964, para. 7). Loos elaborates this difference further when he describes his distinction between who he calls either a "craftsman" or a "draughtsman," characterizing the former as the receiver of accumulated knowledge over generations rooted in a particular culture, while the latter is concerned only with making images having "lost contact with his time" capable now only of decoration (Loos 1985, 105). In this way, the "untrained" peasant farmer is capable of applying a more genuine and uncontaminated approach to constructing his/her dwelling, one that is more connected, more in tune and more grounded with, and within, the surroundings.

The other primary type of architectural origin story places the "primitive" in a less revered position, effectively unable to deal with environmental demands. The nineteenth-century French theorist and architect Eugéne-Emmanuel Viollet-le-Duc ascribes the "primitive" as having no such innate ability to effectively house him/herself. In his fantastical, yet encyclopedic, book *The Habitations of Man in All Ages*, he describes the unending journey of two supernatural characters Doxius and Epergos, who observe the development of various building cultures around the globe throughout human history. The book's prologue begins with a description of Doxious and Epergos observing the plight of early humans, whom they refer to as "creatures" but also "not animals like the others" (Viollet-le-Duc 1876, 1–2). These early humans are crouched under a bushy tree whose limbs have been pulled down and held to the ground by soil. When a storm comes, they are inundated with rain and wind, capable only of heaping up dead branches and reeds to partially cover them against the elements (Figure 1.2). Epergos, seeing their misery, decides to show them how to build a basic shelter.

[Epergos] selects two young trees a few paces apart. Climbing one of these, he bends it down by the weight of his body, pulls towards him the top of the other with the help of a hooked stick, and thus joining the branches of the two trees, ties them together with rushes. The creatures that have gathered round him look on wondering. But Epergos does not

34 Technological Mediation

FIGURE 1.2 Eugene-Emmanuel Viollet-le-Duc, the first shelter, 1876. Reprinted from Eugene-Emmanuel Viollet-le-Duc. *The Habitations of Man in All Ages*. trans. Benjamin Bucknall (London: Sampson Low, Marston, Searle, & Rivington, 1876) 5, fig. 1.

mean them to remain idle, and makes them understand that they must go and find other young trees in the neighbourhood. With their hands and with the help of sticks they uproot and drag them to Epergos; who then shows them how they should be inclined in a circle by resting their tops against the first two trees that had been fastened together. Then he shows them how to fill in the spaces with rushes, branches, and long grass interlaced; then how their roots should be covered with clay, and the whole structure successively; leaving an opening on the side opposite to the wind that brings the rain.

(Viollet-le-Duc 1876, 5–7)

It was this supernatural education that provided these "creatures" the ability to live-in-the-world as human-beings now capable of building a proper hut, and therefore think rationally, leading to the creation of civilizations and countless other culturally specific architectural habitations (Figure 1.3). The entirety of the book moves forward in time from this initial origin moment in a debate between the two characters on the effects of this first act of architectural

FIGURE 1.3 Eugene-Emmanuel Viollet-le-Duc, the first hut, 1876. Reprinted from Eugene-Emmanuel Viollet-le-Duc. *The Habitations of Man in All Ages*. trans. Benjamin Bucknall (London: Sampson Low, Marston, Searle, & Rivington, 1876) 6, fig. 2.

knowledge transmission and whether it was a justifiable act or a subversion of the original "Creator's work." As described by the architectural historian M. Fil Hearn, Viollet-le-Duc's recounting of this origin story "was to demonstrate that architecture began when rational planning and procedure were applied to the problem of the need for shelter." Implying "that the scheme for the first building was revealed, coming as a gift from a higher intelligence, much as fire had been the gift of Prometheus" (Hearn 1990, 23).

While the desire to describe architecture's origin no doubt reflects a genuine curiosity to understand more completely our beginning, the contrasting implications of Loos's and Viollet-le-Duc's architectural origin narratives makes clear these stories have also been guided by less than historical motives, often seeking to reinforce specific ideas about contemporary architecture. One of the clearest origin stories told in this regard is from Marc-Antoine Laugier in his 1753 text *Essai sur l'architecture* (*Essay on Architecture*).

> The savage, in his leafy shelter, does not know how to protect himself from the uncomfortable damp that penetrates everywhere; he creeps into a nearby cave and, finding it dry, he praises himself for his discovery. But soon darkness and foul air surrounding him make his stay unbearable

again. He leaves and is resolved to make good by his ingenuity the careless neglect of nature. He wants to make himself a dwelling that protects but does not bury him. Some fallen branches in the forest are the right material for his purpose; he chooses four of the strongest, raises them upright and arranges them in a square; across the top he lays four other branches; on these he hoists from two sides yet another row of branches which, inclining towards each other, meet at their highest point. He then covers this kind of roof with leaves so closely packed that neither sun nor rain can penetrate. Thus, man is housed.

(Laugier 1977, 11–12)

Laugier's written description of this origin hut was intended through its emphasis on rational simplicity and conception from nature, as a clear rebuke of French Rococo's exuberant saturation of form and decoration of the time.[3] As he states later in the first chapter: "It is true that I take away from architecture much that is superfluous, that I strip it of a lot of trash of which ornamentation commonly consists and only leave it its natural simplicity" (Laugier 1977, 36). While his *Essai* doesn't put forth any architectural design principles not already stated by others, a fact Laugier saw as advantageous in that he could rely on accepted notions and principles (Herrmann 1962, 47), what was unique about his origin narrative was the intention for it to be used toward future architectural design, not simply a means to better understand the past.

He was the first to present the hut as a structure of vital importance for the present...Its momentous significance lay for him in the fact that it provided a badly needed norm by which present-day architecture should and could be guided.

(Herrmann 1962, 48)

The continued interest in Laugier's hut may in part be due to the compelling frontispiece engraving included in the second edition of the book, produced by Charles Eisen (Figure 1.4). It portrays a female figure, the personification of architecture, seated on the ruins of classical stone architectural building elements, pointing toward a structure created from the natural timber elements of the forest. The image illustrates Laugier's rationalist ideas toward a pure inception of form, without decoration and stripped down to the essential elements: column, entablature and pediment, all derived from, and in concert with, nature. One intriguing difference to note between the frontispiece and the description of the hut in Laugier's text concerns the vertical supports. In Laugier's description, they are simply the strongest "fallen branches" raised upright, but in the engraving, they are actual living trees, rooted in the ground and alive, extending above the roof to form a living canopy, with some branches cut, presumably to construct the hut's roof. These differences, while subtle, suggest

In Pursuit of Comfort 37

FIGURE 1.4 Marc-Antonie Laugier, frontispiece to second edition of *Essai sur l'architecture*, 1755. Engraving by by Charles Eisen. Reprinted from Marc-Antonie Laugier. *Essai sur l'architecture: avec une dictionnaire des termes et planches qui en facilitent l'explication* (Paris: Dunchesne, 1755) ii.

at least two interpretations: (1) that the architect has tamed, designed, shaped, engineered the forest to meet human habitation needs or (2) that the architect has selectively and respectfully intervened within the forest to produce an interdependent ecological collaboration. There is also perhaps a third possibility, one capable of providing a synthesis between human and natural systems, as reflected in the research work of Ferdinand Ludwig resulting in the definition of a new type of hybrid origin. Ludwig's experimental Baubotanik tower installation provides a temporary steel tube scaffolding structure composed into a series of platforms reaching nine meters tall, which support the growth of 102-meter high silver willows (*sallx alba*). These young willows are organized in a way so they will intergrow with one another (inosculation), creating over time a timber-framed tower structure that can independently support horizontal platforms. The scaffolding is a guide for future growth, but the process of inosculation is also unpredictable; it is one of natural occurrence that Ludwig sets up and provokes through his strategic arrangement and design. Principles of natural growth processes are redirected toward the development of a structure, albeit somewhat unpredictably.[4]

Another example of this third possibility is the temporary hut pavilion installation designed by the research studio OMG! (O'Donnell Miller Group), a collaboration between architects Caroline O'Donnell and Martin Miller, installed in 2017 at Art Omi in Ghent, NY. The project is composed of a series of self-similar plywood components, capable of slotting together to produce a structure that maximizes volume while minimizing the amount of physical material. These components were CNC milled using a single pass of the drill bit, to produce a layered fluted texture along their surfaces. The components were assembled into a lattice structure adopting the form of gable roof house, similar in profile to Laugier's hut (Figures 1.5 and 1.6). However, OMG! doesn't differentiate between the fundamental elements of column, entablature or pediment, but rather relies on the designed intelligence of their component to assemble into the archetypal form. Additionally, four Maple saplings are planted within the lattice structure; over time these saplings will grow and overtake the hut, accelerating its intentionally designed degradation and ultimate decomposition. Open areas in the lattice structure contain additional "pots" made of a custom hemp, tree sap, sawdust and biodegradable resin compress as well as others made out of cow manure, all intended to eventually fall to the ground, nourishing the further growth of the saplings and the hut's overall deconstruction.

The project cultivates a controlled collaboration between the architectural structure, the "primitive" gabled roof hut and the living trees. This relationship is temporal and evolving; the hut accepts its lack of control, embracing its own designed decomposition and transformation. Here architecture's collaboration with nature is in balance, in productive correlation capable of moving beyond the simply sustainable, toward an idea of broader life affirmation. OMG!'s primitive hut is the product of conflicting realities and begins to suggest an

In Pursuit of Comfort   39

FIGURE 1.5   OMG! (O'Donnell Miller Group), *Primitive Hut*, a growing / decomposing pavilion at Art Omi, concept rendering, Ghent, NY, 2017. Image courtesy of OMG.

FIGURE 1.6   OMG! (O'Donnell Miller Group), *Primitive Hut*, a growing / decomposing pavilion at Art Omi, photo of completed pavilion, Ghent, NY, 2017. Photograph by Brian Havener. Photograph courtesy of OMG.

architectural origin narrative that provides the possibility of engendering a "Terrestrial" architectural habitation of the twenty-first century filled with questions of accelerating environmental degradation, alongside an acceleration in the means of making through advanced digital fabrication techniques and ecologically collaborative design thinking.

Other alternative architectural origin examples of a "Terrestrial" approach to habitation can be found elsewhere in several historical works by non-architects. André Leroi-Gourhan's anthropological study of late Paleolithic stand-alone[5] dwelling structures, built not of pure natural elements derived from the forest, but from the remains of hunted mammoths, reusing the bones, tusks, hides and innards (Figure 1.7), provides such an example.

> At Kostienki, near Kiev, a veritable Solutrean village was discovered. It has a row of open-air hearths surrounding storage-pits and habitations. One hut is fairly well preserved. It consisted of two adjoining oval-shaped rooms dug into the ground to a depth of about a yard and having a diameter of five or six yards. A bench circled the rooms, serving as both a seat and a bed. On the bench was a column of mammoth tusks, set up to support the roof. Sod or turf must have been placed on a layer of big mammoth bones, especially shoulder and pelvic bones, to form the roof.
> (Leroi-Gourhan 1957, 106–107)

In this instance, the animal provided sustenance for the human body, while simultaneously providing many physical raw materials from which humans could assemble habitable enclosures. This "reconstruction" of the animal body as an instrument of environmental mediation, of sheltering, suggests a radical conceptualization of the animal not only as a *source* of sustenance, but also a possible *site* to inhabit. This approach resulted in a deep respect for these animals, a

FIGURE 1.7 Ice age shelter composed of Mammoth bones, Mezhirich, Ukraine, ca. 13,000 BC. Images by lemmy-caution. Courtesy of flciker.

regard for them not as merely resources, but as brothers, sisters, fathers, deities to be revered and shown gratitude for their sacrifice.[6] However, even despite this reverence, it has become increasingly apparent that the mammoths and other "megafauna" of the Paleolithic period, likely did not die out until human-beings migrated into their territories to hunt them. While sudden shifts in climate likely played a part, human actions appear to be the most likely factor in their extinction.[7] This demonstrates how even when revered and respected as family or deity, and seeking balanced collaboration, unchecked human actions may have deadly consequences for other beings living-in-the-world-ecology.

★ ★ ★

As has been discussed thus far, there have been generally two different fundamental attitudes regarding early human's architectural strategies for technological mediation of the environment, one borne of instinctual responses and one of rational forethought. In his extensive exposition of architectural origin narratives, historian Joseph Rykwert describes these two paths in his book *On Adam's House in Paradise* first, as expressed by Mies, Mendelsohn, Choisy and others, they were the result "of man slowly adapting the various makeshift arrangements which the inclemency of the weather imposed upon him" – progress through the direct creation of a *physical* shelter from unconscious instinctual utility and survival-in-the-world (Rykwert 1981, 21), or, as second expressed by Leroi-Gourhan and generally by Le Corbusier, they were the result of a *conceptual* rationality – "It is the difference of conception, the attachment of meaning to his task, that distinguishes man's first attempts in that direction from those of the instinctually driven beasts" (Rykwert 1981, 22). These two attitudes, though not wholly exclusive to one another, do imply very different ideas about architecture's origin – one determined by reactive responses to shifting environmental landscapes, developed informally over time, the other a conscious premeditated act of unadulterated "reason," what Rykwert describes as reflecting the "unity of mankind," and the resultant "primacy of reason" (Rykwert 1981, 28). The literal history of man's architectural origin likely lies somewhere between these two trajectories, and consequently, architects have referenced both together in support of their specific architectural prerogative.

One such case is Leon Batista Alberti's fifteenth-century treatise *On the Art of Building in Ten Books*; beginning in the first book, he states that "the whole matter of building is composed of lineaments and structure" (Alberti 1988, 7). Alberti argued that the purpose of lineaments lies in the somewhat ambiguous notion of determining the "correct" or "infallible" way of putting together the numerous parts of a building into a "graceful order" of "lines and angles" (Alberti 1988, 7) originating and "deriving from the mind" (Alberti 1988, 422). A rational conception of an abstract order imposed over every aspect of the building. However, it was his description of the six fundamental elements related to all buildings: locality, area, compartition, wall, roof and opening,

42 Technological Mediation

which best illustrates his conception of the relationship between structure and environment, as it pertains to an architectural origin. He demonstrates the essential qualities of these six elements in the origin story he recounts:

> In the beginning, men sought a place to rest in some region safe from danger; having found a place both suitable and agreeable, they settled down and took possession of the site. Not wishing to have all their household and private affairs conducted in the same place, they set aside one space for sleeping, another for the hearth, and allocated other spaces to different uses. After this men began to consider how to build a roof, as a shelter from the sun and the rain. For this purpose they built walls on which a roof could be laid – for they realized that in this way they would be the better protected from icy storms and frosty winds; finally they opened windows and doors in the walls, from floor to roof, so as to allow entry and social gathering within, and also to let in the sunlight and the breezes at the right time, as well as to let out any moisture and vapor that may have formed inside the house.
>
> *(Alberti 1988, 7–8)*

This description presents a well-coordinated set of relationships between the environment, structure and human inhabitants. And while the lineaments provided a "correct" geometric order, what was most important was the cooperative organization of these physical elements, "that the harmony [between parts] is such that the building appears a single, integral, and well-composed body, rather than a collection of extraneous and unrelated parts" (Alberti 1988, 23–24). Through these six coordinated elements, human-beings were able to live-in-the-world, actively selecting, occupying and building within a "locality" of agreeable climate, with signs of "good air and pure water"[8] to ensure sustained health and well-being. While Alberti extensively describes all the elements throughout his first book, it is the *physical* element of the roof that he declares most critical.

> Roofs are the most important elements; for not only do they help to maintain the good health of the residents be defending them from rain, and keeping out the night, and above all keeping out the summer sun, but they provide excellent protection for the whole building as well.
>
> *(Alberti 1988, 26)*

And in Book Two, he says:

> In particular, great attention should be paid to ensure that the design of the roof is the best possible. For unless I am mistaken, the roof of its very nature was the first of all building elements to provide mankind with a

place of shelter: so much so that it was for the sake of the roof that the need arose not only for the wall and all that goes with it, but also for anything structured below ground....

(Alberti 1988, 34–35)

If the lineaments described an underlying order "deriving from the mind," then the roof expressed the most basic human tendency to create a protective barrier between oneself and the forces of environment. According to Rykwert, the most poetic origin of such a double-pitched roof came from Filarete's fifteenth-century *Treatise on Architecture*, in which he recounts Adam being cast out of Eden, covering his head with his hands from the first rain marking the first action of architectural invention[9] (Rykwert 1981, 119) (Figure 1.8).

Like Alberti before him, Le Corbusier offers several ideations underlying architectural origins, one of instinctual preference for a particular "soil" fostering a *physical* response to mediate the environment, and another based

FIGURE 1.8 Filarete, Adam covering his head with his hands from the first rain, ca. 1464. Reprinted from Filarete. *Treatise on Architecture, Volume 2: The Facsimile* (New Haven: CT: Yale University Press, 1965) Book I, folio 4v.

fundamentally on *conceptual* geometrical rationality and order. Writing in *Vers Une Architecture* (*Towards a New Architecture*), he states:

> Primitive man has brought his chariot to a stop, he decides that here shall be his native soil. He chooses a glade, he cuts down the trees which are too close, he levels the earth around; he opens up the road which will carry him to the river or to those of his tribe whom he has just left; he drives the stakes which are to steady his tent. He surrounds this tent with a palisade in which he arranges a doorway. The road is as straight as he can manage it with his implements, his arms and his time. The pegs of his tent describe a square, a hexagon or an octagon. The palisade forms a rectangle whose four angles are equal. The door of his hut is on the axis of the enclosure – and the door of the enclosure faces exactly the door of the hut.
> *(Le Corbusier 1986, 69) (Figure 1.9)*

The many affirmations of the engineer's approach to design in contrast to the architect throughout *Vers Une Architecture* makes apparent Le Corbusier's preference for the rational conception of the primitive hut toward the formulation of a

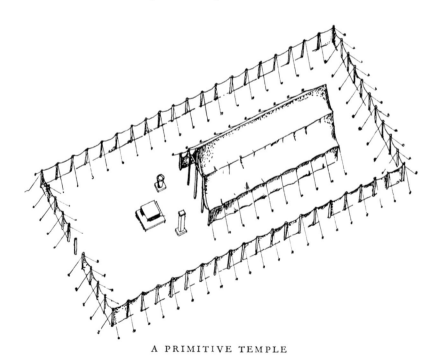

A PRIMITIVE TEMPLE

FIGURE 1.9 Le Corbusier, a primitive temple, [1923] 1986 (Le Corbusier, *Towards a New Architecture*, p. 71). © F.L.C. / ADAGP, Paris / Artists Rights Society (ARS), New York 2019.

"modern" architectural project. The engineer was one who based his work not on the preference for different decorative styles, but rather on "mathematical calculation," "economy," "physical necessity" and "cold reason." Le Corbusier makes a similar point in his 1928 book *Une maison – un palais* (*A House – A Palace*), in which he includes multiple sketches of primitive structures as a kind of underlying historical foundation, or rationale, to support the winning entry he and Pierre Jeanneret made to the 1927 competition for the Palais des Nations building in Geneva, Switzerland[10] (Vogt 1998, 185). Along with these sketches, Le Corbusier states: "Here now the primitive house: Here man reveals himself as a creator of geometry; he is incapable of acting without geometry"[11] (Le Corbusier 1928, 38).

Le Corbusier's preference for an architectural origin founded upon geometrical rationality may be best understood through what he calls "regulating lines," and perhaps not so coincidently his recounting of this early dwelling as quoted above starts the chapter in *Vers Une Architecture* called "Regulating Lines." In reference to the plan of the primitive house or temple, he says, "They are the product of measurement. In order to construct well and distribute your efforts to advantage, in order to obtain solidity and utility in the work, units of measure are the first conditions of all" (Le Corbusier 1986, 70). And he goes further still, making the claim that man's instincts toward building are to produce order through geometrical principles.

> But in deciding the form of the enclosure, the form of the hut, the situation of the alter and its accessories, he has had by instinct recourse to right angles – axes, the square, the circle. For he could not create anything otherwise which would give him the feeling that he was creating. For all these things – axes, circles, right angles – are geometrical truths, and give results that our eye can measure and recognize; whereas otherwise there would be only chance, irregularity and capriciousness. Geometry is the language of man.
>
> *(Le Corbusier 1986, 72)*

This co-opting of man's instinct toward the rational conception of architecture measured by the "feeling" of creation is what he means when he describes architecture as a "pure creation of the mind,"[12] a fundamentally *conceptual* pursuit that man had lost but needed to return to if he was to truly become Modern.

Historian Adolf Max Vogt, in his book *Le Corbusier – Noble Savage*, examines Le Corbusier's sketches of primitive structures from *Une maison – un palais*, grouping them according to building types and giving special attention to the two sketches of the *crannog*, drawn with cubic geometries elevated over a lake, in an effort to demonstrate Le Corbusier's preference for purity of form (Vogt 1998, 189 and 202) (Figure 1.10). Vogt comments that they're "mysterious" and "highly astonishing," asking the question: "Whoever heard that the earliest human shelters, supposed to represent the most elementary survival strategy, could afford, of all things, the luxury of the nearly pure form of a cube and a

46 Technological Mediation

FIGURE 1.10 Le Corbusier, sketches of early structures grouped according to the primary forms of box, tent, flat roof and vaulted building types, 1928 / 1998 (original sketches from Le Corbusier, *Une maison – un palais*, p. 39, 41, 43, 45, 47; regrouped and redrawn by Adolf Max Vogt, *Le Corbusier, the Noble Savage*, p. 189). © F.L.C. / ADAGP, Paris / Artists Rights Society (ARS), New York 2019.

flat roof cover?" (Vogt 1998, 190). Despite Vogt's question of their historical accuracy, these sketches indeed reflect a critical development in Le Corbusier's modernist subjectivity of pure form and the liberation of the ground place. Vogt argues that these *crannog* sketches were almost certainly drawn in some version much earlier than during the Palais des Nations competition, and were specifically selected and redrawn for the publication of *Une maison – un palais* (Vogt 1998, 191 and 218). Most likely, they date to the time period of his early education in La Chaux-de-Fonds instructed by his regionalist teacher Charles l'Eplattenier, an advocate of the early history of Switzerland and its indigenous structures which resembled the Irish *crannogs*[13] (Figure 1.11).

What cannot be overlooked in a discussion of the *crannog*, as it relates to model for adaptive environmental mediation, is the question Vogt later asks: how do these structures function during inclement weather with such large openings? (Vogt 1998, 215). There are also basic questions about how the flat roofs would have adequately shed water and how the proportions altered by Le Corbusier from Sir William Robert Willis Wilde's original description[14] would actually produce habitable interior space. Vogt suggests the possibility of a raw hide curtain hung in front to block the wind and rain, which may have

In Pursuit of Comfort   47

FIGURE 1.11   Le Corbusier, huttes des crannoges d'Irlande, 1928 (Le Corbusier, *Une maison – un palais*, p. 39). © F.L.C. / ADAGP, Paris / Artists Rights Society (ARS), New York 2019.

been a likely solution, but this is not an element Le Corbusier includes. What's most important to Le Corbusier is their purity of form, the liberation of the horizontal plane and a dignity of honest intentions by these "primitive" builders rather than their environmental aptitude or engagement.

> Just as Rousseau maintains that the first human beings were *good,* Le Corbusier maintains now that the first hut has *dignity* and therefore is the *equal* of a palace. This is the decisive *anchoring* of Le Corbusier's argument, which enables him too to measure the world from its primeval beginnings rather than from the present.
>
> *(Vogt 1998, 158)*

This measuring of the past however serves as a particular "origin" not for an architecture of environmental mediation, but for the specific story of modernity Le Corbusier was trying to create, and trying to convince the world was the answer to the many concerns of the early twentieth century (Chapter 2 further explores the implications of this geometrical pursuit as it relates to a further technological mediation of the environment). There is a deep irony in harkening back to a time of the primitive hut as a model for modernity. Whether the result of instinctual *physical* responses or *conceptual* forethinking, the actions of the "primitive" by definition are outside the sphere of modernity's interior, yet it is precisely because of this dislocation that architects have looked to their constructions as a means for justifying their actions toward the creation of a particular future, toward a particular remaking of the world.

In large part, these architectural origin narratives have provided a powerful tool for architects because, regardless of the underlying trigger – instinct or forethought – they each describe the humanization of space, of the world itself.

André Leroi-Gourhan characterized dwelling as the creation of a distinctly "humanized space" (Leroi-Gourhan 1993, 318–322) reflecting the

> taking possession of time and space through the intermediacy of symbols, to a domestication in the strictest sense of the term, since they lead to the creation of controllable space and time within the home and radiating outward from the home.
>
> *(Leroi-Gourhan 1993, 314–315)*

This "domestication" of space was revolutionary in its ability to conceptualize the human place within the natural rhythmicity of *the* world, by remaking it into his/her *own* world, turning " humanized time and space into a theatrical stage upon which the play of nature was humanly controlled" (Leroi-Gourhan 1993, 315). For Le Corbusier, this remaking of *the* world is embodied through the creation of architecture itself. "Architecture is the first manifestation of man creating his own universe, creating it in the image of nature, submitting to the laws of nature, the laws which govern our own nature, our universe" (Le Corbusier 1986, 73–74). While the act of architectural creation may have helped humanize the world, it has also come at a steep price as we're now experiencing in a time of climate destabilization, environmental degradation and mass species extinction. But must it impose itself without concern? Without respect? Without empathy? Perhaps we need a new origin story that addresses these questions. The conception of a Terrestrial *architectural* "dwelling place" requires humans to admit they too are *a part of the world*, borne out of a dynamic co-productive relationship between themselves, the web of life and their constructed environments of habitation

Leroi-Gourhan refers to the human aspect of such actions as "socialization." He argues that the replacement of the "chaotic rhythmicity of the natural world" with a more regularized and controllable cadence derived from a shared network of symbols is "the principal element of human socialization," the system in which we communicate and inter-act, but also how we have chosen to remake our world (Leroi-Gourhan 1993, 315). This system of socialization goes hand in hand with the development of the dwelling.

> Organization of inhabited space is not only a matter of technical convenience but also, by the same token as language, the symbolic expression of globally human behavior. In all known human groups the habitat meets the threefold requirement of creating a technically efficient environment, establishing a framework for the social system, and providing a starting point for the work of ordering the surrounding universe.
>
> *(Leroi-Gourhan 1993, 319–322)*

A "Terrestrial" architectural origin narrative validates the role "socialization" and dwelling have played in remaking the world, but it also demands this correspondence occur not just between human-beings, but also more broadly as a correlation *with* the "chaotic rhythmicity of the natural world" and all its constituent beings, not in lieu of it. This suggests a collaborative remaking of *a* world, beyond an ideation of anthropocentric sustainability and toward a "Terrestrial" experience of total "being with" the-world-ecology.

★ ★ ★

The Roman architect Vitruvius emphasized the fundamental role socialization played in his architectural origin story instigated by a specific event: the discovery of fire. He describes that in the aftermath of a chance initiation of a forest fire, humans drew near to the remaining flames realizing how comfortable it was to be within its warming proximity. This realization of the comforting effects of fire brought men/women to gather, spurning acts of communicative signing, and facilitating rudimentary acts of vocal communication, the shared naming of common things and the construction of the first shelters (Figure 1.12).

FIGURE 1.12 Cesare Cesariano, the discovery of fire, 1521. Reprinted from the illustrated 1521 italian language edition of Vitruvius Pollio, Ceasare Cesariano, and Gotardo da Ponte. *De architectura libri dece* (Como: Gotardo da Ponte, 1521) 31v.

50 Technological Mediation

> Therefore it was the discovery of fire that originally gave rise to the coming together of men, to the deliberative assembly, and social intercourse. And so, as they kept coming together in greater numbers into one place, finding themselves naturally gifted beyond the other animals in not being obliged to walk with faces to the ground, but upright and gazing upon the splendor of the starry firmament, and also in being able to do with ease whatever they chose with their hands and fingers, they began in that first assembly to construct shelters.
>
> *(Vitruvius 1960, 38)*

The claim that fire is a necessary precursor to socialization, the development of the primitive hut and ultimately to civilization itself,[15] marks a third architectural origin narrative type. In this narrative, the flame, whether provided by chance from nature or gifted by Prometheus, draws human-beings together by way of creating a localized thermal environment instigating the need to protect and maintain its eternal ignition through architectural intervention. The primal role of fire and the construction of a structure to protect it was echoed in the nineteenth century by German architect Gottfried Semper, who, in his 1851 book *The Four Elements of Architecture,* wrote:

> The first sign of human settlement and rest after the hunt, the battle, and wandering in the desert is today, as when the first men lost paradise, the setting up of the fireplace and the lighting of the reviving, warming, and food-preparing flame. Around the hearth the first groups assembled; around it the first alliances formed; around it the first rude religious concepts were put into the customs of a cult. Throughout all phases of society the hearth formed that sacred focus around which the whole took order and shape.
>
> *(Semper 1989, 102)*

It was the first of the four elements of architecture, the "moral" element, reflected in the gathering of men and women around the hearth, that was responsible for Semper's development of the other three: the roof, the enclosure and the mound, which served to protect the flame's integrity "against the three hostile elements of nature" (Semper 1989, 102). For Semper, like Alberti before him, the roof was the most predominant architectural construction as it not only directly protected inhabitants from inclement weather, but provided man the ability "to protect his hearth" (Semper 1989, 110–111) and preserve the flame. Lawrence Wright, in his 1964 book *Home Fires Burning*, recounts the history of domestic heating and cooking in England and reflects on fire as perhaps the most important element in early human's dwelling life.

> Man's supremacy in the animal kingdom is usually attributed to his use of tools, but it might be said to stem from his taming of fire. Few of his

tools, or of any other articles in his home, have ever been made without its use at some stage. Nor might the home itself have come into being, but for the fire that gave reason for taking food "home" to cook and eat it. Fire also enabled food to be preserved, and so gave leisure for thought... Once established, the camp-fire would become the focus of assembly, and a shield against attack by mastodon or mosquito.

(Wright 1964, 3–5)

Wright surmises two origin narratives of fire and dwelling, the first whereby "In winter the camp-fire would be moved nearer to the [habitation] pit or hut, and one especially cold night, some daring innovator may have dragged the embers indoors" (Wright 1964, 6). This possibility regards fire as a supplementary component toward the adjustment of an already defined architectural interior. The second is more in line with Vitruvius and Semper, reflecting the essential role fire played toward the creation of architecture, proposing that "rather than the hearth moving into the house, the house began as a circular screen round the hearth" (Wright 1964, 6). In this way, the first architectural construction was a solution for protecting the flame, which was understood as the fundamental agent of environmental mediation and the production of a habitable interiority. The ability to protect it was critical as Wright makes the distinction between the relatively simple ability needed to "tend" a fire in comparison to the more difficult achievement to "make" one. "This duty of keeping the home fires burning became a sacred one, associated in all periods with the rituals of the undying fire, the divine spark, the runner with the torch, the flame on the alter"[16] (Wright 1964, 7). Since this time of architectural origins, man's protection and maintaining of the flame through the architectural edifice has been fundamentally disconnected, largely losing its social and cultural significance. Through the steady progression of technological advancements, many of which came through mechanical means as opposed to architectural,[17] like the furnace, boiler, radiator and stove, the flame became marginalized and largely out of sight. Additionally, developments in the sources of fuel from which to foster the flame also evolved – wood, char-coal, sea-cole, peat, coke, oil and eventually electricity – allowed for the complete outsourcing of its creation and maintenance to "hidden" systems of ducts, pipes and fans.

With further advancements in electrical power generation, distribution and application in the first half of twentieth century, the architectural surround was no longer needed in the same way that it once was to defend and protect the flame, it became more of a container, or insulator, for a "conditioned" interior environment of habitation generated by mechanical heating and ventilation technologies. It was with the advancement of a complete air-conditioning management system – first developed in response to specific industrial processes requiring specialized interior atmospheric conditions for production – that the potential for creating and maintaining a comfortable modern interior became

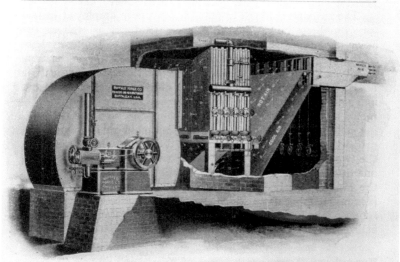

VENTILATION

Three-Quarter Housing Fan, Left-Hand Top Horizontal Discharge, Blowing Air Through and Underneath Heater into Brick Plenum Chamber

FIGURE 1.13   This 1902 schematic drawing shows the likely air-conditioning system installed at Sackett & Wilhelms, a Brooklyn, New York, printing company desperate to find a solution to the humidity problems plaguing its printing processes. Image courtesy of Carrier. Reprinted from E. B. Schultz. *Weathermakers to the World: The Story of a Company, the Standard of an Industry* (Carrier Engineering Corp, 2012).

total[18] (Figure 1.13). In many developed countries of the West, especially in the post-war US, the increase in practical integration of these "mechanical services" into the newly constructed stick-built homes, dramatically shifted the inhabitant's desire and expectation for greater degrees of internal comfortability.[19]

The British architectural historian Reyner Banham called attention to this observation, in his 1965 essay "A Home is Not a House," citing the resolutely American tendency toward the production of "hollow shells" of habitation. They were materially inefficient regulators of internal and external environmental conditions, which helped to solidify an American dependence upon the techno-mechanical subsidy of heat, light and power required to make them livable (Banham 1965, 73). Writing more thoroughly on this history a few years later in his seminal 1969 book *The Architecture of the Well-tempered Environment*, Banham describes the American pursuit and use of these mechanical technologies as compared to Europe in the following way:

> The history of environmental management by the consumption of power in regenerative installations, rather than by simple reliance on

conservative and selective structures, is thus a predominantly American history, at least in its pioneering phases...The problems were those of lightweight structures in extreme climates wherever Americans built in wood, and the advantages were those of the relatively lightweight culture that many Americans took westward with them into a zone of abundant power.

Of all these considerations, the lack of encumbrances of a massive culture (physically or figuratively speaking), may have been the most important. It is striking how often events in the USA are not so far in advance of Europe technically, but the Americans appear to have been more aware of what they were doing, and thus to make a better job of it.

(Banham 1969, 26–27)

The classification of "Regenerative" is the label Banham uses to refer to those structures that predominantly rely on a mode of "applied power," to create a thermally desirable interior environment of habitation, as opposed to those that conserve it through their embodied physical material, or selectively admit desirable environmental conditions and limit others (Banham 1969, 23). For Banham, this American predisposition away from "a rock" (avoidance) and toward "a campfire" (interference) might actually "return Man nearer to a natural state"[20] (Banham 1965, 75).

Man started with two basic ways of controlling environment: one by avoiding the issue and hiding under a rock, tree, tent or roof (this led ultimately to architecture as we know it) and the other by actually interfering with the local meteorology, usually by means of a campfire, which, in a more polished form, might lead to the kind of situation now under discussion. Unlike the living space trapped with our forebears under a rock or roof, the space around a campfire has many unique qualities which architecture cannot hope to equal, above all, its *freedom and variability*.[21]

(Banham 1965, 75)

The campfire results in a "controlled" space that is also flexible as opposed to one that is simply "uniform." It supports or even sponsors the inhabitant to action, providing choice – "it is simply an environment suited to what you are going to do next" (Banham 1965, 79) (Figure 1.14). The campfire constructs habitable space directly through a gradient of localized thermal differentiation as opposed to indirectly through the use of physical barriers. It's dynamic, in direct and continuous collaboration with the surrounding environmental conditions, creating an awareness rather than an obfuscation of the external world, to provide greater variability and potential forms of habitation.

54 Technological Mediation

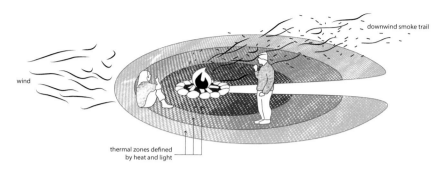

FIGURE 1.14 Environmental spatial conditions produced around the campfire. Drawing by Alex Witteman.

> The output of heat and light from a campfire is effectively zoned in concentric rings, brightest and hottest close to the fire, coolest and darkest away from it, so that sleeping is an outer-ring activity, and pursuits requiring vision belong to the inner rings. But at the same time, the distribution of heat is biased by the wind, and the trail of smoke renders the downwind side of the fire unappetising, so that the concentric zoning is interrupted by other considerations of comfort or need.
>
> *(Banham 1969, 20)*

While the campfire in its initial development may have provided the conditions for socialization, "freedom and variability" and even spirituality, its eventual technological *capitalization*, through the development of specialized mechanical systems intent on producing thermal uniformity, has resulted in our total dependence on these services in order to be able to live-in-the-world-ecology.

The more recent integration of these heating, ventilating and air conditioning (HVAC) technologies with personalized digital control systems have, in the American context as well as in other wealthy nations, become increasingly imbedded into our constructed environments of habitation, perhaps most overtly through the emergence of the "smart" home. This development, while engaging with human "needs" so to speak, has actually cultivated a greater desire and expectation for spaces of habitation to be overly accommodating, comforting and passive, leading to a yearning for ongoing *radical stability* in our interior thermal environments, and reinforcing a sedentary architectural inhabitation.[22] The array of evolving contemporary home technologies rather than facilitate one's growth and personal development often suppress it, resulting in less thought, less variability, less stimulation and arguably a less healthy lifestyle. The effect of these "smart" technologies is not to stimulate, but anesthetize any real need for action. While they've been marketed to consumers as ultra-convenient altruistic timesavers, or even devices of empowerment helping the home owner to remotely monitor the home through a "smart" phone while he/she is away, there's been a recent trend in their use as tools of domestic harassment and abuse. In a *New York Times* article from June 2018 titled "Thermostats, Lock and Lights: Digital Tools of Domestic Abuse," the newspaper conducted more than 30 interviews of domestic abuse victims, their lawyers, shelter workers and emergency responders describing how new digital "smart" home technologies have been used as tools for harassment. "Abusers – using apps on their smart phones, which are connected to the internet-enabled devices – would remotely control everyday objects in the home, sometimes to watch, listen, other times to scare or show power" (Bowles 2018). These smart technologies of ultra-convenience have been turned against their inhabitants, producing an environment of trauma and intimidation rather than care. It has literally caused some inhabitants to feel like they're going crazy, and, as one emergency shelter administrator put it, "[Victims] feel like they are losing control of their home" and after they spend time out of the home environment at the shelter, "they realize they were being abused" (Bowles 2018). While these cases reflect a small percentage of people's experiences using "smart" home technologies, cases of such abuse continue to increase as technology becomes cheaper, more available and our dependence on them becomes more prevalent.

What is clear from these architectural origin stories, regardless of early human-being's actual underlying motivations concerning the construction of an interiorized habitable space, is that we have reached a point today where instinct, rational forethought and socialization have all been subverted by the advancement of the building industry and broader forces of capitalization in the name of ongoing *radical stability* and personal thermal comfort. In the developed world most acutely, because of the increase in technological integration, inhabitants have become more detached and isolated from the possibilities of a dynamic, flexible and inter-active "Terrestrial" inhabitation. Where the campfire began as an instigator of these aspects, cultivating socialization, "freedom and variability," and maintaining a direct correspondence with its environmental context, its total mechanization and now digitalization, has resulted in greater isolation and uniformity of space and experience. Where once the necessary environmental "smoothing out" would have required biologically adaptive physical and/or behavioral adjustments to achieve an ongoing balance, which over time may have helped to generate a movement toward further development and/or differentiation, now our technological (and indirectly economic systems) make these adaptive shifts on our behalf. Before exploring the implications of these possibilities more thoroughly later on in the book, the next chapter will turn its attention toward a discussion of a specific instance of early twentieth-century wall transformation related to the development of advanced technological environmental management strategies and a further isolation between the interior and exterior atmospheres of habitation.

56 Technological Mediation

Notes

1 For a brief overview of Earth system science, see Tim Lenton, *Earth system science: A very short introduction* (Oxford: Oxford University Press, 2016). And, for a more extensive reference, see Michael C. Jacob, Robert J. Charlson, Henning Rodhe and Gordon H. Orians, eds. *Earth system science: From biogeochemical cycles to global change*, 2nd ed., International Geophysics Series, vol. 72 (San Diego: London, Academic Press, 2000).

2 "Terrestrials in fact have the very delicate problem of discovering how many *other beings* they need in order to subsist. It is by making this list that they sketch out their *dwelling places* (the expression allows us to shift away from the word 'territory,' a word too often limited to the simple administrative grid of the state)"; see Latour (2018, 87). And "By the way, it is perhaps time to stop using the word 'ecology' except to designate a scientific field. There are only questions of dwelling places inhabited with or defended against other terrestrials that share the same stakes"; see Latour (2018, 90).

3 Laugier is specifically critical of various buildings and architects of the time for their irrational organizational strategies, superfluous forms and decorative elements. He critically references the façade of St. Gervais, façade at St. Sulpice, the Chateau de Versailles, the work of Bernini and so on; see Laugier (1977, 27, 28 and 76, 30, 80).

4 See http://www.ferdinandludwig.com/baubotanik-tower/articles/baubotanik-tower.html.

5 As opposed to those early shelters made below overhangs or within caves.

6 In conversation with Bill Moyers in their PBS multi-episode interview special, the mythologist Joseph Campbell described the rites and reverence demonstrated by early hunters when participating in the act of killing another living-being for substance; see Joseph Campbell and Bill Moyers, *The power of myth*, ed. Betty Sue Flowers (New York: Anchor Books Doubleday, 1988) 93–94.

7 See Lewis J. Bartlett, David R. Williams, Graham W. Prescott, Andrew Balmford, Rhys E. Green, Anders Eriksson, Paul J. Valdes, Joy S. Singarayer and Andrea Manica, "Robustness despite uncertainty: regional climate data reveal the dominant role of humans in explaining global extinctions of late Quaternary megafauna," *Ecography* 39 (2016): 152–161.

8 Expanding on the ideas of agreeable climate, Alberti says, "For while there is no doubt that any defect of land or water could be remedied by skill and ingenuity, no device of the mind or exertion of hand may ever improve climate appreciably; or so it is said"; see Alberti, trans. Rykwert, Leach and Tavernor (1988, 9).

9 See Filarete and John R. Spencer, *Treatise on architecture: Being the treatise by Antonio Di Piero Averlino, known as Filarete* (New Haven, CT: Yale University Press, 1965) Vol. 1, 10/Book 1, Folio 4V.

10 The historian Adolf Max Vogt makes the point that Le Corbusier's interest in primitive structures originated from both his early educational experiences as well as his knowledge of the subject from previous architectural theorists and historians, like Rousseau, Laugier and Ledoux, and that with the publication of *Une maison – un palais*, "the problem of first origins moves to the center"; see Vogt (1998, 195).

11 Translation from Vogt (1998, 188).

12 Le Corbusier uses this phrase several times throughout *Vers Une Architecture* and uses it as the title for one of its last chapters "Architecture: III. Pure Creation of the Mind."

13 For a more detailed account of the parallel between the Irish crannog and the Swiss alpine lake hut, see Vogt (1998, 203–209).

14 Le Corbusier seems to have adjusted the width dimension of the *crannog* in his sketches, limiting it so his volumes appeared more vertically proportioned, "upright" and "dignified"; see Vogt (1998, 213–214).

15 Vitruvius goes on to describe how early man/woman learned from his/her neighbors, improving his/her primitive abilities into an expertise of building trades, but also other modes of thought and art; see Vitruvius, trans. Morgan (1960, 40).
16 Writing in the 1960s, Wright mentions that there were "inns and cottages still where, they claim, the fire has not gone out for a century or more"; see Wright (1964, 8).
17 Though some did continue to provide architectural significance like the hearth and chimney.
18 For a full history on the technological development of air-conditioning and its impact on the design of spaces, see Salvatore Basile, *Cool: How air conditioning changed everything* (New York: Fordham University Press, 2014), and Margaret Ingels, *Willis Haviland carrier, father of air conditioning* (Garden City, NY: Country Life Press, 1952).
19 The capitalization of these services into new market sectors was also reinforced by a commercialized narrative of the victorious soldier's return home after the war with the hope of realizing the American Dream defined by home ownership, modern appliances of convenience, the affordable automobile, alternative synthetic materials and new entertainment like broadcast television.
20 This is the major provocation of Banham's "A Home is Not a House" essay, supposing that a radical type of mobile living unit, à la Buckminster Fuller's Standardized Living Unit "that actually worked," might embrace totally the American detachment from the Monumental building culture toward a completely new kind of living – both technologically advanced, but free to roam and situate itself in-the-world.
21 Italics added here for emphasis.
22 Products, just to name a few, include: The Nest Learning Thermostat, Phillips HUE connected LED automated light system, Ring Video Doorbell, Google Home and the Amazon Echo with Alexa, Brilliant Control, August Smart Lock and countless others.

References

Alberti, Leon-Batista. 1988. *On the art of building in ten books.* Trans. Joseph Rykwert, Neil Leach, and Robert Tavernor. Cambridge, MA: The MIT Press.
Banham, Reyner. 1965. A home is not a house. *Art in America* 2: 70–79.
———. 1969. *The architecture of the well-tempered environment.* Chicago, IL: The University of Chicago Press.
Bowles, Nellie. 2018. Thermostats, locks and lights: Digital tools of domestic abuse. *New York Times*, June 23. https://www.nytimes.com/2018/06/23/ technology/ smart-home-devices-domestic-abuse.html (accessed May 13, 2019).
Hearn, M. F. 1990. *The architectural theory of Viollet-le-Duc: Readings and commentary.* Cambridge, MA: The MIT Press.
Herrmann, Wolfgang. 1962. *Laugier and eighteenth century French theory.* London: A. Zwemmer Ltd.
Huxtable, Ada Louise. 1964. Architectless architecture – Sermons in stone. *The New York Times,* November 15. https://www.nytimes.com/1964/11/15/archives/architectless-architecture-sermons-in-stone.html (accessed March 14, 2020).
Latour, Bruno. 2017. *Facing Gaia: Eight lectures on the new climatic regime.* Cambridge: Polity Press.
———. 2018. *Down to earth: Politics in the new climatic regime.* Trans. Catherine Porter. Cambridge: Polity Press.

58 Technological Mediation

Laugier, Marc-Antonie. 1977. *An essay on architecture*. Trans. Wolfgang and Anni Herrmann. Los Angeles, CA: Hennessey & Ingalls, Inc.

Le Corbusier. 1928. *Une maison – un palais. A La Recherche D'une Unité Architecturale*. Collection De "L'esprit Nouveau." Paris: G. Crès et cie.

———. 1986. *Towards a new architecture*. Trans. Frederick Etchells. New York: Dover Publications, Inc.

Leroi-Gourhan, André. 1957. *Prehistoric man*. Trans. Wade Baskin. New York: Philosophical Library, Inc.

———. 1993. *Gesture and speech*. Trans. Anna Bostock Berger. Cambridge, MA: The MIT Press.

Loos, Adolf. 1910. Architecture. In *The architecture of Adolf Loos: An arts council exhibition*, 104–109. Trans. Wilfried Wang, ed. Yehunda Safran and Wilfried Wang. London: The Arts Council of Great Britain, 1985.

Rudofsky, Bernard. 1964. *Architecture without architects: An introduction to non-pedigreed architecture*. New York: The Museum of Modern Art.

Rykwert, Jospeh. 1981. *On Adam's house in paradise: The idea of the primitive hut in architectural history*. 2nd ed. Cambridge, MA: The MIT Press.

Semper, Gottfried. 1989. *The four elements of architecture and other writings*. Trans. Harry Francis Mallgrave and Wolfgang Herrmann. Cambridge: Cambridge University Press.

Viollet-le-Duc, Eugéne-Emmanuel. 1876. *The habitations of man in all ages*. Trans. Benjamin Bucknall. Boston, MA: James R. Osgood and Company.

Vitruvius Pollio, Marcus. 1960. *The ten books on architecture*. Trans. Morris Hicky Morgan. New York: Dover Publications, Inc.

Vogt, Adolf Max. 1998. *Le Corbusier, the noble savage: Toward an archaeology of modernism*. Trans. Radka Donnell. Cambridge, MA: The MIT Press.

Wright, Lawrence. 1964. *Home fires burning: The history of domestic heating and cooking*. London: Routledge & Kegan Paul.

2

WALL PERFORMANCE

Two Views of Nature, the Visual and the Visceral

> Our problem is this: men live on the earth. Why? How? Others will answer
> you. My task, my search, is to try to save these men of today from misfortune,
> from catastrophes, to establish them in conditions of happiness, of everyday
> happiness, of harmony. It concerns especially reestablishing or establishing
> harmony between men and their environment. A live organism (man) and
> nature (the environment), this immense vase containing the sun, the moon, the
> stars, indefinable unknowns, waves, the round earth with its axis inclined on
> the ecliptic producing the seasons, the temperature of the body, the circulation
> of blood, the nervous system, the respiratory system, the digestive system, the
> day, the night, the solar cycle of twenty-four hours, its implacable but varied
> and beneficent alteration, etc.
>
> (Le Corbusier 1991, vii)

This statement by Le Corbusier concerning his self-described responsibility as
an architect to create conditions "of everyday happiness, of harmony" between
organism and nature, man and the environment, may be even more pressing
today than ever, in this moment beyond climatological-ecological "crisis". His
words come from the preface to the 1960 second printing of his book *Précisions
sur un état présent de l'architecture et de l'urbanisme* (*Precisions on the Present State of Architecture and City Planning*), first published 30 years prior to record in print a series of ten lectures he delivered in Buenos Aires while on tour in South America.
These lectures, while a kind of culmination of much of his thinking throughout
the 1920s,[1] were also delivered at a definitive moment of transition in his career (McLeod 1996, 89). He had solidified a mature purist theory of modern
architecture, based on a rejection of past historicisms promoted by the academy,
alongside an embrace of twentieth-century construction technologies like steel,

60 Technological Mediation

reinforced concrete and glass. And he had actualized this modern approach through the completion of several multi-unit residential projects, Pessac and Weissenhof-Siedlung, as well as in a number of private residential commissions, most notably La Roche-Jeanneret, Cook and Stein. Despite these accomplishments toward the creation of a new architecture, in the year prior to travelling to South America he had published a book, *Une maison – un palais* (*A House – A Palace*), which advocated for the value and intelligence of different vernacular dwellings, most emphatically the fisherman's hut, but also the crannog discussed in Chapter 1, among others, affirming their purity and honesty of construction as a means of historically grounding his ideas concerning a rational and unadorned modern approach. Aspects of these sentiments were carried forward into his thinking in *Précisions*; his previous censorship of any "emotional, or nostalgic flights of fancy" was relaxed as he began to provide a more explicit emphasis on the value of poetry, lyricism and folklore[2] (McLeod 1996, 90). So, while these lectures did provide a comprehensive overview of his early modernist ideas,[3] they also reflected his "turning away from machinist imagery towards a celebration of the simplicity, dignity and 'spirit of truth,' to be found in humble working people and very simple vernacular buildings" (Benton 2015, A8).

More generally, the Buenos Aires lectures were delivered during a time architectural historian Alan Colquhoun has described as Le Corbusier's "*grands travaux* of the interwar years" (Colquhoun 1989, 125), articulated in the design of four large-scale public buildings.[4] These projects were all based on a compositional principle of "elementarization" using linear bars and centroidal volumes, each element containing a different function, composed in flexible configurations capable of negotiating a complex urban fabric. Colquhoun describes Le Corbusier's approach in these public buildings as "an open-work of slender prisms defining the spatial limits of the ensemble, while at the same time implying its possible extension" (Colquhoun 1989, 133). At the end of 1928, Le Corbusier, with his partner and cousin Pierre Jeanneret, secured the second commission of the *grands travaux* that would provide the opportunity to realize their modernist ideas in the fulfillment of a large, programmatically complex, urban sited public building. The commission was to design the administrative offices and social club for the Central Union of Consumer Cooperatives' Headquarters (Centrosoyus), located in Moscow, USSR. Importantly, the design for the building would also demonstrate another kind of transitional moment concerning Le Corbusier's isolation of the interior atmosphere, embracing internalized mechanical atmospheric management technologies, which he asserted would provide "only one house for all countries, the house of *exact breathing*" (Le Corbusier 1991, 64). This statement reflects a kind of global reconsideration of the potential, and dependence upon, active interior atmospheric management technologies toward the creation of comfortable habitations regardless of geographic location and climatological circumstances – one that must be hermetically sealed, detached and mediated from its environmental context.

In the current moment of catastrophic changes, as human-beings begin to better understand how to bring themselves into habitational "harmony" with the total "Terrestrial" collective "being-with," this chapter reconsiders the primary element of environmental mediation within the *architectural* "dwelling place," the wall. While the roof might have been man's first technological response toward prohibiting the extinguishment of the flame, the wall, with its greater overall area of enclosure, various solar orientations and demands related to the accommodation of apertures for the interchange of people, light and air, it may provide the greatest impact toward the re-making of a terrestrially aligned *architectural* "dwelling place." The development and articulation of Le Corbusier's proposed *pan de verre* (window wall) in the Centrosoyus building is the apogee of his thinking developed in the 1920s for effectively lighting a building and achieving geometric purity of form – "a *100* per cent solution" (Le Corbusier and Pierrefeu 1948, 105). However, it's also a "solution" fundamentally dependent upon active interior atmospheric management technologies for the effective creation and sustainment of a habitable interior environment. This approach reflects a transition toward a "harmony" with the external environment principally concerned with neutralization, disconnection and isolation of the interior from the exterior, facilitating an aesthetic collaboration (visual), rather than an inter-active exchange (visceral). So, while Le Corbusier's attitude concerning architecture's technological mediation of the environment evolved greatly during the 1930s, his approach developed in the 1920s helped define and reinforce a fundamental modern lineage of the *pan de verre* dependent upon active systems of environmental management and interior isolation that remain predominant today.[5]

★ ★ ★

With the advent of new techniques and technologies of construction developed during the nineteenth century, their appropriation and implementation toward the advancement of a modern twentieth-century architecture instigated a radical departure, a "revolution" as Le Corbusier often characterized it, from all previous building cultures. The initial use of steel and reinforced concrete column grid construction techniques was experimented with in the early skyscrapers and industrial warehouse buildings that went up in the latter half of the twentieth century in US cities like Buffalo, Chicago, Detroit, New York and St. Louis, by architects and engineers such as Ernest L. Ransome, Willian Le Baron Jenney and Adler & Sullivan.[6] However, it was the collective advancements of the early Modernists, like Walter Gropius, Le Corbusier and Mies van der Rohe, in the first decades of the new century that came to be best known for exploiting these techniques toward a modern aesthetic and spatial agenda. While they were not the first to technically disconnect the structural system from a system of enclosure, they were among the first to exploit this decoupling toward the explicit creation of a new modern architecture, free from the academicism and stylizations of the past.[7] This modern approach advocated for a liberation of the building plan and the facade toward the organizational, spatial and aesthetic freedom. With this internal advance of flexibility, the role of the enclosure system – the walls – was removed totally from their past need to "hold up" the building, precipitating the desire for better lighting of spaces and consequently for greater transparency of the building's vertical surface. Though most of Le Corbusier's realized architectural projects of the 1920s, including some dating to his time in La Chaux-de-Fonds before he made the permanent move to Paris in 1917, embraced the use of a reinforced concrete structural grid, these works had not yet fully realized the radical wall implications embodied by the disconnection between structure and enclosure.[8] Le Corbusier himself readily admitted in *Précisions* – discussing the development of "the Dom-Ino houses" in 1914/1915 – that he had failed to recognize the full potential for implementing the *pan de verre* as an intentional conscious act. "I tried innumerable combinations of plans within these structural frameworks. Everything was possible. Automatically I had made ribbon windows or window walls. But I didn't realize it" (Le Corbusier 1991, 93).

The specific ideas of Le Corbusier and Jeanneret's use of these new methods of construction toward a modern aesthetic and spatial construct, a theoretical repositioning of architecture toward a "new order," were clearly laid out in their 1926 essay "Five Points Towards a New Architecture," included in the *Almanach de l'Architecture modern*. These points were: (1) supports (pilotis), (2) roof gardens, (3) free designing of the ground-plan, (4) horizontal window and (5) free design of the façade, collectively resulting in the creation of "an entirely new kind of building" (Le Corbusier and Jeanneret 1926, 99) and "a fundamentally new aesthetic" (Le Corbusier and Jeanneret 1926, 100) (Figure 2.1). The "five points" reflected a reconsideration of architectural design principals, priorities and aesthetics, fitting of the emerging second machine age, but outside of a few specific moments in several residential projects from the 1920s[9] Le Corbusier and Jeanneret stopped short of implementing a completely glazed wall enclosure system. It was not until the end of the decade in the final design of the Centrosoyus building that they proposed their first comprehensive application of a thermally active, double layer *pan de verre*. Historian Tim Benton described this situation as follows:

> In the Purist villas, the type solution for the windows was the *fenêtre en longueur* [strip window], reaching from wall to wall, framing the landscape and providing space below for cupboards and radiators. But with projects for Centrosoyus (1928–29), the Swiss Pavilion (1929–32), and the Salvation Army building (1929–33), Le Corbusier experimented with the *pan de verre* (window wall).
>
> *(Le Corbusier and Tim Benton 2012, 284)*

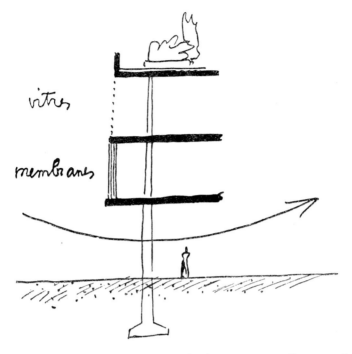

FIGURE 2.1 Le Corbusier, four functions of architecture – standing, carrying, covering, enveloping, 1948 (Le Corbusier and Francois de Pierrefeu, *The Home of Man*, p. 109). © F.L.C. / ADAGP, Paris / Artists Rights Society (ARS), New York 2019.

Benton goes on to describe how the *pan de verre* originated in the double glass wall enclosure of the great auditorium Le Corbusier and Jeanneret included within the Palais des Nations competition proposal, with a space big enough for workmen to circulate between the two layers. However, its application was localized to only the most important auditorium space of collective gathering; the corresponding rectangular office bars and smaller meeting rooms adopted the *fenêtre en longueur*, a horizontal layering of alternating ribbons of ashlar stone and steel-framed plate glass. Yet Le Corbusier was acutely aware of the disconnection between wall and floor; in *Une maison – un palais*, he included an illustration of a typical wall section detail of a rectangular office bar from the Palais de Nations competition proposal with the following description:

> The facade no longer bears the floors; *it is carried by the floors*. The structural columns are set inside 1.25m from the facade. The facade is *completely free*. The windows are *continuous*, never without interruption. Each piece *theoretically* achieves the perfect illumination. The windows slide laterally.[10]
>
> *(Le Corbusier 1928, 102)*

64 Technological Mediation

This described approach is consistent with Le Corbusier and Pierre Jeanneret's "five points" argument, embracing the modern advancements of concrete, steel and plate glass, but maintains a ribbon window to capture a horizontally framed view of Lake Geneva and the natural landscape beyond. It's worth noting that despite being one of the several entries awarded first prize in the competition by an international panel of architects (Boesiger 1956, 161), their entry was disqualified for the specific reason that the office volumes were elevated upon pilotis atop automobile parking[11] (Le Corbusier 1991, 45 and 48).

It was in the aftermath of disappointment over the Palais des Nations competition that Le Corbusier received a written invitation in May 1928 to participate in another international competition to design the Centrosoyus office building. In Soviet Russia, Le Corbusier saw a potentially sympathetic audience for his ideas, where at that time many artists and intellectuals had been maintaining a detailed knowledge of the Paris art scene (Cohen 1992, 3). The Soviets were also exposed to his writings and projects through "early translations of articles in *L'Esprit Nouveau* or reports concerning [his] own publications, town-planning projects, and architectural realizations; and they reached both radical milieux and the more prosaic professional circles" (Cohen 1992, 17). Architectural historian Kenneth Frampton described Le Corbusier's perception of the Soviet state at that time as follows:

> Le Corbusier approached the Soviet Union as though it were the only truly modern nation that now possessed the political and techno-economic means to transcend the demise of vernacular culture through the unequivocal adoption of a scientific, machine-age civilization, with all that this entailed.

> *(Frampton 2001, 90)*

It was clear that, from the onset of his work in the USSR, Le Corbusier felt the Soviets were not only willing but also capable of implementing an aesthetically ambitious and technologically innovative design for the Centrosoyus building. For their part, the Moscow leadership requested specifically that the architects bring to the project all the efficiency that modern techniques have brought to the construction industry[12] (Le Corbusier and Jeanneret 1929, 162).

The Centrosoyus building was to serve as a state office building and was conceived right before the start of the Soviet's first "five year plan" (1928–1932), which focused on rapid industrialization and the collectivization of agriculture.[13] The building's character was intended to both evoke an official central administrative exterior presence and style (Cohen 1992, 64) as well as negotiate a relatively complex program and urban context. Le Corbusier describes the functions of the building as follows: "The program called for the provision of modern offices for 3500 employees. In addition, there are communal facilities such as a restaurant, lecture halls, theater, club, physical culture, etc. The building is a unity comprising both work and recreation"[14] (Boesiger 1989, 35). It was cited on an irregularly shaped urban plot, to be bounded on three sides by roadways of varying density (Colquhoun 1989, 134–139) and also needed to accommodate a variety of movements on the ground floor – people coming and going to their offices as well as occasional large numbers of workers making their way to the great hall for group meetings (Le Corbusier 1991, 46). Lecturing in Buenos Aires on October 5, 1929, in a lecture titled "Techniques are the very basis of poetry they open a new cycle in architecture," Le Corbusier describes his conceptualization of these issues of movement and program in the following way:

> It is necessary to regulate the crowds entering and leaving all at the same time…A set of pilotis covers the site entirely, or almost. These pilotis carry the office building, which starts only at the second floor. Under it one circulates freely, outdoors or in rooms opening onto a big space, fed by the two entrances and creating the "forum"…The analysis is quite clear; such a building has two aspects. The first, an arrival in disorder, on a vast horizontal plane on ground level: it is a lake. The second aspect that of stable, motionless work, sheltered from noise and coming and going, everyone at his place and controllable: whereas it is rivers, means of communication, that lead to offices.
>
> *(Le Corbusier 1991, 45–47)*

Pilotis were incorporated into the second iteration of the project as a primary solution to the needs of circulation on the ground floor and to visually emphasize the building's *prismatic* composition of elevated volumes. This perception would be further heightened with the eventual implementation of the *pan de verre* applied to the primary longitudinal building faces along Miasnitskaia Street and the planned boulevard to the southwest. The summation of Le Corbusier's intent regarding the volumetric organization of the Centrosoyus building is also well described in his October 5 lecture:

> I have already begun, in referring to the Centrosoyuz of Moscow, to formulate one of my important convictions; that what happens on the ground concerns circulation, mobility, and what happens above, inside the building, is work, is motionless. This will presently become an important principle of city planning. I conserve the grass and the herds, the old trees, as well as the ravishing views of landscapes, and above them, at a certain level, on a horizontal slab of concrete, on top of the pilotis descending to their foundations, I raise the *limpid* and *pure prisms* of utilitarian buildings; I am moved by a high intention, I proportion the *prisms* and the spaces around them; I compose in the atmosphere. Everything

66 Technological Mediation

counts: the herds, the grass, the flowers in the foreground on which one walks caressing them with one's eyes, the lake, the Alps, the sky…and the divine proportions.[15]

(Le Corbusier 1991, 49)

The building was to be functionally logical in its elemental organization of different programmatic volumes, intended to be perceived from the exterior as a series of well-composed simple forms commanding a kind of clarity and resolute character indicative of the Soviet state, but also not dependent upon an overt monumentality. The French architectural historian Jean-Louis Cohen, who has written extensively on the work of Le Corbusier in Soviet Russia, describes the building's character in comparison to a competition entry made by architect Peter Behrens as follows: "[Le Corbusier's] response to the demand for 'grandeur' stands in stark contrast to Peter Behrens's entry, whose monumentality was grounded in 'unity and massiveness'" (Cohen 1992, 75). Le Corbusier and Jeanneret proposed a balance between purity of form and resoluteness of character without being overpowering or oppressive, a quality that was reinforced through the materialization of the primary building facades as fully transparent glazed window walls creating a device Cohen refers to as a "picturesque architectural landscape seen…from the *outside*." This was made possible through a breaking with the traditional office building organization around a central courtyard, to instead propose "a new type of edifice capable of engendering a series of angular planes" (Cohen 1992, 77). Le Corbusier, on this point, states:

Against the sky, there is the impeccable edge of a crystal prism, encircled by the volcanic stones of the roof terrace parapets. This clean profile is one of the most admirable conquests of modern techniques (suppression of roofs and cornices).

(Le Corbusier 1991, 58) (Figure 2.2)

Although the exact locations and arrangements of the prismatic volumes within the site were adjusted throughout the design process, taking into account changes in the program and the alteration of site boundaries,[16] the general approach to the composition of prismatic volumes remained consistent. The same, however, cannot be said of the primary building facades as the implementation of the *pan de verre* was an aspect of the project that seemed to develop gradually. Le Corbusier and Jeanneret's initial competition entry proposed a kind of horizontal layering of alternating bands of glass and stone across the primary building facades,[17] and the shorter side walls were largely solid stone, a very similar arrangement to their Palais des Nations competition proposal. This general approach persisted through several more iterations, with an increasing area and emphasis on the glazing of the primary building faces. In revisions after the third stage of the competition, having officially

FIGURE 2.2 Le Corbusier, rectangular prism sketches, "the outside is always inside," October 5, 1929 (Le Corbusier, *Precisions on the Present State of Architecture and City Planning*, p. 78, fig. 64, 65, 66, 67). [F.L.C doc# 33519]. © F.L.C. / ADAGP, Paris / Artists Rights Society (ARS), New York 2019.

secured the commission, a color-rendered elevation of the building facade along Maisnitskaia Street dated to the beginning of 1929 shows a two-thirds to one-thirds ratio between the horizontal windows and stone surface in the middle area of the façade, while on the ends of the bar the glazing was increased to full height with only a stone sill marking each floor (Figure 2.3). The final design iteration for the window wall proposes a double membrane made up of a gridded exterior surface of uninterrupted continuous glazing across the whole face; the exterior layer is offset approximately 10 inches (25 cm) from the interior glazed surface which was divided into three differently proportioned areas with a framing element emphasizing the horizontality of the middle zone that captured the view. Additionally, there was a floor to ceiling curtain running the length of the window walls to provide shading. The resulting effect was to provide from the exterior a pure solid prism of glass inset within a continuous "frame" of stone running around the entire prismatic volume and from the interior a continuous horizontally framed view out to the surrounding context. This final configuration of the Centrosoyus' *pan de verre*

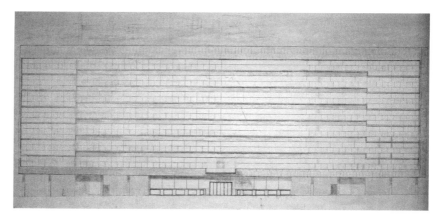

FIGURE 2.3 Le Corbusier and Pierre Jeanneret, *Centrosoyus,* facade study, beginning of 1929. [F.L.C. doc# 16235]. © F.L.C. / ADAGP, Paris / Artists Rights Society (ARS), New York 2019.

was reached in early 1929, well represented in a physical model of that time (Figure 2.4) as well as in a perspective view taken from Maisnitskaia Street, which, along with the plans, were all put on public display at rue de Sévres[18] on January 30, 1929. These materials were then subsequently published for the first time in their final form in the April 1929 issue of *Cahiers d'Art* along with a description of the building which aimed to emphasize both the technical and formal aspects of the building (Cohen 1992, 82–85).

Le Corbusier's evolution in thinking from the horizontal strip window to the *pan de verre* is described in his own words in the following excerpt, again from his October 5 lecture:

> Nothing remains of all the architectural sights to which we have been accustomed by centuries of tradition. Should we then give up, by virtue of academic codes, the immense benefits of the ribbon windows that give the best light to the interiors, that allow all the subdivisions possible from floor to floor?...
>
> I have built many of these "ribbon windows"; my attention has been drawn to the sills that still do not seem frank to me, to these lintels that still seem too expensive to me...One day, this truth appears: a window is made for lighting, *not for ventilation*. To ventilate let us use ventilation devices; that is mechanics, physics...
>
> The examination of my symbolic section shows *facades* reduced to some ribbons 30 centimeters high. Well, let us go without them, *let us get in front of them*. By means of brackets we are going to hang vertical steel sections, well adjusted, really vertical, 25 centimeters in front of these ribbons of concrete. Then, across them, inside or outside, horizontal steel sections at

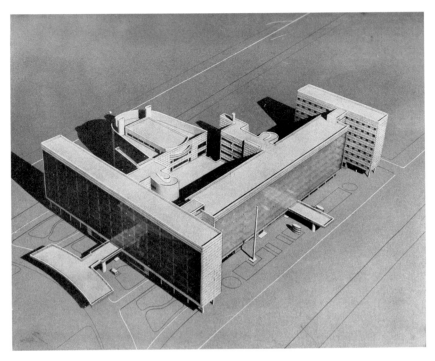

FIGURE 2.4 Le Corbusier and Pierre Jeanneret, *Centrosoyus,* study model, beginning of 1929 (Le Corbusier and Pierre Jeanneret, *Œuvre Compléte, 1910–1929*, vol. 1, p. 211). © F.L.C. / ADAGP, Paris / Artists Rights Society (ARS), New York 2019.

distances determined by the glass or plate glass sizes available on the market. Here then in front of the façade is a "window wall." The façade is a window wall. But, as there is no need for all four sides of a building to be glass, I shall build window walls, stone cladding (veneer, brick, artificial panels of cement or other materials), and mixed walls (small windows or glass panes scattered like portholes in the stone cladding).

(Le Corbusier 1991, 54–55) (Figure 2.5)

While the aesthetic and formal implications of the *pan de verre* solution helped to meet Le Corbusier's aspirations for the creation of "limpid and pure prisms," it initiated significant questions concerning the wall's ability to function as a fundamental means for dealing with the issue of environmental mediation and interior atmospheric management, especially in a climate like Moscow where temperatures could reach well below freezing for sustained periods of time.[19] Le Corbusier and Jeanneret realized that if the only function of the wall was now to let light into the building, then treated air could be provided by mechanical services (air-conditioning) and the glazing could be fixed (von Moss 1979, 93).

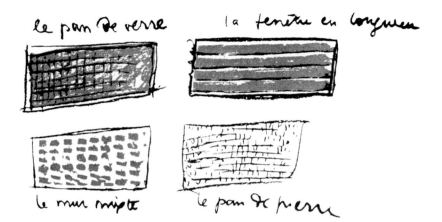

FIGURE 2.5 Le Corbusier, the window wall, the ribbon window, the mixed wall, nonbearing masonry or masonry cladding, October 5, 1929 (Le Corbusier, *Precisions on the Present State of Architecture and City Planning*, p. 59, fig. 33a). [F.L.C. doc# 33504]. © F.L.C. / ADAGP, Paris / Artists Rights Society (ARS), New York 2019.

To meet these interior atmospheric needs, they proposed an ambitious, and technologically unproven, solution, the result of earlier ideas as much as it was momentary inspiration. As recounted by Jean-Louis Cohen, from the initial competition entry the general solution to the problem of heating and cooling the building was to be composed of a closed-circuit central heating, cooling and ventilation system (Cohen 1992, 65). The system was called the *aération ponctuelle* and was credited to the engineer Gustave Lyon, their previous collaborator who had proposed a similar system for the Palais des Nations competition. The system delivered "regulated air" (Le Corbusier 1947, 17–18) at a rate of 80 liters per person per minute and at a constant temperature of 18°C, distributed by fans through a proposed in-floor duct system (Le Corbusier and Jeanneret 1929, 162–163). While Lyon's system reasonably addressed the regulation and distribution of conditioned air throughout the building, the proposed *pan de verre* presented another problem. The thinning mass of the construction radically limited the embodied insulating value of the wall during the winter, while simultaneously amplifying the amount of solar radiation emitted into the building during the significantly warmer summer months. Le Corbusier and Jeanneret's solution was to propose a double layer of glazing, which was to also incorporate a dedicated thermoregulating element between the two layers of glass,[20] to modify the air temperature within the cavity depending upon external thermal conditions. This resulted in a kind of buffer, what they called a *murs neutralisant* (neutralizing walls), around the entire building, capable of counterbalancing the exterior temperature and effectively maintaining the desired interior temperature of 18°C facilitated by Lyon's *aération ponctuelle* (Figure 2.6).

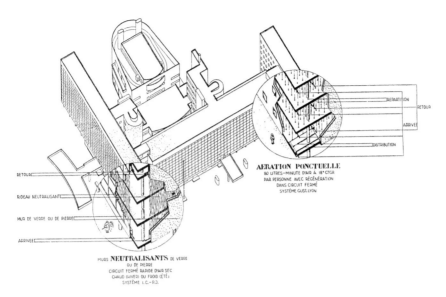

FIGURE 2.6 Le Corbusier, Pierre Jeanneret and Gustave Lyon, principles of *mur neutralisants* and of *aeration punctuelle*, 1928 (Le Corbusier and Pierre Jeanneret, *Œuvre Compléte, 1910–1929*, vol. 1, p. 210). [F.L.C. doc# 15690]. © F.L.C. / ADAGP, Paris / Artists Rights Society (ARS), New York 2019.

These systems as proposed for the Centrosoyus building were first described in detail in the *Cahiers d'Art* publication of the project:

> it's precisely this fight against the intense Moscow winter temperatures (reaching down to 40 below 0°C) that drove the creation of the *isothermal* building, which is equally efficient in hot and cold weather. This type of building is truly versatile, yielding equal results in tropical and polar regions alike. The combination of Gustave Lyon's patent for "aération ponctuelle" (on-demand ventilation) and Le Corbusier and Pierre Jeanneret's patent for "murs neutralisants" (neutralizing walls) has revolutionized traditional building heating systems. The process called "aération ponctuelle" consists of a closed, fan-operated pure air circuit maintained at 18°C with a rate of 80 liters per person per minute. This slowly circulating air is re-purified by scientific procedures and re-enters the airstream after having been returned to a constant 18°C. This is true as well in the winter as in the summer.
>
> The "murs neutralisants" process consists of the installation of paired membrane-walls, or curtain walls, leaving between the two walls a gap of no more than 10 centimeters. These curtain walls make up the building's envelope. They are constructed from glass, bricks or stone, or a combination of glass and bricks. Inside the gap between the outer and inner walls, air that is either very hot (wintertime) or cooled (summertime)

72 Technological Mediation

flows at adjustable speeds. This air, whether heated or cooled, represents a well-enclosed cube and need not be of breathable air quality. It is this very air mass that combats the exterior elements, be they the heat or the cold.

The net effect is that full walls of glass substitute for walls with windows (a considerable reduction in cost).

There is no longer any need for active heating. Only air circulation remains (a considerable reduction in initial investment and operating costs).[21]

(Le Corbusier and Jeanneret 1929, 162–163)

The combination of these two strategies as a solution for the production of "conditioned air"[22] was generally referred to by Le Corbusier as the system of *respiration exacte* (exact breathing), a title derived at least in part by his fascination with the physiological process of respiration. Writing in his 1933 book *La Ville Radieuse (The Radiant City)*, Le Corbusier describes the importance of the lungs and their need for "exact air" ("God-given air") to most effectively respirate, something he argued was currently being compromised by the polluted air of the city ("the devil's air").

For the past several years, while pursuing step after new step the genuine goals of architecture – or, to put it more exactly, having my eyes opened little by little to the duties of architecture, to the sacred and solemn tasks of architecture – I have realized that the key to life is the lung: a man who breathes well is an asset for society. I have arrived at the site of synthesis, the constructive idea, certainty: the need to provide exact air. And I have found the means to do it.

The invention? The discovery that if architecture follows certain paths, it can provide city dwellers with good, true God-given air, for the salvation of their lungs.

(Le Corbusier 1967, 40)

And a similar sentiment can be found at the end of his October 5 lecture:

A house: a lit-up floor.
What for? To live on.
What is the basis of life? *Breathing.*
Breathing what? Hot, cold, dry, damp?
Breathing pure air at a constant temperature and a regular degree of humidity.

(Le Corbusier 1991, 64)

The specific origins of the system as proposed in the Centrosoyus building seems to date back well before its design. Though Le Corbusier himself was somewhat unclear on the subject; in his October 5 lecture, he describes the idea of the double-glazed façade window wall as originating with the L'Esprit Nouveau pavilion of 1925, and then, later in 1927, a "double row of ribbon windows for the offices" were designed for the Secretariat building proposed in the Palais des Nations competition as well as a full window wall for the assembly hall (Le Corbusier 1991, 55). Yet, writing years later in his 1937 book *Quand les cathédrales étaient blanches* (*When the cathedrals were white*), he recounts this evolution of interior atmospheric management in a chapter section titled "conditioned air," describing the work of Gustave Lyon and his own ideas on the subject.

> In that auditorium [Pleyel Hall] Gustave Lyon had provided "regulated air" for three thousand auditors. The first accomplishment of the kind in Europe. His studies in providing pure air, which began a long time ago, were independent of the experiments which were made also in the USA. For our Palace of the League of Nations of 1927, we had applied the same method and had combined it with an invention of my own going back to 1916: "neutralizing walls." These walls make it possible to cancel out the cooling effects of the large glazed surfaces characteristic of the new architecture. In 1929, on my return from Moscow, I had established definitively the theory of the "neutralizing wall" and had combined it, in our Centrosoyus Palace (standing today not far from the Kremlin), with the "regulated air" of Gustave Lyon. The combination was called *"conditioned air."*
>
> *(Le Corbusier 1947, 18)*

This call back to 1916 is a reference to the Villa Schowb completed that year in La Chaux-de-Fonds. While it did not yet express the purist aesthetic pursued by Le Corbusier and Jeanneret during the 1920s,[23] it did utilize an internal reinforced concrete frame structure and incorporated a two-story glazed opening on the major Southern facing garden wall of the salon. This glazed infill wall was constructed with two layers of glass separated by an air space that contained intermediate heating pipes "to obviate cold down-draughts due to the chilling of air against the window in winter" (Banham 1969, 158–159), essentially acting as a localized neutralizing wall to better insulate the two-story salon space. In the Centrosoyus building, Jean-Louis Cohen describes that the decision to use the combined system of the *aération ponctuelle* to provide "regulated air" to the office interiors and the *mur neutralisant* to heat and cool the exterior envelope came to Le Corbusier during his stay in Moscow in October 1928. He recounts this moment in a letter Le Corbusier sent to Pierre in Paris at that time:

> Pierre, rework the whole window system. We might perhaps use double glazing and heat between the panes. See G. Lyon and laboratory.

74 Technological Mediation

> Study one hot-water heating for the offices; one hot-air heating per double glazed partition to keep out the cold.[24]

(Cohen 1992, 82)

Regardless of its exact origins, the realization of the *respiration exacte* in the Centrosoyus building as proposed by Le Corbusier and Jeanneret never came to fruition. Additionally, over the course of the building's prolonged construction, not being completed until 1936, other details concerning the construction of the facade were also changed such as the use of thicker metallic frames for the double glazing and, because of high-quality glass shortages, two different colors of glass – white and green – were used for the windowpanes (Cohen 2008, 55). Despite Le Corbusier's initial optimism toward the Soviet Union's "political and techno-economic means," the system of *respiration exacte* as proposed was rejected by the Soviet authorities as experimental and too costly, given the state's financial situation in early 1930 when the final construction drawings were being completed, though this decision was not without thermal implications[25] (Cohen 1992, 90–93) (Figure 2.7). During this time, Le Corbusier undoubtedly believed in the effectiveness of the system, seeking outside technical confirmation of its performance from the American Blower Corporation, who provided a somewhat unfavorable letter dated January 24, 1930, questioning the effectiveness of the approach and assessing the system as having "high running and maintenance costs" as compared to current alternative methods (Cohen 1992, 93). At the urging of Gustave Lyon, performance tests of the proposed *mur neutralisant* system were conducted at the laboratories of the Saint-Gobain Glass Factory, who issued reports in 1931 and 1932 that seemingly supported the system's effectiveness, prompting Le Corbusier in *La Ville Radieuse* to write: "Exact respiration (neutralizing wall and internal circuit) is confirmed by experimentation!" (Le Corbsuier 1967, 44). However, Reyner Banham makes an astute point concerning the Saint-Gobain experiments when he more accurately identifies that the specific passages of laudation from the reports quoted by Le Corbusier actually come only from a more general article about the "intentions" of the system, one that uses twice as much glass, "but not from the article which reports the conduct and results of the test" (Banham 1969, 160–161). The more specific test report included scant praise for the effectiveness of the system, and provided "a scrupulous and prosy account of how the tests were set up, the equipment used, the adjustments and measurements made"[26] (Banham 1969, 161). While Le Corbusier's ambitious ideas concerning the development of an alternative mechanical heating and cooling system (*respiration exacte*) surely reflects his general embrace and advancement of twentieth-century technological progress, it was his desire for greater purity of form and the expression of a modern aesthetic that seemed to motivate his technological demands most strongly. Writing in 1935 as part of a four-part article published

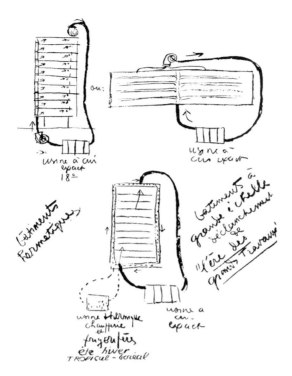

FIGURE 2.7 Le Corbusier, sketches of the machines for air exacte, October 5, 1929 (Le Corbusier, *Precisions on the Present State of Architecture and City Planning*, p. 65, fig. 44, 45, 46). [F.L.C doc# 33527]. © F.L.C. / ADAGP, Paris / Artists Rights Society (ARS), New York 2019.

for the Czechoslovakian journal *Tchéco-Verre* (a trade journal devoted to the manufacture and use of glass and similar materials), he recognizes the need to further develop technical solutions to deal with the challenges of the *pan de verre*, a pursuit he seemingly still felt was worthwhile at this time if it was capable of satisfying "the essential needs of human nature," a possibility he clearly still believed.

> If the glass wall were only a technical achievement that confronted mankind with a new disorder, it might be better not to continue in this spirit of expectant discovery. But if, on the other hand, the glass wall satisfies the essential needs of human nature, carrying with it the possibility of multiple architectural solutions – diverse, flexible, varied, and enjoyable – then we would feel especially encouraged that it is our duty to pursue the path of discovery.
>
> *(Le Corbusier and Benton 2012, 295)*

76 Technological Mediation

And

> Glass that, from inside the building, is as pure as a clear sky and that, from outside, provides distinct angles, a sense of flow, brilliance, and fluid movement. Glass that gives a sense of perfection. What a wonderful material to perfectly express part of the spirit of the Modern Age!
>
> *(Le Corbusier and Benton 2012, 297)*

And

> ...the introduction of glass into contemporary architecture as a fundamental material brings a clarity, a sharpness, a sort of absolute potential of architectural combinations that are realized for our pleasure and, in my view, express one of the essential characteristics of the machine age: purity. Purity, based on contemporary aesthetics!
>
> *(Le Corbusier and Benton 2012, 300)*

There is little doubt of Le Corbusier's disappointment by the decision not to pursue the proposed heating and cooling technologies in the Centrosoyus building, instead relying on conventional system of radiators.[27] Of it, in *La Ville Radieuse*, he says:

> The U.S.S.R. writes me: "In the cities we are planning, there will be neither dust nor toxic gases." (Really!) And the U.S.S.R., stigmatizing "exacte respiration" as a monstrous and unnatural idea, wanted our Centrosoyus Palace in Moscow to be filled with *stagnant air.*
>
> *(Le Corbusier 1967, 40)*

And, in an updated description of the project in his second volume of the *Œuvre Compléte* published in 1935: "Unfortunately the Russian authorities did not accept the principle of 'respiration exacte' which had been devised especially for this building. The solution could have been much more frank and clear; the glazing of the facades purer"[28] (Boesiger 1989, 35). These strong oppositional words illustrate clearly his underlying intentions regarding these mechanical systems toward their collective production of pure air, space and form.

Architectural historian Kenneth Frampton describes this disappointment as even more total, generally shaking Le Corbusier's convictions as to the progress of the second machine age and the possibility of purely technological solutions to questions of environmental mediation.

> Le Corbusier's preoccupation with the curtain wall [*pan de verre*] at this time, as it appeared in both the Centrosoyuz and the Cité de Refuge, was accompanied by a conviction as to the necessity of central air-conditioning.

That such advanced technology was clearly beyond the capacity of either the building industry or the engineering profession of the early 1930s may well account for his subsequent loss of faith in the manifest destiny of the machine age. Central air-conditioning was virtually unknown in France at the time – a technological limitation that was hardly helped by his postulation of a system that he called *respiration exacte,* whereby a building was supposed to be heated and cooled by tempered air being distributed throughout via an all-enveloping plenum, integral with its outer skin.

(Frampton 2001, 101)

The failure to execute the system of *respiration exacte* in both the Centrosoyus building and the Cité de Refuge in Paris led him to move away from a primary dependence on mechanical technological systems to maintain a habitable interior atmosphere.[29] However, his "predilection for closed systems" (Banham 1969, 162) as an inevitable solution for the creation of habitable "limpid and pure prisms" is of significance to the general question and history concerning the greater impact of technological mediation of the external environment, and the isolation of an interior atmosphere from exterior conditions.

Writing about the various issues concerning urban planning in the USSR, Le Corbusier describes in a statement dated July 1931, included in *La Ville Radieuse,* just how strongly he considered the potential impact of such air-conditioning systems as well as the fundamental need to close up the building from all external air infiltration.

These plans necessitate the installation of "correct breathing" or air-conditioning plants inside the buildings, as innovation that I consider to be fundamental, revolutionary, and extraordinary in its consequences. This "correct breathing" installation necessarily implies that the façade of the building shall be of air-tight plate glass.

(Le Corbusier 1967, 145)

In his historical recounting of the "ad hoc" technological advancements in air-conditioning advanced by Willis Carrier in the United States, Banham describes that, by the late 1920s, Carrier could already have offered Le Corbusier "a sophisticated plant that would deliver levels of performance beyond his conception" (Banham 1969, 163). What is significant concerning the Centrosoyus building is not the mechanical technological systems proposed (this is really a different history altogether), but rather the implications of an all glass, hermetically sealed, wall system as it relates to a contemporary conceptualization of a "Terrestrial" *architectural* "dwelling place" and the radical reorientation toward the external environment it provoked – a filtered and regulated interior atmosphere, distant and detached from its external environment. While the *pan de verre* proposed by Le Corbusier and Jeanneret provided the potential for a purer

78 Technological Mediation

outward expression of form, it somewhat paradoxically produced a more expansive, yet more distanced, *visual* connection to nature "out there," an experience they seemed keen on cultivating. The presence of natural elements beyond the building's enclosure – "the ravishing views of landscape" – was considered integral to the Centrosoyus' engagement with the external context. From the initial proposal, vegetation was included on top of the roof of the central office bar, also pushing the volumes back from the street to allow for a larger zone of trees in front and around the building. When working in the calm and "stable" offices, one could look out into the treetops, pleasant and serene, forgetting perhaps entirely that one was within an urban environment (Figures 2.8 and 2.9).

During the time of the Centrosoyus project, Le Corbusier's attitude concerning the relationship between architectural edifice and external environment is described by Tim Benton in his new introduction to the 2015 reprint edition of *Précisions*, when he questions Le Corbusier's idea of the "lieu de toutes les measures." Benton translates this phrase as "the place of all measures" as opposed to the previous English translation, the "point of all dimensions." This difference is critical for Benton because Le Corbusier often used the verb *mesurer*

FIGURE 2.8 Le Corbusier and Pierre Jeanneret, *Centrosoyus,* as per wall section at the *pan de verre,* January 1930. [F.L.C. doc# 15744]. Redrawn by author. © F.L.C. / ADAGP, Paris / Artists Rights Society (ARS), New York 2019.

FIGURE 2.9 Le Corbusier and Pierre Jeanneret, *Centrosoyus,* office interior perspective drawing, October 20, 1928 (Le Corbusier and Pierre Jeanneret, *Œuvre Compléte, 1910–1929,* vol. 1, p. 208). © F.L.C. / ADAGP, Paris / Artists Rights Society (ARS), New York 2019.

to mean "evaluate," intending its use here to refer to an "aesthetic judgement" and not physical dimensions (Benton 2015, A32). Le Corbusier describes numerous examples of the "lieu de toutes les measures" in *Précisions* describing it as the sublime relationship between the passivity of horizontal natural formations, like "the ocean and sky," "the sinuousness of the sandy beaches" (Le Corbusier 1991, 75) and the contrasting vertical formations within it, "a vertical rock" (Le Corbusier 1991, 75) as well as the intentional acts of building by man (Benton 2015, A32). Le Corbusier refers to this relationship as one of contrast: "The vertical gives meaning to the horizontal. One is alive because of the other. Such are the powers of synthesis" (Le Corbusier 1991, 75), but also one of inter-action:

> I perceive that the project we are designing is neither alone nor isolated: that the air around it constitutes other surfaces, other grounds, other ceilings…A project is not made only of itself: its surroundings exist. The surroundings envelop me in their totality as in a room. Harmony takes its origins from afar, everywhere, in everything.
>
> *(Le Corbusier 1991, 77)*

However, when looking at his sketches of the "lieu de toutes les measures," it's impossible not to interpret his reasoning as one that implicitly repositions the surrounding environment as a kind of aesthetic backdrop to the architectural edifice. These sketches show the same house, a "simple rectangular prism," situated within different natural conditions (Figure 2.2) – "a flat plain," "low wooded hills," "the wild outlines of the alps" and "a street crossing" (Le Corbusier 1991, 77) – and while he argues the house is changed because of these different contexts, it's really only the aesthetic collaboration between the pure form of the prism and the varying natural context that provides a changeable value to his measure. Benton describes the relationship in this way: "It is the interaction between the masculine form and the feminine nature which engenders the aesthetic effect" (Benton 2015, A33). Despite such exchange as described by Le Corbusier, the relationship is largely a *visual* one, a "harmony" between architecture, man and environment, made possible through the implementation of mechanical technologies of mediation that make possible such pure prismatic form. Interestingly, in his 7th Buenos Aires lecture from October 15, 1929, titled "A House – A Palace" Le Corbusier does suggest an alternative capable of fostering "physiological sensations" and spiritual feelings – a *visceral* inter-active experience.

> Architecture is a series of successive events going from an analysis to a synthesis, events that the spirit tries to transmute by the creation of relations so precise and so overwhelming that deep physiological sensations result from them, that a real spiritual declaration is felt at reading the solution, that a perception of harmony comes to us from the clear-cut mathematical quality uniting each element of the work to the others and the whole to that other entity which is the environment, the site.
>
> *(Le Corbusier 1991, 160)*

And, writing specifically about the Centrosoyus building in *Cahiers d'Art*, he describes the "moving" potential of the project in a similar way:

> Architecture at its core is composed of moving relationships. What allows us to perceive these relationships are volumes, surfaces, and lines that are both clean and clearly discernable. Our artistic excitement or response relies entirely upon the quality of the relationships existing between these various geometric elements.[30]
>
> *(Le Corbusier and Jeanneret 1929, 163)*

Although for Le Corbusier this *visceral* potential is ultimately dependent upon "smooth planes of glass and stone" and a greater geometric or mathematical "quality" in relationship to the surrounding natural context, it does open up an alternative approach for architecture's conceptualization relative to its environment. This approach aims to leverage these technological support systems of mediation to strategically amplify and inter-act with the external environment to co-productively affect inhabitants and their physiology. This is a very different relationship than that of the dislocated and disembodied *visual* connection to nature "out there" provided by the *pan de verre*, or Le Corbusier's initial explanation of the aesthetic harmony brought about by the contrast presented in the "lieu de toutes les measures." The further implications of these two ideas of wall performance – one dependent upon a strict mechanically controlled, "air-tight" and hermetically sealed interior atmosphere, and the other a physiologically engaging and dynamically responsive relationship between exterior environment and interior atmosphere – as they relate to the possibility of life affirmation or life denial, will be explored further in the next chapter through a detailed examination of two specific architectural typologies.

Notes

1 In the final written statement in the book titled "An Aside", Le Corbusier states, "I think that these ten lectures at Buenos Aires will be, for me, the last on the subject of 'the architectural revolution fomented by modern techniques'"; see Le Corbusier, trans. Aujame (1991, 267).

2 Historian Mary McLeod also makes the point that in the year following the lectures, 1930, during the construction of Villa Savoye, Le Corbusier designs two very different residential projects: the Errázuris House in Chile with an exposed log structure and stone boulder floor, and the Mandrot house at Le Pradet, which utilized a heavily rusticated exposed stone construction; see McLeod (1996, 89).

3 Ideas that art historian Tim Benton describes in his new introduction to the 2015 reprint of *Précisions* effectively changed "the face of Modern architecture."

4 The projects discussed as such by Colquhoun were the Palais des Nations, the Centrosoyus, the Cité de Refuge and the Palais de Soviets. Colquhoun describes all of these projects needing to satisfy the following requirements:

> (1) the need for the building to adapt to a specific site within a given urban context; (2) the need to create a building of symbolic presence; and (3) the need to establish the building as the representative of a type.
>
> (Colquhoun 1989, 125)

5 For a brief overview of this lineage, see Chapter 9, "Towards full control," and Chapter 10, "Concealed power," of Reyner Banham's 1969 book *The Architecture of the Well-tempered Environment.*

6 For a historical analysis of this history in the development of US industrial buildings as it relates to the development of Modernism, see Reyner Banham, *A concrete Atlantis: U.S. industrial building and European modern architecture, 1900-1925* (Cambridge, MA: The MIT Press, 1986).

7 See Walter Gropius and Adolph Myer's 1911 design for the Fagus factory in Ahlfeld an der Leine, their model factory design exhibited in the 1914 Deutsche Werkbund exhibition in Cologne, and their entry into the Chicago Herald Tribune skyscraper competition of 1922; Le Corbusier's 1914/1915 proposals for a standard frame (*L'ossature standard*) system of reinforced concrete construction – the Domino, his proposals of the early 1920s for multi-unit apartment blocks (*immuebles villas*) and standardized dwelling units (*la maison standardisée*); and Mies van der Rohe's proposals for the Friedrichstrasse Glass Skyscrapers from 1920–1922 and his proposal for a concrete office building of 1922. The work of Peter Behrens and Auguste Perret was also influential in the use of these technologies toward a Modernist expression. As general references, see Chapters 11–14 in Kenneth Frampton, *Modern architecture: A critical history* (New York: Oxford University Press, 1980), and Chapters 3, 5 and 8 in Alan Colquhoun, *Modern architecture* (New York: Oxford University Press, 2002).

8 Much of his focus concerning the use of reinforced concrete systems was toward the economic and rational approach for housing the masses, a point he stressed many times in *Vers une Architecture*, reflected in the selection of projects included in the second to last chapter of the book titled "Mass -Production Houses."

82 Technological Mediation

9 Where a large expanse of glass does exist in their works of the 1920s, it typically occurs in more localized areas as an infill surface carved out of the building mass like in the Maison Citrohan (1920 and 1922), the entry slot of space between the main house and the vertical circulation in the Villa Besnus (1922) and the Maisons en serie pour artisans (1924), or it occurs in specific double height spaces like in Ozenfant's painting studio (1922), the entry mezzanine in the Maison La Roche-Jeanneret (1923) or the Villa Church (1927) and the main living space in the Pavillon de L'Esprit Nouveau (1925). One exception to this can be found in the unbuilt Villa Mongermon, Paris, (1924) whose schematic design drawings do show a three story continuously glazed front facade wall. Reyner Banham observes that Le Corbusier did implement areas of full height glazing throughout the 1920s; it was typically in studio-type rooms that called for diffuse Northern light "as a going tradition from Paris studio-house vernacular practice"; see Banham (1969, 152).

10 "La façade ne porte plus les planchers; *elle est portée par les planchers*. Les poteaux de structure sont à 1 m. 25 à l'intérieur de la façade. La façade est *entièrement libre*. Les fenêtres sont *continues,* sans jamais d'interruption. Chaque pièce réalise l'éclairement *théorique,* parfait. Les fenêtres coulissent latéralement"; translation from the French by author.

11 Le Corbusier states explicitly, "The president of the Geneva government told me that because of my pilotis, I was kicked out of the League of Nations competition" and "High up in the League of Nations hierarchy it was said, 'No, the Secretariat, the committee members cannot work on top of automobiles'"; see Le Corbusier, trans. Aujame (1991, 45 and 48). Le Corbusier also describes his consternation and eventual lawsuit against the League of Nations over the unfair treatment in the competition process in the first volume of his *Œuvre complete*; see Boesiger (1956, 161).

12 Translation from the original French provided by Marianne Okal.

13 Over a period of 25 years, the Soviet Union implemented a series of five-year economic initiatives to help focus and plan the economic growth and development of the communist nation.

14 Translation from the French by the Foundation Le Corbusier, cited from: http://www.fondationlecorbusier.fr/corbuweb/morpheus.aspx?sysId=13&IrisObjectId=4689&sysLanguage=en-en&itemPos=12&itemSort=en-en_sort_string1%20&itemCount=79&sysParentName=&sysParentId=64 (accessed August 6, 2019).

15 Italics added here for emphasis.

16 The basic evolution of the building's organization on the site, starting from the first competition entry submission in the spring of 1928, is well documented by Jean-Louis Cohen; see Cohen (1992, 81), illustration #104.

17 It's worth noting that Le Corbusier and Pierre Jeanneret did not make a hierarchical distinction between the building's two primary faces as they related to the urban context. As recounted by Jean-Louis Cohen citing a handwritten note Le Corbusier and Jeanneret attached to the initial competition submission plans sent to Moscow: "There is, in fact, no predominant façade. The block along Miasnitskaia Street and the one on the future boulevard are of one and the same architectural value"; see Cohen (1992, 65); cited in note #19 as: Le Corbusier and Pierre Jeanneret, "Plan pour l'édification des bâtiments du Centrosoyuz de Moscou," Paris, July 1928, handwritten document, p. 1, Foundation Le Corbusier.

18 This is the address of Le Corbusier and Pierre Jeanneret's office in Paris at that time.

19 A similar critique is posed by Reyner Banham concerning Le Corbusier's Pavilion Suisse building, designed several years after the Centrosoyus building, but maintains a similar design approach; see Banham (1969, 155).

20 They proposed this system also be implemented in the stone-clad walls as well.

21 Translation from the original French provided by Marianne Okal.

22 In his book *Quand les cathédrales étainet blanches* (*When the cathedrals were white*), Le Corbusier discusses this specific point in a section called "conditioned air" when he describes the work of Gustave Lyon and his own ideas about interior atmospheric management; see Le Corbusier (1947, 17–21).

23 Instead, it adopted a kind of eastern character, receiving the nickname of the "maison turque" by local residents, and organized its facades "like Beaux-Arts compositions"; see Von Moos (1979, 19–20).

24 Jean-Louis Cohen cites this letter as "Le Corbusier, note written in Moscow, October 1928, FLC"; see Cohen (1992, 82), note# 59.

25 On this point, Stanislaus von Moos states that "the funds were lacking for the establishment of the necessary mechanical devices and, as might be expected, it was hot inside the Centrosoyus in the summer and cold in the winter"; see von Moos (1979, 93).

26 There has been at least one recent study conducted on the proposed system of *respiration exacte* and *mur neutralisant*, which sought to compare the results of the 1931 Saint-Gobain tests with a digital computational fluid dynamics (CFD) model analyzing the performance of a similar system that was proposed for the Cité de Refuge south-facing glazed wall. The conclusion of the study states that according to the CFD simulations, the systems would have worked together if executed as proposed in the Cité de Refuge building, and that *mur netralisant* should be considered a valid active thermal system for buildings; see C. Ramírez-Balas, J.J. Sendra, R. Suárez, E.D. Fernández-Nieto and Narbona-Reina, "The Mur Neutralisant as an active Thermal System: Saint Gobain Tests (1931) versus CFD Simulation (2015)" (conference paper, Editorial Universitat Politécnica de Valéncia, November 2015).

27 "Timorous Moscow stuck to current practices and rejected our 'conditioned air'; behind our immense sheets of glass they installed radiators, as is customary"; see Le Corbusier (1947, 18).

28 Translation from the French by the Foundation Le Corbusier, cited from: http://www.fondationlecorbusier.fr/corbuweb/morpheus.aspx?sysId=13&IrisObjectId=4689&sysLanguage=en-en&itemPos=12&itemSort=en-en_sort_string1%20&itemCount=79&sysParentName=&sysParentId=64 (accessed August 6, 2019).

29 As Reyner Banham recounts the failure to implement these systems as intended in both the Centrosoyus and the Cité de Refuge – which was designed after, but whose construction was completed several years before the Centrosoyus – prompted Le Corbusier to develop what Banham calls "one of the few last *structural* innovations in the field of environmental management," the *brise-soleil*. This was a sun-shading device – a screen – that was not reliant upon a mechanical system and could not so easily be eliminated from a project because of budget concerns; see Banham (1969, 155–158).

30 Translation from the original French provided by Marianne Okal.

References

Banham, Reyner. 1969. *The architecture of the well-tempered environment*. Chicago, IL: The University of Chicago Press.

Benton, Tim. 2015. Introd. *Precisions on the present state of architecture and city planning*. By Le Corbusier. Trans. Edith Schreiber Aujame. Reprint of the original American edition. Zurich: Park Books.

Boesiger, Willy, ed. 1956. *Le Corbusier et Pierre Jeanneret, Œuvre Compléte 1910–1929*. 6th ed. Zurich: Editions Girsberger.

———, ed. 1989. *Le Corbusier et Pierre Jeanneret, Œuvre Compléte 1929–1934*. 11th ed. Zurich: Les Editions D'Architecture.

84 Technological Mediation

Cohen, Jean-Louis. 1992. *Le Corbusier and the mystique of the USSR: Theories and projects for Moscow, 1928–1936*. Princeton, NJ: Princeton University Press.

———. 2008. Le Corbusier's Centrosoyuz in Moscow. *Future Anterior* 5 (summer): 52–61.

Colquhoun, Alan. 1989. The strategies of the *Grand Travaux*. In *Modernity and the classical tradition: Architectural essays 1980–1987*, 121–161. Cambridge, MA: The MIT Press.

Frampton, Kenneth. 2001. *Le Corbusier*. New York: Thames & Hudson, Inc.

Le Corbusier. 1928. *Une maison – un palais. "A La Recherche D'une Unité Architecturale.* Collection De "L'esprit Nouveau." Paris: G. Crès et cie.

———. 1947. *When the cathedrals were white: A journey to the country of timid people*. Trans. Francis E. Hyslop, Jr. New York: Reynal & Hitchcock.

———. 1967. *The Radiant City: Elements of a doctrine of urbanism to be used as the basis of our machine-age civilization*. Trans. Pamela Knight, Eleanor Levieux, and Derek Coltman. New York: The Orion Press.

———. 1991. *Precisions on the present state of architecture and city planning*. Trans. Edith Schreiber Aujame. Cambridge, MA: The MIT Press.

Le Corbusier and Francois de Pierrefeu. 1948. *The home of man*. Trans. Clive Entwistle and Gordon Holt. London: The Architectural Press.

Le Corbusier and Pierre Jeanneret. 1926. Five points towards a new architecture. In *Programs and manifestos on 20th-century architecture,* English ed. Ulrich Conrads, trans. Michael Bullock, 99–101. Cambridge, MA: The MIT Press, 1970.

———. 1929. Maison de l'Union des Coopératives de l'U. R. S. S. á Moscou. [U.S.S.R. Cooperative Union House in Moscow] *Cahiers d'art* 4: 162–68.

Le Corbusier and Tim Benton. 2012. Glass, the fundamental material of Modern architecture, Trans Paul Stirton. *West 86th: A Journal of Decorative Arts, Design History, and Material Culture* 19, no. 2 (Fall-Winter): 282–308.

McLeod, Mary. 1996. Review: Precisions: On the present state of architecture and city planning by Le Corbusier. *Journal of the Society of Architectural Historians* 55 (1): 89–92.

Von Moos, Stanislaus. 1979. *Le Corbusier elements of a synthesis*. Cambridge, MA: The MIT Press.

3

OF LIFE AND DEATH

The Interior Atmosphere-Environments of the Greenhouse and the Gas Chamber[1]

> The more we see of architecture, the more we are forced to realise that the only progress in the field is in making more fit environments for human activities, and that no building that can't offer this is really worth a second look as architecture, even though it may be a handsome sculpture, *á la* Kahn, or the cleverest erector toy in the world, Wachsmann-fashion.
>
> (Banham 1962, 59)

Both the greenhouse and the gas chamber are extreme examples of architecture as a form of technological mediation of the external environment with the aim of creating a specifically tuned interior atmosphere-environment. As proposed by British architectural historian Reyner Banham in his 1962 essay "The Environmentalist", the productive future for architecture was one focused on creating "more fit environments" for human inhabitation as opposed to formalist compositions or engineered efficiencies. To further consider Banham's statement, this chapter will examine two opposing typologies of interior atmospheric design, the greenhouse and the gas chamber, each relying on an approach to design grounded in the mediation of the exterior conditions through a highly calibrated architecture of technological environmental mediation and construction. The greenhouse, while certainly augmented by mechanical systems of climate control, maintains a degree of flexible operability necessary to meet changing solar, ventilation and thermal needs of inhabitants, while the gas chamber, aiming to fundamentally suppress these needs, relies on a strict mechanically controlled, "air-tight" and hermetically sealed interior atmosphere.

The greenhouse is a building typology dedicated to the sustainment and amplification of life – specifically plant-life. While there have been many techniques developed throughout history to "force" the development and production of fruit or vegetable crops, either in advance of or beyond their natural growing season,[2] there is evidence that humans have been constructing structures for the purpose of creating artificial climates dedicated to the sustainment of plants since as early as the fifth century BC in Greece (Hix 1974, 9). The development of the greenhouse as an architectural typology, however, generally has its origins during the Renaissance, as garden design gradually gained prominence, reflected in the many garden villas built near or north of Rome, and as the first methodological botanical gardens began to be established throughout Europe in the late fifteenth and early sixteenth centuries (Hix 1974, 9). As many different varieties of citrus native to Southeast Asia, like oranges, limes and lemons were brought into ancient Europe over the centuries (Woods and Swartz Warren 1988, 3), the more Northern parts of Italy and central Europe required some type of system to protect them from the colder winter months. In many cases the solution was to plant the fruit trees in large pots which could be moved indoors or into dry underground caves for wintering (Woods and Swartz Warren 1988, 4–5). Some of the first dedicated structures intent of creating an artificial interior climate specifically for plants began as temporary wood constructions fitted around and between those trees that had been planted outside directly in the ground and organized into rows (Figure 3.1).

> This principle was in widespread use, as ground-planted trees are taller and bushier with more flowers and fruit, and in many ways easier to grow for they do not need constant watering. The disadvantage was that erecting the winter house every year must have been a major performance....
> *(Woods and Swartz Warren 1988, 5)*

FIGURE 3.1 Salomon de Caus, portable wooden orangery, 280ft long and 32 feet wide, constructed for the Elector Palantine in Heidelberg, put up each year in late September (about Michaelmas) and taken down in the Spring at Easter. Reprintned from Salomon de Caus, Illustrations de Hortus Palatinus (Francfort: T. de Bry, 1620) planche 5.

These temporary structures would also have likely incorporated a heat source of some kind activated at times of great cold; an open fire or brazier was used in heating orangeries as early as the sixteenth or seventeenth century (Hix 1974, 30) as well as other portable combustion stoves. Another early means for creating more hospitable interior atmosphere-environment for plants was the development of "hotbeds," a simple glass frame structure enclosing a dung- or tan bark-filled trench covered over with soil. To reduce the cost of assembly and disassembly, these temporary structures began to be conceived as more permanent, with fewer removable parts. The plants were surrounded on three sides by permanent walls leaving the south side and the roof as separate elements that could be removed during the summer months (Kohlmaier and von Sartory 1986, 43) and more generally for ventilation. One significant advantage of a more permanent structure was that it could be constructed more tightly, reducing draughts and increasing the efficiency of the heating system employed, which often required great effort to keep up during the coldest months of the year. With increased interest in garden design, burgeoning global engagement, competitive aristocracies and university institutions, the "glasshouse" came into prominence around 1700 alongside the stone-walled orangery (Kohlmaier and von Sartory 1986, 43). Many advancements in the development of greenhouse design took place in colder climates of central and northern Europe, like France, Belgium, Germany and Holland, where the nobility and bourgeoisie developed a keen interest in the cultivation of Mediterranean, subtropical and tropical plants, like citrus trees and palms (Kohlmaier and von Sartory 1986, 43). It was, however, in the United Kingdom during the height of empire and global colonialism in the eighteenth and nineteenth centuries that the greenhouse was most radicalized architecturally as well as atmospherically into the iconic houses of iron and glass most familiar today. As the empire spread far and wide, access to exotic botanicals proliferated, and as these unique plants were taken back to England, their continued survival in such a foreign climate demanded greater architectural and technological innovations.

The lead up to this nineteenth century apex of the typology was a period of significant technological advancement, facilitated through two primary developments: (1) more sophisticated systems of heating and (2) the maximization of solar exposure through an increased use and configuration of glass. These developments transformed what originated as simple protective structures into the advanced interior atmospheric generator of the modern greenhouse – what the influential Scottish botanist and garden designer J. C. Loudon[3] coined as creating an "artificial climate"[4] (Hix 1974, 29). Once conceived as a permanent structure, greater investment and planning into a dedicated stationary heating system then made sense. These early systems were developed from other domestic heating technologies of the time period, originating from simple in-room iron stoves (Figure 3.2) to more elaborate extended flue systems (Figure 3.3).

INTERIOR OF LEAN-TO HEATED BY MUSGRAVE'S SLOW COMBUSTION STOVE.

FIGURE 3.2 Plant-house heated by Musgrave's iron slow combustion stove. Reprinted from Shirly Hibberd. *The Amateur's Greenhouse and Conservatory* (London: Groombridge and Sons, 1873) 40.

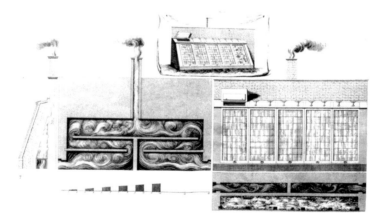

FIGURE 3.3 Dutch forcing-frame with brick back wall flue proportioned for proper draw and maximum length of smoke path. Reprinted from Pieter de la Court van der Voort. *Byzondere Aenmerkingen over Het Aenleggen Van Pragtige En Gemeene Landhuizen, Lusthoven, Plantagien En Aenklevende Cieraeden* (Leiden: Abraham Kallewier; Jan En Herman Verbeek; Pieter Vander Eyck, 1737).

These elongated flues were incorporated into the floor or northernmost back wall, but despite the level of integration, these systems still had a variety of issues that impeded their overall performance. As architectural historian John Hix describes:

Gardeners still had to fill the stoke holes of many small furnaces through-out the night during severe weather. Flues drew with difficulty, and temperature control was often impossible and because they were so inefficient, the flue systems consumed vast quantities of coal and peat. When walls of the flues cracked, noxious fumes and smoke escaped into the house. Furthermore, there was a constant struggle to increase the length of the flues within the floor or back wall and still get the flue to draw.

(Hix 1974, 32)

While these extended flue systems were widely used by the end of the eighteenth century, the next significant technological heating development took place at about this time – the use of steam heat generated from a central boiler then contained and/or distributed by a system of pipes, vaults, masses of stone or even by being bubbled through water tanks underneath the planting beds (Hix 1974, 35). Although initially not in favor of such steam systems, by 1817, in his text *Remarks on the Construction of Hothouses*, J. C. Loudon extolled their capacity to carry heat over long distances at an even temperature, their greater cleanliness and more efficient use of fuel and labor (Hix 1974, 34 and Loudon 1817, 54–59). Advancing rapidly from these steam-based systems were those that used hot water to heat; they proved to be even more efficient, not requiring the water to actually boil into its gaseous state before beginning to circulate through the piping system. In fact, water began to circulate almost as soon as the boiler was fired up, it rose throughout the system as it warmed eventually reaching a cast iron reservoir where it cooled and naturally fell back to boiler to be reused (Hix 1974, 39) (Figure 3.4). In addition to various advancements in boiler design, Thomas Fowler and James Kewley produced an alternative system called a thermosiphon, which was developed from the siphon principle able to circulate hot water more easily by permitting the location of the water supply to be either above or below the boiler, effectively creating a never-ending circuit (Hix 1974, 40). In some cases, a gutter system might be integrated into the structure as means for collecting external precipitation, perpetually feeding the system.

Coinciding with various technical innovations in the production of glass, the second major development during the eighteenth and nineteenth centuries was the greater recognition for the significance sunlight plays in the growth and sustainment of plants, resulting in the desire for more transparent surfaces and maximization of solar exposure. The greater availability of plate glass for architectural applications provided a means for increasing the transparency of building surfaces, resulting in larger operable glazed window panels within the vertical wall surfaces and also the incorporation of glass into the roof surface (Hix 1974, 16). What advanced from these two strategies of glass incorporation was a kind of blending of the front wall and roof surface into a single south-facing glass surface, initially a single lean-to surface capable of maintaining a more

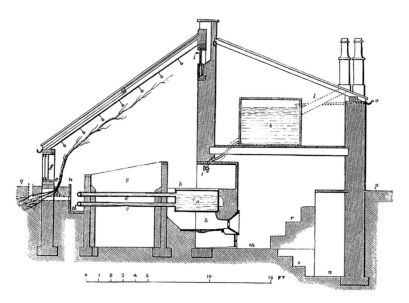

FIGURE 3.4 Charles McIntosh, section through vinery and pine-pit at Dalkeith Palace. It shows the coal fired furnace that heats up a boiler above which then feeds horizontal heating pipes running around to warm the hothouse. Rainwater was also collected along the back roof and stored in a cast-iron cistern that fed the boiler and watered the plants. Reprinted from Charles McIntosh. *The Book of the Garden* (Edinburgh and London: William Blackwood and Sons, 1853) 308, fig. 414.

perpendicular angle to the winter sun – a concept J. C. Loudon also examined in *Remarks on the Construction of Hothouses* through an illustrative comparison of 12 greenhouses constructed over the previous almost 100 years (Figure 3.5). Loudon provides much insight regarding the numerous historical points of view on the issue of determining the most desirable angle and configuration of the glazing for the greenhouse. In reference to the design ideas of Philip Miller, a botanist, chief gardener and greenhouse designer at the Apothecaries' Garden at Chelsea, London, from 1722 to 1771, Loudon makes a critical point concerning the significance of needing to understand more specifically the intended use and planned plant-life the greenhouse was to support before making decisions about the final glazing configuration. Of Miller he wrote:

> Had the demand among the opulent for early and high-flavoured fruits been as great then as it is now, it is probable so intelligent a writer and general observer would have made a nicer distinction between houses for general purposes, or maintaining an artificial climate during the whole year; and such as are only intended to mature crops of fruit at particular seasons.
>
> *(Loudon 1817, 9)*

Of Life and Death **91**

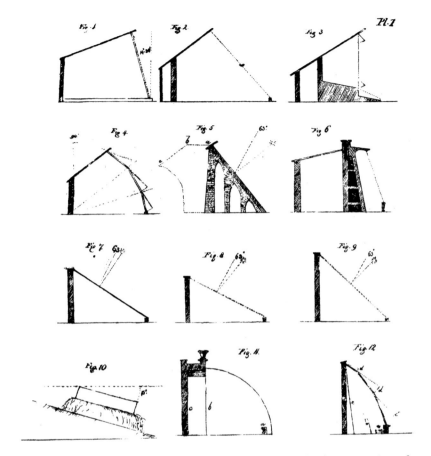

FIGURE 3.5 J. C. Loudon, Comparison of 12 historical hothouse sections from 1699 to 1817 showing the relationship between the southern sloping roof angle of inclination and solar exposure. Reprinted from J. C. Loudon. *Remarks on the Construction of Hothouses* (London: Printed for J Taylor by R. and A. Taylor, 1817) 93, plate 1.

With these observations in mind as it relates to solar exposure, the section of the greenhouse, in particular the slope of the primary south-facing wall, could be calibrated based upon an understanding of fostering a perpendicular angle between the glazing and the sun's radiation specific to the latitudinal location of the structure, the type of fruit or crop being cultivated and the time of the year desired for ripening. In this way, the articulation of the architecture is directly informed by the necessary requirements of the plant-life inhabiting the interior and mediating the particular external environmental conditions to create the most desirable interior atmosphere-environment related to the sustainment and production of the plant-life.

92 Technological Mediation

Further on in *Remarks*, Loudon discusses an 1815 proposal by Sir George Mackenzie that sought to apply these principles to a more generalized solution to maximize the amount of solar radiation during all times of day and throughout the year. To achieve such results, Mackenzie proposed a one-quarter sphere or "semidome" geometry (Loudon 1817, 15–16) that was the first proposed curvilinear glass roof intended for a horticultural application (Hix 1974, 19). Loudon was certainly impressed but also critical of Mackenzie's proposal, stating:

> But though the semidome cannot be adopted as a forcing-house without considerable disadvantages, yet it may be used in some cases even for maturing fruits; and as its appearance is most elegant, and it admits of a happy combination of lightness with strength in the construction; it may be considered, with the improvements of which it is susceptible, as a most valuable acquisition to the horticultural architecture of this country.
>
> *(Loudon 1817, 21)*

He proposed a number of improvements to different aspects of the design, specifically concerning the distance of the trellis from the glazing, the semidome's dimensional proportions, the potential for collecting unwanted condensation at the flat apex of the dome and most significantly that perpendicular light was only possible at one point along the surface at any one time (Hix 1974, 20; Loudon 1817, 17-22). He also voiced his preference for a complete fully detached dome, an "acuminated solid of revolution of glass on all sides," which he regarded as a more "elegant single object" than the semidome and capable of "admitting light in every direction" (Loudon 1817, 21). To address the deficiencies in Mackenzie's semidome, Loudon proposed his own version, acuminating the apex and flaring out the base; "a campanulated house, fifty feet high, intended for large trees in the centre, and smaller articles towards the circumference" (Loudon 1817, 22) (Figure 3.6). In a further development of his own accord that he called a "forcing-house for general purposes," Loudon proposed a "ridge and furrow disposition of glass" capable of being applied as vertical glazing or as roofing (Loudon 1817, 23). The benefits of such pleating, a simple, but ultimately radical configuration of the glass panels, was to maximize the perpendicular alignment of the glass with two daily solar meridians, one taking place earlier in the morning and another later in the afternoon, both moments when the sun's rays are less intense. During the middle of the day, solar rays wouldn't be perpendicular with any glass surface, but its power is also at its most intense, so Loudon argued "the loss sustained will be more than counterbalanced by the earlier and later meridians, which give a double chance of obtaining the sun's full influence in cloudy weather, and prolong his influence in clear weather" (Loudon 1817, 24) (Figure 3.7). Architect and scholar William M. Taylor has characterized that the purpose of the forcing-houses designed by Loudon and proposed by Mackenzie "was to regulate the forces of nature, not to reproduce them…Nature was itself

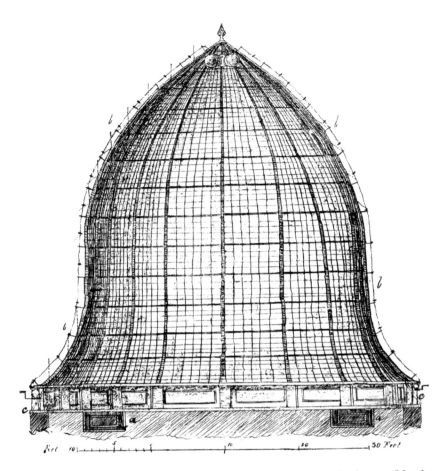

FIGURE 3.6 J. C. Loudon, section drawing of a campanulated hothouse, fifty feet high to contain taller trees in the center and smaller plants around the perimeter. Reprinted from J. C. Loudon. *Remarks on the Construction of Hothouses* (London: Printed for J Taylor by R. and A. Taylor, 1817) 97, plate 3.

envisioned as an entity separate from the various technological means intended to engage it…" (Taylor 2004, 64), and Hix writes that "Loudon's conceptions had the sophistication of an engineer creating environment control machines" (Hix 1974, 20). Significantly, Loudon's proposal of the ridge-and-furrow glazing configuration greatly influenced the most recognized greenhouse designer of the nineteenth century, Joseph Paxton.

As interests had shifted from the Baroque garden of the seventeenth and early eighteenth century to the more idealized English garden, exotic plant specimens from African and West Indian locales were introduced; this evolution also coincided with a general increase in the systematic study of botanicals

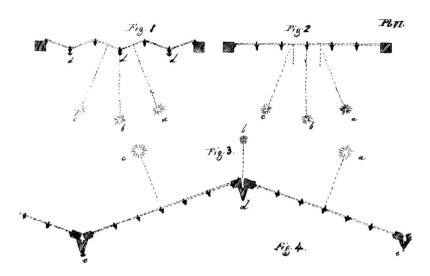

FIGURE 3.7 J. C. Loudon, ridge and furrow roof section showing the relationship to maximum solar exposure. Reprinted from J. C. Loudon. *Remarks on the Construction of Hothouses* (London: Printed for J Taylor by R. and A. Taylor, 1817) 103, plate 6.

and flora of the tropics (Kohlmaier and von Sartory 1988, 43). During this time of expedition and further colonial expansion, as exotic specimens became more prevalent in England: "The palm collection, once an expression of culture and wealth, became a part of the middleclass scene"[5] (Kohlmaier and von Sartory 1988, 43). With this expansion of interest and accessibility also came a literal expansion in the size of the architectural edifice meant to house such specimens: "The hitherto low and narrow glasshouse now changed into a spacious conservatory" (Kohlmaier and von Sartory 1988, 43). It was the further material innovation and technological refinement of construction,[6] alongside the previous 150 years of typological development, that made possible the creation of a tropical indoor climate for exotic plants, consequently producing the most iconic glasshouse structures of the nineteenth century. It was the gardener and greenhouse designer of modest beginnings, Joseph Paxton, the seventh son of a small Bedfordshire farmer, born at Milton Bryant (Jewitt and Hall 1881, 386), who at age 15 became a garden boy at Battlesden, the seat of Sir Gregory Page-Turner (Chadwick 1961, 15), who became the most well-known designer of these glass structures. Still, today, his grand works, like the Great Conservatory at Chatsworth (1836–1840), and his two versions of the Crystal Palace, first constructed at Hyde Park (1851) and then reconstructed on Sydenham Hill (1856), have often been considered among the most important buildings of the second half of the nineteenth century.[7] It was, however, a relatively modest structure by comparison his Victoria Regia House at Chatsworth which Reyner Banham regarded as his most substantial architectural achievement. It's precision in creating a specific and intentioned interior atmosphere-environment concerned with supporting life, but also its structural and technological precisions, that set it apart from his other grander constructions. Banham described the Crystal Palace as "little more than a byproduct, an epiphenomenon, of [Paxton's] output of controlled environments for 'the vegetable tribe,'" proclaiming the Victoria Regia House as "Paxton's masterpiece" (Banham 1962, 62). The structure preceded the Crystal Palace by one year and influenced greatly both the roof structure and cast-iron façade of the massive exhibition building[8] (Kohlmaier and von Sartory 1988, 225).

The Victoria Regia House at Chatsworth, completed in 1850 for the Duke of Devonshire, was designed specifically to support the most exhilarating aquatic plant of the mid-nineteenth century, the South American giant water lily then named *Victoria regia* (now known as *Victoria amizonica*). Specimens and drawings of the plant were brought back for the Geographical Society from British New Guiana in 1837 by Sir Robert Schomburgk, creating great interest and imagination in the minds of many exotic botanical collectors (Hix 1974, 50; Holway 2013, 8–11). Despite such interest, the plant proved very difficult to cultivate outside its native tropical habitat; seeds were planted at Kew Gardens in 1849, but did not develop beyond seedlings (Hix 1974, 50), and consequently, the attainment of its bloom became the great prize for gardeners and botanical collectors of the day. Despite its laudation in mid-nineteenth-century Britain, Banham describes his own personal assessment of the plant as follows:

> *Victoria Regia* was a typical botanical white-hunter's prize specimen of the period – the largest, dreariest, showiest and most pointless aquatic plant ever negligently produced by the processes of natural selection. But also the most demanding environmentally and the most instructive structurally – and Paxton responded to its overblown challenge by creating the extreme micro-climate it demanded, packaged in a structure modelled on that of the plant itself.
>
> *(Banham 1962, 62–63)*

Despite Banham's lackluster enthusiasm for the lily, his assessment provides a sense of not only the plant's environmental need for an exceptionally well-controlled interior atmosphere-environment but also the unique potential of its natural "structure" to inform Paxton's solution for a roof system design that was strong but also light as well as materially efficient and highly transparent. In a lecture to the Royal Society of Arts in November 1850, Paxton himself conceded that the inspiration for the roof structure, similar in approach to the modern space-frame, did indeed come from the plant itself.[9] In his comprehensive book *The Works of Sir Joseph Paxton*, George Chadwick describes the structural significance of the lily's leaves in the following way: "The leaves of the great lily were formed of a flat upper surface supported by a series of webs like miniature cantilevers touching only intermittently; yet they would bear a

96 Technological Mediation

considerable weight, as Paxton found when he put it to the very practical test of placing his own daughter Annie, then seven, on one" (Chadwick 1961, 101).

While Paxton had proposed a version of a flat ridge-and-furrow roof for a conservatory on Lord Burlington's estate ten years prior, and later built a smaller version of it on to Adam Washington's house at Darley Dale near Matlock (Hix 1974, 50), it was in the Victoria Regia House at Chatsworth where "Paxton's roofing system had reached its final perfection: the simplest, lightest, and most economical form of roofing then seen" (Chadwick 1961, 101). In a description of the building published on August 31, 1850, in *The Gardener's Chronicle*, Paxton compared the house's roof design to his earlier conservatory on the Chatsworth estate in the following way: "since that period the improvements in different branches of manufacturers have enabled me to make the present Lily-house (though comparatively small) of a much more light and elegant appearance" (Paxton 1850, 549). Paxton achieved this lightness and elegance through the efficiency of the overall design, creating a hierarchy between the different horizontal members arranged perpendicular to one another and on two different planes – one plane composed of his integrated and adjustable "Paxton gutters" and the other running in the opposite direction were the primary support girders.

> The four 54-foot master joists, which extended over the pool in 34-foot clear spans, were wrought iron beams 5 inches deep, reinforced by 1-inch-diameter round steel bars. They were supported on eight hollow cast-iron columns 3 ½ inches in diameter. The Paxton gutters, spanning 11 ½ feet, lay across these master joists and carried the ridge-and-furrow roof.
>
> *(Kohlmaier and von Sartory 1988, 226)*

It was however not the roof system's material efficiency or strength per se that was of greatest consequence to the lily, it was the resulting transparency achieved through such a light weight and thin member system that was most consequential. "Paxton's aim to make a building that would exploit to the full its load-bearing capacity, partly for the sake of economy but particularly to achieve maximum transparency of the roof" (Kohlmaier and von Sartory 1988, 226). These lighter, thinner and less frequent load-bearing elements provided both a maximization of openness for glazing, which also allowed for compartments of the roof that could "open by simple machinery, for the purpose of ventilation" (Paxton 1850, 548), collectively contributing to a literal and phenomenal atmospheric lightness within the interior. Combined with the fully glazed façade walls, made up of separate equally spaced cast-iron columns six feet six inches center to center and connected by cast-iron arches, the exterior vertical surfaces of enclosure became almost equally dematerialized. The façade columns were intentionally set forward of the glazing surface creating a subtle compressed depth to the façade, emphasizing the vertical elements and separating out the various layers of the enclosure.[10]

Of Life and Death 97

This separation of the facade layers was effectively made possible because of the disconnection between the envelope and the roof structural system. While the two systems were seemingly tied together through the horizontal fascia that wraps around the building, which helped to conceal the profile of the ridge-and-furrow roof structure creating a more uniform expression of the cornice around the building, they also operated on different modular proportions independent of one another. On the short side of the building, the principle roof girders and the façade columns did not align, other than both being centered at the midpoint of the elevation; on the long side of the building, the horizontal gutters did align with every vertical façade column (Figure 3.8). The roof structural system dimensions appear to be somewhat of a reflection of the internal organization and dimension of the central pool, the two middle columns falling directly on the perimeter circumference of the central pool, while the outermost columns on either side fall within the secondary shallow pools, remaining equidistant to the others and caring little for the peripheral organization of the plan. The vertical building surfaces, however, seem to be the result of the desired elevational expression of verticality, shallow layering and equally dimensioned

The Victoria Regia.

FIGURE 3.8 Joseph Paxton, *Victoria Regia House* at Chatsworth, interior, engraving. Reprinted from Llewellynn Frederick William Jewitt and S.C. Hall. *The Stately Homes of England* (London: Reeves and Turner, 1881) 388. Image scan courtesy of the Walter Havighurst Special Collections & University Archives, Miami University Libraries, Oxford, OH.

bays across the length – an almost modernist approach to the vertical surface as a uniform wrapper. The misalignment of the supportive girders with the longitudinal walls is rather curious, given that Paxton's other houses of this kind generally maintained a simple continuity between plan, section and elevation as a fundamental part of the system of construction and assembly.[11] In the Victoria Regia House at Chatsworth, it seems the utilization of this two-way multi-layer "space-frame" roof type effectively allowed for a structural disconnection between the roof and the recessed vertical building surfaces. Whether Paxton was aware of the future potential for such a disconnection between roof and wall is not clear, but this separation was reinforced by the slight projection of the roof cornice as graphically articulated in the building section drawing published in the *Gardener's Chronicle* article in 1850 (Figure 3.9).

Although many of the technical architectural components of the greenhouse had been developed, at least in principle, in Paxton's previous projects and/or proposals, the *Victoria regia* plant presented a set of requirements distinct from the other greenhouses he had designed. It was a species of "water-lily," described as the "Queen of Aquatics," requiring predominantly aquatic medium, typically residing in shallow waters with its shoots extending down to the soil below.

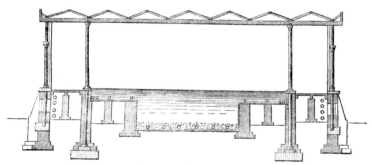

TRANSVERSE SECTION.

END ELEVATION.

FIGURE 3.9 Joseph Paxton, *Victoria Regia House* at Chatsworth, section and elevation. Reprinted from Joseph Paxton. "Description of the Victoria Regia House at Chatsworth." *The Gardener's Chronicle* 10, (August 31st, 1850) 548.

Of Life and Death 99

In an October 1839 conversation with Sir Robert Schomburgk provided the Duke of Devonshire and Joseph Paxton a description of the exotic plant.

> For his part, Paxton wanted to know every detail of the water lily's habitat and manner of growth, so the conversation turned technical…Schomburgk recited facts and figures that he knew so well, noting that the largest leaf that he measured had been six and half feet in diameter, with a rim five and a half inches high. Each plant had upwards of half a dozen such leaves. He also described the silt of the river bottom in which *Victoria regia* rooted, as well as correcting his earlier description of the habitat being a "currentless basin." In actually, it did have a current, though it was very slight.
>
> (Holway 2013, 133)

There had been earlier examples of greenhouses proposed and built for aquatic plants, one as early as 1807 designed by G. Tod and recounted in his book *Hothouses, Greenhouses, and Aquaria etc.* (Hix 1974, 48). Though never built, Loudon had also proposed a well-developed design for a dedicated aquatic plant house in his *Encyclopedia of Gardening* included in the 1822 first edition of the tome (Figure 3.10). At the time of the completion of Paxton's Victoria Regia House in 1850 none had been built or proposed that were as finely tuned and calibrated to the construction of an interior environment conducive to this most difficult of water lily species. After all, it was in the end Paxton, even before the dedicated house had been built at Chatsworth, who was the first to be able to effectively grow and eventually bloom the species, presenting the

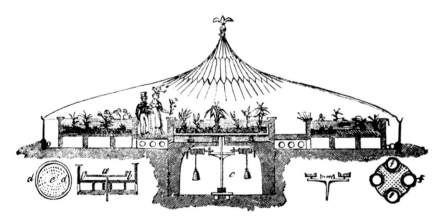

FIGURE 3.10 J. C. Loudon, section through proposed mechanical tropical aquatic house. Reprinted from J.C. Loudon. *Encyclopedia of Gardenin* (London: Printed for Longman, Rees, Orme, Brown, Green, and Longman, 1822) 927, fig. 423.

100 Technological Mediation

first English-grown bloom and leaf to the Queen and Prince Albert at Windsor castle on November 8, 1849 (Hix 1974, 50).

Paxton's sectional design of the aquatic tanks and the technical systems required to create the necessary thermal conditions of the pools as well as the interior atmosphere-environment were equally as sophisticated as his structural design for the ridge-and-furrow glazed roof structure. George Chadwick describes them succinctly in the following way:

> Apart from the main tank there were eight smaller tanks in the angles of the house which held other aquatics: *Nymphaea, Nelumbium* and *Pontederia*. The main tank had a central deeper part, 16ft. in diameter, which contained the soil for *Victoria*; embedded in the soil were 4 in. diameter iron heating pipes, whilst 2 in. diameter lead pipes were placed in the shallow part of the tank. The house as a whole was heated by a system of 4 in. iron pipes running round inside the basement walls. Thirty openings between the piers of the basement wall allowed for low-level ventilation, and opening lights in the roof "made to open by simple machinery" gave additional ventilation when required. Four small water-wheels were provided in Victoria's tank to give gentle motion to the water and a cold water supply was placed above each so that the water temperature could be modified as required, (average tank temperature 83°-85°F, house 80°-90°F).
>
> *(Chadwick 1961, 102)*

The conception, design and execution of the lily house reflected an architecture singularly focused on the propagation and affirmation of life, in the case the very specific life of the South American giant water lily, but certainly extending Paxton's "environmentalist" thinking toward other possible inhabitants, including human-beings, is equally possible. While the aforementioned "smart home" discussed in Chapter 1 might, according to some, reflect just such a strategy, it in fact cultivates an interior environment often completely foreign to the affirmation of human life, instead promoting new forms of sedentation, capitalization, marginalization and subjugation. To extend Paxton's "environmentalist" approach would be to rethink many of the parameters of design to help better cultivate human experience, human physiology, human psychology, but also importantly is the possibility of cultivating a better relationship with the changing external ecological environment within which all life resides. For Banham what was so significant about Paxton was his ability to maintain an eighteenth century "broad, holistic vision of the landscape" and "some sense of ecological wholeness in the human environment," while continuing to provide a nineteenth century "enquiring, experimental grasp of technology" toward advancing the quality and effectiveness of the artificial environments he created (Banham 1962, 60–61). This is the approach that prompted Banham to describe Paxton as "the first great environmentalist," a necessary and fundamental alternative to what he referred to as the "School of Philadelphia" and its "phoney monumentalism" of the early 1960s (Banham 1962, 64). What the "environmentalist" approach exemplifies, as described by Banham, is a radical reconsideration of how architecture understands itself as means for the construction of specific life-affirming interior environments as well as holding a deep connection to the collectivity of external environmental conditions. To extend this approach further, requires an *explication* of the surrounding external environmental conditions, specifically the atmosphere-environment, as a possible inter-active locus of design.

★ ★ ★

The potential to construct an inter-active architecture through the explication of the environment is itself a neutral endeavor, capable of being used toward the propagation of life as much as toward its extermination. The contemporary Austro-German philosopher Peter Sloterdijk has pinpointed what he claims is the modern explication of the atmosphere-environment to a singular historical event that took place in the time between the development of the two architectural typologies under discussion, the greenhouse and the gas chamber. In his book *Terror from the Air*, Sloterdijk describes the twentieth century's "discovery of the 'environment'" through the inaugurating use of toxic chlorine gas on April 22, 1915, by the Germans against unsuspecting French-Canadian troops in the northern Ypres Salient (Sloterdijk 2009, 10). For Sloterdijk, the creation of this "unlivable milieu" marks the fundamental moment when, through intentioned design and technical application, the atmosphere-environment became *explicit*, no longer suppressed as simply "background givens," but now itself the potential locus of design (Figures 3.11 and 3.12). As Sloterdijk states:

> by means of gas terrorism, modern technics crossed over into the design of the non-objective – it came to include the explication of *latent* topics such as physical air quality, artificial atmosphere additives, and other factors of climate creation for places of human-dwelling. It is precisely this process of progressive explication that binds terrorism with humanism.[12]
> *(Sloterdijk 2009, 24–25)*

For Sloterdjik, the event at Ypres Salient marks the confluence of the three defining aspects of the twentieth century: terrorism, product design and environmental thinking, a triad of atmosphere-explication and reactionary action intent on surprise, destruction and death. This binding of terrorism and humanism now remains ever present, because to explicate the atmosphere-environment, a fundamental condition for human life, is to reveal that

102 Technological Mediation

FIGURE 3.11 World War I French soldiers making a gas and flame attack on German trenches in Flanders, Belgium. Photograph courtesy of Photographs of American Military Activities, ca. 1918 – ca. 1981, created by the War Department, Army War College, Historical Section, World War I Branch, made available in the holdings of the National Archives and Records Administration, catalogued under the National Archive Identifier (NAID) 530722. https://catalog.archives.gov/id/530722.

FIGURE 3.12 United States, Army, Signal Corps, "The gas attack," six U.S. soldiers, with five of them wearing gas masks and the other one holding his throat. Probably used for training purposes, ca. 1918/1919. Photograph courtesy of Library of Congress, Prints & Photographs Division, American National Red Cross Collection, [LC-USZ62-90494].

something once invisible, taken as a given, has now, through acts of terror or war, become the possible locus for design – now, through intentioned design, capable of either affirming or denying life itself. After the war ended in November 1918, the "non-objective" design of the atmosphere-environment intent on death continued virtually undeterred, utilized toward numerous "productive" applications in industry, and even toward the implementation of a higher standard of health and cleanliness intended to benefit humanity. The "peaceful use" of these gas technologies and their further development into new products was quickly leveraged for profit, being recast as innovative and totalizing solutions to pest control, including bed bugs, the common mosquito, flour moths and lice (Sloterdijk 2009, 30).

Despite the development and use of toxic gas as a weapon for the battlefields, these peacetime applications reinstated thinking in both the scientific and legal establishments for its potential use as a "humane" form of capital punishment in the United States, an alternative to hanging, firing squad and electrocution. In fact, this thinking predated the war by some time; starting in the late nineteenth century, Americans were interested in more humane alternatives for administering the death penalty. The New York State commission, who issued a report in 1888 evaluating various potential methods of execution, briefly considered the basic idea of using lethal gas as a humane method but did ultimately recommended electrocution as the preferred method of death (Banner 2002, 196). There was a second brief consideration of lethal gas shortly after this time when some early electrocutions brought disturbing results. The Medical Society of Allegheny County, Pennsylvania, in the winter of 1896–1897, concluded that poisonous gas would be more humane than electricity, and that hypothetically if a prisoner's cell could be made airtight, then the lethal gas could be released at night when the prisoner was asleep (Banner 2002, 196). "The benefits to the prisoner would be twofold: he would die without experiencing pain, and he would be spared the anxiety of attending a ceremony devoted to his own death" (Banner 2002, 196). However, as electrocutions started to run more smoothly, interest in using lethal gas and the development of a cell capable of creating such an "unlivable" atmospheric milieu faded. This changed in early March 1921 when the legislature of Nevada, a sparsely populated western state largely controlled by mining interests, quickly passed the Humane Execution Bill allowing for execution by lethal gas, which was then signed into law by Governor Emmet D. Boyle on March 28, 1921 (Christianson 2010, 63). While the bill did not provide specifics about how exactly to administer the lethal gas, or even what specific gas should be used, its signing did require that a suitable cell be constructed and "it specified that the warden, a competent physician, and six other citizens must witness the execution" (Christianson 2010, 63–64), effectively leaving all other details for the prison officials to work through (Banner 2002, 197). According to reports in *The New York Times* newspaper, contemporaneous to the bill's signing as well as from proponents of the law, the expectations were that condemned prisoners would be administered the lethal gas one night "while asleep in their cells, without ceremony, in the sight of a small number of spectators. They reasoned that death while sleeping would be more humane than even the electric chair" (Banner 2002, 197).

Attention then turned toward the design of a space capable of effectively administering the lethal gas through the creation of the corresponding "unlivable" atmosphere-environment while still allowing spectators to view the execution but also protecting them from its detrimental effects (Figure 3.13). This last, very real consideration for the safety of spectators was only necessary with the use of lethal gas as a method of execution and reflects how the explication of the atmosphere-environment required a very different conceptual understanding of the potential for architecture to effect human inhabitants in ways previously unconsidered. While the idea of administering the gas during sleep sought to uphold the narrative, and even possibly the action, of a more humane method of execution, it generally proved to be impractical.

FIGURE 3.13 Rawlings state prison in Wyoming lethal gas chamber: "The gas chamber in which Wyoming's condemned criminals will be executed in future. Poison pellets are dropped into a jar under the chair to which the prisoner is strapped," manufactured in Denver, CO, shown November 17, 1936. Photograph reprinted with permission of the Associated Press.

> To satisfy the twin goals of humanity and visual display would have required an airtight cell large enough to live in for several days, with thick glass windows along one wall, and with two systems of valves, one for ventilation during the prisoner's last days and the other for releasing the gas. Prison officials settled for a small airtight chamber, just large enough to hold a wooden chair, with a window through which spectators could see the prisoner's head.
>
> *(Banner 2002, 197)*

The small physical size of the chamber, the limited ability to accommodate spectators and the necessary technical expertise required to carry out the gas executions, all demanded that the event take place within the existing confines of the prison itself instead of outside within the public sphere, which was historically the tradition with hangings.[13] While electrocution also shifted the space of execution into the prison, the possible adverse effects to spectators by threat of the gas chamber malfunctioning and its technical requirements of operation greatly reduced the number of possible spectators. This change in location and lack of public participation effectively reframed the literal and symbolic meaning of fulfilling the death sentence, shifting the onus of the action from one of community justice to one of state authority and power (Banner 2002, 206). In North Carolina, the first state East of the Mississippi and the first Southern state to adopt lethal gas as a method of execution, a legislator put forth an amendment that called for "'mobile executions' by means of a portable gas chamber that would be carried around by truck, in order to facilitate the process for local officials and residents and allow for public executions" (Christianson 2010, 108). The measure however was not adopted on the grounds that it was "undignified." Later the concept was separately developed by the Nazis, who converted vans into sealed mobile gas chamber units, employing them starting in September 1941, not as a means to maintain public participation but rather for the convenience and stealth mobility it provided (Piper 1994, 176, n.5).

A decade after executions by lethal gas were being carried out in Nevada, its accepted use began to spread, and so did knowledge of how to most efficiently, and seemingly effectively, carry out the action. The sequence of effects enacted by the prisoner during the execution were even so predictable that in the state of Missouri the prison physician had a preprinted form listing out each step with blank spaces to record the time it had occurred. "Prison officials knew for certain that the head would fall forward, then backward, and then forward again. Even electrocution was not this predictable, not this clinical" (Banner 2002, 202). The fact that within a matter of seconds from inhaling the gas most prisoners appeared to just fall asleep[14] and the procedure's predictability both reinforced the idea of the gas chamber as a "matter of practical social reform" (Christianson 2010, 1). In this sense, as Sloterdijk described, the use of the gas chamber as first developed in Nevada reflected a "sense of humanity" through the realization of a "modern" explication of a human-being's dependency on a specific atmosphere-environment. As he says: "In this field, 'modern' can be defined as that which promises to combine a high level of efficiency with a sense of humanity – in the case at hand, through the use of a quick-acting poison administered to delinquents" (Sloterdijk 2009, 39).

Despite having its "practical" origin in the terror gas attacks of World War I, the creation of an atmosphere-environment intent on death facilitated through the contained and technologically mediated construction of a specific built environment made it possible to reframe this action, not as one of war but one of humanity – both for the prisoner destined to be executed and in the fulfillment of justice for the victims afflicted. Historian Scott Christianson describes this transformation in the following way:

> Although the world had recently undergone the horrors of chemical warfare, advocates of gassing claimed that the poor soldiers on the battlefield had suffered more because of low concentrations and other conditions, whereas a lethal chamber would provide highly concentrated doses in an enclosed space, thereby ensuring a quick and painless death.
>
> *(Christianson 2010, 63)*

Despite its increased adoption exclusively in Western and Southern states (Banner 2002, 199) over the following two decades after its first use in 1921, its continued use had many challengers who questioned its effectiveness and ability to deliver a peaceful death.[15] In the aftermath of World War II, as a greater understanding of the Nazi atrocities became known and their use of the gas chamber as a mechanism for mass human extermination fully came to light, its use as a means to administer capital punishment in the United States had "acquired an extremely bad reputation" (Christianson 2010, 171), the perception of its so-called humanity radically shattered.

The Nazis' implementation of the gas chamber as a mechanism for the destruction of life through the construction of a specific interior atmosphere-environment was, from a technological point of view, in line with the earlier developments of lethal gas as a method of capital punishment in the United States. The Nazi's use was even in many ways less advanced, relying often on the retrofitting and conversion of existing structures to carry out the action[16] without concern for those being killed or the need to accommodate spectators. Their use of the method cared only for how to most expediently induce mass death; there was no pretense of humanity. The Nazi gas chamber was a mechanical "answer" to the "question" of how to most efficiently and effectively conduct mass execution, the genocide of Jews, gypsies, political dissidents, prisoners of war and any other minority group felt to be unworthy – there was no justice being served through the advancement of death, it was only death (Figure 3.14).

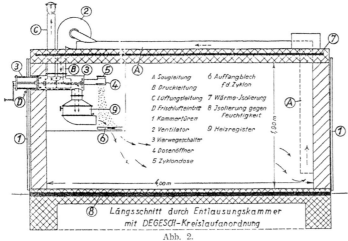

FIGURE 3.14 Longitudinal section drawing of a delousing chamber. Reprinted from RG-11.001M.03, Zentralbauleitung der Waffen-SS und Polizei Auschwitz (Fond 502), Waffen-SS and Polizei. Zentralbauleitung in Auchwitz, United States Holocaust Memorial Museum Archives, Washington, DC.

In conclusion to this chapter let us briefly examine a somewhat perverse example of historical confluence between the Nazi's gas chamber and the greenhouse typology. Alongside the conquests of greater Europe, the Nazi's maintained an agenda for the creation of an expansive agricultural estate to be located in the eastern Upper Silesia in Poland, in and around the camp Auschwitz-Birkenau. While the use of the gas chamber was carried out in various camps throughout the German-controlled territory of World War II, Auschwitz-Birkenau was selected as a primary location for its initial testing, development and implementation on a mass scale; beginning in 1942, it became the largest of the extermination centers where the "Endlösung der Judenfrage," the final solution to the Jewish question (i.e. extermination) was to be carried out (Auschwitz-Birkenau State Museum). Alongside the massive concentration camp, this area of Southern Poland was subject to a re-Germanification campaign, enacted through a process of forced displacement of indigenous Poles and the resettlement by ethnic Germans. The resettlement of this predominantly peasant farmland was important both strategically, to "create a wedge between the Poles and the Czechs who, it was feared were in communication through the Moravian Gap" (Dwork and van Pelt 1996, 182), and symbolically. The Nazis regarded this region as a part of their lost medieval German heritage, part of the German East, having been under Polish occupation for the last 500 years. Upon the resettlement of the area by ethnic Germans, Heinrich Himmler, commander of the SS and controller of the Nazi concentration camps, became enamored by the idea of transforming the region into a number of bucolic agricultural estates whose establishment could be facilitated by the labor of the projected 10,000 inmates of Auschwitz-Birkenau (Dwork and van Pelt 1996, 189–190).

> It was the metamorphosis of the camp into an agricultural estate worked by slaves that caught [Himmler's] fancy; it fitted his fantasy of the German East, and he was enraptured by the vision of Auschwitz playing a central role in the reclamation of that area.
>
> *(Dwork and van Pelt 1996, 190)*

In addition to massive infrastructure projects related to water drainage and road construction, the inmates were also tasked to build various buildings in which agricultural experiments could be carried out related to plant cultivation and cattle breeding – by 1943, there were barns, pigsties and a number of different experimental greenhouse stations that had been constructed (Figures 3.15 and 3.16). Himmler imagined that the agricultural estate would provide training for the relocated German farmers and serve as nurseries for corn, berries, fruits and other garden seeds as well as various livestock (Dwork and van Pelt 1996, 188). While the greenhouse stations were used for experimentation in plant cultivation, many were also used for cultivating flowers to adorn the tables of the Auschwitz-Birkenau SS soldiers as well as to provide them fresh vegetables throughout the year. In this way, the creation of atmosphere-environments conducive to the propagation of life made possible

FIGURE 3.15 Auschwitz, Poland, construction of greenhouses, south of Camp I, 1941. Photograph courtesy of Yad Vashem, Photo Archive, Album # FA157/128, Item ID 51270. Photography by SS photographer. https://photos.yad-vashem.org/photo-details.html?language=en&item_id=51270&ind=174.

FIGURE 3.16 Auschwitz, Poland, a prisoner working in a greenhouse, south of Camp I, 1941. Photograph courtesy of Yad Vashem, Photo Archives, Album #FA157/131, Item ID 46428. Photography by SS photographer. https://photos.yadvashem.org/photo-details.html?language=en&item_id=46428&ind=53.

through the design and construction of the greenhouse building had been indirectly co-opted for the sustainment of the Nazi world system and mass extermination epitomized in the gas chamber, both directly built on the backs of camp slave labor. A number of these experimental greenhouse structures still stand today in ruins, serving as both the literal and symbolic confluence of architecture's "environmentalist" potential to cultivate life and death through systems of technological mediation of external conditions and the construction of specific interior atmosphere-environments. While in some ways both are extreme examples of such an architecture, the gas chamber is without comparison as a sinister and destructive application of such an approach, even if intended as humane means for implementing capital punishment or the outright mass murder of a people. The greenhouse however offers much potential toward an "environmentalist" strategy that may move beyond the false rhetoric of the early modernist conceptions of the standardized human body and the cultivation of the ideal inhabitant, to instead provide an active participatory role in the lives of human-beings toward their individually evolving potentials as unique living-beings. Its intentioned design may instead help to support, stimulate, challenge and even foster bio-physical responses beneficial to human well-being and the possibility for *coping* and *adapting* our collective "new" world. There must also be a consideration for how this "environmentalist" potential might move beyond the singular individual human inhabitant, extending outward to

110 Technological Mediation

include the broader *ecological* environmental context comprised of many other non-human living and non-living-beings. This consideration and more generally the question of alternative approaches to how we might choose to live-in-the-world-ecology is the primary focus of the next part of this book.

Notes

1 A previous version of this chapter was presented at the 108th annual meeting virtual conference of the Association of Collegiate Schools of Architecture (ACSA), held June 15–18, 2020.
2 The main concept is to increase the temperature of the soil and the amount of solar exposure.

> Using all the techniques at their disposal, Roman gardeners employed the principle of forcing growth by making hot-beds, either by digging pits in the ground, or by constructing raised beds surrounded by a low brick wall and filling them with manure. A third option was to make a bed on wheels, a giant wooden wheelbarrow that could be trundled in and out.
>
> (Woods and Warren 1988, 3)

3 For an extensive history of the life and work of John Claudius Loudon see Melanie Louise Simo, *Loudon and the Landscape: From Country Seat to Metropolis 1783–1843* (New Haven, CT: Yale University Press, 1988).
4 Historian John Hix states his appreciation for this phrase because of its "positive" or even "arrogant" belief in technology reflective of this time period; also see Loudon (1817, 2).
5 In the second half of the nineteenth century in England the greenhouse became a fixture of the Victorian house itself becoming a prefabricated commercialized product, industrialized and marketed to the masses, see Hix (1971, ch.7). Alongside these developments of industry also came a proliferation of technical manuals and handbooks related to greenhouse design and construction for amateurs, for one such example see Shirley Hibbard, *The amateur's greenhouse and conservatory: A handy guide to the construction and management of plant-houses and the selection, cultivation, and improvement of ornamental greenhouse and conservatory plants* (London: Groombridge and Sons, 1883).
6 Such as the development of cast iron, the cost reduction and continued improvement of glass manufacturing and the incorporation of the aforementioned central heating systems.
7 This is a point Reyner Banham explicitly discusses in his essay "The Environmentalist" challenging the acceptance of the Crystal Palace specifically as "the first great monument of modern architecture," instead arguing that despite its advanced use of materials and methods, its "architectural conception had vastly more to do with the period before 1851 than the period after it." This argument concerning the Crystal Palace's proper place in history did not take away from Banham's regard for Paxton's eighteenth-century holistic view of the natural environment as a designer capable of constructing highly effective interior climates of botanical habitation; see Banham (1962, 57–64).
8 Paxton describes how the Victoria Regia House proved specifically inspirational toward the design of the Crystal Palace. "It occurred to me that it [the Crystal Palace] only required a number of such structures as the Lily-house repeated in length, width, and height, to form, with some modifications, a suitable building for the exhibition of 1851"; see Paxton (1850, 549).

9 See Paxton's lecture to the Royal Society of Arts, November 1850. *Transactions*, vol. LVII, 1850–1851, p. 1.
10 Again, from Paxton's description in *The Gardener's Chronicle* of 1850: "By this section it will be seen that the upright sashes are placed behind the cast iron columns, so that the shafts of the pillars are isolated"; see Paxton (1850, 548).
11 Most notable in his other ridge-and-furrow roofed greenhouse at Chatsworth, details of which are illustrated in *Paxton's Magazine of Botany* of 1834, but this continuity is also clearly demonstrated in his Great Conservatory at Chatsworth built in 1836–1840 and the two later versions of the Crystal Palace.
12 Italics added here for emphasis.
13 Stuart Banner makes the argument in his book *The Death Penalty: An American History* that the limitations of the physical space required for economic efficiency and the safety of spectators as well as what seemed to be the desire by States limiting viewings primarily to state officials contributed to the insular nature of the lethal gas method of execution. He also makes the point that like the electric chair, the gas chamber reinforced the small world of capital punishment as an exclusively male domain; see Banner (2002, 204).
14 This was not however true for every person and seemed to depend on one's physical stature and ability to resist the initial effects of the gas.
15 "By December 1937 national discussion about the pros and cons of lethal gas had become so widespread that *Reader's Digest* published a comparison of the arguments." One side argued that it was "practically foolproof" and the other that the method was "neither painless nor easy to watch"; see Christianson (2010, 121).
16 The first use of lethal gas in a chamber at Auschwitz took place in late 1941, when Zykon B, originally utilized for delousing and pest fumigation, was used on 250 "incurable" inmates and 600 Soviet prisoners of war. The gas was administered in the existing basement of block 11, which proved problematic for the Nazis as it lacked ventilation needed to clear the space after the gas had been administered effectively and was at too great a distance from the existing crematorium; see Jean-Claude Pressac and Robert-Jan Pelt, "The machinery of mass murder at Auschwitz" in *Anatomy of the Auschwitz death camp*, ed. Yisrael Gutman and Michael Berenbaum (Bloomington: Indiana University Press 1994) 209, and Christianson (2010, 152).

References

Auschwitz–Birkenau State Museum. History KL Auschwitz-Birkenau. http://auschwitz.org/en/history/kl-auschwitz-birkenau/.

Banham, Reyner. 1962. The environmentalist. *Program* 2 (Spring): 57–64.

Banner, Stuart. 2002. *The death penalty: An American history.* Cambridge, MA: Harvard University Press.

Chadwick, George F. 1961. *The works of Sir Joseph Paxton, 1803–1865.* London: The Architectural Press.

Christianson, Scott. 2010. *The last gasp: The rise and fall of the American gas chamber.* Berkeley, CA: University of California Press.

Dwork, Debórah and Robert Jan van Pelt. 1996. *Auschwitz 1270 to the present.* New York: W. W. Norton & Company.

Hix, John. 1974. *The glass house.* Cambridge, MA: The MIT Press.

Holway, Tatiana M. 2013. *The flower of empire: An Amazonian water lily, the quest to make it bloom, and the world it created.* New York: Oxford University Press.

Jewitt, Llewellynn Frederick William and S. C. Hall. 1881. *The Stately Homes of England.* London: Reeves and Turner.

Kohlmaier, Georg and Barna Von Sartory. 1986. *Houses of glass: A nineteenth-century building type.* Cambridge, MA: MIT Press.

Loudon, John Claudius. 1817. *Remarks on the construction of hothouses: Pointing out the most advantageous forms, materials, and contrivances to be used in their construction; Also a review of the various methods of building them in foreign countries as well as in England.* London: Printed for J. Taylor by R. and A. Taylor.

Paxton, Joseph. 1850. Description of the Victoria Regia House at Chatsworth. *The Gardener's Chronicle* 10 (August 31): 548–549.

Piper, Franciszek. 1994. Gas chambers and crematoria. In *Anatomy of the Auschwitz death camp,* ed. Yisrael Gutman and Michael Berenbaum, 157–182. Bloomington: Indiana University Press.

Sloterdijk, Peter. 2009. *Terror from the air.* Trans. Amy Patton and Steve Corcoran. Los Angeles, CA: Semiotext(e).

Taylor, William M. 2004. *The vital landscape: Nature and the built environment in nineteenth-century Britain.* Aldershot, Hants, England: Ashgate.

Woods, Mary and Arete Swartz Warren. 1988. *Glass houses: A history of greenhouses, orangeries and conservatories.* New York: Rizzoli International Publication.

PART II
Environmental Identification

Our naming of the current volatile human epoch as the Anthropocene, recognized as a time of anthropocentric global warming, environmental degradation, species extinction and climate change (of which buildings and the constructed environment more broadly have played a significant part), has resulted in, as Bruno Latour has put it, a "profound mutation in our relation to the world." This change is ongoing, with the level and extent of its destructive effects dependent upon our past, current and future actions. A model and concept of sustainability has been the architectural disciplinary response, aiming to reduce the energy consumption, carbon footprint, pollution generation and environmental degradation of the constructed environment, these goals proposed largely to be achieved through greater anthropocentric technological advancements. While admirable, the ability to achieve a truly sustainable model of habitation with and within the earth-system, the world-ecology, remains elusive (if even possible) as the global economic system of capital production, accumulation and exchange remains unchallenged. This system of capital is dependent upon perpetual growth, the perpetual consumption of resources and spaces, all of which are finite within the effectively closed system of the world-ecology. Part II, "Environmental Identification," questions various aspects of the sustainability model and its disciplinary relevance in the current moment beyond climatological-ecological "crisis." It explores an alternative approach at multiple scales, relying not on greater efficiency, effectiveness or even reciprocity but rather on an alternative self-conceptualization and self-realization of the "ecological self." This approach recognizes the inherently ecological basis of being and living "in-the-world-ecology" dependent upon individual environmental identification. It reconsiders our abilities for coping and adapting to the changing conditions beyond climatological-ecological "crisis," in relationship to a conceptual reframing of how we might choose to inhabit the world-ecology, and only made possible through an understanding based upon correlation and ultimately co-production, between "us" and the total collective "being-with" all living-beings.

4

BACK HOME FROM THE FRONTIER

Considering an Eco-Effective Approach to Design

> Along with the possibility of the extinction of mankind by nuclear war, the central problem of our age has therefore become the contamination of man's total environment with such substances of incredible potential for harm – substances that accumulate in the tissues of plants and animals and even penetrate the germ cells to shatter or alter the very material of heredity upon which the shape of the future depends.
>
> Some would-be architects of our future look toward a time when it will be possible to alter the human germ plasm by design. But we may easily be doing so now by inadvertence, for many chemicals, like radiation, bring about gene mutations. It is ironic to think that man might determine his own future by something so seemingly trivial as the choice of an insect spray.
>
> (Carson 1962, 8)

This assessment, provided by marine biologist and conservationist Rachel Carson in her vital and immensely influential 1962 book *Silent Spring*, called attention to a broad public audience the toxic consequences of human actions on and within the various environments he/she inhabits. However, to fully understand the implications of Carson's observations concerning these toxic actions, a further distinction must be made between the concept of *environment*, which generally considers the external, or surrounding, conditions in isolation to an organism, and the idea of *ecology* or an *ecosystem*, which both express the relationships between organisms and their external surroundings. Ecology as an idea was supported in the late eighteenth and early nineteenth century by the work of the German explorer and scientist Alexander von Humboldt whose writings concerning the relationships between specific plant species and their environmental climate would go on to influence many naturalists, scientists and thinkers of the following several generations including

116 Environmental Identification

Darwin, Thoreau and Haeckel. Carson's work is fundamentally *ecological*, bringing to light several profound realizations concerning the deleterious effects of our twentieth-century use of poisonous chemicals in the various environments we call home. First, *Silent Spring* exposed to the masses how these human-made and/or human-applied toxic chemicals, even if used in supposedly safe diluted quantities and targeted only to combat various unwanted non-human "vermin" or "pests," could, when applied regularly, accumulate over time to reach toxic concentrations across many levels of an ecosystem. Second, Carson revealed that these toxic chemicals may travel beyond the local ecosystem of application, through air, water and natural organism migrations, to contaminate previously separated locales and even what she refers to as the "total environment." "Seldom if ever does Nature operate in closed and separate compartments" (Carson 1962, 42). It's important to recognize – as she describes in the quotation to start this chapter – that these adverse effects are not limited to the non-human living-beings of an ecosystem, but may also have profound consequences for humans. Considering the many linkages made by humans across many different ecosystems, toward the growth of food, the raising of livestock, the consumption of water and general habitation, we are not immune to the detrimental effects of these human-made and/or human-applied toxic chemicals, even when "responsibly" used.[1]

In this sense, Carson's research prompts a similar realization as Peter Sloterdijk's observations discussed in Chapter 3 concerning the twentieth century's radical *explication* of the atmosphere-environment. In fact, quite literally many early pesticides were the result of research and development undertaken during the interwar period as wartime technologies were reconsidered for "peaceful" application and profit. They became "answers" to various pestilence concerns, like lice, or invasive and/or detrimental insect species (Sloterdijk 2009, 30) (Figures 4.1 and 4.2). The destruction inflicted by the two great wars only reinforced the perceived peacetime ability to alter and control the environment through technological prowess, now fully radicalized by twentieth-century industrial means, and more generalized peace. The ecological observations made in *Silent Spring* reflect an even broader environmental explication than the one articulated by Sloterdijk, to now include seemingly every aspect of man's environment of habitation – a kind of *ecological explication* that reveals all living and non-living "beings" as possible receptors of human design, whether intended or inadvertent. This is not to imply our actual dominion over the world-ecology, but simply that it cannot escape being affected by our actions (i.e. the epoch of the Anthropocene).

While today Carson has become the most well-known early "environmentalist" advocate of the second half of the twentieth century an equally prolific contemporaneous critical voice, Murray Bookchin, began to raise many of the same concerns in his book *Our Synthetic Environment* published a few months earlier than *Silent Spring* in early 1962. Writing under the pseudonym Lewis Herber, Bookchin does not mince words regarding his concerns for the toxic

FIGURE 4.1 Council worker dusting DDT (Dichloro-Diphenyl-Trichloroethane) on mosquito breeding water by using a hand operated machine, Brisbane, Australia, 1949. Photograph courtesy of Brisbane John Oxley Library, State Library of Queensland. Negative #157560.

FIGURE 4.2 Ford tri-motor spraying DDT (Dichloro-Diphenyl-Trichloroethane). Western spruce budworm control project. Powder River control unit, Oregon, 1955. Photograph courtesy of USDA Forest Service, Pacific Northwest Region, State and Private Forestry, Forest Health Protection. Collection: Portland Station Collection; La Grande, Oregon. Image: PS-1430. Photography by R.B. Pope, date: July 1955.

effects of human actions on the natural and constructed environments we inhabit. On the use of insecticides and the ecological basis for their negative effects, he says the following:

> Insecticides commonly aggravate the very problems they are meant to solve. The ecological difficulties they create lead to the use of increasingly toxic preparations, until a point is reached where the insecticides

118 Environmental Identification

> threaten to become more dangerous in the long run to the human species than the insects for which they are intended. The need to rescue a crop from agricultural mismanagement gains priority over the health and wellbeing of the consumer...It would seem to be a form of ecological retribution that the very forces man has summoned against the living world around him are being redirected by a remorseless logic against the human organism itself.
>
> *(Herber 1962, 110)*

Taking a closer look at a specific example Carson's examination of Clear Lake, California, demonstrates this *ecological explication* through the contamination and toxic consequences pertaining to one environmental element within the localized ecosystem: water and the "chains of life it supports" (Carson 1962, 46). She describes how, starting in 1949, the application of the insecticide chemical DDD (a chlorinated hydrocarbon and close relative to DDT) was used to combat the gnat species *Chaoborus astictopus*, which naturally inhabited the lake. Although a close relative of mosquitoes, these gnats were not bloodsucking insects, but were nevertheless considered a nuisance by the recreational users of the lake who deemed it necessary to eradicate them (Carson 1962, 46). Control efforts were carefully planned and researched resulting in a heavily diluted application of the insecticide which worked well for a number of years. However, despite initial success, it eventually lost its effectiveness, and in 1954, a second treatment was sprayed, this time at a higher concentration[2] (Carson 1962, 47). The lake was also inhabited in the winter months by the western grebe, a species of bird attracted to it as a breeding ground and as an ample source of fish. During the winter following the second application of the insecticide, as western grebes began to die, it became clear that the gnat population was not the only form of life within the ecosystem of the lake being adversely affected by the chemical applications. A third treatment of the DDD insecticide was applied in 1957 as the gnat population persisted, and, as in previous years, more western grebes also died (Carson 1962, 47). As Carson describes, "when someone thought to analyze the fatty tissues of the grebes, they were found to be loaded with DDD in the extraordinary concentration of 1600 parts per million" (Carson 1962, 47). In a relatively short time of a matter of years, through the consumption of toxified fish, who had been feeding upon toxified plants and plankton, the DDD chemicals migrated through all levels of the lake's ecosystem, its deleterious effects continuously amplified as concentrations became ever greater up the food chain, transforming whole organisms into reservoirs of poison. Although measurements of the water indicated no trace of DDD shortly after its application, "the poison had not really left the lake; it had merely gone into the fabric of the life the lake supports" (Carson 1962, 48), and this remained so for years well after the last insecticide application. The ecosystem's intrinsic interconnectedness was succinctly described by Carson through the fundamental element of water.

> Water must also be thought of in terms of the chains of life it supports – from the small-as-dust green cells of the drifting plant plankton, through the minute water fleas to the fishes that strain plankton from the water and are in turn eaten by other fishes or by birds, mink, racoons – in an endless cyclic transfer of materials from life to life. We know that the necessary minerals in the water are so passed from link to link of the food chains. Can we suppose that poisons we introduce into water will not also enter into these cycles of nature?
>
> *(Carson 1962, 46)*

Understanding the role of just this one element – water – illustrates the essential ecological point that various entities (living and non-living) do not exist-in-the-world in isolation, they are held together in ongoing dynamic inter-active relationships to form interpenetrating and interdependent ecosystems. Individual species of plants, insects, birds and even humans cannot be singularly considered and still be fully comprehended – it is equally as necessary to understand their correspondences as it is their individual attributes. Adopting an ecological point of view however, is not without its own set of consequences that humans must accept if we are to develop a more considerate approach to how we choose to live-in-the world. Bookchin puts it this way: "An ecological point of view that emphasizes the use of organic materials and the practice of biocentric control admittedly restricts man. It requires him to reconstruct the agricultural situation along more natural lines, to defer to the dictates of ecology rather than those of economics" (Herber 1962, 61). This last point concerning the need to adjust our economic priorities is critical and one that will be discussed more in-depth in the next chapter.

Rachel Carson's biographer Linda Lear, writing in an introduction to the 40th anniversary edition of *Silent Spring*, points out that it was Carson's concept of the "ecology of the human body" that provided a fundamental departure in how we think about our actions, and the inherent connections between the natural environment and human health. "*Silent Spring* proved that our bodies are not boundaries. Chemical corruption of the globe affects us from conception to death. Like the rest of nature, we are vulnerable to pesticides; we too are permeable" (Carson 1962, xvi). Disturbingly these *unintended* detrimental effects are often latent, residing below the surface of conscious registration, our human vulnerability concealed until it's too late to even make the connection back to the toxic source of our ailing.[3]

With the publication of *Silent Spring*, Carson, a woman scientist, outside the perimeter of institutionalized environmental science or government agency, and writing in a voice specifically intended for a public audience, not surprisingly faced an onslaught of criticism from the chemical industry, who assaulted her character, intellectual ability and gender. Despite these criticisms, her argumentation helped facilitate a critical social repositioning, helping to awaken

120 Environmental Identification

FIGURE 4.3 Rachel Carson speaking before Senate Government Operations subcommittee studying pesticide spraying, 1963. Photograph courtesy of Library of Congress, Prints & Photographs Division, NYWT&S Collection, 1963, https://www.loc.gov/item/94505448/ [LC-USZ62-111207].

a collective consciousness within the emerging generation of younger citizens becoming aware of environmental degradation and who were more skeptical of the government's moral authority on such matters. Lear states that it was in many ways Carson's outsider status from the scientific establishment that resonated so much with the public, giving voice to many citizens already sounding the alarm about the destructive effects of toxic chemicals being applied in their communities. This public resonance ultimately made it impossible for the establishment institutions and industries to dismiss her voice (Figure 4.3).

Despite this public awareness and some positive institutionalized changes since Carson's voice was heard,[4] the ongoing explication of the *ecological environment* has continued to create a "new" world defined by pollution, global warming, climate instability and species extinction – all phenomena for which buildings have contributed significantly. According to the most recent 2018/2019 report issued by the World Green Building Council, the *operational* carbon emissions of buildings accounts for 28% of global carbon emissions and their *embodied* carbon emissions and construction account for a further 11% (World Green Building Council 2019, 12). The emissions are largely due to the implementation of fossil fuel-dependent heating, ventilating and air-conditioning systems (HVAC) necessary to create more livable interior milieus (see Chapters 1 and 2), alongside the processes of construction and the rapid global increase in the use of other modern building materials like steel, but especially concrete[5] (Figures 4.4 and 4.5). The natural resource extraction processes needed to acquire fossil fuels and the mineral resources necessary for manufacturing synthetic materials as well as the production of electricity needed to run the HVAC building systems have also contributed greatly (Williamson, Radford, and Bennetts 2003, 86–88). And, the chemical technologies developed

(a)

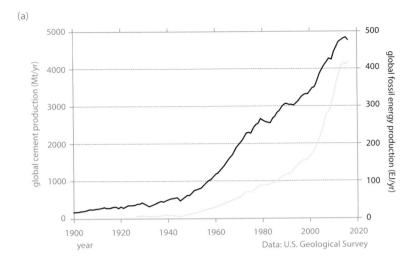

(b)

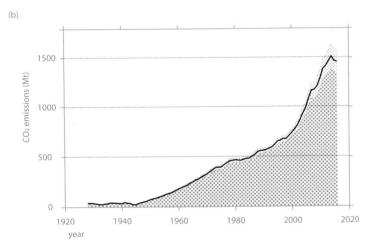

FIGURE 4.4 (a) Global cement and fossil energy production from 1900 to 2016; (b) Global process CO_2 emissions from cement production, with 95% confidence level reflecting data availability and reliability. Data for (a) based upon U.S. Geological Survey, 2014, Cement statistics, in Kelly, T.D., and Matos, G.R., comps., Historical statistics for mineral and material commodities in the United States: U.S. Geological Survey Data Series 140, accessed April 21, 2020, http://minerals.usgs.gov/minerals/pubs/historical-statistics/, and S. H. Mohr, J. Wang, G. Ellem, J. Ward, and D. Giurco. "Projection of world fossil fuels by country." *Fuel* 141 (2015): 120–135, https://doi.org/10.1016/j.fuel.2014.10.030 (b) Redrawn by author, from Robbie M. Andrew, "Global CO2 emissions from cement production," Earth Syst. Sci. Data, 10, 195–217, figs. 1 and 2, https://doi.org/10.5194/essd-10-195-2018, accessed April 20, 2020.

122 Environmental Identification

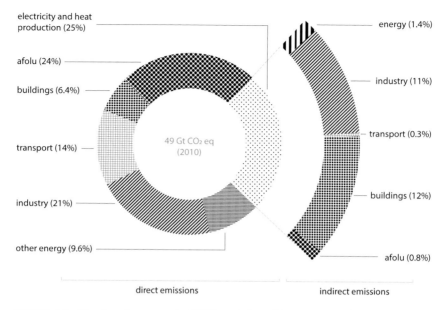

FIGURE 4.5 Total anthropogenic GHG emissions (GtCO$_2$eq/yr) by economic sectors. Redrawn by author from IPCC, 2014. *Climate Change 2014: Mitigation of Climate Change. Contribution of Working Group III to the Fifth Assessment Report of the Intergovernmental Panel on Climate Change*, edited by O. Edenhofer, R. Pichs-Madruga, Y. Sokona, E. Farahani, S. Kadner, K. Seyboth, A. Adler, I. Baum, S. Brunner, P. Eickemeier, B. Kriemann, J. Savolainen, S. Schlömer, C. von Stechow, T. Zwickel and J.C. Minx (Cambridge and New York: Cambridge University Press) 8, fig. SPM.2.

in the first half of the twentieth century have since been applied beyond the pesticide industry, to become pervasive in how we manufacture everything, including the constructed environments we inhabit. The use of synthetically produced and petroleum-based building materials, interior finishes and furnishings of all kinds have directly instigated numerous deleterious effects on many inhabitants through the process of off-gassing, or their breakdown into airborne particles which can be inhaled, resulting in toxic interior containers of habitation[6] (Environmental Protection Agency). Bookchin has strongly argued that this general toxification of the environment through its construction is fundamentally a result of the densification, urbanization and standardization of how we choose to inhabit the world.[7] The building of vast urban conglomerations results in

> replacing a highly complex, organic environment with a simplified, inorganic one...steadily restoring the biosphere to a stage which will be able to support only simpler forms of life. If this great reversal of the evolutionary process continues, it is by no means fanciful to suppose that the

preconditions for higher forms of life will be irreparably destroyed and the earth will become incapable of supporting man himself.

(Bookchin 1965, 89–90)

He describes an effective alternative as a reconstructive anarchist approach based upon physical and social decentralization, adopting an ecologically based model through the concepts of a "balanced community, a face-to-face democracy, a humanistic technology and a decentralized society" which taken collectively "now constitute the preconditions for human survival" (Bookchin 1965, 91).

While Bookchin's 1960's assessment of society's relationship to the constructed environments we create and inhabit provides an expansive radical repositioning of how we might choose to live-in-the-world-ecology, the lead-up to the new millennium, has seen most of its momentum swing toward technocratic solutions through the creation of less toxic alternatives in material use and production as well as greater energy efficiency and reduction in overall building emissions generated from the construction and daily operation. These approaches have coalesced into numerous individual technologies and strategies which have been largely consolidated under the name of "sustainability" or, as they have been referred to more generally, "green design." Though it's not always clear what's exactly meant by the use of the term "sustainability," as its meaning seems to vary depending upon the specific circumstances, context and intended audience for which it's used, generally speaking, it recognizes that the collective actions of industrial civilization play a significant role in degrading and toxifying both the ecological and constructed environments we inhabit, and it seeks to reduce such negative impact through a more equitable approach to design. Perhaps the most generally referenced definition comes from the World Commission of Environment and Development, an independent body set up by the United Nations, who, in their 1987 report "Our Common Future," stated: "Sustainable development seeks to meet the needs and aspirations of the present without compromising the ability to meet those of the future" (World Commission of Environment and Development 1987, 40). But how really might such egalitarian ambitions of posterity be met today within the rapidly changing conditions of the world-ecology, beyond climatological-ecological "crisis" and the underlying global system of capital production, accumulation and exchange?

The Australian architects Terry Williamson, Antony Radford and Helen Bennetts, writing on the very first page of their book *Understanding Sustainable Architecture*, describe how architects and architectural discourse have applied various labels to projects intended to connote a more positive relationship with the surrounding environmental context. Monikers like "green," "ecological," "ecofriendly," "low energy," "solar" and "passive," among others, aim to succinctly describe a project's environmentally beneficial intent and desire to achieve such an outcome (Williamson, Radford, and Bennetts 2003, 1).

Not long ago a major part of the image of good architecture was a building that was *suitable* for its environmental context – one that would

124 Environmental Identification

> adequately protect the inhabitants from the climate. More recently it is "the environment" that has been seen as needing protection. The concept of good architecture has shifted to encompass the notion of a building that is *sensitive to* its environment – one that will adequately protect the environment from the potential pollution and degradation caused by human habitation. In many ways the built environment, the very means by which we attempt to create secure conditions, is itself seen as becoming (or having become) a source of danger and threat.
>
> *(Williamson, Radford, and Bennetts 2003, 1)*

Accepting this shift in how we evaluate architecture's relationship to its environmental context reflects the need to question more broadly the industrialization of how we make things. As well as how the underlying system of global capital accumulation, production and exchange fundamentally regards the environment as a resource to be exploited rather than to engender through respectful "sensitive" relations. While sustainable design principles include a variety of strategic design and building practices (i.e. community engagement, increased walkability, site optimization, adaptive reuse and building life-cycle analysis, etc.), the dominant focus within sustainable architectural discourse has largely concerned itself with the reduction of energy consumption and lowering the carbon impact through the incorporation of different technological "solutions" (i.e. energy star appliances, high efficiency light bulbs, building-integrated wind turbines, photovoltaic panels, low VOC and/or recycled materials, water harvesting systems, green roofscapes, etc.). While these technologies are undoubtedly a positive advance toward reducing human impact on the earth-system, their predominance as the principle means for creating "sustainable" architectural solutions largely maintains the status quo regarding how we choose to live-in-the-world-ecology and the system of capital that supports it. In fact, these technologies have themselves often been capitalized toward developer-driven marketing strategies aimed at the consumer's moral desire for "responsible" lifestyle choices. This approach reflects a kind of packaging of the building with sustainable elements ("high-tech gadgets") that, while helping to reduce energy use and carbon emissions, are also expressly intended to convey the *image* of a more environmentally "sensitive" building (Williamson, Radford, and Bennetts 2003, 25). This strategic *image* recalibration has more generally been given the name "green-wash," first coined by Jed Greer and Kenny Bruno in their book *Greenwash: The Reality behind Corporate Environmentalism* (Greer and Bruno 1996, 11). The practice has not just been limited to savvy real-estate developers, corporate product development teams or "progressive" politicians, but, as Greer and Bruno describe, it's fundamentally a tactic used by transnational corporations for decades to portray their actions, however detrimental in reality, as being in harmony with the earth-system and the ecological environment – compensating for them by way of "good" environmental deeds.

> By the late 1980s…transnational corporations could no longer deny their role in environmental degradation. Instead, they embraced the environment as their cause and co-opted its terminology in advertisements and corporate policies. While little had changed in practice, the greenwash counterstrategy was born.
>
> *(Greer and Bruno 1996, 14)*

Perhaps not surprisingly it has been those corporations whose industries are most often, or inherently, in direct conflict with the earth-system and its ecologies, like chemical, oil, coal, automotive, logging and commercial fishing, who have most readily utilized this "greenwashing" tactic to make consumers feel better about buying their products or using their services.[8] More recently however, there's been a shift within the oil industry toward direct acquisition and/or investment in renewable energies like solar, wind and biofuels, though these investments remain modest compared to their overall operational budgets.[9] This somewhat rapid about-face has little to do with social consciousness and is more driven by a recognition to diversify their positions as the demand for a low carbon-based energy system becomes increasingly heightened.[10]

In his edited collection of essays, *Prismatic Ecology*, Jeffrey Jerome Cohen, professor of English and Medieval Studies, proposes a purposeful broadening of the color spectrum of ecological thought "beyond green" to include many other colors reflective of other, less "bucolic" approaches to ecological thinking and design. He argues in his introductory essay that the use of "green" as the dominant color filter through which to comprehend the environment, ecosystems or the world is creatively limiting and unnecessarily selective, failing to move beyond an anthropocentric conception of the world-ecology to reinforce the long-standing bifurcation between nature and culture (Cohen 2013, xx), a separation that assures our continued detachment and intention to control the earth-system for our individual benefit – even through actions of conservation and preservation. Cohen's interest is to explore a more expansive coloration of ecocriticism, while "green ecologies" tend to blend the "romantic, the pastoral, and the georgic" which "dwell on the innate plentitude that nature offers, mourning its commodification and disruption" (Cohen 2013, xx), "prismatic ecologies" have the capacity to "[break] monochromatic light into a multitude of colors [offering] a suggestive entryway into concepts of nonanthropocentric ecologies, where the *oikos*[11] is not so much a bounded home as an ever-unfinished world" (Cohen 2013, xxii-xxiii) – i.e. the "Terrestrial" *architectural* "dwelling place." Most importantly Cohen raises the following question: "Green has become our synonym for sustainability, but such a colorful ascription begs the question exactly what mode of being we are attempting to sustain, and at what environmental cost" (Cohen 2013, xx).

★ ★ ★

126 Environmental Identification

In the concluding paragraph of *Silent Spring*, Rachel Carson makes a clear assessment as to the root problem concerning human-beings' twentieth-century relationship to the world-ecology: "The 'control of nature' is a phrase conceived in arrogance, born of the Neanderthal age of biology and philosophy, when it was supposed that nature exists for the convenience of man" (Carson 1962, 297). Concerning this specific passage, the eco-philosopher Warwick Fox writes:

> The effect of Carson's critique was to suggest to many people that what was needed first and foremost in regard to ecological problems was not bigger and better technical solutions but rather a thorough rethinking of our most fundamental attitudes concerning *our place* in the larger scheme of things.[12]
>
> *(Fox 1995, 5)*

The need to reconceptualize "our place" in the world rather than mere image production or moderate reductions in energy consumption through technological incorporation may provide more substantive and lasting productive change. In many countries, the technology-focused approach to conceiving of the design and the implementation of a "sustainable" architectural project has been institutionalized by the discipline through various certification programs like the LEED (Leadership in Energy and Environmental Design) developed in the US beginning in 1993 and BREEAM (the Building Research Establishment Environmental Assessment Method) developed in the United Kingdom and first published in 1990 – both widely used internationally. These programs generally provide a predetermined set of criteria that a building must meet to acquire credits that contribute to an overall rating for the building's planning, design, construction and performance. While certainly having benefits related to overall energy consumption, quality of indoor environments, building life-cycle planning and even taking into account some aspects of the social, cultural and community impact of development,[13] these certifications as practiced also tend to reinforce a detached technocratic approach emphasizing the specification of "appropriate" certified materials and high-efficiency building systems. Though beneficial in reducing the energy impact of buildings, these institutionalized certification programs ultimately reinforce the narrative that with enough advancements in "green" engineering, we can effectively ride out the climatological-ecological "crisis," without actually changing much of anything about the way we choose to live-in-the-world or the system of capital that supports it.

In the years since the new millennium, architect William McDonough and chemist Michael Braungart have advanced an alternative sustainable approach they call "Cradle to Cradle" which aims to more holistically reconsider architectural design within an expanded field of production. However, despite this more expansive design consciousness, they do still fundamentally honor "commerce as the engine of growth and innovation, as *the* way to make the planet far more productive than it is right now" (McDonough and Braungart 2013, 21).

Writing in their 2002 book *Cradle to Cradle: Remaking the Way we Make Things*, they advocate for working with global commerce and transnational corporations toward implementing what they call an "eco-effective" relationship between the constructed and ecological environments we inhabit.

> Our questioners often believe that the interests of commerce and the environment are inherently in conflict, and that environmentalists who work with big businesses have sold out. And businesspeople have their own biases about environmentalists and social activists, whom they often see as extremists promoting ugly, troublesome, low-tech, and impossibly expensive designs and policies...
>
> Eco-effectiveness sees commerce as the engine of change, and honors its need to function quickly and productively. But it also recognizes that if commerce shuns environmental, social, and cultural concerns, it will produce large-scale tragedy of the commons, destroying valuable natural and human resources for generations to come. Eco-effectiveness celebrates commerce *and* the commonweal in which it is rooted.
>
> *(McDonough and Braungart 2002, 149–150)*

Their critique is principally focused on the design, materialization and production of *things* – buildings but also everyday products – proposing to re-engineer the chemical compositions of the materials from which things are made as well as the related systems and methods of manufacturing. They regard "eco-efficiency," the term they use to describe the most common conception of sustainability, as fundamentally flawed, because simply being "less bad" only slows down the exploitation and degradation of the environment.

> Whether it is a matter of cutting the amount of toxic waste created or emitted, or the quantity of raw materials used, or the product size itself (known in business circles as "dematerialization"), reduction is a central tenet of eco-efficiency. But reduction in any of these areas does not halt depletion and destruction – it only slows them down, allowing them to take place in smaller increments over a longer period of time.
>
> *(McDonough and Braungart 2002, 53–54)*

McDonough and Braungart's proposed "eco-effective" model challenges designers to design products not for a single lifespan (cradle to grave), but rather for many (cradle to cradle). They categorize all products as participating in either *biological* and/or *technological* nutrient cycles which, if designed and manufactured within a Cradle to Cradle model, may feedback into themselves and/or each other indefinitely. In the current system of consumer capital production, accumulation and exchange, this rarely, if ever, takes place. Once a product has been discarded after its initial lifespan, the material elements of which it's composed are either "contaminated, wasted or lost" through the lack of adequate

128 Environmental Identification

retrieval systems, or by their initial manufacturing into "monstrous hybrids." McDonough and Braungart define these hybrids as "mixtures of materials both technical and biological, neither of which can be salvaged after their current lives" (McDonough and Braungart 2002, 99). Even in utilizing methods of recycling, the process of material disentanglement generally requires significant additional energy and/or chemicals, resulting in lesser-performing, lower-quality material dilutions, or further hybrids. This compromise in material integrity greatly reduces future commercial applications, that is, downcycling, and in some cases, this process of recycling even results in a net loss of energy compared to if one simply discarded the product into a landfill or burned it in an incinerator.

> Just because a material is recycled does not automatically make it ecologically benign, especially if it was not designed specifically for recycling. Blindly adopting superficial environmental approaches without fully understanding their effects can be no better – and perhaps even worse – than doing nothing.
>
> *(McDonough and Braungart 2002, 59)*

The current global system of capital production, accumulation and exchange not only tolerates but often encourages the use of these monstrous material hybridizations as they may be cheaper to initially manufacture, and their single-use lifespans relegate them to "throwaway" objects intended for consumers to buy a new one the next time it's needed. Some corporations even encourage consumers to discard outdated versions of a product before its lifespan is complete; industrial design and manufacturing has even named this practice as "planned," "built-in" or "premature obsolescence."[14] Targeted advertising campaigns, the continuous implementation of product "advancements" or even the outright manipulation of products to make older versions less functional over time[15] is a tenant of consumer capitalist culture. This leads to more waste, more demand for high-quality "virgin" resources and more energy to produce the replacement products. As McDonough and Braungart argue, "eco-effective" design proactively considers how materials are engineered and how products might be specifically designed, assembled and disassembled to maintain each individual component's embodied material value without degradation, the goal being to maintain the indefinite participation within the technological and biological nutrient cycles of all components, thereby producing zero waste. In their proposed "eco-effective" model, when a product reaches the end of its current lifespan it can be returned to a manufacturer, disassembled into reusable parts or materials and then used for future manufacturing and production purposes. If participating in the technical stream, it would maintain its inherent material integrity, not having been made into a "monstrous hybrid," or, if in the biological stream, it could simply be composted to provide nutrients for the growth of future living-beings. McDonough and Braungart sum up

Back Home from the Frontier **129**

this principle with the adage "waste equals food" (McDonough and Braungart 2002, 92), and this reconceptualization of zero-waste is fundamental to the Cradle to Cradle design approach and what has more broadly been referred to as the development of a circular economy.[16]

> *To eliminate the concept of waste means to design things – products, packaging, and systems – from the very beginning on the understanding that waste does not exist.* It means that the valuable nutrients contained in the materials shape and determine the design: form follows evolution, not just function.
>
> *(McDonough and Braungart 2002, 104)*

Taking this strategy one step further, McDonough and Braungart suggest that the "eco-effective" design of things implemented to its fullest potential not only can maintain a current nutrient value, whether biological, technological or some combination of both, but may actually provide added value within a particular system, instigating positive effects within an environmental context. These aspirations are fundamentally "ecological" in their thinking, an application of Rachel Carson's observations of the interconnectedness of the environment and human actions. McDonough and Braungart cite a primary example of the cherry tree as an ideal model for this approach:

> Consider the Cherry tree: thousands of blossoms create fruit for birds, humans, and other animals, in order that one pit might eventually fall onto the ground, take root, and grow. Who would look at the ground littered with cherry blossoms and complain, "How inefficient and wasteful!" The tree makes copious blossoms and fruit without depleting its environment. Once they fall on the ground, their materials decompose and break down into nutrients that nourish microorganisms, insects, plants, animals, and soil. Although the tree actually makes more of its "product" than it needs for its own success in an ecosystem, this abundance has evolved (through millions of years of success and failure or, in business terms, R&D), to serve rich and varied purposes. In fact, the tree's fecundity nourishes just about everything around it.
>
> What might the human-built world look like if a cherry tree had produced it?
>
> *(McDonough and Braungart 2002, 72–73)*

And

> As [the cherry tree] grows, it seeks its own regenerative abundance. But this process is not single-purpose. In fact, the tree's growth sets in motion a number of positive effects. It provides food for animals, insects, and microorganisms. It enriches the ecosystem, sequestering carbon, producing oxygen,

130 Environmental Identification

cleaning air and water, and creating and stabilizing soil. Among its roots and branches and on its leaves, it harbors a diverse array of flora and fauna, all of which depend on it and on one another for the functions and flows that support life. And when the tree dies, it returns to the soil, releasing, as it decomposes, minerals that will fuel healthy new growth in the same place.

The tree is not an isolated entity cut off from the systems around it: it is inextricably and productively engaged with them. This is a key difference between the growth of industrial systems as they now stand and the growth of nature.

(McDonough and Braungart 2002, 78–79)

Advocating for designing buildings like a cherry tree, as described above, provides an excess of elements and functional byproducts that may directly or indirectly provide support and/or resources for many other living entities (Figure 4.6). They claim that implementing a Cradle to Cradle approach incentivizes economic growth by effectively eliminating the perceived opposition between nature and industry, resulting in *doing* good, thereby growing and producing more goods, is *doing* "more good." This idea of doing "more good" not "less bad" is what McDonough and Braungart call "upcycling," a concept they've elaborated upon in their 2013 book *The Upcycle: Beyond Sustainability – Designing for Abundance*. This further advancement in thinking inverts the traditional environmentally conscious mindset of trying to limit the negative environmental effects of people, corporations, governments and so on to instead support their positive effects.[17] As McDonough and Braungart rightly express at a moment when human-beings bare the sole responsibility for so much destruction within the world-ecology, it is time for us to have a positive environmental footprint (McDonough and Braungart 2013, 36). The operative word

FIGURE 4.6 William McDonough + Partners, *Method manufacturing facility*, photo of exterior showing wind turbine, solar panels and rooftop greenhouse, Pullman neighborhood, Southside, Chicago, 2015. Photography by author.

they use to express this approach is "abundance," implying the potential to create a wealth of positive effects as a natural byproduct of an "eco-effective" design mindset – that is, the upcycle.

> Using the Cradle to Cradle framework, we can upcycle to talk about designing not just for health but for abundance, proliferation, delight. We can upcycle to talk about not how human industry can be just "less bad," but how it can be more good, an extraordinary positive in our world.[18]
> *(McDonough and Braungart 2013, 11)*

But is more always good? And if we believe that it is, how is it possible as we expand out to consider not just localized inter-actions within an ecosystem but the "total environment"?

For McDonough and Braungart the success of this reorientation, flipping how we think about the potential effects of our collective actions and the systems of production we employ within the world-ecology, continues to be fundamentally dependent upon economic growth.

> The most effective transformational foundation of Cradle to Cradle is, to the surprise of some, not environmental. Nor is it ethical. It is economic. If Cradle to Cradle fails as a business concept and innovation engine, then it fails, period. It succeeds when it celebrates economic growth, which in turn grows ecological and social revenue. It succeeds when it upcycles the economy, and ecological and ethical benefits accrue.
> *(McDonough and Braungart 2013, 189)*

There is little doubt that a Cradle to Cradle, "eco-effective" and upcycling approach provides a radical and positive advancement in the design and manufacture of *things*, capable of positively impacting the world-ecology, at least in the short term, but this overt dependence on continuous economic growth (presumably of the current capitalistic model, just with "eco-effective" goods as its basis of exchange) still sits atop unstable ground. As a singular entity, the cherry tree as a model for design and growth may hold strong; however, even as a beautiful, compelling and concise analogy, it may literally not see the forest for the trees. The illustration of the cherry tree in isolation fails to fully recognize the implications of its implicit and boundless desire to expand and proliferate endlessly over time. Even if many of those blossoms fail to become new trees, instead serving as resources for other living entities, some do not fail, some succeed and proliferate one tree into many. In this way, McDonough and Braungart's approach seems to miss the mark concerning another ecological principle of balance or dynamic equilibrium.[19] Placed within the *real* context of a constrained ecosystem, or even the planet, the tree's unending desire to proliferate is inevitably checked by other competing organisms, primarily

132 Environmental Identification

other trees fighting across the same finite limits for the same natural resources needed to sustain themselves. Although in constant flux, these factors are important ecological checks that maintain a "natural" dynamic balance of individual and collective growth. The continuous *positive* growth necessary to fuel the capital-based system does not seem to fully acknowledge that, on a deep level, the world-ecology we inhabit is physically finite, with real limits and boundaries to its elements and extents. Even if one believes a Cradle to Cradle, "eco-effective" and upcycling approach to how we inhabit the planet may support a human population of "10 billion living comfortably and fruitfully in a Cradle to Cradle world" (McDonough and Braungart 2013, 33), then, to borrow one of McDonough's own commonly asked questions, after humans reach this number, and continue to proliferate, "what's next?"

★ ★ ★

To begin to effectively consider such a question ultimately requires a zooming out capable of better understanding the interconnected *energetic* relationships that underlie all aspects of being and working within the "total" world-ecology. Energy is not the only means of adequate measure, but when it comes to thinking about sustainable practices it is certainly the most common denominator capable of comprehending and comparing dynamic relationships between all kinds of living and non-living entities within the "total" world-ecology which operates at a scale and complexity beyond our current cognitive and experiential capacities. Even a focused examination of continuously dynamic matter-energy flows and inter-actions within a localized territory, like a building, still requires a global understanding which includes all historically embodied energies at various scales. The architect and environmental historian Kiel Moe critically frames this reality in the following way:

> Architects do not yet see that buildings occupy temporal and spatial scales that span from the molecular to the territorial, from the instantaneous transfer of energy to flows of matter that are millions of years long. Architects do not yet comprehend that within these states and bonds, building has a designed velocity and momentum.
>
> *(Moe 2017, 19)*

This intrinsic movement, fluctuation, fluidity and ongoing formation of a building as described through its matter-energy flows is what Moe refers to, in reference to the observations of philosopher Brian Massumi, as "incorporeal" – as a dimension of architecture that "reveals as much about the social, economic, ecological, and intellectual state of architecture as do…the individual instances of specific object-buildings." And in a more literal way, he states, "In the process of building, materials and energy converge in one place for a finite duration and then are eventually redistributed back out into the world. Building is movement" (Moe 2017, 21). The word he uses to refer more broadly to this process of temporal building coagulation is "convergence."[20]

His book *Empire, State & Building* aims to describe the total material and energy flows across the entire history of inhabitation of the specific Manhattan block that currently contains the Empire State Building. This detailed graphic documentation and analysis of the historical material energetics for this one urban parcel resulted in an expansive book, revealing the various interconnected global systems and complexity of material movements, phases of construction, technologies, developments and demolitions over time. What was fundamental for Moe was to understand the "incorporeal" aspects of these architectural developments throughout the history of the urban block, to reveal the latent global matter-energy flows. His intent was to challenge architects to reframe their conception of the building to understand it as the temporal result of a process that in and of itself has great influence on global "social, economic, ecological, and intellectual" conditions.[21] Moe's extensive micro and macroanalysis provides architects, engineers and environmental scientists a way to better understand more completely the thermodynamic impact of the matter-energy flows of buildings, yet his examination of one single block is fairly overwhelming, let alone if it was applied to the total built environment.

To more reasonably capture such a broad assessment, a systems-based method of analysis may provide the necessary degree of resolution and vantage point from which to most effectively evaluate the built environment's energetic relationship within the world-ecology. The environmental scientist Howard Odum in his seminal book *Environment, Power and Society* first published in 1971,[22] sought to provide such a systems-based alternative that was relatively objective, and capable of describing the dynamic relationships between energy, society and the constructed and ecological environments we inhabit. This approach is largely rooted in a "general" systems approach developed a generation or so before Odum in the work of Ludwig von Bertalanffy, among others, who sought a model of understanding that could more easily compare complex and diverse systems (like a living organism[23]), not through reducing them to their most basic units, but rather through the use of isomorphies[24] capable of maintaining their "wholeness" and "organization" (Bertalanffy 1951, 303). "Isomorphies are basic for the use of models and model conceptions in science…General Systems Theory will be an important means to facilitate and to control the application of model-conceptions and the transfer of principles from one realm to another" (Bertalanffy 1951, 306). Odum's systems-based methodology utilized an illustrative strategy of graphic diagramming to visualize as well as reveal the underlying energy-based inter-connections between the various aspects of a specific system, and between systems through isomorphic relationships (Figure 4.7). His method adopted a "macroscopic" or "whole systems" view, capable of simplifying concepts by rising above exponentially increasing internalized complexities

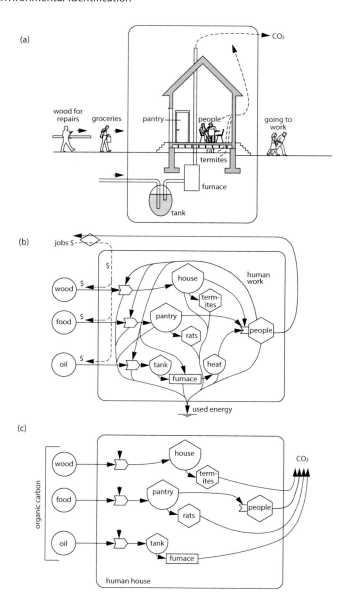

FIGURE 4.7 Energy circuit diagrams of a house: "(a) Sketch; (b) systems diagram showing the storages of house structures, pantry and oil furnace, 3 outside energy sources, work by people inside, work and money earned from an outside job, and dissipation of used energy through the heat sink; (c) same system showing the inflows of organic carbon and outflow of carbon dioxide." Redrawn by author and reproduced by permission from Columbia University Press. Reprinted from Howard T. Odum, *Environment, Power, and Society For the Twenty-First Century: The Hierarchy of Energy* (New York: Columbia University Press, 2007) 29, fig. 2.11.

(Odum 2007, 2–3). "A whole system view is one of the tools of the macroscope. By drawing the main parts and connecting the parts with pathways, we learn to think about wholes, parts, and processes at the same time" (Odum 2007, 16). From the macroscopic vantage point, it was possible to quantify all aspects of a system into material and/or energy flows, thus making it possible to compare and evaluate how systems of all types inter-act and the various relationships between component parts, inputs and outputs. An ecosystem, a car, a human-being or even the "total" world-ecology, could be described, compared and evaluated, but also interrelated through the hierarchy of energy.

> Any phenomenon is controlled both by the working of its smaller parts and by its role in the larger system of which it is a part.
> The work that results from energy flow is inherently hierarchical, with many calories of one kind required to produce a few calories of another. Much of the organization of the geobiosphere and the human economy is understandable from the energy hierarchy concepts.
>
> *(Odum 2007, 3–5)*

In this systems-based approach to understanding energetic relationships, their hierarchical expression reflects the various processes of transformation and consolidation, providing the possibility for great difference while maintaining specific relational correspondences between parts. This approach can be directly applied to the evaluation of the constructed environment as it relates both to internal energy performance of parts, but more importantly how those matter-energy flows inter-act with elements "outside" the internal boundaries – the surrounding energetic context. And may suggest further insights about how human-beings may more effectively understand their energy impact, and therefore modify, how they choose to live-in-the-world-ecology.

Within the inter-active energy dynamics of a complex system, there often emerges a predictable cycle of energy movement, growth, development, climax and decline, which Odum describes through the ecological concept of *succession* and over multiple cycles of what he more generally terms a "pulsing paradigm." He describes how ecological systems in their early stages of development grow rapidly without much diversity – rapid colonization – but in the later stages, they transfer their energy into sustaining more complex structures and diversity instead of growth – this stage is referred to as the climax (Figures 4.8 and 4.9). But the climax state is not permanent because the circumstances from which that state arose are also inevitably changing. He claims the tendency of the most successful and sustaining systems are actually those that adopt a pulsing pattern.[25] This pulsing ensures to some extent that the system maintains the potential to actively respond to changing circumstances either from internal shifts or external stimuli, which would otherwise disrupt its function. The current disciplinary model of sustainability, and even a Cradle to Cradle, "eco-effective," upcycling approach, all essentially aspire to maintain the climax state

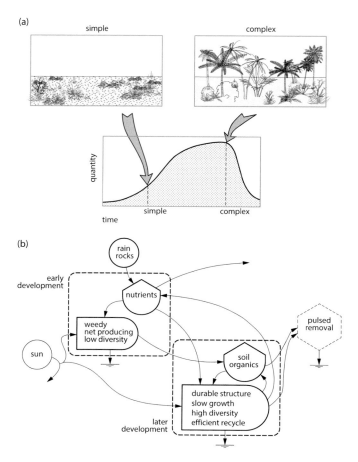

FIGURE 4.8 Systems diagram of a pulsing ecosystem and mechanisms: "Growth and diversity of succession, climax and restart that begins with available energy and nutrients to be colonized. Power is maximized at first by low-diversity overgrowth and net production and later by durable structures, high–diversity division of labor, and efficient recycle. (a) Growth curve and diversity sketches; (b) simplified energy systems diagram with dashed frames to indicate the parts of the system that are important in the 3 regimes." Redrawn by author and reproduced by permission from Columbia University Press. Reprinted from Howard T. Odum, *Environment, Power, and Society For the Twenty-First Century: The Hierarchy of Energy* (New York: Columbia University Press, 2007) 55, fig. 3.12.

indefinitely through an economic system of capital production, accumulation and exchange that is fueled by continued technological innovation and perpetual growth. As Odum describes, this prospect is energetically unfeasible over the long run: "The ecological model of succession and climax has now been applied to national policy under the name *sustainability*. But seeking a constant level of civilization is a false ideal contrary to energy laws" (Odum 2007, 54).

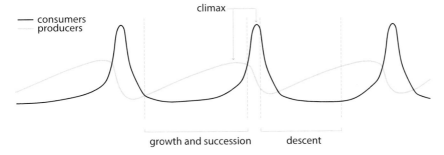

FIGURE 4.9 Pulsing paradigm graph showing the cycle of growth, diversification, succession, climax and collapse. Drawing by author.

While McDonough and Braungart argue for an alignment with the current global system of capital, regarding it as the primary propellent behind the implementation of their "eco-effective" ideas, the writer and ecological thinker Paul Hawken has argued for a "restorative economy"[26] modeled on and toward the principles of ecology itself,[27] capable of substantially reducing the impact human-beings have on environment through reinforcing productive actions at all levels of society, culture and the economy (Hawken 1993, 209–210). While his approach sounds similar to the Cherry Tree analogy as proposed by McDonough and Braungart, there is one key difference – it fundamentally reprioritizes the pursuit of the economy away from exclusively human concerns, turning instead more broadly toward the non-anthropocentric.

> What ecology offers is a way to examine all present economic and resource activities from a biological rather than a monetary point of view, including the impact that our present lifestyle will have on generations henceforth.
>
> (Hawken 1993, 205)

And

> A restorative economy is not going to lead to a life of dulling comfort and convenience. We have to recognize that we've reached a watershed in the economy, a point at which "growth" and profitability will be increasingly derived from the abatement of environmental degradation, the furthering of ecological restoration, and the mimicking of natural systems of production and consumption.
>
> (Hawken 1993, 210)

This restorative approach to living-in-the-world-ecology is dependent upon a new economic set of priorities that must "serve and nurture" those currently disadvantaged or on the periphery rather than take advantage or exploit them.

It intends "to reconstruct, know, or revive" the ecologies lost through industrialization and the pursuit of the global system of capital production, accumulation and exchange (Hawken 1993, 214). This is an alternative pursuit that "harmonizes the relationship between commerce and nature" (Hawken 1993, 215). Embodying such a pursuit, the work of architect Anna Heringer demonstrates a noteworthy alternative to the technologically motivated "sustainable" architectural project, whether through technological performance or as "sensitive" image. Her work evokes a deeply natural and local grounding through the predominant use of indigenous materials like earthen mud or bamboo. While also utilizing traditional building techniques, it cultivates a kind of stewardship through the inhabitant, community knowledge and local economic impact. She describes her work as imbuing an "emancipatory approach" (Drouet and Lacrouts 2019), relying on the use of local labor and materials intent on initiating and/or maintaining local commerce, knowledge, training and community empowerment. Located in the rural Northern town of Rudrapur of densely populated Bangladesh, the METI school was her first completed and perhaps most well-known project, exemplifying her holistic design values and providing an example of Hawken's ideas to "serve and nurture" the peripheral through an alternative set of considerations (Figures 4.10, 4.11, and 4.12). As Heringer states in a 2019 interview in *Domus* magazine: "I always ask myself: Does my approach hurt the planet? Who profits? Will it cause inequity? Will know-how be increased or decreased?" (Drouet and Lacrouts 2019). In conjunction with the NGO Dipshikha, the intention of the project was to "help [rural] people learn about the value of the village" and the operation of the school "instills in

FIGURE 4.10 Anna Heringer and Eike Roswag, *METI School*, photo west elevation, Rudrapur, Dinajpur district, Bangladesh, 2006. Photograph by Kurt Hoerbst. Photograph courtesy of Kurt Hoerbst.

FIGURE 4.11 Anna Heringer and Eike Roswag, *METI School*, photo upper floor classroom spaces combined into a multifunctional hall, Rudrapur, Dinajpur district, Bangladesh, 2006. Photograph by Kurt Hoerbst. Photograph courtesy of Kurt Hoerbst.

FIGURE 4.12 Anna Heringer and Eike Roswag, *METI School*, photo exterior detail, Rudrapur, Dinajpur district, Bangladesh, 2006. Photograph by Kurt Hoerbst. Photograph courtesy of Kurt Hoerbst.

140 Environmental Identification

the children self-confidence and independence with the aim of strengthening their sense of identity."[28] The building was constructed primarily out of mud, providing a locally resourced, completely biodegradable, circular, zero carbon emission material that "offers many job opportunities and is environmentally and socially equitable" (Drouet and Lacrouts 2019). Heringer describes moving from concrete to mud as having the potential to "save society," as its use does not enrich a few select foreign manufacturers, but instead supports local craftsman and local economies, and provides zero carbon emissions. In both a literal and theoretical way, the use of mud embodies a "Terrestrial" approach to design and construction of the *architectural* "dwelling place," literally grounded, but also engaged and empathetic to the "total" collective through a deep connection to its immediate "place."

In October 2013, Heringer was an integral force in the formulation of a collaborative statement – "The Laufen Manifesto for a Humane Design Culture" – which described an alternative approach to the design and construction of the built environment, aiming to advance global equality and to "improve the ecological, social, and aesthetic quality of the built environment, while developing more effective design strategies to anticipate predicted future growth on a global scale" (Heringer et al. 2013). It provided the following seven points toward achieving these goals: (1) Collaborating Eye to Eye, (2) Designing Work, (3) Unfurling Beauty, (4) Identifying the Local, (5) Understanding the Territory, (6) Educating Designers and (7) Shaping Policy (Heringer et al. 2013). What's perhaps most striking about this manifesto is that it's not specifically advocating for particular design attributes but rather the process of design as it relates to both the consideration of a particular localized context as well as the desired effects of such a design beyond the explicit architectural intervention itself. What matters most is the intentional action of design as it relates to "how we want our world to be" (Heringer et al. 2013). Heringer's design for the Ways of Life house reflects such an approach (Figure 4.13), proposing it as a prototype dwelling strategy that remains highly localized, specific to a particular climatic and ecological context in which it's placed but also maintains a basic strategy capable of successfully operating in a variety of locales, recalibrating itself depending on the immediate environmental, cultural and social conditions. While much of the strength of her approach provides a radical reorientation of priorities away from traditional forms of global building and commerce, there remain questions of how this approach might negotiate more complex urban sites or operate at higher densities. Perhaps the answer is to question the need to achieve such arrangements in the first place. Referring to Bookchin's reconstructive anarchist argument the most "effective" solution, especially in the post-climatological-ecological "crisis" world, may be to question the value of physical and social centralization itself. Heringer admits that mud may not be suitable for all contexts but makes the point that, irrespective of scale, implementation or even context, architects

Back Home from the Frontier **141**

FIGURE 4.13 Anna Heringer and Stegano Mori, *Ways of Life: Fachwerk Capriccio*, concept drawings and sketches included in the Universität Kassel exhibition "Ways of Life – Experimenta Urbana" a co-event with documenta14, curated by Christoph Hesse and Neeraj Bhatia, Kassel, Germany, 2017. Images courtesy of Anna Heringer.

should "value local resources," support craftsmanship (Drouet and Lacrouts 2019) and make design choices at every level that are grounded from a place of empathy. Like the ecosystems within which we live and participate, the reality human-beings must confront concerning an empathetic approach to "our place" living-in-the-world-ecology is one of uncontrollable cyclical change as opposed to technological control. Though it may be disturbing during times of transformation, embracing a pulsing approach of adaptation may actually be the most "stable" path forward toward our survival living in this "new" world beyond climatological-ecological "crisis".

Notes

1 For example, in reference to soil, Carson states the following:

> Seemingly moderate applications of insecticides over a period of years may build up fantastic quantities in soil. Since the chlorinated hydrocarbons are persistent and long-lasting, each application is merely added to the quantity remaining

142 Environmental Identification

from the previous one. The old legend that "a pound of DDT to the acre is harmless" means nothing if spraying is repeated.

(Carson 1962, 58)

2 Murray Bookchin makes the point more generally when he says:

The discovery of DDT led to widespread belief that insect pests could be eradicated by relying exclusively on the use of chemical agents. This belief was severely shaken when it was found that a number of harmful species were producing strains that were resistant to existing insecticides…As long as present methods of control are employed, new insecticides will be required every few years just to hold the line in man's chemical war against the insect world.

(Herber 1962, 58–59)

3 "The fact that the suburbanite is not instantly stricken has little meaning, for the toxins may sleep long in his body, to become manifest months or years later in an obscure disorder almost impossible to trace to its origins"; see Carson (1962, 24).

4 In the years following the publication of *Silent Spring*, numerous meaningful governmental responses and regulations were enacted, such as the National Environmental Policy Act (1969), the establishment of the Environmental Protection Agency (1970), the Clean Air Act (1970, 1990) and the Clean Water Act (1972, 1977, 1987), the Endangered Species Act (1973), Safe Drinking Water Act (1974) and the Resource Conservation and Recovery Act (1976), to name only a few.

5 According to data from the US Bureau of Mines and the US Geological Survey – Minerals handbook, in the last 50 years the US production of cement increased by about 25%, while the global production increased by about 600%, due in large part to the rapid growth of China; see U.S. Geological Survey, 2014, Cement statistics, in T.D. Kelly and G. R. Matos, comps, Historical statistics for mineral and material commodities in the United States: U.S. Geological Survey Data Series 140, http://minerals.usgs.gov/minerals/pubs/historical-statistics/ (accessed April 21, 2020). And as stated by David Wallace-Wells "If the cement industry were a country, it would be the World's third largest emitter." See Wallace-Wells (2019, 180).

6 Importantly, in 1968, the Occupational Safety and Health Administration (OSHA) adopted standards for threshold limit values related to one's exposure to specific toxins developed by the American Conference of Governmental Industrial Hygienists (ACGIH), creating the nation's first permissible exposure limits for indoor workplace environments; see Ronald V. Gobbell, Steve M. Hays and Peter D. Cappel's National Council of Architectural Registration Boards Monograph *Indoor Environment,* The American Institute of Architects Continuing Education Systems, 2015: 59.

7 See Lewis Herber [Murray Bookchin], *Our Synthetic Environment* (New York: Alfred P. Knopf, 1962); and Lewis Herber [Murray Bookchin], *Crisis in Our Cities: Death, Disease, and the Urban Plague* (Englewood Cliffs, NJ: Prentice-Hall, In., 1965).

8 Greer and Bruno's book *Greenwash* in fact documents in detail a series of such case studies from the 1980s and 1990s by corporations like Royal Dutch/Shell Group, Mobil, Dow Chemical, Dupont, Monsanto, General Motors, among many others.

9 See Maxx Chatsko, "Big Oil is Investing Billions in Renewable Energy: Here's Where and How," *The Motley Fool,* June 4, 2018, https://www.fool.com/investing/2018/06/04/big-oil-is-investing-billions-in-renewable-energy.aspx.

10 See Terry Macalister, "Green really is the new black as Big Oil gets a taste for renewable," *The Guardian,* May 21, 2016, https://www.theguardian.com/business/2016/may/21/oil-majors-investments-renewable-energy-solar-wind, and Henry Edwardes-Evans, James Burgess and Emma Slawinski, "Cross currents: Big oil and the enegy transition," *S&P Global Platts Insight,* April 21, 2020, https://blogs.platts.com/2020/04/21/big-oil-energy-transition-power-plays/.

Back Home from the Frontier **143**

11 The word *oikos* is Greek in origin meaning "household," "home" or "place to live," and etymologically serves as the root word for *ecology* coined by German zoologist Ernst Haeckel, who implemented the term *oekologie*; see *Encyclopedia Britannica Online*, s.v. "Ecology" (by Robert Leo Smith and Stuart L. Pimm), https://www.britannica.com/science/ecology (accessed March 24, 2020).

12 Italics added here for emphasis.

13 See the US Green Building Council website: https://www.usgbc.org/.

14 For a broader view of this practice in the tech industry, including some perceived benefits, see Adam Hadhazy, "Here's the truth about the 'planned obsolescence' of tech," *BBC: Future*, https://www.bbc.com/future/article/20160612-heres-the-truth-about-the-planned-obsolescence-of-tech (accessed June 11, 2020).

15 Take, for instance, Apple, a company that routinely phases out various "outdated" devices, no longer supporting their functionality regardless of the ongoing performance of the existing product. Operating software; network functionality; applications; and even the connectors, adapters and chords are constantly being "updated," forcing consumers to keep buying new versions of the product. In March 2020, Apple agreed to pay $500 million to settle a lawsuit accusing the company of intentionally slowing down older models of their iPhone devices to prompt consumers to buy new devices; see Jonathan Stempel, "Apple to pay up to $500 million to settle U.S. lawsuit over slow iPhones" *Reuters*, March 2, 2020, https://www.reuters.com/article/us-apple-iphones-settlement-idUSKBN20P2E7 (accessed March 24, 2020).

16 Since the time of the publication of the *Cradle to Cradle* book, it has been developed into an independent certification process where products are reviewed and analyzed to become Cradle to Cradle Certified™; see https://www.c2ccertified.org/. The concept of a circular economy has also been strongly reinforced by the work of the Ellen MacArthur Foundation; see the 2013 report Towards the Circular *Economy: Economic and Business Rationale for an Accelerated Transition* and more recently in 2018 the establishment of the Platform for Accelerating the Circular Economy (PACE) in conjunction with many other partners including the World Economic Forum, World Resources Institute and the United Nations Environment Programme.

17 On this approach, see Anders Bjørn and Michael Z. Hauschild. "Absolute versus relative environmental sustainability," *Journal of Industrial Ecology* 17, no. 2 (April 2013): 321–332.

18 McDonough and Braungart provide numerous examples from their work, citing the massive green roof of the Ford truck plant in Dearborn, Michigan, a proposal for a NASA Ames office building in California, the redesign of an upholstery textile for Designtex, a division of Steelcase and many others that all produce beneficial consequences from a Cradle to Cadle approach to design on all levels.

> The aftereffects of the projects we took on turned out to be larger than we dreamed. We have been astounded by the enthusiasm and profitability that accompany taking up this thinking. Government regulations drop away when there are no ill effects to minimize. Cradle to Cradle designers and manufacturers know that they are engaged in what the Buddhists call 'right livelihood,' a way of making a living within the framework of right behavior that allows them to happily present themselves to their children.
>
> (McDonough and Braungart 2013, 20)

19 For a detailed examination, see Anders Bjørn and Maria Strandesen, "The cradle to cradle concept – Is it always sustainable?" 2011, https://pdfs.semanticscholar.org/c413/20cdfd6be0c0fee4973c7ec7a6faf9b2b7cd.pdf.

20 See Kiel Moe, *Convergence: An architectural agenda for energy* (London: Routledge, 2012).

21 As Moe describes:

> For the purposes of this book, it is important to grasp that the "thing" we call a "building" is the outcome of a "process" we call "building." Therefore, what

> constitutes building extends far beyond any individual parcel and beyond any individual construction. In every way, building is not so much an autonomous object, but an accumulating center of manifold, contingent process. We need enough irony as architects to recognize the contingencies inherent in building, and begin to address these incorporeal but real attachments.
>
> (Moe 2017, 24)

And even more directly:

> Designers do not document nor analyze the full material and energy corpus of construction endeavors: the ecology of building and urbanization. Distant, untold environments are transformed and produced through the making of buildings, yet shockingly, these environments are habitually dismissed as externalities.
>
> (Moe 2017, 29)

22 Though first published in 1971, Odum was working on a revised edition of the book "for the twenty-first century" when he passed away in 2002. The updated edition was completed by his wife Elisabeth Odum and two colleagues, Mark Brown and Dan Campbell, published posthumously by Columbia University press in 2007, and it is this version that is referenced throughout.

23 See Ludwig von Bertalanffy, *Modern theories of development: An introduction to theoretical biology,* trans. and adapted by J. H. Woodger. (New York: Harper Torchbooks, [1933] 1962) 47–50.

24 On isomorphisms, also see Manual DeLanda, "Immanence and transcendence in the genesis of form," *The South Atlantic Quarterly* 96 (1997): 499–514.

25 "Apparently the pattern that maximizes power on each scale in the long run is a pulsed consumption of mature structures that resets succession to repeat again. There are many mechanisms, such as epidemic insects eating a forest, regular fires in grasslands, locusts in the desert, volcanic eruptions in geologic succession, oscillating chemical reactions, and exploding stars in the cosmos. Systems that develop pulsing mechanisms prevail"; see Odum (2007, 54).

26 Hawken puts forth three basic principles derived from nature: (1) waste-equals-food, (2) change from an economy based on carbon to one based on hydrogen and solar radiation and (3) the creation of systems of feedback and accountability that support and reinforce restorative behavior; see Hawken (1993, 209).

27 "We have operated our world for the past few centuries on the basis that we could manage it, if not dominate it, without respect to living systems. We have sacrificed the harmonious development of our own cultures for enormous short-term gains, and now we face the invoice for that kind of thinking: an ecological and social crisis whose origins lie deep within the assumptions of our commercial and economic systems. The compelling nature of this crisis, however, is its evolutionary nature. The array of choices and problems that face us do not call for a global triage, the further dislocation of cultures, or the division of nations. They are soluble by design, and the basis of that design rests within nature"; see Hawken (1993, 201–202).

28 See "METI school" http://anna-heringer.com/index.php?id=30 (accessed June 11, 2020).

References

Bertalanffy, Ludwig von. 1951. Problems of general systems theory. *Human Biology* 23, no. 4 (December): 303–312.

Bookchin, Murray. 1965. Ecology and revolutionary thought. In *Post-Scarcity Anarchism.* 2nd ed. Montreal/Buffalo: Black Rose Books, 1986.

Carson, Rachel. 1962. *Silent spring*. Fortieth anniversary ed., with introd. by Linda Lear. Boston: Mariner Books, 2002.

Cohen, Jeffrey Jerome, ed. 2013. *Prismatic ecology: Ecotheory beyond green*. Minneapolis: University of Minnesota Press.

Drouet, Laura and Olivier Lacrouts. 2019. Anna Heringer: Ethics before aesthetics. *Domus*, September 6. https://www.domusweb.it/en/architecture/gallery/2019/09/05/anna-heringer-ethics-before-aesthetics.html.

Environmental Protection Agency. Indoor air pollution and health. https://www.epa.gov/indoor-air-quality-iaq/introduction-indoor-air-quality.

Fox, Warwick. 1995. *Toward a transpersonal ecology: Developing new foundations for environmentalism*. New York: Shambhala; Distributed in the US by Random House.

Greer, Jed and Kenny Bruno. 1996. *Greenwash: The reality behind corporate environmentalism*. New York: Apex Press.

Hawken, Paul. 1993. *The ecology of commerce: A declaration of sustainability*. New York: Harper Collins Publishers.

Herber, Lewis [Murray Bookchin]. 1962. *Our Synthetic Environment*. New York: Alfred A. Knopf.

Heringer, Anna, Andres Lepik, Hubert Klumper, Peter Rich, Line Ramstad, Peter Cchola Schmal, Andres Bäppler, Emilio Caravatti, Dietmar Steiner, Christian Werthmann, Martin Rauch, Dominique Gauzin-Müller, Helena Sandman, Enrico Vianello, Rahul Mehrotra, Alejandro Restreppo-Montoya, Susanne Hofmann, Anh-Linh Ngo, Luis Fernandez-Galiano and Alejandro Echeverri. 2013. *Laufen manifesto for a humane design culture*. https://www.ar.tum.de/aktuell/news-singleview/article/laufen-manifesto-for-a-humane-design-culture/.

McDonough, William and Michael Braungart. 2002. *Cradle to cradle: Remaking the way we make things*. New York: North Point Press.

———. 2013. *The upcycle: Beyond sustainability – Designing for abundance*. New York: North Point Press.

Moe, Kiel. 2017. *Empire, state & building*. New York/Barcelona: Actar Publishers.

Odum, Howard T. 2007. *Environment, power, and society for the twenty-first century: The hierarchy of energy*. New York: Columbia University Press.

Wallace-Wells, David. 2019. *The uninhabitable earth: Life after warming*. New York: Tim Duggan Books.

Williamson, Terry, Antony Radford and Helen Bennetts. 2003. *Understanding sustainable architecture*. London: Spon Press.

World Commission of Environment and Development. 1987. *Our common future*. Oxford: Oxford University Press.

World Green Building Council. 2019. *World Green Building Council annual report 2018/2019*. London: World Green Building Council.

5

DWELLING DEEP

Toward a Transpersonal Architecture of Self-Realization!

> Two centuries of capitalism and market nihilism have brought us to the most extreme alienations – from ourselves, from others, from worlds. The fiction of the individual has decomposed at the same speed that it was becoming real. Children of the metropolis, we offer this wager: that it's in the most profound deprivation of existence, perpetually stifled, perpetually conjured away, that the possibility of communism resides.
>
> When all is said and done, it's with an entire anthropology that we are at war. With the very idea of man.
>
> (The Invisible Committee 2009, 16)

It is precisely this revolution in the "idea of man," of the self, articulated above by an anonymous group of French leftists the Invisible Committee, as a response to the alienation caused by our global capitalist economic system that this chapter examines as it relates to an architectural alternative *beyond* the simply sustainable. An alternative capable of challenging how we might choose to live-in-the-world-ecology and engendering a "Terrestrial" *architectural* "dwelling-place." While this book maintains that the current global system of capital production, accumulation and exchange has deeply affected our anthropology, including the constructed environments we design and inhabit, it does not explicitly propose alternative economic models. Rather, it proposes a shift in philosophy and psychology, toward a kind of ecological "communism," a solidarity between human-beings, and other living and non-living beings, a total collective "being-with" including the constructed environments we inhabit. As a pretense to this possibility, one additional energetic point requires attention – capitalism's utilization of cheap energy ("cheap nature") in the form of various fossil fuels and the necessary "frontier-making" inherent to capitalism.[1]

For the majority of the roughly 200,000 years human-beings have inhabited the surface of the earth they have relied on renewable sources of energy – solar, wind, oceanic or earth processes – to fuel their civilizations and populate all types of environmental contexts. While human civilizations based upon renewable forms of energy have on many occasions been destructive ecological forces, the voracity of their energetic presence pre-fossil fuels was limited by the pace required for those renewable energy sources to renew themselves – a kind of *natural* limiting factor. These energy renewal processes are connected to cycles – daily, seasonally, annually, generationally – that, in turn, have fundamentally shaped societies through correlating sequences of succession marked by rapid growth, complexification, climax and downturn.[2] When the need/ demand for energy exceeded the renewable energy sources locally available, or if those energy sources migrated, people either moved locations (nomadism), developed methods for storing energy (agriculture), developed more nuanced methods corresponding to these cycles of storing energy (shifting agriculture) (Odum 2007, 183–186), sought new energy sources (geographic conquest) or the society deteriorated and/or fragmented (collapse).

In his book *The Collapse of Complex Societies*, an expansive historical and intellectual examination of the circumstances and causes of civilizational collapse, the American anthropologist and historian Joseph Tainter described succinctly the specific sequence that complex societies undertake related to the production of resources other than agricultural crops and the relative decline on return as the most readily exploitable sources are used up.[3]

> Complex societies depend on the production of other resources besides agricultural crops. Energy and minerals production, as the modern industrial world is well aware, follows the same productivity curve as subsistence agriculture, and for a similar reason. The fuel resources used first by a rationally-acting human population, and the mineral deposits mined first, are typically those that are most economically exploited, that is, most abundant, most accessible, and most easily converted to the needs at hand. When it subsequently becomes necessary to use less economical resources marginal returns automatically decline.
>
> *(Tainter 1988, 95)*

Although non-renewable fossil fuels like coal, natural gas and oil have been marginally used since ancient times, most often in small amounts for specialized industrial purposes like smelting, but also sometimes for cooking and heating, it was a combination of increased access, alongside the general technological advancements of the burgeoning industrial revolution during the late eighteenth century, which provided the means to utilize fossil fuels at a commercial scale. With the shift to highly concentrated fossil fuel-based sources of potential energy, which required millions of years of environmental work to

148 Environmental Identification

generate, human-beings were effectively no longer energy source limited. This instigated a radical transformation in how humans might inhabit the world-ecology, consequently creating a "flash explosion" of growth in humanity (Odum 2007, 187). "It has been a time of early successional overgrowth, competition, wars of conquest, capitalism, and uniformity" (Odum 2007, 59). From an energetic point of view, fossil fuels have temporarily replaced work that was previously done by plants, animals and rural farmers historically powered by renewable energies.

Humanity, during this time of rapid succession driven by non-renewable fossil fuel utilization, has been responsible for unimaginable technological advancement, growth and relative increase in human prosperity for many, but has also instigated global climate destabilization and unknowable levels of current and future ecological, social and cultural destruction. As human-beings begin to recognize the adverse effects of fossil fuel consumption and consider a shift back toward renewable energy sources, solar radiation is often cited as the most readily available untapped, universally accessible source. However, while its dispersal across the globe is comprehensive, its energy is inherently dilute as compared to fossil fuels. To harness and concentrate it into a comparable fuel, its net emergy yield (embodied energy) is actually quite low (Odum 2007, 69 and 207) (Figure 5.1). Renewables as a "solution" to energy demands and carbon emissions may simply not be feasible, given the scale necessary to effectively harness and concentrate their energies at the level required by current demand.[4] Today, even with increasing advancement in solar collection technologies and decreasing costs, when it comes to total energy consumption by the United States, renewables account for only 11%, of which only 6% is from solar (U.S. EIA June 2019) (Figure 5.2).

Setting the question of energy aside for a moment, what if we *could* somehow overnight meet 100% of our energy needs from renewable sources? What if we were also able to instantly eliminate any further greenhouse gas emissions, invent and implement effective carbon sequestration technologies and eliminate all waste from production processes – what would we do next? How long after this nocturnal transformation before the earth-system's ledger would fall back into the red from overpopulation and the continued consumption of nature? One generation? Two? Three? Twenty? There is undoubtedly a point where the life-supporting "resources" embodied in the earth-system – minerals, nutrients, water, air, soil, physical space – can simply no longer sustain the exponentially increasing demands of an exponentially increasing human population. There is only so much of the earth pie to go around to an ever-greater number of people seeking an equal piece.[5] Howard Odum characterizes humanity's phase of successional overgrowth, made possible by fossil fuels as a "cancer."

> The biggest cancer of them all is the human population itself. Removed from its normal controls by modern medicine, global population has

Dwelling Deep 149

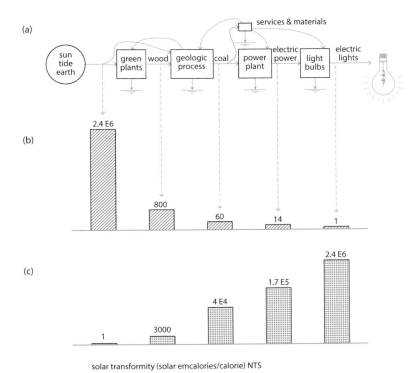

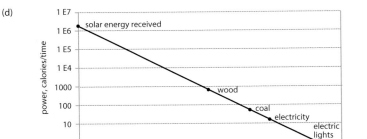

FIGURE 5.1 Energy transformation diagrams: "Example of energy transformation series from solar energy through biomass to electrical lighting. (a) Energy flows and transformations; (b) bar graph representing the decrease of available energy at each step; (c) transformities increasing at higher levels to the right; (d) graph showing power as a function of transformity." Redrawn by author and reproduced by permission from Columbia University Press. Reprinted from Howard T. Odum. *Environment, Power, and Society For the Twenty-First Century: The Hierarchy of Energy* (New York: Columbia University Press, 2007) 70, fig. 4.5.

150 Environmental Identification

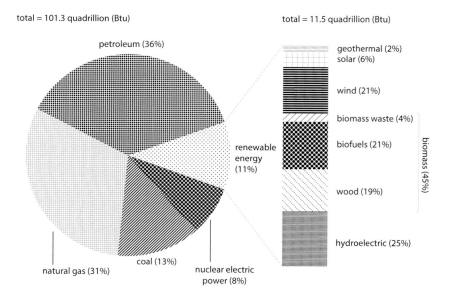

FIGURE 5.2 US energy consumption by energy source for 2018. Redrawn by author. Data based on U.S. Energy Information Administration, Monthly Energy Review, Table 1.3 and 10.1, April 2019, preliminary data.

accelerated past 6 billion. Using fossil fuel, some human populations have gone into a mode of competitive exclusion, consuming resources, setting up subcompetitions in their cultures and races, and generally draining the operating capital of the world toward its collapse.

(Odum 2007, 58–59)

As it specifically relates to the use of renewable energy sources necessary to support the exponential growth of human-beings, Odum states:

> The greater the human population, the smaller the area of forests remaining, and the less time is usually allowed for growth. The global net empower of solar energy decreases with population. As populations have increased, times between shifting agriculture farming have decreased, which reduced yields.
>
> When a dilute renewable energy has to be concentrated to support society, either emergy is used to concentrate the energy spatially or time is allowed for the energy to accumulate in a broadly distributed storage.
>
> *(Odum 2007, 209)*

The inevitability of the human population exceeding the earth's carrying capacity[6] and the resulting death and destruction to follow has long been discussed. At the end of the eighteenth century, the English economist and scholar Thomas Malthus, in his text *An Essay on the Principle of Population as it Affects the Future Improvement of Society*, warned that continued population growth at the current rate was untenable when compared to the rate of food production, a disjunction he argued would lead to greater poverty, famine and suffering. Despite lacking a rigorous statistical empiricism, Malthus's ideas concerning population were incorporated into theoretical systems of economics,[7] but, as his predications of immanent widespread famine and death did not come to fruition, he was widely criticized as an alarmist. Malthus's text was published at a moment just preceding the time when fossil fuels began their ascent as the dominant form of energy use. His thinking failed to anticipate the agricultural revolution facilitated by the development of petroleum-based technological innovations capable of enabling vastly greater crop production. These advancements would be further applied worldwide in the mid-twentieth century instigating the so-called "Green Revolution." In 1968, just before the global effects of the Revolution were fully felt, Paul Ehrlich, a Stanford University entomologist, and his wife Anne, at the urging of the then Sierra Club executive director David Brower,[8] published the book *The Population Bomb*, which provided a modern warning concerning overpopulation. In the book, they argued as Malthus had before them that population, if left uncontrolled, would very soon bring the perils of famine, conflict and suffering across the globe. Though the book was initially ignored, overtime it gained traction, and, also like Malthus, the Ehrlichs were roundly criticized as alarmist propagandists, even crackpots, as the specific scenarios portrayed in the book did not come to pass. It's important to note that the book clearly stated that these descriptions of the future were not "predictions" but rather possible "scenarios" or "stories," told as a means to think about the consequences of human actions.

> Scenarios are hypothetical sequences of events used as an aid in thinking about the future, especially in identifying possible decision points. I'd like to offer three brief scenarios, giving three possible projections of what the next fifteen years or so could look like. Remember, these are just possibilities, not predictions. We can be sure that none of them will come true as stated, but they describe the kinds of disasters that *will* occur as mankind slips into famine decades.
>
> *(Ehrlich and Ehrlich 1968, 72)*

Still today the Ehrlich's maintain that many of their fundamental points are sound and remain relevant. Writing in a 2009 article titled "The Population Bomb Revisited," they admit the scenarios posed in the book were misleading in their timing and were based on inaccurate assumptions concerning the full effects of the Green Revolution[9] and the underestimation in the "resiliency of the world system," but they still dealt with real and relevant issues regarding

152 Environmental Identification

population growth (Ehrlich and Ehrlich 2009, 67). Citing the work of political economist Thomas Homer-Dixon, they stand by the principle ideas of the book:

> The fundamental point of *The Population Bomb* is still self-evidently correct, we believe: the capacity of Earth to produce food and support people is finite. More and more scholars have realized that as our population, consumption, and technological skills expand, the probability of a vast catastrophe looms steadily larger (Homer-Dixon 2006).
>
> *(Ehrlich and Ehrlich 2009, 68)*

Two years after *The Population Bomb* was published, scientists and researchers at the Massachusetts Institute of Technology began a study which focused on the question of humanity's future trajectory related to how we choose to live-in-the-world. The study was sponsored by the Club of Rome, a think tank, whose self-described purpose was to "foster understanding of the varied but interdependent components – economic, political, natural, and social – that make up the global system in which we all live; to bring that new understanding to the attention of policy-makers and the public worldwide; and in this way to promote new policy initiatives and action" (Meadows et al. 1972, 9). The product of that study was a report published in 1972 titled *The Limits to Growth* and it immediately made an impact. The study utilized a specifically developed world model intent on improving an understanding of "long-term, global problems by combining the large amount of information that is already in human minds and in written records with new information-processing tools that mankind's increasing knowledge has produced – the scientific method, systems analysis, and the modern computer" (Meadows et al. 1972, 21). The focus of inquiry was aimed at five specific global trends of concern: "accelerating industrialization, rapid population growth, widespread malnutrition, depletion of nonrenewable resources, and a deteriorating environment" (Meadows et al. 1972, 21) (Figure 5.3). What's critical to note about the study is that it was grounded in a systems dynamics method using a specifically developed computer software program called "World3"[10] that aimed to account for the complex feedback loops and dynamic processes embodied in the total world system. Journalist Christopher Ketcham described the study's approach in his 2017 article "The Fallacy of Endless Economic Growth" as follows:

> Meadows and his team used World3 to examine growth trends worldwide that had prevailed from 1900 to 1970, extrapolating from the data to model 12 future scenarios of global development and its consequences, projected out to the year 2100. They focused on the complex feedback loops – the system dynamics – that play out when we tax the limits of the planet.
>
> *(Ketcham 2018) (Figure 5.4)*

The study sequentially presents simulations from the world model, adjusting variables after each run based on an analysis of the result. Such variables included natural resource availability, industrial output, capital production, food production, pollution, birthrate and death rate. The general conclusion made by the authors of the study was clear:

> Although we have reservations about the approximations and simplifications in the present world model, it has led us to one conclusion that appears justified under all the assumptions we have tested so far. *The basic behavior mode of the world system is exponential growth of population and capital, followed by collapse.* As we have shown in the model runs presented here, this behavior mode occurs if we assume no change in the present system or if we assume any number of technological changes in the system.
>
> *(Meadows et al. 1972, 142) (Figure 5.5)*

In Ketcham's "Fallacy" article, the director of the study Dennis Meadows describes that, even in updated simulations published in 1992 and 2004,[11] which both greatly increased the capacities for future technological advancements, the results were the same as the original study. As Meadows states in Ketcham's interview: "In those later runs we even assumed infinite resources. But guess what? It is still impossible for the human population and consumption to grow exponentially forever" (Ketcham 2018).

As it might be expected, the publication of *The Limits to Growth* study received an immense amount of criticism and push back from many "pro-growth" economists, politicians and business people for whom growth was an unquestionable, fundamental imperative to humanity's *ability* to live-in-the-world, and in particular, in the United States.

> Worse than any specific prediction, however, was that the *Limits* team seemed to be questioning the viability of the American Dream. "*Limits* preaches that we must learn to make do with what we already have," grumbled the economists writing in the *Times*. The study was an affront to the cornucopian credo of mainstream economics, which says that pricing and innovation will always save us from the depletion of sources and the saturation of sinks. If a resource becomes scarce in the marketplace, economists tell us, its price rises, which acts as the signal for society to innovate alternatives because there's money to be made doing so. If a sink is saturated, technology—priced right—will ameliorate the effect, scrub the smokestacks, disperse the oil spills, and so on.
>
> *(Ketcham 2018)*

Today the trajectories provided in the *Limits to Growth* "standard model" appear to have largely tracked quite closely to the growth data reflected in the conditions of the world system since the original publication of the study. Concerning

154 Environmental Identification

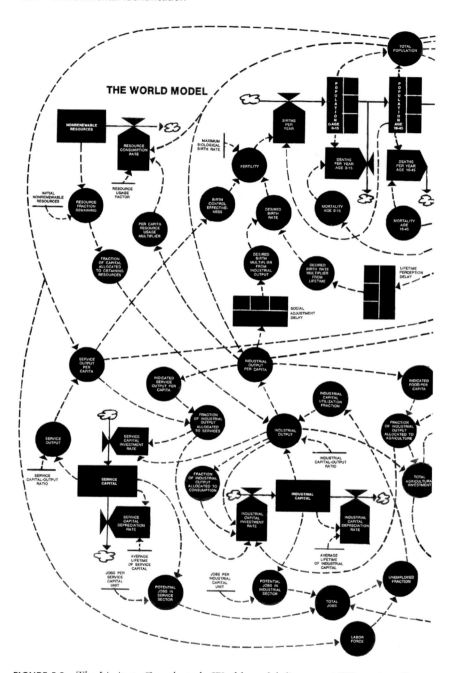

FIGURE 5.3 *The Limits to Growth* study World model diagram, 1972 version. Reproduced by permission from Dennis Meadows. Reprinted from Donella H. Meadows, Dennis L. Meadows, Jørgen Randers, and William W. Behrens III. *The Limits to Growth: A Report for the Club of Rome's Project on the Predicament of Mankind* (New York: Universe Books, 1972) 102–103, fig. 26.

Dwelling Deep 155

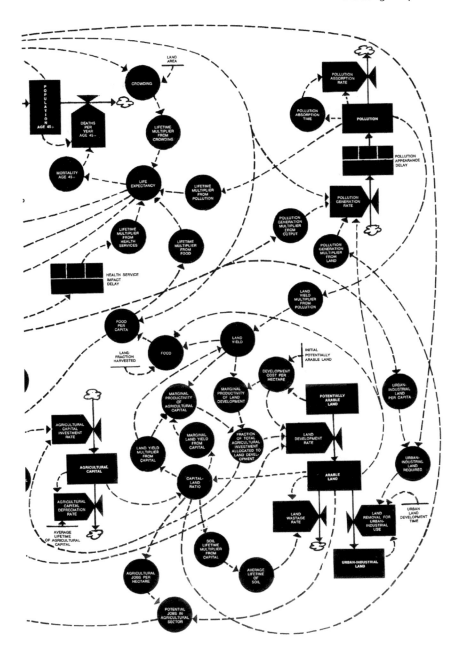

FIGURE 5.3   (Continued).

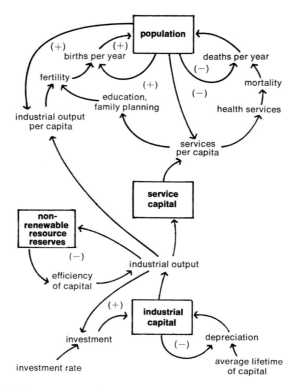

FIGURE 5.4 *The Limits to Growth* study feedback loops of population, capital, services and resources diagram. Reproduced by permission from Dennis Meadows. Reprinted from Donella H. Meadows, Dennis L. Meadows, Jørgen Randers, and William W. Behrens III. *The Limits to Growth: A Report for the Club of Rome's Project on the Predicament of Mankind* (New York: Universe Books, 1972) 100, fig. 25.

The Limits to Growth study alongside the work of the Ehrlich's and Malthus, the environmentalist writer Paul Hawken states:

> The underlying principles informing such cautionary predictions are largely correct, while timing and nature of humankind's destiny with earthly limits is still unknown. This means that the optimists who say we will be taken care of in the future will be correct for the time being, until the day they are wrong, when we will all be in big trouble. The environmentalists, warning of impending catastrophe, will usually be wrong with regard to specific predictions, but are right in principle.
>
> *(Hawken 1993, 204–205)*

Importantly, *The Limits to Growth* study was able to find several runs of the world model that didn't result in collapse by the year 2100. These "stable"

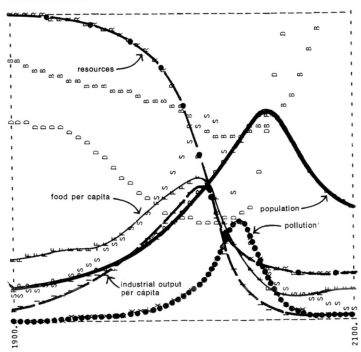

FIGURE 5.5 *The Limits to Growth* study World model "Standard" run diagram, 1972 version: "The 'standard' world model run assumes no major change in the physical, economic, or social relationships that have historically governed the development of the world system. All variables plotted here follow historical values from 1900 to 1970. Food, industrial output, and population grow exponentially until the rapidly diminishing resources base forces a slowdown in industrial growth...Population growth is finally halted by a rise in the death rate due to decreased food and medical services." Reproduced by permission from Dennis Meadows. Reprinted from Donella H. Meadows, Dennis L. Meadows, Jørgen Randers, and William W. Behrens III. *The Limits to Growth: A Report for the Club of Rome's Project on the Predicament of Mankind* (New York: Universe Books, 1972) 124, fig. 35.

runs required the following seven parameter adjustments: (1) population stabilized by setting the birthrate equal to the death rate, (2) and (3) resource consumption and pollution per unit of industrial and agricultural output reduced to one quarter its 1975 level, (4) societal economic preferences shift more toward services and less toward factory-produced material goods, (5) high value given to producing food for all people over the preference for capital accumulation, (6) soil enrichment and preservation made a priority, and (7) the design of goods toward durability, reuse and recycling given greater priority

158 Environmental Identification

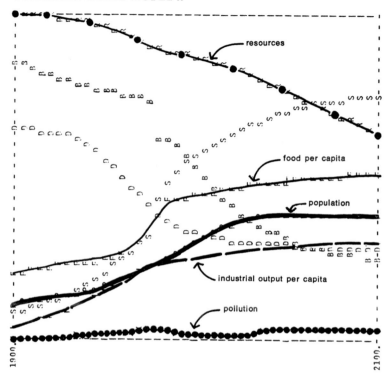

FIGURE 5.6 *The Limits to Growth* study World model II "Stabilized" run diagram, 1972 version. Reproduced by permission from Dennis Meadows. Reprinted from Donella H. Meadows, Dennis L. Meadows, Jørgen Randers, and William W. Behrens III. *The Limits to Growth: A Report for the Club of Rome's Project on the Predicament of Mankind* (New York: Universe Books, 1972) 168, fig. 47.

(Figures 5.6 and 5.7). This path to stability reflects a future not of rampant unyielding growth, grounded in technological developments and free market laissez-faire economics but one that shifts the focus from individual gain, uncontrolled growth and consumption to one of collectivity, supported by respectful interdependence – suggesting a radical departure in how we choose to live-in-the-world-ecology.

> An equilibrium state would not be free of pressures, since no society can be free of pressures. Equilibrium would require trading certain human freedoms, such as producing unlimited numbers of children or consuming uncontrolled amounts of resources, for other freedoms, such as relief

Dwelling Deep **159**

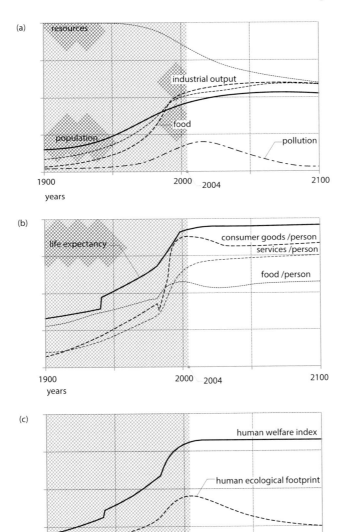

FIGURE 5.7 *The Limits to Growth* study World model "Stabilized" run diagram, 2004 version. (a) State of the World; (b) Material Standard of living; (c) Human welfare and footprint. "In this scenario population and industrial output are limited [ ] technologies are added to abate pollution, conserve resources, increase land yield, and protect agricultural land. The resulting society is sustainable: Nearly 8 billion people live with a high human welfare and a continuously declining ecological footprint."

160 Environmental Identification

> from pollution and crowding and the threat of collapse of the world system. It is possible that new freedoms might also arise – universal and unlimited education, leisure for creativity and inventiveness, and, most important of all, the freedom from hunger and poverty enjoyed by such a small fraction of the world's people today.
>
> *(Meadows et al. 1972, 179–180)*

The tradeoffs needed to initiate and maintain such stability are not ones likely to be made easily; the current systems and concentrations of power benefit too greatly from a "business as usual" or even a "green" approach articulated through global capital production, accumulation and exchange. However, as the earth-system changes and the effects of global warming become more present in everyone's daily life,[12] there have been small signs of change in the values of the global economic system as it relates to business and industry beyond simply "greenwashing."[13]

There has been a growing number of self-described socially and environmentally conscious corporations who have begun to incorporate social and environmental responsibility into their business models. While changes like these are productive steps toward less overall negative environmental impact, there is little doubt these changes alone will not be enough to thwart the current trajectory of humanity radically destabilizing the earth-system. To survive, to ultimately *cope* and *adapt* to this moment beyond climatological-ecological "crisis", what's really necessary is a more fundamental shift in our conception of who "we" are and "our place" living *within* the world-ecology, facilitating actions that *could* lead to some form of collective stability.

★ ★ ★

In our current moment, the ball we've been balancing upon has already begun to roll, its movement already felt – for how long, how far and how fast the ball rolls is still up to us, but regardless of future actions, wherever it stops (if it ever does) will not be the same place from which it started. There really is no amount of carbon sequestration[14] we can reasonably hope to achieve that will reverse many of the catastrophic changes already initiated in the earth-system, even within the context of the more optimistic 2019 IEA World Energy Outlook report showing lower carbon emissions than previously projected by 2040.[15] Irrespective of any further actions taken, "good" or "bad," we are facing a radically different world from the one we previously inhabited and from which we evolved before the dawn of the Anthropocene. As journalist David Wallace-Wells puts it bluntly: "No human has ever lived on a planet as hot as this one; it will get hotter" (Wallace-Wells 2019, 221). He poignantly articulates this "new" world reality in a critique of former California Governor Jerry Brown's comments made during one of the state's wildfire disasters, when the Governor referred to their increasing presence as a "new normal."

The truth is actually much scarier. That is, the end of normal; never normal again. We have already exited the state of environmental conditions that allowed the human animal to evolve in the first place, in an unsure and unplanned bet on just what that animal can endure. The climate system that raised us, and raised everything we now know as human culture and civilization, is now, like a parent, dead. And the climate system we have been observing for the last several years, the one that has battered the planet again and again, is not our bleak future in preview. It would be more precise to say that it is the product of our recent climate past, already passing behind us into a dustbin of environmental nostalgia. There is no longer any such thing as a "natural disaster," but not only will things get worse; technically speaking, they have already gotten worse…The devastation we are now seeing all around us is a beyond-best-case scenario for the future of warming and all the climate disasters it will bring.

(Wallace-Wells 2019, 18–19)

The world is changing whether we like it or not. Even when considering the scenarios described by the Ehrlich's or the "stabilized" world scenarios provided in *The Limits to Growth* studies, all fall somewhat short of fully recognizing the unpredictable consequences of the current moment beyond climatological-ecological "crisis" now reflected in the earth-system.[16] William McDonough and Michael Braungart's forward-thinking Cradle to Cradle, "eco-effective" and upcycling approaches – while remarkable for their advancements in how we conceptualize, design and produce the "things" that makeup the constructed environment – also fall short of radically challenging how human-beings actually choose to live-in-the-world, a necessary adjustment given the finite resources and physical space on the planet. While the sustainment of biological and technological nutrients would surely benefit the ecosphere, their approach is principally dependent upon "human focused" technological innovation, maintaining an anthropocentric ideology of the social, cultural and economic necessities for growth. Howard Odum makes a concise criticism of this general approach in his discussion of the sustainable reinforcement of the environment by the "free market" economy: "To compete in an unregulated economy, business must engage in short-range exploitation or have the resources taken by others. Sustainable economic use requires that either the users organize necessary reinforcements or use public money to pay for them. Free market forces alone cannot reinforce the environment" (Odum 2007, 271). Similar sentiment has been described by the ecological economist Herman Daly, a former Senior Economist in the Environmental Department of the World Bank, whose work has aligned with theories of a steady-state economy helping to establish the discipline of ecological economics. In an essay titled "Sustainable Growth: An Impossibility Theorem," Daly states:

162 Environmental Identification

> In its physical dimensions the economy is an open subsystem of the earth ecosystem, which is finite, nongrowing, and materially closed. As the economic subsystem grows it incorporates an ever greater proportion of the total ecosystem into itself and must reach a limit at 100 percent, if not before. Therefore its growth is not sustainable. The term "sustainable growth" when applied to the economy is a bad oxymoron – self-contradictory as prose, and unevocative as poetry.
>
> *(Daly 1993, 267)*

He goes on to make the explicit point that "sustainable *development*" is possible as long as it's "development without growth," meaning qualitative improvement of a physical economic base within a steady-state (Daly 1993, 268). Growth must be brought into balance with the finite world in which we and all other beings inhabit.[17] There has been more recently a discussion within the architectural and design community around the concept of "de-growth" as a necessary strategy to reach such a balanced steady-state. De-growth has been defined in various ways, but perhaps most succinctly as "a downscaling of production and consumption that increases human well-being and enhances ecological conditions and equity on the planet."[18] This distinction between "growth" and "development," while subtle, is important as it fundamentally changes the way in which we evaluate economic activities and how we approach understanding our impact on, and in, the world-ecology.

Perhaps the most impactful image of such a critique concerning the relationship and limitations between the economy and the world-ecology was described by the economist Kenneth Boulding in his 1966 essay "The Economics of the Coming Spaceship Earth." In the essay, he describes how human-beings have largely conceived of the earth as an "illimitable plane," an *open* frontier of new lands always available beyond the horizon. However, over the course of history, it has become clear scientifically that we are actually inhabiting a "spherical earth and a closed sphere of human activity" (Boulding 1966, 3). Boulding illustrates the necessity for shifting from an *open* to a *closed* economic model[19] with two evocative metaphors, the "cowboy," associated with "reckless, exploitative, romantic, and violent behavior," and the "spaceman," bound to an isolated vehicle (Spaceship Earth[20]) "without unlimited reservoirs of anything" (Boulding 1966, 9). The fundamental difference between these two approaches is how they regard production and consumption. In the illimitable frontier plane economy of the cowboy they are both desirable, the measure of success determined by the amount of throughput,[21] while in the limited sphere economy of the spaceman, the situation is reversed: "The essential measure of the success of the economy is not production and consumption at all, but the nature, extent, quality and complexity of the total capital stock, including in this the state of human bodies and minds included in the system" (Boulding 1966, 9). The spaceman riding in Spaceship Earth cannot survive operating from a position of narcissistic self-interest like the cowboy; he must maintain a healthy and balanced relationship with the other passengers on board. Posterity guides the actions of the spaceman, preventing him from creating an encapsulated "unlivable milieu" as there really is nowhere else to go. To those critics who feel the sacrifice of the future *is* worth the self-indulgence of the present, Boulding provides the following answer:

> The only answer to this, as far as I can see, is to point out that the welfare of the individual depends on *the extent to which he can identify himself with others, and that the most satisfactory individual identity is that which identifies not only with a community in space but also with a community extending over time from the past into the future.* If this kind of identity is recognized as desirable, then posterity has a voice, even if it does not have a vote; and in a sense, if its voice can influence votes, it has votes too. This whole problem is linked up with the much larger one of the determinants of the morale, legitimacy, and "nerve" of a society, and there is a great deal of historical evidence to suggest that a society which loses its identity with posterity and which loses its positive image of the future loses also its capacity to deal with present problems, and soon falls apart.[22]
>
> *(Boulding 1966, 11)*

What's essential to achieving any such posterity within a given economic model is the primary supposition of ecological equality – meaning equality that takes into account not just human-beings or even other constituent living-beings but equally values all substantive aspects of the earth-system itself. This approach doesn't eliminate the possibility for the further *development* of economic opportunity, adequate standards of living or the production of knowledge and culture, but it does eliminate the overarching demand for growth and exploitation that values living-beings according to their perceived usefulness to human-beings. To even begin to achieve such equality, however, requires not just a reconsideration of our economic models but rather a total reframing of the philosophical, psychological and even spiritual conceptualization of "our place" living-in-the-world-ecology.

★ ★ ★

The eco-philosopher Warwick Fox writes the following, in reference to the conclusions of a 1967 paper by medieval historian Lynn White Jr., "The Historical Roots of Our Ecological Crisis," in which White argued for the need to abandon an anthropocentric relationship with the world in order to begin to overcome the current ecological problems:

> From this viewpoint, the continued application of technical solutions while "we" – and especially wealthy, male humans in the financial

164 Environmental Identification

> capitals of the world – essentially carry on with "business as usual" is simply not good enough. What is instead required is a reorientation toward nonanthropocentric – or, in more positive terms, toward an ecocentric – way of being in the world.
>
> *(Fox 1995, 23)*

Since the time a contemporary ecological awareness transpired during the 1960s, ecologists and philosophers have developed many different labels for this type of non-anthropocentric ecological thinking – "ecophilosophy," "environmental philosophy," "environmental ethics" etc. It is from within the subset of this spectrum referred to as the Deep Ecology movement that a "beyond sustainable" non-anthropocentric reconceptualization of the constructed environments we design and inhabit will be explored.

The Deep Ecology movement was initially formulated by the Norwegian philosopher Arne Naess, who first presented the concept in a lecture delivered at the third World Future Research Conference held in Bucharest in September 1972; its first articulation in print took place the following year in the journal *Inquiry* as a summary of his conference lecture in an essay titled "The Shallow and the Deep, Long-Range Ecology Movement" (Fox 1995, 37, n. 63). Naess's initial conceptual formulation of the movement provided a distinction within the more generalized environmentalist community of that time, between the work of ecologists whose approach he regarded as *shallow* – "concerned with fighting pollution and resource depletion" and whose "central objective is the health and affluence of people in the developed countries" – in contrast to those ecologists whose work he considered *deep* – "[who] touch upon principles of diversity complexity, autonomy, decentralization, symbiosis, egalitarianism, and classlessness" (Naess 2005, 7). Within this initial summary text, he presented seven distinct points that described the principles of deep ecology as a movement. These points have evolved since the time of their original publication, but still provide a general overview of *deep* ecological thinking. They are: (1) rejection of a human-in-environment image in favor of the relational, total-field image; (2) accepts in principle biospherical egalitarianism; (3) emphasis on principles of diversity and symbiosis; (4) assumption of an anti-class posture; (5) fight against pollution and resource depletion; (6) emphasis on complexity, not complication; and (7) support of local autonomy and decentralization (Naess 2005, 7–10). Naess ends this summary essay by making several concluding points concerning the application and context for his formulations.

> insofar as ecology movements deserve our attention, they are ecophilosophical rather than ecological. Ecology is a limited science that makes use of scientific methods. Philosophy is the most general forum of debate on fundamentals, descriptive as well as prescriptive, and political philosophy is one of its subsections. By an *ecosophy* I mean a philosophy of

ecological harmony and equilibrium. A philosophy as a kind of wisdom is openly normative; it contains norms, rules, postulates, value-priority announcements, and hypotheses concerning the state of affairs in our universe. Wisdom is policy wisdom, prescription, not just scientific description and prediction.

(Naess 2005, 11)

The inclusion of a decidedly philosophical perspective from which to reflect upon the question of ecological harmony and equilibrium (*ecosophy*) helps to frame the discussion more deeply, providing the capacity to work seriously from what Naess often refers to as "intuition" or "wisdom." As an approach to better understand "our place" living-in-the-world-ecology, including how we design and construct the environments we inhabit – our *architectural* "dwelling-place" – it provides an alternative value system not relegated to the rigid demands of science, technological innovation or economic imperatives but rather toward the potential to cultivate "profound" understandings. Since the time of its initial presentation and publication in 1972/1973, the *shallow* and *deep* ecological spectrum, certainly not the first articulation of a fundamentally non-anthropocentric ecological approach, has become an influential mainstay of ecophilosophical thought and environmental ethics more generally.[23]

A scholar of the Deep Ecology movement, Warwick Fox, in his book *Towards a Transpersonal Ecology: Developing New Foundations for Environmentalism*, has articulated three different senses of Naess's thinking about deep ecology, which he defines as *formal, philosophical* and *popular*. The *formal* sense concerns the structure and approach of Naess's argument, as defined by premise and conclusion chains "asking progressively deeper questions about ecological relationships of which we are a part" (Fox 1995, 92). The questions of "why" and "how" are the most important, leading to "end-of-the-line" assumptions, what Naess refers to as "fundamentals" or "norms," from whence *deep* ecological views are grounded. According to Naess, this approach of systematic questioning "is concerned with the *deepness of premises* used in debates over efforts to overcome the ecological crisis" (Naess 1995, 204). What is critical to recognize in Naess's approach – why he considers it an ecophilosophical movement rather than a scientific one – is because as one goes deeper and deeper with questioning, particularly as it relates to ecological concerns, one inevitably ends up at fields of inquiry typical of philosophy (Naess 1995, 209). Still deeper inquiry endeavors to uncover the most "profound" beliefs and assumptions that are essential to informing our relationships with the world and, if challenged, could result in significant social change.[24] Referencing Rachel Carson's work, Naess argues that the *shallow* movement refrained from discussing *deep* questions, and therefore held no immediate concern over the use of toxic pesticides, seeing no need to prohibit them; it was only after the *deep* questioning by Carson that

166 Environmental Identification

widespread scientific and governmental concerns were raised, leading to eventual policy changes. Naess describes this questioning as follows:

> Few people persistently asked "why?" or "how?" with persistence. But those who did were deeply concerned with the ecological situation. The answers to these questions relate not only to chemistry and biology; they involved increasingly more and more of various aspects of human affairs – economic, technological, social, cultural – and ultimately, philosophical and religious aspects. That is, those who went deeper *both* questioned deeper in the sense of deeper premises, and *suggested deeper changes socially (in a wide sense)*.
>
> *(Naess 1995, 209)*

Although the process of questioning more deeply, whatever its content, inevitably leads to philosophical and/or religious norms, in the *formal* sense it only reflects a system of "asking deeper questions"; it cannot make predictions, provide judgment statements or answers to such questions, and from this premise there is the possibility for many individual deep ecological philosophies (Fox 1995, 94). Sociologist Bill Devall and philosopher George Sessions, strong proponents of Naess's work on the Deep Ecology movement and contributors to its development themselves, described the movement's broad intentions in their 1985 co-authored book *Deep Ecology: Living as if Nature Mattered* in the following way:

> Naess was attempting to describe the deeper, more spiritual approach to Nature exemplified in the writings of Aldo Leopold and Rachel Carson. He thought that this deeper approach resulted from a more sensitive openness to ourselves and nonhuman life around us. The essence of deep ecology is to keep asking more searching questions about human life, society, and Nature as in the Western philosophical tradition of Socrates... Thus deep ecology goes beyond the so-called factual scientific level to the level of self and Earth wisdom.
>
> *(Devall and Sessions 1985, 65)*

It is this expansion of "self" and the embrace of "Earth wisdom" that define the second sense of deep ecology Fox describes as the *philosophical* sense, which specifically articulates Arne Naess's own personal version of deep ecology. Naess refers to it as *Ecosophy T*, a combination of *eco* meaning "environment" or "ecology," which itself came from the ancient Greek word *oíkos* meaning "home" or "dwelling place," and the Greek *sophos* meaning "wisdom," the *T* was used to communicate a variable, emphasizing that his specific formulation of *ecosophy* is just one of many possible versions (Fox 1995, 95). Naess's *Ecosophy T* always begins from the foundational norm of "Self-realization!," a term, according to Fox, which was directly derived from Naess's interpretation of Spinoza's *Ethics* and his psychological definition of "conatus," referring to a being's basic effort to preserve him or herself, typically rendered into English as "self-preservation" (Fox 1995, 105). However, an alternative translation of "conatus" as Naess argues, would be the term "realization" as it better reflects a process of actualizing or expanding the self through greater identification with others rather than its internalization aimed at preserving an already established self-identity (Naess 1997, 97). In a 1986 lecture titled "Self-Realization: An Ecological Approach to Being in the World," Naess provides the simple explanation: "Survival is only a necessary condition, not a sufficient condition of self-realization" (Naess 2005, 520). Fox sums up Naess's interpretation and development of Spinoza's thinking about the self as follows:

> For Naess, Spinoza's philosophy points us toward the realization of as expansive a sense of self as possible. Moreover, it points us toward the *this-worldly* realization of as expansive a sense of self as possible since the world of which we are a part is the sum-total of reality (e.g., there is no *transcendent* God). And this is precisely what Naess means to point to when he employs the term "Self-realization!" as his fundamental norm in Ecosophy T: the this-worldly realization of as expansive a sense of self as possible.
>
> *(Fox 1995, 106)*

Although *Ecosophy T* is largely a philosophical inquiry, its context as it regards the process of individual self-realization lies within the "real" world of things, the "this-worldly" living and non-living beings with which one is in constant inter-action. For Naess, it is important to state that "Self-realization!" is not equivalent to realizing the narrow "ego" or, in its extreme form, a self-centered "ego-trip"; rather, his intended meaning is actually quite the opposite, seeking to broaden and deepen the self through increased *identification* with other beings. This is an approach directly influenced by the teachings of Gandhi and other Bodhisattvas, who, in addition to Spinoza, were most influential in Naess's development of *Ecosophy T*. He even takes the term "self-realization" directly from Gandhi (Fox 1995, 107), associating it with the ideal of Mahayana Buddhism which finds self-realization through serving the world[25] (Fox 1995, 111). In this way, the conception of the narrow ego of the self is transformed into a much greater entity – the "ecological self." Again from his lecture "Self-Realization":

> Traditionally, the *maturity of the self* has been considered to develop through three stages: from ego to social self (including the ego), and from social self to a metaphysical self (including the social self). In this conception of the maturity of the self, Nature is largely left out. Our immediate environment, our home (where we belong as children), and the identification with

168 Environmental Identification

nonhuman living beings are largely ignored. Therefore, I tentatively introduce, perhaps for the very first time, the concept of *ecological self*. We may be said to be in, and of, Nature from the very beginning of our selves. Society and human relationships are important, but our self is much richer in its constitutive relationships. These relationships are not just those we have with other people and the human community…

Because of an inescapable process of identification with others, with increasing maturity the self is widened and deepened. We "see ourselves in others." Our self-realization is hindered if the self-realization of others, with whom we identify, is hindered.

(Naess 2005, 516)

And, similarly, in the 1988 essay "The Basics of Deep Ecology," Naess describes the ecological basis of the self as follows:

It is taken for granted that the self is basically ecological. Talk about human beings in the environment is misleading, for we are as much out there as inside here. The beauty of a tree is as much in the tree as it is inside us. There is an object, a medium, and a subject, but you cannot separate these three except as abstractions. People with this approach think in these terms: world first, men not apart, friends of the earth, ecological responsibility, the forest for the trees, hug the trees. If we say "the forest for the trees" we acknowledge that a forest is an end in itself; it does not need to serve any narrow human purpose.

(Naess 2005, 14–15)

This fundamental understanding of the most basic norm adopted by *Ecosophy T*, "Self-realization!" provides a fundamental shift toward as expansive a conception of self as possible and a greater *identification* with other living-beings, whereby this shift will naturally inform one's actions toward the betterment of the world-ecology. It is important to note however that identification should not, as Fox explicitly states, be taken to mean *identity*. "What is being emphasized is the tremendously *common* experience that through the process of identification my *sense* of self (my experiential self) can expand to include the tree even though I and the tree remain physically 'separate'" (Fox 1995, 231–232). This expansion of self-identification describes a truly radical departure from a *shallow* concept of ecology and the predominant disciplinary models of sustainability that do not deeply challenge how we think, feel, live, act and ultimately live-in-the-world. These *shallow* models seek to maintain existing social organizations, implementing only minor changes within institutions, reinforcing largely technical innovations toward reducing negative environmental impacts rather than as a means for reforming fundamental human relations with nature and world (Naess 2005, 16).

The *popular* sense of deep ecology, the last described by Fox, presents what Arne Naess refers to as level two views, or the most general ecologically relevant views popularly shared by other ecophilosophical thinkers within the Deep Ecology movement (Fox 1995, 114). It reflects a "general orientation" of basic principles, not necessarily a specific set of "guidelines for action" (Fox 1995, 116). Naess has provided a variety of bullet point lists of these principles since his initial conception of the Deep Ecology movement in the early 1970s (see the original seven-point list quoted earlier).[26] An overview of these general orientation points reflects two primary understandings: all beings on Earth have inherent value independent of their perceived usefulness to human-beings, and human-beings have excessively interfered with non-human life reducing its richness and diversity, something they have no right to do except to satisfy vital needs (Fox 1995, 114–115; Naess 2005, 18–20). It's important to clarify that the use of the term "life" in these lists is intentionally broad, extending beyond the limits of the biotic to suggest a:

> symbiotic attitude on the part of humans not only toward all *members* of the ecosphere but even toward all identifiable *entities* or *forms* in the ecosphere. This orientation is intended to extend, in other words, to such entities/forms as rivers, landscapes, and even species and social systems.
>
> *(Fox 1995, 116)*

And in an article titled "Equality, Sameness, and Rights" Naess states, "I prefer the term *living being* to the term *organism*. The intuitive concept of 'life' (or 'living being') sometimes includes a river, a landscape, a wilderness, a mountain, and an arctic 'waste'" (Naess 2005, 69). This expansion is critical to fulfilling "Self-realization!" but also, perhaps most profoundly, eliminating the divide between the "terrestrial" and all "beings" that inhabit and makeup its spaces. Naess refers to this broader conception of life as a reflection of an "intuitive appreciation" for the equal rights of all "living" beings, reflecting a broadly egalitarian, non-anthropocentric understanding of "our place" living-in-the-world-ecology, abiding by the right for all "life" to "live and blossom" on earth. Again from "Equality, Sameness, and Rights":

> It is therefore a better formulation to say that living beings have a right (or intrinsic or inherent value, or value in themselves) to live and blossom that is the *same* for all. If we speak of differences in rights or value, we do not speak of the rights or value I have in mind. It is not meaningful to speak of the *degrees* of intrinsic or inherent value when speaking of the right of individuals to live and blossom.
>
> *(Naess 2005, 68)*

The implications of this position are wide ranging in how we understand ourselves, how we perceive other living-beings, how we might choose to

170 Environmental Identification

live-in-the-world-ecology. This is especially true when considering the design, fabrication and construction of the built environment created to mediate external conditions and advance our physical biological bodies as well as service our habitation needs, wants and desires. While we have evolved biologically, socially and culturally to be dependent upon these physical constructions, the current moment beyond climatological-ecological "crisis" is in large part the direct result of the destructive anthropocentric model of inhabiting the world-ecology that elevates the value of human-beings above all else. Fox asserts that Naess's *Ecosophy T* should be more generally referred to as "transpersonal ecology," as it "involves the realization of a sense of self that extends beyond (or that is *trans-*) one's egoic, biographical, or personal sense of self…" (Fox 1995, 197). Not coincidently, the term *transpersonal* derives from thinking in psychology, coined during the late 1960s by psychologists Abraham Maslow and Anthony Sutich. They developed this transpersonal approach out of a critique of humanistic psychology, claiming that it was unable to account for human experiences that went beyond the "narrow, atomistic or particle-like" conception of the self, the ego, and could not describe the experiences of individuals who had been able to "transcended self-actualization" (Fox 1995, 294), able to "identify their own good with the good of greater wholes (humankind, the cosmos)"[27] (Fox 1955, 295).

The transcendence of the egoic sense of self toward one equally dependent upon the self-realization of other living-beings ultimately expresses not a philosophical or ethical inquiry but rather a deep *psychological* transformation into the "ecological self," of which the built environment plays an integral part and cannot be separated. Considering Naess's *Ecosophy T* through this lens means that an ethical responsibility for co-productive actions toward the ecosphere – whether intended as sustainable, conservationist or preservationist – no longer makes sense as an applied *moral* imperative; instead, these co-productive egalitarian actions should more accurately be regarded as something akin to "self-defense."[28] Again from his lecture "Self-Realization":

> What is the practical importance of this conception of a wide and deep ecological self? When we attempt to defend Nature in our rich industrial societies, the argument of our opponents is often that we are doing it to secure beauty, recreation and other nonvital interests for ourselves. Our position is strengthened if, after honest reflection, we find that the destruction of Nature (and our place) threatens us in our innermost self. If so, we are more convincingly defending our vital interests, not merely something "out there." We are engaged in self-defense. To defend fundamental *human* rights is vital self-defense.
>
> *(Naess 2005, 522)*

And

The requisite care flows naturally if the "self" is widened and deepened so that protection of free nature is felt or conceived as protection of ourselves.

(Naess 2005, 527)

The psychological transformation inscribed by the deepening and widening of the self, a transpersonal ecological understanding, creates a kind of obsolescence of moral obligations or moral "oughts" (Naess 2005, 526). This directs decision-making toward choices that benefit the community, even if working against a short-term individual benefit – a choice rarely feasible in the current economic model of capital production, accumulation and exchange. And as it correlates to a specifically transpersonal ecological point of view, what's most significant is how this psychological reframing of the self ultimately effects one's actions and behaviors in-the-world. Fox describes the thinking of transpersonal ecologists' as follows:

Their analysis of the self is such that they consider that if one has a deep understanding of the way things *are* (i.e., if one empathetically incorporates the fact that we and all other entities are aspects of a single unfolding reality) then one *will* (as opposed to should) naturally be inclined to care for the unfolding of the world in all its aspects.

(Fox 1995, 247)

This amounts to what Naess, by way of Kant, refers to as a "beautiful act," performing actions the moral laws say are right based on inclination and pleasure, not out of sacrifice or social obligation. Beautiful acts are quite simply actions of benevolence, compassion and empathy toward the world, stemming from one's self-identification with the ecosphere rather than out of guilt, coercion or capital gain.

The deep transpersonal ecological reconceptualization of the self transforms how we understand "our-place" in the world-ecology and thus the actions we might take within it. While that does not mean our actions benefit all beings all the time equally, especially in the face of ongoing environmental degradation, global warming and climate change, it does mean they will be enacted from an non-anthropocentric understanding of our shared world. These actions are not ruled by the benefit of a singular species, or subgroup of privileged individuals within that species; rather, they seek to benefit the collective through the pursuit of "Self-realization!" It is in this sense that we might understand how Naess's *Ecosophy T* may reconcile itself with our current understanding of the Anthropocene and the recognition that human interference has had radical effects at the planetary scale, itself becoming an object of design imagination – what has in recent architectural discourse been generally referred to as the "planetary imaginary."[29] While *Ecosophy T* does not directly operate with such direct

172 Environmental Identification

design intent, what's clear is that with the expanded sense of the "ecological-self" comes different actions, different desires, met through acts of solidarity – beautiful acts – which collectively may transform the world, not through top-down grand plans or engineered utopian visions, but brought about by individual choice made from the egalitarian collective body acting toward itself.

The work of architect Joyce Hwang (Ants of the Prairie) conceptualizes the constructed environment from such a place of mutual "self-respect" toward all living-beings, aiming to cultivate an architecture of "beautiful acts" (Figures 5.8 and 5.9). It in large part focuses on designing architectural systems, interventions, spaces and structures intent on supporting non-human living-beings – from bats to birds to bugs and plants as well as to raise the conscious awareness in human-beings of the need to consider other living-beings outside of themselves. She has referred to some projects as "habitecture" and describes her work more generally as "confronting the pleasures and horrors of our contemporary ecologies."[30] In her essay "Living Among Pests," Hwang addresses habitat loss due to human development and presents the possibility

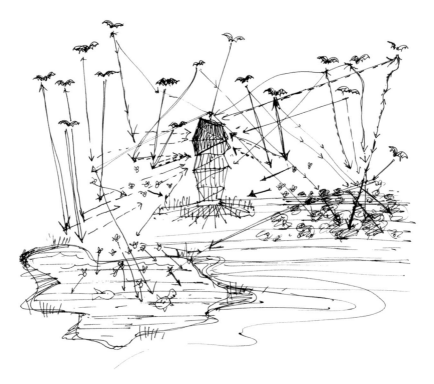

FIGURE 5.8 Joyce Hwang, *Bat Tower*, concept sketch, Griffis Sculpture park, East Otto, NY, 2010. Drawing by Joyce Hwang. Image courtesy of Joyce Hwang.

FIGURE 5.9 Joyce Hwang, *Bat Tower*, photos of completed structure, Griffis Sculpture park, East Otto, NY, 2010. Photographs by Albert Chao. Image courtesy of Joyce Hwang.

of co-habitation between humans and non-human living-beings, not as one of conflict or pestilence but of necessity and possibility – of beauty.

> As architects, we are operating in a landscape of shifting ecological and cultural values. We must not only develop strategies for incorporating diverse habitats into the spatial and built environment, but we must also take on the challenge to radically rethink the spatial and visible dimensions of animals and urban organisms. In the process of doing so, we will not only enable urban citizens to envision the possibilities of living among "pests," we'll also unshackle architecture from some of its time-loaded assumptions and cultural biases. It is only then that architecture can become a vehicle for provoking new priorities, rather than simply responding to them.
> *(Hwang 2013, 61)*

This approach recognizes current and future change as a fundamental reality, provoking the need for a conscious and ultimately adaptive provocation moving beyond simply sustainable design solutions. Hwang's work reflects a deep ecological and transpersonal understanding of the constructed environment, capable of initiating beyond climatological-ecological "crisis" strategies not derived from branding, economics, efficiency or even morality but rather from a deep identification, realization and respect for the "ecological self" (Figure 5.10).

174   Environmental Identification

FIGURE 5.10   Joyce Hwang, *Habitat Wall: Chicago*, photo of installation at the Sullivan Galleries, Chicago, IL, School of the Art Institute of Chicago, completed 2015. Photography by Joyce Hwang. Photograph courtesy of Joyce Hwang.

In the face of inexorable changes to the earth-system presently underway, a conceptualization of sustainable habitation intent only on subverting the damaging effects of human actions, in an attempt to regain some kind of perceived control of the world-ecology, no longer really holds the same relevance or intentionality as it did when we could still claim to be living within the midst of "crisis." Now, squarely on the other side, the intent of this acknowledgment is not to validate a kind of nihilist proclamation of inevitable civilization apocalypse or provide consent toward policies reverting back to indiscriminate exploitation, toxification and degradation of the environment in some kind of last-ditch effort to reap whatever bounties are left before collapse; the purpose is quite the opposite. This self-critique advocates for an alternative conceptualization of "our place" in the world from a "Terrestrial" approach capable of effecting how we construct "Our" *architectural* "dwelling place." Whether by choice or by force, there is a need for a new conception of habitation that moves beyond the outdated anthropocentric notion of controlling nature through technological advance, being more "sustainable" or more "effective." Reconsidering "Our place" requires an non-anthropocentric attitude capable of *coping* and *adapting* to the changing earth-system under our feet and over our heads through the creation of beautiful acts and a recognition and respect for the ecological self rather than deliriously yearning to avert a "crisis" that has already passed us by.

The deep transpersonal ecological understanding of "Our" environment, of "Our" world-ecology, of which human-beings are an integral part, provides not just the formation of a revised conceptual or philosophical imperative;

rather, it presents an entirely different understanding of the self – deeper, wider and integrated. Initiating an alternative understanding in the conception of *who* we are, but also *what* we are, and consequently how we might choose to act, design and inhabit the world-ecology. This is the position that Hwang's work takes, explicitly providing new spaces, new habitats, new territories and new collaborations between how we might choose to live in and with the world-ecology (Figures 5.11 and 5.12).

While this vantage point grounded in mutual and collective self-respect may help to establish a design model more capable of helping us *cope* and *adapt*, it simultaneously generates a new disjunction. If we conceive of ourselves as deeply connected to the ecologies we inhabit, integral to the larger collective of living-beings, how can "we," as human-beings, reconcile the facts of our individual experiences and sensations of life? While our individual psychology may transform to maintain a much more expansive conception of the self, our biology, physiology and personal life experiences – all intimately connected to the ecological and constructed environments we inhabit – are locally limited by our physical sensibilities, producing unique "self-worlds." How can these physiological and ecological conceptions of the self be reconciled? What are

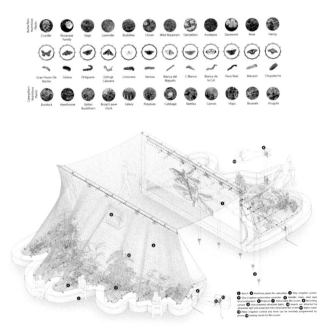

FIGURE 5.11 Joyce Hwang and Nerea Feliz, *Hidden in plain sight*, axon drawing, Matadero, Madrid, Spain, 2019. Image by Double Happiness (Nerea Feliz and Joyce Hwang). Image courtesy of Joyce Hwang.

176 Environmental Identification

FIGURE 5.12 Joyce Hwang and Nerea Feliz, *Hidden in plain sight*, rendering, Matadero, Madrid, Spain, 2019. Image by Double Happiness (Nerea Feliz and Joyce Hwang). Image courtesy of Joyce Hwang.

the direct *biological* and *physiological* manifestations of a deep ecological approach on the formulation of the "ecological self" and the constructed environments we design and inhabit? The last part of this book will begin to examine these questions and their implications for architects, uncovering more intentioned, co-productive and *deep* alignments between ecology, human biology, physiology and "Our" evolving environments of habitation.

Notes

1 Jason W. Moore has referred more broadly to capitalism's pursuit of "cheap nature" in the form of the "Four Cheaps."

> In these centuries [of early modernity] we find the origins of capitalism's Cheap Nature strategy, the very strategy that underpins today's biospheric turbulence. This strategy enables advancing labor productivity in great bursts by means of effecting even greater bursts in the production of the Four Cheaps: labor-power, food, energy, and raw materials.

And

> While all civilizations had frontiers of a sort, capitalism did something very different. Before the sixteenth century, civilizational frontiers – such as feudal Europe's drive east to the Elbe – were more-or-less an output of the system. With the rise of capitalism, frontier-making was much more fundamental: not

merely a safety valve, but a constitutive spatial moment unlocking epoch-making potential of endless accumulation. The extension of capitalist power to new, un-commodified spaces became the lifeblood of capitalism.

(Moore 2015, 62 and 63)

2 "Cultures and civilizations grew and dispersed, first in one place and then in another, as energy resources were accumulated and consumed in frenzied pulses of local, momentary growth. Like ecosystems, human societies alternated between stages of simple overgrowth and climax periods of complexity and diversity. These patterns of society apparently maximized power in both the short run and the long run, like those of other self-organizing systems"; see Odum (2007, 59).

3 Also see Tony Ord, *The Precipice: Existential Risk and the Future of Humanity* (New York: Hachette Books, 2020).

4 See Michael Schellenberger, "Why renewables can't save the planet," *Quillette*, February 27, 2019, https://quillette.com/2019/02/27/why-renewables-cant-save-the-planet/.

5 As it relates to the "modernization project" Bruno Latour describes the shrinking earth pie in the following way: "If the project has become impossible, it's because there is no Earth capable of containing its ideal of progress, emancipation, and development…We must face up to what is literally a problem of dimension, scale and lodging: the planet is *much too narrow and limited* for the globe of globalization; at the same time, it is *too big*, infinitely too large, too active, too complex to remain within the narrow limited borders of any locality whatsoever"; see Bruno Latour, *Down to Earth: Politics in the New Climatic Regime*, trans. Catherine Porter (Cambridge: Polity Press) 16. The reconciliation of global and local is precisely what he means by the "Terrestrial" as a new political actor.

6 "In wildlife management the phrase *carrying capacity* sometimes is used to describe the ability of an ecosystem to sustain a species population without damaging its functions. Carrying capacity for wildlife is the population level for long-range survival"; see Odum (2007, 209).

7 See *Encyclopedia Britannica Online*, s. v. "Thomas Malthus" (by Donald Gunn MacRae), https://www.britannica.com/biography/Thomas-Malthus#ref252180 (accessed March 26, 2020).

8 See Charles C. Mann, "The book that incited a worldwide fear of overpopulation," *Smithsonian Magazine*, January 2018, https://www.smithsonianmag.com/innovation/book-incited-worldwide-fear-overpopulation-180967499/.

9 But did recognize the catastrophic ecological risks such a revolution would likely produce, see Ehrlich and Ehrlich (2009, 67).

10 For an interactive online simulation of the model, see https://insightmaker.com/insight/1954/The-World3-Model-A-Detailed-World-Forecaster.

11 See Donella H. Meadows, Dennis L. Meadows, and Jørgen Randers, *Beyond the Limits: Confronting Global Collapse, Envisioning a Sustainable Future* (White River Junction, VT: Chelsea Green Publishing Company, 1992) and Donella H. Meadows, Dennis L. Meadows, and Jørgen Randers, *The Limits to Growth: The 30-year Update* (White River Junction, VT: Chelsea Green Publishing Company, 2004).

12 "The fact that warming is now hitting our wealthiest citizens is not just an opportunity for ugly bursts of liberal schadenfreude; it is also a sign of just how hard, and how indiscriminately, it is hitting. All of the sudden, it's getting a lot harder to protect against what's coming"; see Wallace-Wells (2019, 74).

13 See "Business Roundtable redefines the purpose of a corporation to promote 'an economy that serves all Americans,'" *Business Roundtable press release*, August 19, 2019. https://www.businessroundtable.org/business-roundtable-redefines-the-purpose-of-a-corporation-to-promote-an-economy-that-serves-all-americans.

178 Environmental Identification

14 For an analysis of current carbon sequestration technologies and their implications see Chapter 4 "Capturing," in Holly Jean Buck, *After geoengineering: Climate tragedy, repair, and restoration* (New York: Verso, 2019).

15 See IEA World Energy Outlook report released on November 13, 2019, https://www.iea.org/reports/world-energy-outlook-2019.

16 "Perhaps the most serious flaw in *The Bomb* was that it was too optimistic about the future…Since *The Bomb* was written, increases in greenhouse gas flows into the atmosphere, a consequence of the near doubling of the human population and the near tripling of global consumption, indicate that the results likely will be catastrophic climate disruption caused by greenhouse heating"; see Ehrlich and Ehrlich (2009, 66).

17 Also see Herman Daly, *Beyond Growth: The Economics of Sustainable Development* (Boston: Beacon Press, 1996) and David Pilling, *The Growth Delusion: Wealth, Poverty and the Well-Being of Nations* (New York: Tim Duggan Books, 2018).

18 See "Research & Degrowth (R&D)." See https://degrowth.org/definition-2/ (accessed March 27, 2020).

19 He makes this point from a "moral, political and psychological" perspective as well as an economic one.

20 The image/concept of the Spaceship Earth is perhaps most familiar for architects from Buckminster Fuller's 1969 book *Operating Manual for Spaceship Earth.*

21 Throughput is the amount of something (materials, data, energy, etc.) that moves through something (machine, system, etc.); see *Merriam Webster's Dictionary Online,* s.v. "throughput," https://www.merriam-webster.com/dictionary/throughput (accessed March 27, 2020).

22 Italics added here for emphasis.

23 For a detailed examination of why Deep Ecology became such an influential and widely used concept, see Chapter Two "Moving Away from Human-Centeredness" and Chapter Three "Why so Influential?" in Warwick Fox's book *Toward a Transpersonal Ecology: Developing New Foundations for Environmentalism.*

24 "But 'deepness' must include not just systematic philosophical deepness, but also the 'deepness' of proposed social changes"; see Naess (1995, 205). While Naess's personal definition of deep ecological thought (Ecosophy T) did provide the structure to address social concerns it's important to note here the overt criticism of the Deep Ecology movement by Murray Bookchin. He argued for a "social ecology" that accepted humanity as a necessary force in the world, but challenged its current forms of hierarchical, class-oriented, and statist institutions that have given rise to a capitalist economy. From Bookchin: "social ecology has the special meaning that ecological crisis that beleaguers us stems from a social crisis, a crisis that the crude biologism 'deep ecology' generally ignores…the resolution of this social crisis can only be achieved by reorganizing society along rational lines, imbued with an ecological philosophy and sensibility"; see Murray Bookchin, "Thinking Ecologically: A Dialectical Approach," in *The Philosophy of Social Ecology: Essay on Dialectical Naturalism* (Montréal: Black Rose Books, 1996) 120.

25 See Arne Naess, "Through Spinoza to Mahayana Buddhism or through Mahayana Buddhism to Spinoza?," in *Spinoza's Philosophy of Man: Proceedings of the Scandinavian Spinoza Symposium 1977,* ed. Jon Wetlesen (Oslo: University of Oslo Press, 1978) 136–158. Also see Fox (1995, 107–114).

26 See chapter 4, note number 53 of Warwick Fox's book *Towards a Transpersonal Ecology* where he describes the development of these lists by Naess and others.

27 "With a sufficiently wide and deep 'self,' *ego* and *alter* are, in a way, transcended"; see Naess (2005, 526).

28 There have been many radical environmentalist groups that operate from such a position of "self-defense." A few examples include Earth First!, Deep Green Resistance (DGR), Sea Shepard Conservation Society, Animal Liberation Front (ALF), Earth Liberation Front (ELF) and Earth Liberation Army (ELA).

29 For various recent understandings of this concept, see James Graham, ed., *Climates: Architecture and the planetary imaginary* (Zurich: Lars Müller, 2016); Rania Ghosn, and El Hadi Jazairy, *Two cosmograms: Design Earth* (Cambridge, MA: SA + P Press, 2016); and Neyran Turan, *Architecture as measure* (Barcelona: Actar, 2020).
30 See http://www.antsoftheprairie.com/?page_id=2 (accessed March 28, 2020).

References

Boulding, Kenneth E. 1966. The economics of the coming spaceship Earth. In *Environmental quality in a growing economy; Essays from the sixth RFF forum*, ed. Henry Jarrett, 3–14. Baltimore, MD: Published for Resources for the Future by the John Hopkins University Press.

Daly, Herman E. 1993. Sustainable growth: An impossibility theorem. In *Valuing the Earth: Economics, ecology, ethics*, eds. Herman E. Daly and Kenneth N. Townsend, 267–273. Cambridge, MA: The MIT Press.

Devall, Bill and George Sessions. 1985. *Deep ecology: Living as if nature mattered*. Salt Lake City, UT: Gibbs M. Smith, Inc.

Ehrlich, Paul, and Anne Ehrlich. 1968. *The population bomb*. New York: Ballantine Books.

———. 2009. The population bomb revisited. *The Electronic Journal of Scientific Development* 1, no. 3: 63–71.

Fox, Warwick. 1995. *Toward a transpersonal ecology: Developing new foundations for environmentalism*. New York: Shambhala; Distributed in the U.S. by Random House.

Hawken, Paul. 1993. *The ecology of commerce: A declaration of sustainability*. New York: Harper Collins Publishers.

Homer-Dixon, Thomas. 2006. *The upside of down: Catastrophe, Creativity, and the renewal of civilization*. Washington, DC: Island Press.

Hwang, Joyce. 2013. Living among pests. *Volume #35: Everything under Control* 35 (April): 60–63.

The Invisible Committee. 2009. *The coming insurrection*. Intervention series 1. Los Angeles, CA: Semiotext(e).

Ketcham, Christopher. 2018. The fallacy of endless economic growth: What economists around the world get wrong about the future. *Pacific Standard*, September 22, https://psmag.com/magazine/fallacy-of-endless-growth.

Meadows, Donella H., Dennis L. Meadows, Jørgen Randers, and William W. Behrens III. 1972. *The limits to growth: A report for the club of Rome's project on the predicament of mankind*. New York: Universe Books.

Moore, Jason W. 2015. *Capitalism in the web of life: Ecology and the accumulation of capital*. London: Verso.

Naess, Arne. 1995. Deepness of questions and the deep ecology movement. In *Deep ecology for the 2st century: Readings on the philosophy and practice of the new environmentalism*, ed. George Sessions, 204–212. Boston, MA: Shambhala Publications, Inc.

———. 1997. *Freedom, emotion and self-subsistence: The structure of a central part of Spinoza's Ethics*. Oslo: University of Oslo Press.

———. 2005. *Deep ecology of wisdom: Explorations in unities of nature and cultures*. Vol. 10 of *The selected works of Arne Naess: Volumes 1–10*, eds. Harold Glasser and Alan Drengson. Dordrecht: Springer.

Odum, Howard T. 2007. *Environment, power, and society for the twenty-first century: The hierarchy of energy*. New York: Columbia University Press.

Tainter, Joseph A. 1988. *The collapse of complex societies.* Cambridge: Cambridge University Press.

U.S. Energy Information Administration. June 27, 2019. *Renewable energy explained.* https://www.eia.gov/energyexplained/renewable-sources/.

———. October 25, 2019. *Frequently asked questions: What is U.S. electricity generation by energy source?* https://www.eia.gov/tools/faqs/faq.php?id=427&t=3.

Wallace-Wells, David. 2019. *The uninhabitable Earth: Life after warming.* New York: Tim Duggan Books.

PART III
Bio-Physical Inter-Action

Architecture at its most fundamental has always provided human-beings a means for better "surviving-in-the-world," maintaining even today a vital potential to help us mediate the adverse aspects of the various natures we inhabit. But, in the moment beyond climatological-ecological "crisis" we now find ourselves, how might architecture further provide a means to effectively deal with the drastic and ongoing changes to the earth-system? How might it help us to not just mediate or even identify with the environments we inhabit, but how might it help us bio-physically cope and adapt to this "new" world? As we've explored in the first two parts, there is every indication that one's engagement with the constructed environments he/she inhabits plays a significant role in many, if not all, aspects of life — in the total collective "being-with" and one's Self-realization!. Part III "Bio-physical Inter-Action" focuses on exploring architecture's ability to stimulate co-productive bio-physical responses with, and within, inhabitants towards coping and adapting, now and in the future. The intent is not to expound upon an architecture of control or manipulation by an authority for the gain of a select few but rather to consider its potential to help facilitate an ongoing process of adaption — a collective liberation in the face of catastrophic changes currently taking shape. Such an approach advocates for the fulfillment of greater freedoms, explorations and variability of experiences capable of co-productive relations with, and within, the changing world and within our physiological, psychological and even spiritual constitutions. The design of the constructed environment provides a unique opportunity for human-beings to impact their own lives and even their own futures, but, equally as such, the lives of those other "beings" with which they inter-act, both directly and indirectly, capable of supporting a deep affirmation for the life of all constituent beings.

6

INVISIBLE WORLDS

Constructing an Architecture of the Sensorium

> Thus, architecture, in the future, will not be judged chiefly by its beauty of rhythm, juxtaposition of materials, contemporary style, etc., etc.; it can only be judged by its power to maintain and enhance man's well-being – physical and mental. *Architecture thus becomes a tool for the control of man's health, its de-generation and re-generation…*
>
> By changing the physical environment, life may be quickened and increased, retarded or destroyed.
>
> (Kiesler 1939, 66)

The need for architecture to be judged by its ability to "maintain and enhance man's well-being" was posed by the Austrian born architect Frederick Kiesler in his remarkable essay "On Correalism and Biotechnique."[1] This approach was derived from his principle idea that the "forms" of natural or artificial entities were the visible result of integrating and disintegrating forces, continuously interacting with one another in visible and invisible arrangements – a state he called *correalism*. "This exchange of inter-acting forces I call *co-reality*, and the science of its relationships, *correalism*. The term 'correalism' expresses the dynamics of continual interaction between man and his natural and technological environments" (Kiesler 1939, 61). His use of the term "technological" is intended to describe the uniquely human ability to create a "third" environment, the "technological" environment, of which architecture is a fundamental part. Kiesler broadly describes that this "third" environment "is made up of a whole system of tools, which man developed for better control of nature"[2] (Kiesler 1939, 63). It is highly specific to humans, implicitly and continuously interacting with the other two: the surrounding "natural" environment and the explicitly "human" physiological environment, whose continuous interactions taken together create the human-being.

184 Bio-Physical Inter-Action

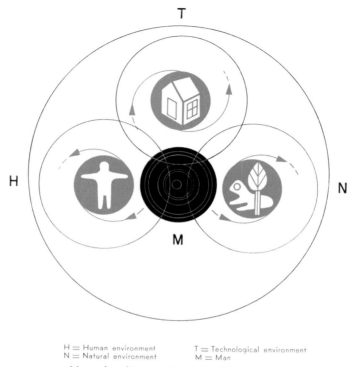

FIGURE 6.1 Frederick Kiesler, Man = Heredity + Environment, diagram, September 1939 (Frederick Kiesler, "On Correalism and Biotechnique. Definition and Test of a New Approach to Building Design," *Architectural Record*, p. 60). © 2020 Austrian Frederick and Lillian Kiesler Private Foundation, Vienna.

> When the biologist speaks of environment, he invariably means the geographical and animal environment. This definition is perhaps accurate for all creatures except man. For man alone has developed a third environment: a *technological* one which has been his steady companion from his very inception. This technological environment, from "shirts to shelter," has become one of the constituent parts of his total environment. Thus, the classification of environment becomes three- instead of two-fold: 1. natural environment, 2. human environment, 3. technological environment.
>
> *(Kiesler 1939, 61) (Figure 6.1)*

This relationship between these three environments was graphically illustrated in the essay as a kind of collaborative Venn diagram which for Kiesler "to maintain and enhance man's well-being" required moving beyond modern architecture's visual modalities of geometry, composition, icon and style, or outmoded

Invisible Worlds **185**

adages concerning a rational approach to form, function and program. While many prominent early modern architects like Le Corbusier did conceive of modern architecture as an integral part to a grand solution for remedying physical and societal ills through greater cleanliness, the mitigation of disease (especially tuberculosis) and the general health of the body,[3] the focus was principally aimed at new solutions for housing the masses, improving urban organization and a kind of standardization of space, even aspiring to an urban Utopian ideal.[4] These early strategies helped to establish and reinforce many design tenants of the Modern movement such as the creation of large expanses of glazing through the utilization of new material technologies,[5] the desire for abundant natural light, unadorned taught white surfaces, the expression of austere geometric forms and the authority of the plan as a logical organizational device.[6]

In contrast, Kiesler sought to "maintain and enhance man's well-being" through his concept of *correalism* derived from various dynamic and intensive qualities, "forces" of design, capable of a direct and evolving inter-active exchange between the three aforementioned environments (natural, human and technological). In this more collaborative and inter-active model of inhabitation and design, Kiesler argued that the "Technological environment, being a part of the complex of environmental forces, must consciously contribute to the extraction and development of man's inherent possibilities into a higher order" (Kiesler 1939, 67). Designing the "technological" environment based upon modernist ideas of functionality, standardization, control and "the *status quo* of man" (Kiesler 1939, 67) would only reinforce those existing conditions with no possibility for adaptive change or further development. For Kiesler taking advantage of the constructed environment's potential to instigate co- productive change required a redefinition of function as "a specific nucleus of actions" leading the designer to deal with "forces, not objects" (Kiesler 1939, 67) (Figures 6.2 and 6.3). In this sense, the design of a formative architectural environment should not be predicated on a set of a priori demands (rational functions), but rather, might emerge as the result of various overlapping systems of exchange capable of accommodating multiple sensations and actions contemporaneously. Architecture becomes the means for generating *evolving environmental potentials* with which, and from which, inhabitants may inter-act, engendering co-productive responses between inhabitant and the constructed environment.

As early as 1926, in a short essay titled "Space City Architecture" Kiesler wrote about the potential for architecture to be less rigidly defined by function, or even physical elements like the ground, walls or foundations, in an attempt to produce "the building that is adequate to the elasticity of the life function" (Kiesler 1926, 98). This sentiment was similarly repeated in many other writings like his 1949 essay "Pseudo-Functionalism in Modern Architecture" when he states:

> Functionalism is determinism and therefore stillborn. Functionalism is the standardization of routine activity. For example: a foot that walks

186 Bio-Physical Inter-Action

FIGURE 6.2 Frederick Kiesler, Study on perception, New York, ink on paper, ca. 1937–1941. [SFP 1211/0]. © 2020 Austrian Frederick and Lillian Kiesler Private Foundation, Vienna.

FIGURE 6.3 Frederick Kiesler, Study on perception, New York, ink on paper, ca. 1937–1941. [SFP 1210/0] © 2020 Austrian Frederick and Lillian Kiesler Private Foundation, Vienna.

(but does not dance); an eye that sees (but does not envision); a hand that grasps (but does not create).

Functionalism relieves the architect of responsibility to his concept. He mechanizes in terms of the current inherited conception of the practical, and little more; only simplifying and rendering ascetic what is already traditional. Actually, however, he does violence to the *freedom* and *self-realization* of the basic functions of living man. The species is known by the total coordination of its functions, not by oesophagus.[7]

(*Kiesler 1949, 57*)

And, in another passage from that same essay, he directly critiques the use and dominance of the plan as incapable of providing an effective means for designing a house which requires a sensorial approach to comprehending the possibilities of a "polydimensional" architecture that must be explored sensorially rather than two-dimensionally through the plan.

A house must be practical. To be practical means to serve. To be serviceable in every respect…But how can a house be practical if the draftsman always begins with the flat ground plan? Our vision is physically flat – we see with one eye (mono-dimensionally) rather than stereoscopically, with two eyes, as a living spatial vision would require.

The ground plan is only a flat imprint of a volume…A house is a volume in which people live polydimensionally. It is the sum of every possible movement its inhabitants can make…

Hence it is fallacious to begin with the floor plan. We must strive to capture a *general sense* of dwelling, and configurate accordingly. This is difficult but not impossible. It is difficult, if only because the space of the house is polydimensional (it is imprisoned on paper, so to speak). But if the design is intrinsically two-dimensional, that is all the more reason why we must not see two-dimensionally, or feel two-dimensionally *a priori*.

(*Kiesler 1949, 59*)

Kiesler's lack of trust in conventional architectural drawings as tools for design and representation, instead favoring large-scale "half-opened models," can almost certainly be attributed to the influence of another prominent Viennese architect, Adolf Loos, with whom Kiesler "learned a lot" (Colomina 2008, 24 and note# 27) and whose development of the *Raumplan*[8] and consequent lack of comprehensive drawings for his designs is well known. In a passage from her book *Privacy and Publicity: Modern Architecture as Mass Media*, Beatriz Colomina quotes Loos's 1910 essay "Architecture" stating that an "established" building is "ineffective in two dimensions," (Loos 1910, 106) meaning that "the drawing cannot convey the 'sensation' of space, as this involves not only sight but also the other physical senses" (Colomina 1994, 269). She also goes on to quote a passage from Richard Neutra in which he recounts how Loos would, in an effort to humanize the design, leave dimensions off his drawings, insisting on making final dimensional decisions for his interiors onsite during construction (Colomina 1994, 269 and Neutra 1954, 300). In many ways, Kiesler's criticism of the functionalist approach could be interpreted as a critique of modernity's belief in the creation of a specific modern *ideal* of the human body, an object of conformity, as established through the process of standardization developed in the late nineteenth and early twentieth centuries by industry through Taylorism, Fordism and later in design itself with the development of standardized human dimensional systems proposed by Ernst Neufert, Henry Dreyfuss and Le Corbusier's Modular.[9] Today these approaches have been further radicalized through the increasing collection of data resulting in an "evidence-based design" approach towards standardization and uniformity of expected norms.[10] For Kiesler, this movement towards standardization leads to a kind of "social standardization," which, in turn, "has given rise to a standardization not only of the parts of houses, but of architectural forms as well" (Kiesler 1949, 60).

Writing in her essay "Endless Drawing: Architecture as Self-Analysis," Colomina describes Kiesler's conception of architecture as deeply personal and psychologically impactful for the inhabitant – characterizing it as a kind of interior "cave" or "womb" (Colomina 2008, 18 and 24) conceived as a personal psycho-analytical experience and expansion. Kiesler referred to this concept as "psycho-function," arguing that different materials, like glass or leather, may instigate a different "psychological effect" and how "Function and efficiency alone cannot create art works. 'Psycho-Function' is that 'surplus' above efficiency which may turn a functional solution into art" (Kiesler 1930, 87). This conception suggested a dynamic space of ongoing inter-action, envelopment and the open possibility for personal development, formation and evolution, a stark contrast to the modernist ideas of passive standardized inhabitation, rigid and orthogonal grids and "pure" forms. If modern architecture sought to advance man into an "ideal" citizen of the world, then Kiesler's architecture was a psycho-analytical space of exploration and individual self-discovery. Not a preplanned choreographed display, but a continuously evolving correspondence that Colomina suggests may also provide a kind of pleasure.

> With the concept of "psycho-function," the material condition of the building and its mechanical operations give way to a form of sensuality understood as psychological pleasure. The architect becomes a kind of therapist unlocking repressions.
>
> *(Colomina 2008, 22)*

And

> Kiesler even described architecture itself as the "skin of the body." The house is the interior of the body itself. Architecture is the sensuous limit of the body.

Kiesler goes one step further than Loos. The sensuality of his house extends from the tactile into the psyche.

(Colomina 2008, 24)

This sensual characterization of Kiesler's architectural ambitions opens up a further departure from a functionalist approach, grounding reciprocity between human-beings and their environments through the senses themselves, through direct psychological and physiological inter-actions.

This suggests a much deeper, more integral potential towards architecture's ability to co-productively engage with and affect human inhabitants, not towards a predetermined ideal "form" but as an individual living, evolving and collaborative human-being (Figure 6.4). In their book *Are we human?*, Beatriz Colomina and Mark Wigley describe Kiesler's alternative approach as replacing modern architecture's "heroic, athletic, muscular body" with "a frail body in need of protection by architecture. Architecture becomes an infinite, uterine cave, nurturing a kind of translucent body" making the claim that "Dissidents like Kiesler expose that modern design is an always failed attempt to repress its

FIGURE 6.4 Frederick Kiesler, Study on human perception, New York, ink on paper, ca. 1937–1941. [SFP 858/0]. © 2020 Austrian Frederick and Lillian Kiesler Private Foundation, Vienna.

own sensuality. It is full of secrets, obsessions, and forbidden pleasures hidden just behind its attempts to project the image of a new normality" (Colomina and Wigley 2017, 176-177). How might architects further advance the potential for such a "sensual" engagement between inhabitants and their constructed environments, beyond simply protecting human frailty and/or mediating its exposure to external environmental hazards, to further co-productively inter-act with inhabitants?

One of Kiesler's few built projects was the prototype Space House completed in 1933 at the Modernage Furniture Company's headquarters on East Thirty-third Street in Manhattan (Phillips 2010, 98), providing an example of his approach in physical form. The project was designed in part as a response to Kiesler's rejection of "the idea of discrete rectangular boxes limited by a structural grid" (Colomina 2008, 26) that he felt dominated Philip Johnson and Henry-Russell Hitchcock's MoMA exhibition *The International Style* from the year previous. In the text that accompanied the Space House installation "Notes on Architecture: The Space-House," Kiesler is specifically critical of Modernist architects like "Corbusier, Mies, Oud, and others"[11] (Colomina 2008, 26) whom he accuses of initiating the architectural design from "the idea of the house," its function, not recognizing it as the resultant of a confluence of three different aspects – "social, tectonic and structural" (Kiesler 1934, 23). In comparison, he describes how the Space House, as a "One-Family-Shelter," was designed and built to demonstrate "Architecture as Biotechnique. (The interrelation of a body to its environment: spiritual, physical, social, mechanical)" (Kiesler 1934, 23). Functionality was relative, secondary to the responsiveness of the *architectural environment* and its embedded potentials. The house was literally flexible, rejecting static fixed elements like dividing walls and even doors, to instead accommodate the changing needs of inhabitants and help facilitate variable social conditions. Architectural theorist Stephen Phillips characterizes the house this way:

> As described by Kiesler in a series of unpublished sketches and notes, the Space House "contracted" to provide seclusion for a single individual or "expanded" to support group interactions. The house was not intended to be fixed in time but to be keyed to the changing and evolving requirements of its inhabitants. Kiesler's design for the Space House sought to envelop dwelling within architecture geared to the changing interactions of work, rest, or play.
>
> *(Phillips 2010, 98)*

The concept of "Biotechnique" is primary to Kiesler's conception of an "elastic" approach to the design of an *architectural environment* and its relational potentials with inhabitants, but it is important to note, as Phillips does, that Kiesler did not invent the term entirely, versions of it having been used prior by Sir Patrick Geddes (Biotechnics), Moholy-Nagy (biotechnique) and Lewis Mumford (biotechnic).[12] Kiesler recognized Geddes's early use of the term, but only as it relates to *"nature's* method of building, not of *man's"* (Kiesler 1939, 67). Regardless of its specific origins, Kiesler's definition and use of the term "biotechnique" as it applied specifically to the design of the *architectural environment* and man's correalist inter-action with and within it, provided a stark contrast to the burgeoning wave of Modernist functionalism sweeping over architectural discourse at that time.

In an attempt to more rigorously explore the potential of these correalist inter-actions, Kiesler founded the Laboratory of Design Correlation at the Columbia University School of Architecture in the autumn of 1937, which was built on a model of multidisciplinary design exploration, experimentation and testing the possibilities of "biotechnique" (Kiesler 1939, 70). Phillips describes the laboratory as follows:

> The laboratory invented new ways to modulate the built environment in response to multiple spatial habits of perceiving bodies in motion as situated and evolving through time. Their forms were designed to be "elastic" – mobile and flexible – able to expand and contract to perform multiple dwelling tasks. Kiesler's laboratory was at the forefront of a design research culture interested in harnessing human perception and behavior in order to facilitate new and evolving systems of capital production and proves an important precedent to educational models interested in the study of mass behavior, visual and corporeal affect, responsive systems, and relational organic structures (Phillips 2010, 93).

While the Laboratory of Design Correlation was permanently shut down in 1941 (Phillips 2010, 113), during its short existence Kiesler sought to better understand and test the inter-active relationship between bodies-in-motion and the environments they inhabit.[13] "In time, Kiesler believed everything eventually becomes networked, relational, and continuous. Correalism as the science and biotechnique as the method, Kiesler argued, would facilitate the production of a total environment, a *Gesamtkunstwerk* of effects…" (Phillips 2010, 99–100). The most fully materialized outcome of the research lab was the design and fabrication of a prototype Mobile-Home-Library. This project reflected a reconceptualization of the typical bookcase, basing its redesign upon biotechnical principles that aimed to create a more integrated and physiologically aligned book storage strategy, capable of accommodating current needs, but also allowing for future adaptability (Figure 6.5). Kiesler describes it as "a *new standard type* and from it we have developed many *variations* adapted to the special needs of the social economy" (Kiesler 1939, 71).

The possibility of extending a correlational approach and biotechnical method beyond the design of the furniture object is a prospect made apparent in the many drawings and physical models Kiesler produced from 1947 to 1961 concerning his unbuilt "endless" house project.[14] This expansion conceives of the body not as a mobile object inhabiting a static physical space, but rather more

192 Bio-Physical Inter-Action

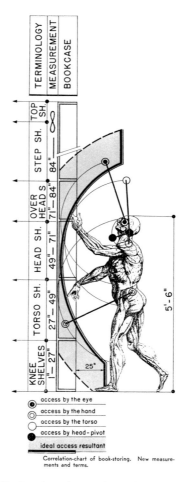

FIGURE 6.5 Frederick Kiesler, Correlation chart of book-storing, drawing, September 1939 (Frederick Kiesler, "On Correalism and Biotechnique. Definition and Test of a New Approach to Building Design," *Architectural Record*, p. 71). © 2020 Austrian Frederick and Lillian Kiesler Private Foundation, Vienna.

deeply as a set of interrelated psychological, physiological *and* environmental systems, maintaining continuous sensual inter-action and feedback between one another. These biological systems principally operate below the conscious surface, selecting and collecting environmental information through the specifically human sensorial apparatuses, thereby constructing "a" world that is the direct product of those immediate sensual experiences. In this sense, even individuals within a species group, who generally maintain the same fundamental set of sensorial constitutions, individually maintain varying abilities, sensitivities and experiences. Therefore, each individual, in all practical terms, constructs and inhabits his/her own individual world – his/her own perceptual and historically specific "bubble."

The Estonian zoologist Jakob von Uexküll conceived of a similar idea through what he called "Umwelt" theory, described succinctly in his short 1934 text "Streifzüge durch die Umwelten von Tieren und Menschen Ein Bilderbuch unsichtbarer Welten" ("A Stroll Through the Worlds of Animals and Men: A Picture Book of Invisible Worlds"). This work adopted a non-anthropocentric vantage point from which to reveal how animals as subjects perceived and processed their surroundings into unique "bubbles" or "self-worlds." An organism's "self-world" is comprised of unique perceptual and effector worlds which together form a closed unit which von Uexküll called the organism's "Umwelt" (Uexküll 1957, 6), and it is the umwelt that most specifically describes the conditions with, and within which, an organism lives its life (Figure 6.6). In this sense, quite literally every species group and really every individual living being independently experiences "the" environment, "the" world, in a unique way relative to their own specific subjectivity as articulated through their own particular sensorial apparatuses, past experiences and socio-cultural milieu.

Italian philosopher Giorgio Agamben describes an important distinction concerning the inter-action between these self-worlds as described by von Uexküll:

> Where classical science saw a single world that comprised within it all living species hierarchically ordered from the most elementary forms up to the higher organisms, Uexküll instead supposes an infinite variety of

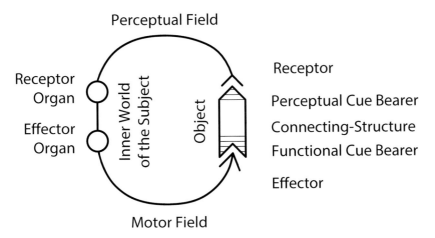

FIGURE 6.6 Jakob von Uexküll and G. Kriszat, functional cycle of perception, diagram, 1934. Redrawn and translated by author from Professor J. Baron Uexküll and G. Kriszat. *Streifzüge durch die Umwelten von Tieren und Menschen; Ein Bilderbuch unsichtbarer Welten, Verständliche Wissenschaf*t, V. 21 (Berlin: Julius Springer, 1934) 7, Fig. 3.

perceptual worlds that, though they are uncommunicating and reciprocally exclusive, are all equally perfect and linked together as if in a gigantic musical score...Thus, Uexküll calls his reconstructions of the environments of the sea urchin, the amoeba, the jellyfish, the sea worm, the sea anemone, the tick (these being their common names), and the other tiny organisms of which he is particularly fond, "excursions in unknowable worlds," because these creatures' functional unity with the environment seems so apparently distant from that of man and the so-called higher animals.

Too often, he affirms, we imagine that the relations a certain animal subject has to the things in its environment take place in the same space and in the same time as those which bind us to the objects in our human world. This illusion rests on the belief in a single world in which all living beings are situated. Uexküll shows that such a unitary world does not exist, just as a space and a time that are equal for all living things do not exist.

(Agamben 2003, 40)

This non-anthropocentric approach to understanding the worlds of non-human organisms provides a departure from a conceptualization of "the" environment or "an" environment – both understood as a priori constructions independent of the organism – to a conception of "its" environment. A unique environmental "bubble" constructed through an assemblage of perceptual-effectual cues intrinsically connecting individual subjectivity to environmental "carriers of significance" – the receptor signs (*Merkzeichen*) that are perceptible by means of an organism's specific sensorial systems (Uexküll 1957, 9) (Figure 6.7). While von Uexküll maintained that "all animals, from the simplest to the most complex, are fitted into their unique worlds with equal completeness"

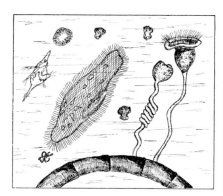
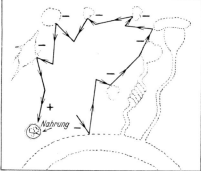

FIGURE 6.7 Jakob von Uexküll and G. Kriszat, Environment and Umwelt of the Paramecium, diagram, 1934. Reprinted from Professor J. Baron Uexküll and G. Kriszat. *Streifzüge durch die Umwelten von Tieren und Menschen; Ein Bilderbuch unsichtbarer Welten, Verständliche Wissenschaft*, V. 21 (Berlin: Julius Springer, 1934) 34, fig. 17.

(Uexküll 1957, 11), he also recognizes that these worlds are "linked" indirectly through perceptual cues (*Merkmal*), which include the actions of other organisms; thus, while solitary, each organism maintains a continuous dialogue with the "external" conditions and other beings outside of itself. Architect Caroline O'Donnell, in the introduction to her book *Niche Tactics*, draws a productive comparison between Le Corbusier's "soap bubble" description of a harmonious architecture derived from a properly regulated interior and the "self-world" bubbles articulated by von Uexküll that are externally derived.

> Von Uexküll's bubble, considered as a model for architecture, could not be more opposed to its Corbusian cousin. While Le Corbusier's bubble represents an architecture formed from internal forces, Von Uexküll's bubble points to an architectural organism which "perceives" and thus responds to a select set of external forces. Moreover, Le Corbusier's bubble is the object of architecture itself, floating in a void, whereas Von Uexküll's bubble reaches out, wraps around, and draws in many excerpts of its environment.
>
> *(O'Donnell 2015, 6)*

Taken together, Kiesler's proposition for a "polydimensional" and "psycho-functional" architectural space of co-relational interactions, with von Uexküll's articulation of the organism's unique construction of a "self-world" through the sensorial engagement with "external forces," presents the possibility for architects to conceive of a "Terrestrial" *architectural* "dwelling place" that is both individually specific, yet in continuous and evolving dialogue with other "self-worlds" – providing a possible means for living, *coping* and *adapting* in this "new" world. For the architect who adopts such a conception, what are the means, materials and design strategies he/she might utilize to construct such an inter-active "place"?

To begin to answer this question, architect Sean Lally (Weathers) makes the point that as organisms detect changes in the "objective" space of their surroundings differently, they will choose to inhabit their "self-world" differently.

> The sensory perceptions of any given creature – its ability to sense a rate of change in its surroundings and therefore make decisions about its own movement in that setting – can make the same locale unique from one creature to the next.
>
> *(Lally 2014, 155)*

For Lally, it is an organism's ability to sense the continuous variations and changes of its surroundings over time that provides architects a new means for cultivating co-productive organism-architecture-environment inter-actions through what he calls "material energies."[15] These energies provide the possibility for soft boundaries with gradient edges, flexible and evolving spatial configurations. Similarly, former NASA engineer and architect Michelle

Addington has advocated for reconceptualizing the building envelope away from an objective physical barrier of external-internal mediation toward a dynamic and transient thermodynamic boundary – "a region in which change occurs" (Addington 2017, 82). She argues that there's been an unwarranted privileging of the surface in architectural design, whether considered as formal exploration, as performative system or as the originator of architectural effects.

> This privileging of the surface emanates from an *a priori* belief that performance is rooted in and perception is determined by geometry. Geometry relentlessly tethers the built environment to static artifacts. And even though we cannot trace a line of causation from the objective precision of the geometrically constructed surface to either the subjective perception of the imagined space or the actual behavior of the constructed wall, we unconditionally accept that the surface is the progenitor – the author – of the resulting effects.
>
> *(Addington 2017, 79–80)*

An alternative is for architecture's surface materialization to be understood not as a kind of hard static wrapper, simply mimicking the outline of the physical body – another skin – but rather that it be "conceived as multiple and layered contour gradients" (Lally 2014, 158). As Lally describes, human-beings are "capable of perceiving gradient energy changes," but our construction and habitation of the world today is dominated by the visual and to a lesser degree the haptic, both largely resulting in expectations of the architectural construct as needing to have "visually perceivable edges and tactile boundaries" (Lally 2014, 157). Addington also argues that most architects would likely consider the architectural boundary and the thermodynamic boundary to be analogous as a means for mediating between two distinct environmental conditions, interior and exterior, yet she rightly points out this assumption fails to acknowledge the temporality of the thermodynamic boundary, a fundamental aspect of its definition (Addington 2017, 83). Lally's proposed design for a residence called the SIM House in 2006 leverages material energy gradients and the temporality of the internal environment through "a shift in energy from the kinetic to potential" (Lally 2007, 27) capable of producing a multiplicity of responses to various conditions of living. He describes these living scenarios as being instigated through "elastic and networked structures of organization (systems of display, illumination and air flow and temperature) as a method to develop configurations that, while dominant, exist simultaneously within form until activated" (Lally 2007, 27). These systems are fully integrated into the project's ceiling/roof design which provides the loose spatial and formal configuration of the house. It was imperative for Lally to utilize advanced simulative software to visualize the fluid dynamics of air temperature and air movement, helping provide feedback as to how these networked environmental systems behaved in relationship to various configurations and material properties (Figures 6.8 and 6.9).

Invisible Worlds **197**

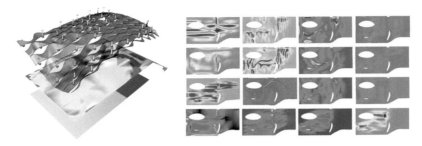

FIGURE 6.8 Sean Lally (Weathers), *SIM House*, simulative thermal studies exploring the various dynamic gradient conditions activated by the different material energies embedded within the roof surface, 2006. Image courtesy of Sean Lally WEATHERS, 2006.

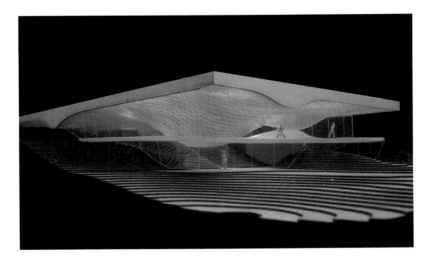

FIGURE 6.9 Sean Lally (Weathers), *SIM House*, physical model study showing the undulation and cellular formation of the roof surface, 2006. Image courtesy of Sean Lally WEATHERS, 2006.

Like the static building envelope, the typical implementation of modern heating, ventilating and air-conditioning (HVAC) systems, concerned with producing stable and uniform interior climates within a predetermined thermal "comfort zone," significantly negates the possibility for inhabitant growth in response to changing or gradient conditions of interior atmosphere (also see Chapter 1). On this point, Addington makes the following analysis:

> The incredible array of thermal behaviors – temperature / density stratifications; transient conditions; wide ranging velocities; laminar and turbulent flows; buoyant plumes; convective, conductive and radiant

transfer; mass transfer, and randomly moving objects – are all mixed together and diluted in the black box. Indeed the human body becomes an
almost unwelcome perturbation that disrupts the efficient functioning of
the HVAC system.

(Addington 2017, 84)

Conceiving and designing the "Terrestrial" *architectural* "dwelling place"
based upon gradient energies and a reconsideration of architectural boundaries
generates the capacity for it to interface dynamically with inhabitant sensorial
systems. In keeping with Kiesler's "elastic" architectural environment and von
Uexküll's conception of *umwelt*, this is an approach that may directly convey
information to inhabitants through multiple stimuli, to provoke previously
unrealized possibilities of action and flexible habitation. Lally suggests that the
architectural environment could even be designed to heighten an inhabitant's sensorial abilities through what he calls "amplification." This reflects a kind of
enhancement of individual sensorial systems as well as the possibility of providing extra-sensory abilities to access stimuli normally out of range and, in turn,
provide an expanded field of possible actions.

In order for various energies in the environment to be useful as information, the body needs to be able to perceive them. Our surroundings do
not suffer from a lack of such information coursing through them; the issue is more that humans are not always able to sense that distinct material
and act upon the information it contains.

(Lally 2014, 156)

To effectively consider Lally's "amplification" approach, the different ways
human-beings take in and receive perceptual information must be appreciated.
The specifics of these bio-physical sensorial mechanisms will directly affect
how architects might design aspects of the constructed environment intent on
amplifying existing stimuli or even to provide access to new ones. This approach effectively creates "carriers of significance" received by an inhabitant's
sensorial receptors in the form of energy or chemicals, thereby expanding the
individual's construction of its *umwelt*. Those signals received by receptors as
energy (i.e. light, heat, pressure, etc.) are translated into data that is then sent
to the brain for processing, an essential process referred to as transduction.[16]
Depending upon how a receptor translates the initial informational stimuli,
the brain then makes decisions about how to react, usually autonomically, like
in respiration or internal thermal regulation but sometimes with direct conscious intention demonstrated through behavioral responses or even in advance
through the premeditated activities of utilizing tools, growing food or building
shelter.[17] If signals are received as chemicals, they may be capable of react-
ing biochemically directly with or on the central nervous system to induce

physiological responses.[18] These energy and chemical stimuli have the potential to effectively become new "materials" for the architect to deploy, constructing new spaces, boundaries and experiences of environment.

As discussed already the environments we inhabit, whether constructed or natural, provide information – stimuli – which we receive and respond. The deeper physiological effort of the body has always been to maintain an internal state of continuity that allows it to function effectively and efficiently, maintaining a general internal level of stability, health and well-being. This concept referred to as homeostasis is one articulated in modern terms in the twentieth century by Walter B. Cannon most thoroughly in his 1932 book *The Wisdom of the Body*. A key difference between the concepts of simply maintaining equilibrium, as compared to homeostasis, is that equilibrium is a static condition of equality within a closed system, where homeostasis reflects a complex dynamic equilibrium of an open system across a threshold. Though first conceptualized by Claude Bernard and presented to the Académe des Sciences in 1865 in his *Introduction á l'étude de la medicine expérimentale* (*An Introduction to the Study of Experimental Medicine*), the modern use of the term homeostasis was introduced by Cannon,[19] which he defined in the following way:

> The coordinated physiological processes which maintain most of the steady states in the organisms are so complex and so peculiar to living beings – involving, as they may, the brain and nerves, the heart, lungs, kidneys and spleen, all working cooperatively – that I have suggested a special designation for these states, *homeostasis*.
>
> *(Cannon 1963, 24)*

Cannon later refers to Bernard's claim that an individual's ability to maintain its "milieu interne" across a great number of different changing external environmental stimuli directly corresponds to the organism itself (Cannon 1963, 287). He makes the point that the level of ability an organism exhibits towards effectively maintaining a homeostatic internal state directly reflects its level of evolutionary development and, consequently, a greater level of freedom and independence of action regardless of the external conditions. "And the course of evolution of higher organisms has been characterized by a gradually increasing control of the functions of that *milieu* as an environmental and conditioning agency" (Cannon 1963, 287), an agency in which architecture now plays an integral part.

Through the development and design of the *architectural environment*, human-beings have displaced aspects of this internal homeostatic strategy to the outside of the body; it serves to effectively buffer detrimental external environmental stimuli through the creation of a mediated interior space of habitation, thereby reducing to some extent the responsibility of those internal physiological systems. In keeping with Lally's concept of "amplification" alongside the use of energy and chemical stimuli as new "materials" for design, the *architectural environment* acts not only as a buffer, but could also serve to strengthen desirable stimuli and/or selectively introduce new stimuli with the intent of bio-physically activating humans in co-productive ways. This possibility for an architectural design approach of multi-sensorial stimulation may, through habitation, effectively remake or reconstruct the individual "self-worlds" in which we each live and, if extended outwards, even possibly the larger collective world-ecology.

★ ★ ★

> Having a body includes having a world, one of a particular kind. This is a world in which elements or events are dispersed and sited. The body, through its senses and its movements, configures the world or, more precisely, each body generates a person who originates, read co-originates, the world.
>
> *(Arakawa and Gins 1994, 18)*

Artists Shūsaku Arakawa and Madeline Gins describe above their conception of how the "body" makes, or what they call "configures," the "world" through its imbedded sensorial systems — a multi-sensorial approach that maintains an ongoing set of co-originating inter-actions. Extending these multi-sensorial potentials of construction out further to consider how the *architectural environment* may stimulate bio-physical effects, both consciously through determined action but also at the deeper level of the unconscious or the autonomic, would require architects to radically reconsider their approach to its design. In the companion book to their 2018 Cooper Hewitt exhibition "The Senses: Design Beyond Vision," curators Ellen Lupton and Andrea Lipps describe the potential effects of such an approach in the following way:

> Sensory design considers not just the shape of things but how things shape us — our behavior, our emotions, out truth. Sensations respond to an insistent, ever-changing environment. When our body presses into the cushioned surface of a chair, both body and chair give and react. We grab objects in order to use them as tools for breaking, bending, mashing, or joining together other objects and materials. Tools are active extensions of our sense of touch. Tasting food is more than a chemical response — it involves the muscular, skeletal action of crushing and transforming matter. We use our senses to change our world.
>
> *(Lupton and Lipps 2018, 15)*

This sensorial approach to the conceptualization and materialization of the *architectural environment* would need to embrace those energy and chemical sensorial stimuli typically regarded as technical afterthoughts within the design process, elements like light, air composition, temperature and relative humidity, as aspects fundamental to architecture's formation and construction. In the context of their description of Nietzschean esthetics and the current advancements within the life sciences, architects Philippe Rahm and Jean-Gilles Décosterd in their 2002 essay "Physiological Architecture" describe how our relationship to the world today is less about representation and more a matter of "internal modification of the mechanisms for perceiving and generating form" (Rahm and Décosterd 2002, 4). They go as far as to redefine our understanding of the art object, its definition and its ability to interface between external and internal environments.

> In this evolution, the art object no longer merely emerges from a representation of the external world, but also from a physiological stimulus exercised directly on the metabolism. The function of the senses tends to expand. They are no longer limited to receiving information that would then be culturally or psychologically decoded by thought. Rather, they are becoming an interface in the transmission of biological, chemical, physical, and electromagnetic information between the external and the internal environments, between the extra-corporeal space in which information is emitted by objects outside our body and corporeal space, that of the nervous and endocrine systems.
>
> *(Rahm and Décosterd 2002, 4–5) (Figure 6.10)*

This approach allots the architect an opportunity to inculcate a more active inter-action between the *architectural environment* and those individuals who inhabit its spaces towards the direct stimulation of co-productive bio-physical effects. In this way the architectural surround, which buffers and contains, might not be thought of as a singularly defined construction, intent on producing equilibrium and uniformity of experience, but rather a dynamic, layered and multi-sensorial physical construction of continuous engagement. As previously suggested by Addington and described by Lally, "a multilayered series of sensory edges that extend beyond the skin" (Lally 2014, 172) made from "material energies" and is simply "a region in which change occurs" (Addington 2017, 82). Rahm and Décosterd describe this transformation in the following way:

> What is taking shape through this research is a possible re-engagement of the human being in the sensory world. Light and climate are acquiring a physical weight, which goes beyond mere visual mediation, and are becoming a genuine architectural material in the formulation of our space, our bodies, and our emotions.
>
> *(Rahm and Décosterd 2002, 10)*

Since forming his independent architectural design office, Philippe Rahm has further developed a contemporary theory for an architecture reconceived from

202 Bio-Physical Inter-Action

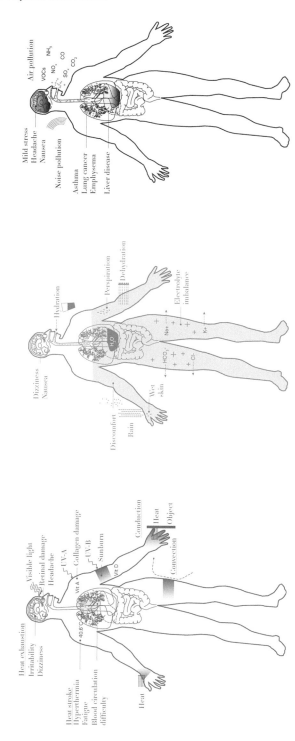

FIGURE 6.10 Philippe Rahm architectes, *Central Park*, human physiological diagrams. Image courtesy of Philippe Rahm architectes.

Invisible Worlds **203**

the basis of a multi-sensorial and physiologically engaging architectural project. He has described his approach as adopting an extreme openness towards reality, referring to these "material energies" of "relative humidity levels, the temperature gradient, light intensity, and spectrality [as] the elements of architectural language that are called into question in producing an architectural project" (Rahm 2008, 171). Like Kiesler before him, this approach no longer adheres to spatial or functional requirements as the motivation for designing architecture; instead, it is the effect of an interior climate on human physiology which provides the primary force behind design and the reception of the *architectural environment*. Rahm uses words like "meteorology" or "weather" to describe his projects, considering the definition, construction, materialization and experience of his architecture as the literal creation of internalized climates. In 2006, Rahm titled his installation at the Canadian Center for Architecture (CCA) "Interior weather," which aimed to both produce and measure the construction of fluctuating internal climatic conditions to produce a "micro-geography." The installation was specifically interested in testing how the fluctuating confluences of three climatic factors – temperature, light intensity and relative humidity – might challenge twentieth-century ideas about the use and program of spaces (Rahm 2006a, 118) (Figure 6.11). In this way, the definition, design and construction of a space composed of these fundamental meteorological elements was intended to open up the possibilities for how a person might perceive the constructed environment through a multi-sensory and/or sensual experience, capable of provoking alternative and evolving conceptions of use.

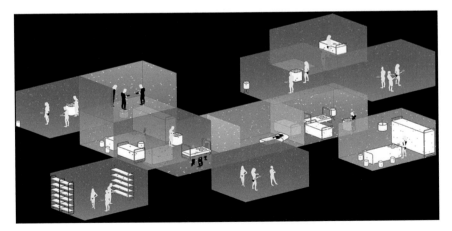

FIGURE 6.11 Philippe Rahm architectes, *Interior Weather,* drawing showing multiple interior climatic conditions, installed as part of Canadian Centre for Architecture (CCA) exhibition "Environment: Approaches for Tomorrow," curated by Giovanna Borasi and Mirko Zardini, Montreal, Canada, 2006. Image courtesy of Philippe Rahm architectes.

Again like Kiesler, Rahm aims to define use not through preconceived spatial planning or divisions related to socio-cultural expectations, but rather by associating different climatic conditions with various bio-physical needs related to particular functional tasks. One gallery space of the installation was used to simulate a constant fluctuation of these three climatic factors, continuously modifying them in real time and generating data from their interactions.

> The situations are then interpreted from different points of view: physiological, social, functional, etc. These interpretations initially draw on recognized physiological values, such as the relationship between the temperature of the space and the type of bodily activity or clothing it suggests, or between light intensity and hormonal activity. The data are then feely reinterpreted in "fictions" suggesting new spatial practices, new forms of social behavior, and new urban and architectural forms.
>
> (Rahm 2006a, 120) (Figure 6.12)

This approach is a rejection of the adage coined by Louis Sullivan in the late nineteenth century of "form follows function," or the later reworking of the

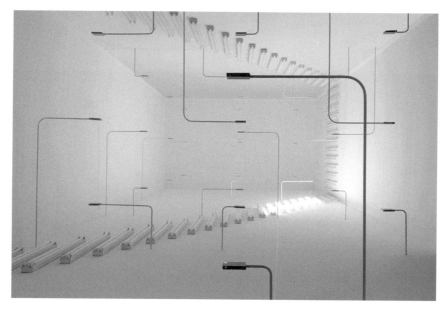

FIGURE 6.12 Philippe Rahm architectes, *Interior Weather,* image of installation, installed as part of Canadian Centre for Architecture (CCA) exhibition "Environment: Approaches for Tomorrow," curated by Giovanna Borasi and Mirko Zardini, Montreal, Canada, 2006. Image courtesy of Philippe Rahm architectes.

saying by Louis Kahn of "function follows form" to instead one of "form and function follow climate" (Rahm 2006b, 152).

The meteorological is explored in many of Rahm's projects developed since his earlier collaborations with Décosterd, and is well illustrated by several residential project proposals. His design for Mollier Houses, proposed in 2005 to be built on a lake in Vassivière en Limousin, France, contends that various activities undertaken in the domestic environment require, and are the result of, the relationship between the level of water vapor (relative humidity) and temperature. Rahm chose to use this one specific climatic relationship to facilitate the design for the houses, resulting in the total reorganization of domestic programs. This approach disregarded the traditional individualization of rooms intended to accommodate singular functions to instead redefine the spaces according to their necessary level of relative humidity, from the driest to the most humid.

> The problems of the degree of humidity in the air, its regulation within the home, and the distribution of air in space according to its temperature density, define, by their physical and sensory nature, the organization of the building in plan and section. New typologies of habitat appear, unexpected, not based on modern house planning, with its divisions between day and night, intimate and public, but emerging from the sensual and physiological results of the treatment of building techniques. Climates for living in.
>
> *(Philippe Rahm architectes 2019a)*

The spaces were scaled accordingly with the driest being the smallest and the wettest the largest, then organized concentrically in plan and offset vertically in section to best take advantage of the natural air flows on the site for ventilation, heating and cooling (Figure 6.13). Different domestic functions were then assigned to one of the spaces simply corresponding to its respective moisture and temperature requirements. The result was a reorganization of the typical program spaces where elements of the kitchen and bathroom were part of the same space because they both required a greater level of relative humidity. In this way, the house didn't program domestic spaces separately by use, but rather according to the inhabitant's bio-physical needs, effectively creating new programmatic correspondences and alternative domestic possibilities.

Taking a similar approach, but this time focusing on the climatic parameter of temperature, Rahm designed and installed an apartment prototype, which he called "Domestic Astronomy," at the Louisiana Museum of Modern Art's exhibition "Green Architecture for the Future" in Humlebæk, Denmark, in 2009. The installation occupied a gallery space of 225 square meters and sought to reconsider the typical arrangement and organization of domestic spaces through the creation of a temporal interior atmosphere, defined principally by temperature and the related process of convection (Figures 6.14 and 6.15). Like the Mollier Houses, rather than starting from a premeditated notion of a spatial compartmentalization to delineate individual functions, "Domestic Astronomy" adhered to the thermal

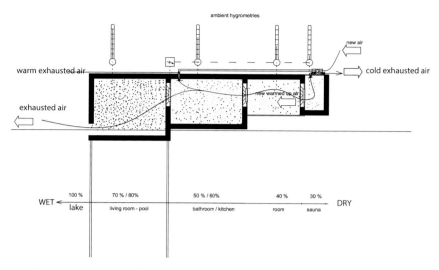

FIGURE 6.13   Philippe Rahm architectes, *Mollier Houses*, section drawing showing route of the air ventilation and repartition of the vapor, Vassivière en Limousin, France, 2005. Image courtesy of Philippe Rahm architectes.

expectations of different spaces, but spatially organized them in relationship to temperature. Using this principle, the space was continuous as was the atmosphere it contained, but through the manipulation of heat and light, various atmospheric conditions were created to define spaces suitable for various domestic activities and also anticipated the type of clothing inhabitants would be wearing in each atmosphere. "Accordingly, the spaces where one is naked will be heated more intensely while the spaces through which one merely passes or those where one is dressed more warmly must be colder" (Philippe Rahm architectes 2019b). The project also took advantage of the physical properties of air movement within the space related to temperature differentials – convection – specifically harnessing heat energies that rise to the ceiling. In this way, the design approach resulted in a vertical rather than a horizontal configuration, utilizing energy that would otherwise be lost to create a more energy efficient domestic space, but also one that prioritized energy as a primary generator of the design.

> Our purpose today is to take into account these physical disparities in the distribution of temperatures in the space and to take advantage of them in order to transform the way of inhabiting space by leaving the exclusivity of a horizontal mode of habitation in the interior for a vertical mode of inhabitation where one can inhabit different thermal zones, different strata, different altitudes.
>
> *(Philippe Rahm architectes, 2019b)*

Invisible Worlds **207**

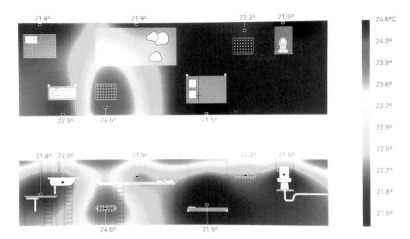

FIGURE 6.14 Philippe Rahm architectes, *Domestic Astronomy*, thermal section diagram, installed as part of the Louisiana Museum of Modern Art exhibition "Green Architecture for the Future," curated by Kjeld Kjeldsen, Humlebæk, Denmark, 2009. Image courtesy of Philippe Rahm architectes.

FIGURE 6.15 Philippe Rahm architectes, *Domestic Astronomy,* photo of installation, installed as part of the Louisiana Museum of Modern Art exhibition "Green Architecture for the Future," curated by Kjeld Kjeldsen, Humlebæk, Denmark, 2009. Photograph courtesy of Philippe Rahm architectes.

Therefore, the most critical design decision was to determine the location and source of radiant heat, in conjunction with the anticipated process of convection within the space. The only heat source within the installation was achieved through the diagonal placement of two sets of electric lights – one incandescent and the other compact fluorescent – harnessing the otherwise discarded radiation emitted by the activation and use of these light bulbs. The actual light emitted by the bulbs was conceived simply as a convenient consequence to their function as the primary heat source. Rahm referred to this as a "collusion between heat and light" (Philippe Rahm architectes 2019b), responsible for creating the dynamic interior meteorology that both describes and prescribes the interior atmosphere, and thus how the different domestic spaces organize themselves in space and time. The diagonal placement and location in section, as well as the two different types of bulbs, created in the space a "thermal plug" higher up, facilitating the heated air below to spread out horizontally, instigating the creation of thermal variations and consequently different domestic functions depending on one's location in the space and the variable intensity of the bulbs. The intent was not to recreate the natural world within the interior, but rather to construct an interior environment that takes advantage of the integrated flows between different inhabitants, energies and spaces.

> Our purpose today is to reintroduce in the interior a sort of second astronomy whose purpose will be in no way naturalistic but on the contrary will come directly from the center of artificial means of creating artificial interior climates of modernity. It is in this way that we propose to reassemble a whole, to recompose in a single unit, the different climatic elements separated by the techniques of the building industry for constructing a global interior ecosystem as a new sort of astronomy of the interior where temperature, light, time, and space recombine into one single atmosphere, a single temporality, a geography.
>
> *(Philippe Rahm architectes 2019b)*

This approach embodies much of Kiesler's correalist and "psycho-functional" project as well as, through its evolving multi-sensorial climatic stimuli, an energetic definition of space capable of providing new forms of "freedom and variability," [20] and new ways of living in correspondence with direct bio-physical inter-actions. Of Rahm's work in general, journalist Erin Bucknell writes, "By combining science with a deep awareness of the body, Rahm's multi-sensory architecture performs a pedagogical function, wherein its occupants are no longer passive users of space but active learners about the changing climate they inhabit" (Bucknell 2018).

Perhaps the most sensorially complex and expansive project Rahm has completed to date, taking into account not just the sensorial and physiological systems of human inhabitants, but also the complex inter-actions with an existing and proposed urban fabric and green space, is his design of the Central Park and Meteorological Garden, located in Taichung City, Taiwan, and completed in July 2015. The project is located on a 70-hectare area of land – the site of a former airport north of the city center – intended to provide a new urban green space supporting various sports, leisure and tourist activities within this developing area of the city. Given the city's naturally intense subtropical environment of high heat and high humidity, Rahm aimed to mitigate these harsh climatic conditions through the insertion of a series of natural and artificial "climatic devices" into the Central Park space (Rahm 2017, 88). This approach required a high level of contextual knowledge about the climatological factors of the existing site area as well as the surrounding urban context. Rahm chose to focus on the three most impactful existing climatic conditions affecting the habitation of the park: heat, humidity and atmospheric pollution. Using a computational fluid dynamic (CFD) simulation model, he first produced "gradation climactic maps" that document the variation and intensity of each parameter throughout the existing park site area.

> The three maps intersect and overlap randomly in order to create a diversity of microclimates and a multitude of different sensual experiences in different areas of the park that we could freely occupy depending the hour of the days or the month in the year. At a certain place for example, the air will be less humid and less polluted but it will still be warm, whilst elsewhere in the park, the air will be cooler and dryer, but will remain polluted.
>
> *(Rahm 2017, 89) (Figure 6.16)*

From this more nuanced localized understanding of the dynamic atmospheric conditions of the site, Rahm then developed the specific "climatic devices" that could be strategically inserted throughout the park to lower, reduce, invert and diminish the excessive heat, humidity and pollution within selected localized areas identified through the simulations (Rahm 2017, 89) (Figure 6.17).

Depending on the existing atmospheric condition in question, these "climatic devices" can be loosely organized into those that cool, dry or depollute, each taking a different form of either natural means, like the simple addition of a specific species of tree with leaves or frond particular to shading, sheltering, evaporating, absorbing or filtering, or a variety of artificial architectural pavilion structures. These architectural insertions generally operate on atmospheric phenomena like convection, conduction, evaporation or reflection as well as simply blocking and filtering unwanted elements (Rahm 2017, 90). While the natural strategies are all achieved through the selection and planting of specific tree species with desirable atmospheric effects, the artificial architectural solutions are more varied, assigned names like "Antycyclone" and "Underground breeze," both emitting cold air produced through an underground heat exchange, or "Dry cloud" and "Desert wind," both blowing air dried by silicate gel more capable of absorbing excess humidity, and "Ozone eclipse," which blows in filtered air without pollutants (Figures 6.18 and 6.19).

210 Bio-Physical Inter-Action

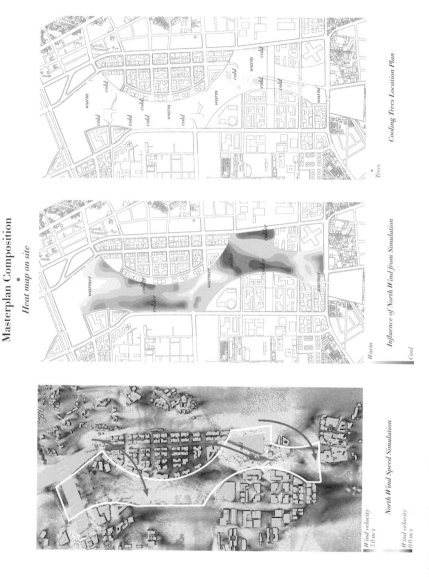

FIGURE 6.16 Philippe Rahm architectes, *Central Park, The Meteorological Garden*, diagrams of masterplan composition, Taichung, Taiwan, 2012–2020. Philippe Rahm architectes, Mosbach paysagistes, Ricky Liu & Associates. Images courtesy of Philippe Rahm architectes.

Invisible Worlds **211**

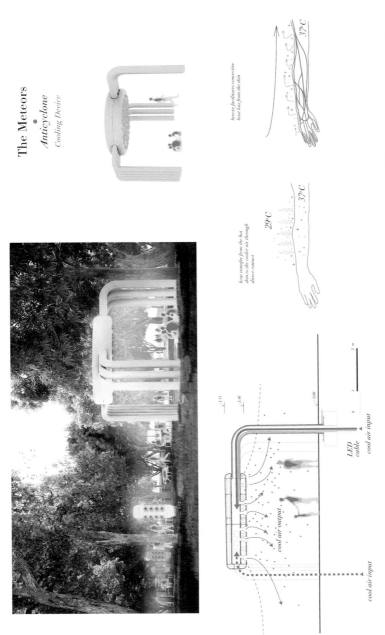

FIGURE 6.17 Philippe Rahm architectes, *Central Park, The Meteorological Garden*, diagrams of Anticyclone cooling device, Taichung, Taiwan, 2012–2020. Philippe Rahm architectes, Mosbach paysagistes, Ricky Liu & Associates. Images courtesy of Philippe Rahm architectes.

212 Bio-Physical Inter-Action

FIGURE 6.18 Philippe Rahm architectes, *Central Park, The Meteorological Garden*, photo Cold Light radiation cooling device, Taichung, Taiwan, 2012–2020. Philippe Rahm architectes, Mosbach paysagistes, Ricky Liu & Associates. Images courtesy of Philippe Rahm architectes.

FIGURE 6.19 Philippe Rahm architectes, *Central Park, The Meteorological Garden*, photo Stratus Cloud evaporative cooling device Taichung, Taiwan, 2012–2020. Philippe Rahm architectes, Mosbach paysagistes, Ricky Liu & Associates. Images courtesy of Philippe Rahm architectes.

Through the strategic dispersal of these "climatic devices" throughout the park, previously, slight differentials in temperature, humidity and pollution were amplified, achieving micro-climates of habitation (Figure I.8). Rahm, however, makes clear that his design intent was not to dictate a plan for how people (or other living beings) *should* inhabit the park, but rather that through insertion of these devices the existing climatic conditions could be modulated to increase the possibility for greater comfort and sensual experience based upon individual preference.

> According to the density and quantity of climatic devices in a given area, we create spaces more or less enjoyable, more or less comfortable, thus the different climatic properties sometimes overlap, separate, regroupe, densify, dilute, generating a variety of atmospheres where the users can choose and appropriate as they see fit.
>
> *(Rahm 2017, 105)*

In this sense, the design of the Central Park and Meteorological Garden is not about mediating the existing atmosphere-environment to create spaces dedicated for one type of human habitation; instead, it aspires to create further variation, flexibility of use and preference depending upon one's particular physiological, psychological and energetic state. It acknowledges the fluctuating and dynamic reality of both the ecological and constructed environments, accepting this quality not as something to overcome and control, but to amplify and inter-act with. This attitude describes an alternative approach for architects operating within a world beyond climatological-ecological "crisis" currently undergoing radical changes. It reflects a position of active multi-sensorial engagement and localized interventions intent on the amplification of habitable conditions, and not the desire or demand for an impossible domination of nature "out there." It cultivates local specificities that build upon the existing dynamic conditions of both the ecological and constructed environments for the benefit of both, and simultaneously preserves variability.

The final two chapters will further explore the articulation of an architectural theory of design founded upon the amplification of human sensorial systems as well as the recognition of a correalist understanding of our evolving *architectural environments* of habitation, to consider the possibility for architecture to engage with inhabitants, and co-productively inter-act with them. This possibility extends the *architectural environment* beyond operating as an active *participant* to instead become an active *stimulator* of bio-physical effects capable of impacting current and future inhabitant states of development. Sean Lally describes such a potential succinctly when he says, "Architecture no longer needs to be reflexive to knowledge learned about the body; it can now precipitate the body's development!" (Lally 2014, 175). It must however be immediately stated that the intention behind discussing such a possibility for bio-physical stimulation through designed environmental conditions and inter-actions is not

214 Bio-Physical Inter-Action

to advocate for an architecture of greater panoptical control in the service of "bio-power"[21]; rather, its aim is to advocate for the co-productive potential of such an approach towards the fulfillment of greater "freedom and variability" within the architectural construct, providing inhabitants the ability to explore and create their own "Terrestrial" *architectural* "dwelling place." This approach is capable of more co-productive relations with, and within, the changing world-ecology but also with, and within, our physiological, psychological and even spiritual constitutions, supporting a deep affirmation for the life of all constituent beings.

Notes

1 The essay was first published in the September 1939 issue of *Architectural Record*, but as stated in a note on the first page of the article the groundwork for the piece was laid earlier in an unpublished manuscript titled "From Architecture to Life" from 1930, and first presented in its present form at a Symposium on Science and Design held by the alumnae association of MIT on June 6, 1938.

2 This definition is similar to Mumford's use of the word technics; see Lewis Mumford, *Technics and Civilization* (New York: Harcourt Brace Jovanovich, 1963) 52.

3 "Nineteenth-century architecture was demonized as unhealthy, and sun, light, ventilation, exercise, roof terraces, hygiene, and whiteness were offered as means to prevent, if not cure tuberculosis. The publicity campaign of modern architecture was organized around contemporary beliefs about tuberculosis and fears of disease"; see Colomina and Wigley (2017, 112).

4 As it relates to Le Corbusier's early urban planning reform proposals see his 1924 book *Urbanisme* (*The City of Tomorrow*) and his book *La Ville Radieuse* (*The Radiant City*) published in 1933. Also, see Chapter Three "The City of Tomorrow 1910–1933," Kenneth Frampton, *Le Corbusier* (New York: Thames & Hudson Inc., 2001) 46–57.

5 Most specifically, reinforced concrete and steel.

6 On this point, see Le Corbusier, *Towards a new architecture*, trans. Frederick Etchells (New York: Dover Publications, Inc., 1986) 47 and 198.

7 Italics added here for emphasis.

8 In his book *Modern Architecture: A Critical History* architectural historian Kenneth Frampton defines Loos's concept of "raumplan" as "'plan of volumes,' a complex system of internal organization that culminated in the split-level houses realized towards the end of his life" and described its apotheosis in the Moller and Müller houses through "the torturous manipulation of the available volume of the prism as though it were just so much raw material from which to create dynamic composition in section." See Kenneth Frampton, *Modern Architecture: A Critical History* (New York: Oxford University Press, 1980), 93–94. And for a more nuanced definition see Johan van de Beek, "Adolf Loos – patterns of town houses," in *Raumplan Versus Plan Libre: Adolf Loos and Le Corbusier, 1919–1930*, ed. Max Risselada (New York: Rizzoli, 1987), 27–46.

9 This desire was incorporated into various residential projects by many early modernists, like Le Corbusier, Walter Gropius, Marcel Breuer, R. M. Schindler and Richard Neutra, but also coincided with the general Modernist approach; see Chapter eleven "Designing the Body," Colomina and Wigley (2017, 166–177).

10 In this more empirical, more scientifically minded approach to design the utilization of data is intended to inform and ultimately substantiate specific design strategies and elements for the benefits of those who inhabit these spaces, relying on typical norms. For a general overview of evidence-based design, see D. Kirk Hamilton

and David H. Watkins, *Evidence-based design for multiple building types* (Hoboken, NJ: John Wiley & Sons, Inc., 2009).

11 "The radicalism of Kiesler's architecture, detached from any sense of ground or stasis, separated Kiesler from the architects of the modern movement"; see Colomina (2008, 24).

12 See Phillips (2010, 117, n. 15, and 97). Kiesler also makes the claim in a note in "On Correlation and Biotechnique" that he used the term in a treatise on "Town Planning" as "Vitalbau," published in *De Stijl*, no. 10/11 in 1925, but it was not published in America until May 1934 in *Hound and Horn*; see Kiesler (1939, 67, n.★).

13 This line of thinking likely originates both from Adolf Loos as well as from Kiesler's early experiences in avant-garde theater as a teacher of stage design and practices and later as manager and scenic director at the Julliard School of Music where he worked from 1934 to 1957; see Phillips (2010, 93–94).

14 For a more detailed overview of the Endless House project, see the publication *Friedrich Kiesler: Endless House*, produced in conjunction with a 2003 exhibition "Endless House" at the Museum für Moderne Kunst Frankfurt am Main; see *Friedrich Kiesler: endless house/Friedrich Kiesler-Zentrum* Wien (Ostfildern-Ruit: Hatje Cantz, 2003). And for a more general discussion of Kiesler's "endless" theme throughout his work, see Dieter Bogner and Peter Noever, eds., and MAK-Center for Art Architecture, Los Angeles, *Frederick J. Kiesler: Endless space* (New York: Hatje Cantz, 2001).

15 Lally defines *material energies* as "the stimuli and information within our surrounding context that the human body can perceive. More specifically, material energies produce the boundaries and edges that define space"; see Lally (2014, 95).

16 See *Encyclopedia Britannica Online*, s.v. "Senses" (by Michael Land), https://www.britannica.com/science/senses (accessed March 31, 2020).

17 Humans may be regarded as the most prolific species able to engage with the *conscious* construction of their environment; however, it should be noted that many other species also demonstrate such actions. There are ants that gather and mulch leaves creating garden beds where they sow fungal spores to grow their food; many species of birds make nests, but many also use tools like the Green Heron that creates fishing lures to entice small fish to the surface; bearded capuchin monkeys place nuts on pitted stone anvils before precisely hitting them with large rocks to extract the nuts; and various ape species such as Chimpanzees, Bonobos and Orangutans build complex nest-like constructions in the trees to nap, keep away insects and stay warm.

18 See *Encyclopedia Britannica Online*, s.v. "Senses" (by Michael Land), https://www.britannica.com/science/senses (accessed March 31, 2020).

19 See Steven J. Cooper, "From Claude Bernard to Walter Cannon. Emergence of the concept of homeostasis," *Appetite*, 51 (2008) 419–427.

20 As previously described in Chapter 1 by Reyner Banham.

21 As explored extensively in the work of Michel Foucault; see *Discipline and Punish: The Birth of the Prison*, trans. Alan Sheridan (New York: Vintage Boks, 1979); *The Birth of Biopolitics: Lectures at the Collège de France, 1978-1979*, trans. Graham Burchell (Hampshire, UK: Palgrave Macmillian, 2008); and as it specifically relates to modern architecture see Sven-Olov Wallenstein, *Biopolitics and the Emergence of Modern Architecture* (New York: Princeton Architectural Press, 2009).

References

Addington, D. Michelle. 2017. The unbounded boundary. In *Thermodynamic interactions: An architectural exploration into physiological, material, territorial atmospheres*, ed. Javier García-Germán, 79–87. New York: Actar Publishers.

Agamben, Giorgio. 2003. *The open: Man and animal.* Trans. Kevin Attell. Stanford, CA: Stanford University Press.

Arakawa and Madeline Gins. 1994. *Architecture: Sites of reversible destiny (Architectural experiments after Auschwitz-Hiroshima)*. Art and Design Monographs. London: Academy Editions.

Bucknell, Erin. 2018. Architecture you can smell? A brief history of multi-sensory design. *Metropolis*, October 11. https://www.metropolismag.com/architecture / multisensory-architecture-design-history.

Cannon, Walter B. 1963. *The wisdom of the body*. New York: WW Norton & Company Inc.

Colomina, Beatriz. 1994. *Privacy and publicity: Modern architecture as mass media*. Cambridge, MA: The MIT Press.

———. 2008. Endless drawing: Architecture as self-analysis. In *Drawing Papers 77: Frederick Kiesler co-realities*. New York: The Drawing Center, 16–32.

Colomina, Beatriz and Mark Wigley. 2017. *Are we human? Notes on an archaeology of design*. Zürich: Lars Müller Publishers.

Kiesler, Frederick. 1926. Space city architecture. In *Programs and manifestos on 20th-century architecture*, English edition, ed. Ulrich Conrads, trans. Michael Bullock, 98. Cambridge, MA: The MIT Press, 1970.

———. 1930. *Contemporary art applied to the store and its display*. New York: Brentano's.

———. 1934. Notes on architecture: The space-house. In *Frederick J. Kiesler selected writings*, eds. Siegfried Gohr and Gunda Luyken, 23–29. Stuttgart: Verlag Gerd Hatje, 1996.

———. 1939. On correalism and biotechnique: A definition and test of a new approach to building design. *Architectural Record* 86 (September): 60–75.

———. 1949. Pseudo-functionalism in modern architecture. In *Frederick Kiesler 1890–1965*, ed. Yehuda Safran, 56–60. London: The Architectural Association, 1989.

Lally, Sean. 2007. Potential energies. In *Softspace: From a representation of form to a simulation of space*, eds. Sean Lally and Jessica Young, 25–37. London: Routledge.

———. 2014. *The air from other planets: A brief history of architecture to come*. Zürich: Lars Müller Publishers.

Loos, Adolf. 1910. Architecture. In *The architecture of Adolf Loos: An arts council exhibition*, 104–109. Trans. Wilfried Wang, ed. Yehunda Safran and Wilfried Wang. London: The Arts Council of Great Britain, 1985.

Lupton, Ellen, and Andrea Lipps. 2018. *The senses: Design beyond vision*. New York: Cooper Hewitt, Smithsonian Design Museum and Princeton Architectural Press.

Neutra, Richard. 1954. *Survival through Design*. New York: Oxford University Press.

O'Donnell, Caroline. 2015. *Niche tactics: Generative relationships between architecture and site*. New York: Routledge.

Philippe Rahm architectes. 2019a. Description of the Mollier Houses, 2005. http:// www.philipperahm.com/data/projects/mollierhouses/index.html.

———. 2019b. Description of the "domestic astronomy" installation at the Louisiana Museum of Modern Art, 2009. http://www.philipperahm.com/data/projects/domesticastronomy/index.html.

Phillips, Stephen. 2010. Toward a research practice: Frederick Kiesler's design-correlation laboratory. In *Grey Room* 38 (Winter): 90–120.

Rahm, Philippe. 2006a. Interior weather. In *Environ(ne)ment: Approaches for-tomorrow*, trans. Marie Aquilino, Guillemette Morel Journel, John Tittensor and Alice Winkler, 118–121. Milan: Canadian Centre for Architecture/Skira.

———. 2006b. Form and function follow climate. In *Environ(ne)ment: Approaches for-tomorrow*, trans. Marie Aquilino, Guillemette Morel Journel, John Tittensor and Alice Winkler, 152–159. Milan: Canadian Centre for Architecture/Skira.

————. 2008. In architecture, precisely. In *Precisions: Architecture between Sciences and the Arts*, eds. Ákos Moravánszky and Ole W. Fischer, 166–195. Berlin: Jovis Verlag.

————. 2017. Jade Mateo Park. In *Thermodynamic interactions: An architectural exploration into physiological, material, territorial atmospheres*, ed. Javier García-Germán, 88–107. New York: Actar Publishers.

Rahm, Philippe and Jean-Gilles Décosterd. 2002. Physiological architecture. In *Physiological architecture: Published for the exhibition at Swiss pavilion as part of the 8th International Architecture Exhibition at Venice 2002*, 2–16. Basel: Birkhäuser.

Uexküll, Jakob von. 1957. A stroll through the worlds of animals and men: A picture book of invisible worlds. In *Instinctive behavior: The development of a modern concept*, trans. and ed. Claire H. Schiller, 5–80. New York: International Universities Press, Inc.

7

BEYOND THE PROSTHESIS

Architectural Augmentation and Human Evolution

> Man, alone among all organisms, knows that he evolves and he alone is capable of directing his own evolution. For him evolution is no longer something that happens to the organism regardless but something in which the organism may and must take an active hand. The possibility and responsibility spread from the new evolution to the old. The accumulation of knowledge, the rise of a sense of values, and the possibility of conscious choice, all typical elements in the new evolution, also carry the means of control over organic evolution, which is determinate but is determined, in part, by factors that can be varied by the human will…
>
> The infantile fantasy of becoming whatever we wish as fast as we please is simply unrealistic in a material cosmos, but this is obviously no argument against the fact that we do have a measure of conscious control over what becomes of us.
>
> (Simpson 1967, 291-292)

As the prominent American paleontologist George Gaylord Simpson stated in his book *The Meaning of Evolution*, human-beings are the only organism consciously aware of their own evolution and thereby have some ability to "take an active hand" in its process. We know we are not static, unchanging beings; we are aware that we "live-in-the-world," adapting and thus providing the potential to co-productively impact our trajectory as living-beings. While language and culture certainly maintain fundamental channels for such advancements, the evolving environments of habitation that we design and construct may play an equally formative part. The seventeenth century's shift in the physical sciences toward a reductionist, predictable and mechanically causal experimental method resulted in a simplified linear conception of environment, creating the post-enlightenment idea that it could be rationally controlled. Although this reductionist model has produced substantial scientific advancements toward problems studied in isolation (particularly in the fields of physics, chemistry and molecular biology), it provides only an approximate conception of the "real" world. This Cartesian model understands a system through its constituent parts, reducing the complexity of interrelationships and representing them inexactly to make them easier to comprehend; in this model environment is regarded as something to overcome. Throughout his career, the evolutionary biologist and geneticist Richard Lewontin has been one of the most prominent and outspoken critics of genetic determinism (a result of Cartesianism in biology), voicing great concern over the fact that, because of its perceived scientific successes, environmental reductionism has been regarded as more than a method of investigation and, rather, an accurate reflection of how things really are. Not a representation of reality, but reality itself (Levins and Lewontin 1985, 2–3). For Lewontin, environmental conditions could not be separated from the definition of the organism, as both were dynamically interrelated throughout the *process* of evolutionary development. The continued persistence of genetic determinism in biology, and its detrimental social implications, prompted Lewontin to publish a paper in 1974 titled "The Analysis of Variance and the Analysis of Causes," perhaps the most influential contribution to the literature concerning the interpretation of behavioral genetics (Griffiths 2006, 179) in which he challenged the supremacy of additive causal relationships between genotype, environment and phenotype (Figure 7.1). He resurrected the concept of the *Reaktionsnorm* (Norms of Reaction) (Figure 7.2), first put forth by the German zoologist Richard Woltereck at the beginning of the twentieth century, which is capable of including the *total* potentials embodied within a genome, not just at an ideal or selective instance, describing more fully its ability to provide various responses to changing environmental circumstances.[1]

Rethinking human development through an understanding of the *Reaktionsnorm* suggests that a designed architectural environment we construct could be conceived not simply as a functional extension of the phenotype, a kind of prosthesis, but if designed as an *active* environmental subjectivity, it could help us *cope* and *adapt* to "Our" changing "new" world. The intent being not to control behaviors or traits, but rather that through such a reconceptualization, a "Terrestrial" *architectural* "dwelling place," it might provide inhabitants many different stimulating potentials with which to co-productively interact. This chapter will consider how the interactions between the genotype and phenotype may be influenced through the conscious design of the constructed architectural environment configured toward the creation of more egalitarian possibilities for "freedom and variability."[2] Further, it will consider more specifically the underlying genetic phenomena capable of substantiating how these interactions could cultivate more enduring adaptive responses.

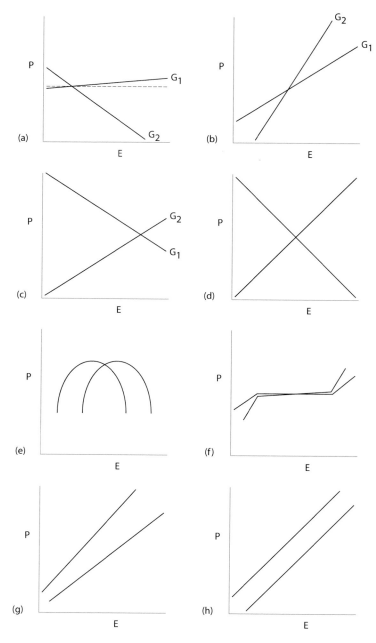

FIGURE 7.1 Reaction norms examples, phenotype (P) is drawn as a function of environment (E) reflective of different genotypes (G_1 and G_2). Redrawn by author. Reproduced by permission from the *American Journal of Human Genetics*, 26, Richard C. Lewontin, "The Analysis of Variance and the Analysis of Causes," 405, Figure 1, a–h, Copyright Elsevier (1974).

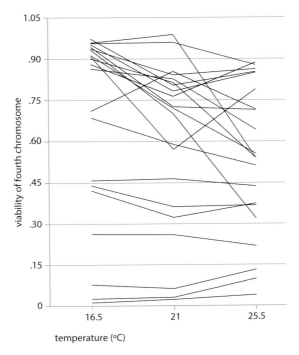

FIGURE 7.2 Example of actual reaction norms for viability of fourth chromosome homozygotes of *Drosophila pseudoobscura*. Redrawn by author. Reproduced by permission from the *American Journal of Human Genetics*, 26, Richard C. Lewontin, "The Analysis of Variance and the Analysis of Causes," 410, Figure 2, Copyright Elsevier (1974).

This ability to design and construct aspects of our environments of habitation, alongside the awareness of our own evolution described by Simpson, provides a radical opportunity to co-productively affect our own biology as well as our surrounding ecological context through architectural intervention. This possibility requires a very different approach in comprehending and implementing the generative design parameters of architecture, calling into question the means, methods and design of its construction. A recognition that we live-in-the-world-ecology and the ambition of constructing a collaborative and "Terrestrial" *architectural* "dwelling place" provides the possibility of moving beyond sustainment through technological mediation of the environment, or even mutual identification with it, to instead consider the possibly of bio-physical inter-action and physiological stimulation capable of helping us *cope* and *adapt*. In his book *Survival Through Design*, a wide-ranging compilation of thoughts concerning how the built environment effects and shapes inhabitants,[3] architect Richard Neutra cites the mid-twentieth century empirical research of Dr. D. B. Harmon on the effects of optical environmental

222 Bio-Physical Inter-Action

conditions of classroom design on school children as a decisive example of the potential for the built environment to stimulate a diverse set of physiological and psychological effects. Dr. Harmon published a comprehensive overview of the multi-year study in a 1951 paper titled "The Co-ordinated Classroom," describing how the visual factors of light distribution patterns, brightness contrast, light intensity, light source location and each student's specific line of vision toward the blackboard contributed to both eye difficulties or impairments, but also other seemingly unrelated conditions like malnutrition, chronic infections, posture problems, chronic fatigue and nose, throat and ear ailments (Harmon 1951, 26; Neutra 1954, 308). The reasoning behind such connections was the fact that the body is an integrated system of systems, as Neutra describes: "The visual adaptation to this task and the adaptation to it of the whole body appeared intimately fused" (Neutra 1954, 309). Dr. Harmon describes this interrelationship between the constructed environment, the human-being and specific body systems more broadly in the following way:

> Whether the shift of body balances or the adaptations made are organically good or bad depends largely on the total pattern or arrangement of stimulating forces existing in a specific environment; the degree and duration of those forces; the relations between the various patterns of behavior each of the distributions of the various forces bring forth: and, the body's capacity to "take" the stresses these forces and conflicts of forces set up in the organism – that is, the body's capacity to shift its internal economy and modify its structures in order to find a balance with or utilize these external forces, without depriving itself of energies or structural efficiencies needed for other immediate or later uses.
>
> *(Harmon 1951, 5)*

For Neutra, "concrete research" like Dr. Harmon's proved a clear relation between architectural design and specific physiological stimulations within inhabitants that were largely interrelated across multiple body systems. "Noticeable morphological and histological changes of the living sense organ itself proved startling and intimate consequences of the architect's design" (Neutra 1954, 310). This was an opportunity, but also a responsibility, for architects to design and construct environments of habitation with the knowledge of its possible physiological effects. Again Neutra:

> Having once recognized that a sensory stimulation such as the one producing vision does not simply end there, we can appraise with awe the complex investigations into all parts and layers of the physiological being and entity that will be possible and perhaps unavoidable in deciding on the merit or demerit of a formal and technical design.
>
> *(Neutra 1954, 311)*

To begin to further uncover such possibilities, a comparison of the designs for two projects – one of bio-physical sustainment (prosthesis) and one of bio-physical inter-action (stimulation) – will provide an initial point of departure to consider how a collaborative relationship between a constructed environment, genotype and phenotype may provide a co-productive conception of the "Terrestrial" *architectural* "dwelling place."

★ ★ ★

The Oxygen House designed by Douglas Darden was one of ten unbuilt allegorical projects he published in his 1993 book *Condemned Building: An Architect's Pre-text*, and it provides the first example of an architecture of bio-physical sustainment (prosthesis). The house was specifically designed for a singular fictional inhabitant, Burnden Abraham, an ex-train signalman who sustained a severe lung injury, forcing him to live in an oxygen-rich atmosphere-environment to survive. The design's parameters have been explicitly reprioritized toward the support of life, creating an adaptive internal atmosphere-environment intent on *sustaining* the specific physiological action of respiration. The adaptive potential of the constructed environment in this case is one of radical compensation toward the ongoing sustainment of Burn-den Abraham's life and his specific physiological conditions. Although not a direct *physical* extension, like a prosthetic limb or implant, the house would operate as a prosthetic *atmosphere* of bio-physical sustainment.

In the story Darden provides about the development of the Oxygen House design he describes how Burnden Abraham acquired the land from the railroad company at the precise location where his accident took place, wishing to locate the house over the train track on the exact spot of his injury three years prior (Darden 1993, 143). The house was to serve as both a literal atmospheric support system helping to sustain his life, a monument to his survival, but also an architectural marker of his trauma. When the oxygen provided by the house to keep him alive ran out, he would die and the house would then become his final resting place, his tomb, a monument to his passing. Architect Jean LaMarche describes this kind of duality in Darden's project, as an exploration of architecture's "underbelly,"[4] and the Oxygen House specifically in the following way:

> Other projects examine the assumption that architecture domesticates our fears by positing how it also locates our fears;…that architecture represents an irreconciliation and a reconciliation with nature; that it displaces as well as takes possession of a place; that it confronts and accommodates; that it objectifies and fulfills desire;…and in the *Oxygen House*, the last project, that a house is for living as well as for dying.
>
> *(LaMarche 1998, 162)*

224 Bio-Physical Inter-Action

Darden explicitly describes the dual nature of the house's trajectory succinctly in a short side caption in *Condemned Building*, when he writes: "A house is for ~~living~~. A house is for dying" (Darden 1993, 141). This dual perspective of the building, first as a dwelling and then as a tomb, speaks of the intensity with which it was designed as an architectural prosthesis for life, but also a reminder of the dependence human-beings, impaired or not, maintain toward the constructed environments of habitation they create. However, as LaMarche describes, upon Abraham's death the house would literally be transformed:

> the oxygen "tent" would collapse, the resident would finally be wrapped like a shroud in the membrane of the tent and would be buried in the base of the lift; the willow would be uprooted, raised and replanted in the drum base. The architecture, therefore, would allow for the transformation which, like a conceptual mobius strip, replaces death with life and life with death.
>
> *(LaMarche 1998, 169)*

Darden's process for generating the design of the Oxygen House, like all the projects included in *Condemned Buildings*, was intentionally originated from a collage of historical images and engravings of various technologies, mechanisms and antique machinery. Oxygen House was specifically derived from train mechanisms, antique water containers and the Hindenburg zeppelin, which Darden enlarged and composed together into what he called a "Composite Ideogram" (Darden 1993, 148). He referred to this process as a "Dis/Continuous Genealogy,"[5] and it was this composition that set the guidelines for the form, organization and to a large extent, the aesthetic quality of the house – a kind of machine for living *and* dying (Figures 7.3 and 7.4). Despite this compositionally focused starting point, Darden's own words from a passage of notes on the project titled "House for a man kept alive under an oxygen tent," are quite revealing as to his underlying intentions for the project.

> The contest of <u>endurance</u> initiated by the geometry can be described literally as the capacity to hold his breath in an atmosphere exhausted by codified volumes.
>
> The project is thus a concerted exercise in the control of breathing.
> *(Douglas Darden papers and drawings 1979–1995b)*

And in another untitled set of notes, Darden states the project in the following way:

> I began to wonder what would happen if a house no longer simply accommodated a person's life, but was actually crucial for life's sustenance. It seemed to me then that the house would not only have to anticipate the

Beyond the Prosthesis 225

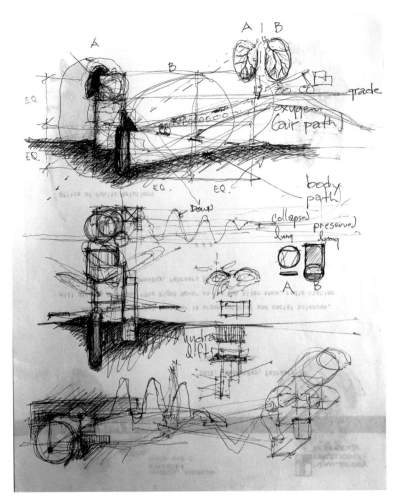

FIGURE 7.3 Douglas Darden, *Oxygen House*, concept sketches. Reproduced by permission from Allison (Darden) Collins. Image courtesy of Douglas Darden papers and drawings, 1979–1996, Series I: Condemned Building, Subseries 10: Oxygen House, Box 04: Folder 05, Generative Material, Avery Architectural & Fine Arts Library, Columbia University.

longevity of the person living there, but it would also have to account for the inhabitant's death. The house would be a sort of contest which could literally be described as the capacity to hold one's breath.
(Douglas Darden papers and drawings 1979–1995b)

Despite its allegorical message of facing death through the physical manifestation of an architectural edifice, the Oxygen House was concerned with quite

226 Bio-Physical Inter-Action

FIGURE 7.4 Douglas Darden, *Oxygen House*, composite ideogram, 1993. Reproduced by permission from Allison (Darden) Collins. Image courtesy of Douglas Darden papers and drawings, 1979–1996, Series I: Condemned Building, Subseries 10: Oxygen House, Box 04: Folder 05, Generative Material, Avery Architectural & Fine Arts Library, Columbia University.

literally sustaining the life of its particular inhabitant. It was a life-extending, life-perpetuating construction, a prosthesis capable of augmenting the atmosphere-environment toward Abraham's survival. This is why when he dies the house may no longer serve this purpose; like its solitary inhabitant, it too must transform into a monument to *his* life. In the archive of Darden's papers concerning the design of the Oxygen House, in a folder titled "research materials" a photocopy of two pages from Walt Whitman's poem "Song of the Open Road" of his seminal collection *Leaves of Grass*, includes a handwritten note by Darden that says, "antithesis of these lines for house" (Douglas Darden papers and drawings 1979–1993a), and the two sets of Whitman's lines highlighted read as follows:

> I inhale great draughts of space,
> The east and the west are mine, and the north and the south are mine.
> I am larger, better than I thought,
> I did not know I held so much goodness.

Beyond the Prosthesis **227**

And

> Now if a thousand perfect men were to appear it would not amaze me,
> Now if a thousand beautiful forms of women appear'd it would not
> astonish me.
> Now I see the secret of the making of the best persons,
> It is to grow in the open air and to eat and sleep with the earth.
>
> (Whitman 1899, 123)

The last line holds the greatest resonance to Darden's note as the Oxygen House was designed as an exclusively interior atmosphere-environment, removed from the earth and not of the "open air".

There is one additional connection to life and death embodied in the design of the Oxygen House worth noting, as recounted by Darden in an untitled document in his archived papers dated May 25, 1993, Denver, Colorado:

> Long before I knew that I had cancer and was able to come to terms intellectually with the disease inside me, my body was struggling to work out its own sensed understanding of the mortal flesh. The friction between this incomplete understanding and my simultaneous ignorance drove the project's creation.
>
> *(Douglas Darden papers and drawings 1979–1993b)*

And in a letter to the architect Robert Miller dated July 20, 1991, he says:

> I have no way of knowing for sure, but I believe now that when I designed <u>Oxygen House</u> my body KNEW that I had cancer. I was acting out my own difficult connection to that mysterious thing we call LIFE.
>
> This to me is all that architecture IS: By designing a building the architect asks us to envision a certain attitude towards life and what it means to be alive.
>
> *(Douglas Darden papers and drawings 1979–1993b)*

While surviving for over six years after his initial diagnosis, well beyond the expectations of doctors, Douglas Darden passed at the age of 44 from a rare form of leukemia in April 1996 (LaMarche 1998, 165). His proposal for the Oxygen House contains the essence of the bio-physical architectural project with the purpose to *sustain* life, as a prosthesis, both literally through the construction of an oxygen-rich atmosphere-environment and symbolically through marking and preserving memory (Figure 7.5).

While Darden's Oxygen House was conceived to compensate for the specific physiological disability of the fictitious man, the project's reconsideration as a container for a specific constructed interior atmosphere-environment – the literal composition of the "air" – as something *to be designed* – is a radical shift in keeping

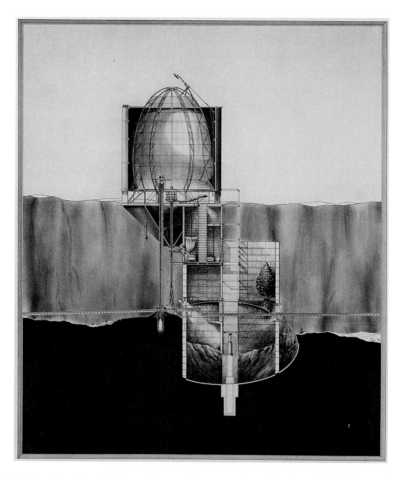

FIGURE 7.5 Douglas Darden, *Oxygen House*, section drawing, 1993. Reproduced by permission from Allison (Darden) Collins. Image scan courtesy of Douglas Darden papers and drawings, 1979–1996, Series I: Condemned Building, Subseries 10: Oxygen House, Box 04: Folder 06, Generative Material, Avery Architectural & Fine Arts Library, Columbia University.

with Peter Sloterdijk's observations on the explication of the environment as a "non-objective," object of design, as discussed in Chapter 3. The potential of such a reconsideration of design parameters and further explication of the environment toward bio-physical engagements could be applied not only to compensate or counteract inhabitant "deficiencies," but also through the advancement of greater "freedom and variability,"[6] might actively foster co-productive physiological effects toward "Our" ability to *cope* and *adapt* in this "new" world.

★ ★ ★

The second project in this comparison utilized a similar set of parameters like the Oxygen House, focusing on the precise construction of an interior atmosphere-environment related to the action of breathing, but with radically different intentions. Installed within the Swiss Pavilion at the 2002 Venice Biennale, the Hormonorium was the result of a collaboration between architects Philippe Rahm and Jean-Gilles Décosterd (Figure 7.6). The installation was focused entirely on the literal recreation of the specific "alpine-like climate" of mountains, achieved through the adjustment of the physical air composition, temperature as well as the type and source of light within the space (Décosterd and Rahm 2002, 321). To achieve the necessary environmental effects, the architects constructed a translucent false floor out of Plexiglas capable of allowing the passage of UV light from a series of 528 fluorescent tubes. The tubes emit a "white light that reproduces the solar spectrum, UV-A and UV-B" from below the floor's surface, simulating the effect of it being reflected off the snow-covered ground and "not blocked by the eyelids, the eyelashes or the natural tilt of the head" (Philippe Rahm architectes). The alpine atmosphere is also naturally thinner, composed of a lower oxygen content; to achieve this, Décosterd and Rahm increased the level of nitrogen within the space effectively reducing the percentage of oxygen in the air from 21% to 14.5%, a level consistent with an altitude of around 3,000 meters (Philippe Rahm architectes).

The installation as a spatial construct defined by visual, formal or semiotic cues is purposefully bare; there is nothing physical *in* or *of* the space other than the Plexiglas floor and a series of symmetrically placed solid rectangular volumes that serve as benches. Otherwise the space itself was empty, painted entirely white and lacking any signals as to its purpose (Figure 7.7). In fact, Décosterd and Rahm's intention behind the design of the Hormonorium as well much of their other collaborative work at this time was precisely to undermine such

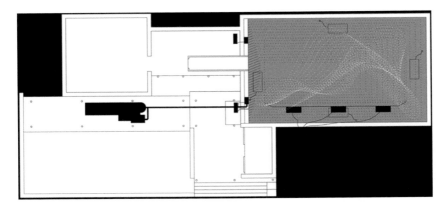

FIGURE 7.6 Philippe Rahm and Jean-Gilles Décosterd, *Hormonorium*, plan drawing of installation at the 8th Biennale of Architecture, Swiss Pavilion, Venice, Italy, 2002. Image courtesy of Philippe Rahm & Jean-Gilles Décosterd.

230 Bio-Physical Inter-Action

FIGURE 7.7 Philippe Rahm and Jean-Gilles Décosterd, *Hormonorium*, photo of installation at the 8th Biennale of Architecture, Swiss Pavilion, Venice, Italy, 2002. Photograph by Jean-Michel Landecy. Image courtesy of Philippe Rahm & Jean-Gilles Décosterd.

questions of form and function altogether – or at least as a primary parameter of assessment (see Chapter 6). Writing in the introductory text to the 2006–2007 exhibition at the Canadian Centre for Architecture titled "Environ(ne)ment: Approaches for Tomorrow," curator Givanna Borasi describes Philippe Rahm's approach in this way:

> In the case of Philippe Rahm, the proposition involves the close observation and documentation of elemental conditions like temperature, humidity, and light, all of which have a direct physical and emotional impact on human life. In Rahm's manifesto "Form and Function Follow Climate," these conditions are deployed as new instruments for determining architectural space keyed to human comfort and behaviour, but also to energy efficiency.
>
> *(Bosari 2006, 39)*

Similarly, the Hormornorium operates with a different set of objectives and materials, what Bolari calls "elemental conditions." These conditions are not static, but rather dynamic and inter-active with each other, with the external environment and with inhabitants. The art critic Guy Tortosa, in reference to the Hormonorium, but also more generally about the work of Décosterd and Rahm, describes the design approach in the following way:

> Based specifically on data from medical research, the practice of Décosterd and Rahm associés is related to a new type of "construction site," a "construction site" that could be called invisible because it consists of replacing the heavy components of the dominant, allopathic, expansionist and polluting architecture with the new materials of an architecture, which they characterize, depending on the circumstances, as gentle, elementary, chemical or sensory.
>
> *(Tortosa 2002, 60)*

While this approach surely reflects a radical departure from the rationalist, formalist or semiotic focused discussion that has filled architectural discourse for much of the twentieth century, Tortosa eludes to an even deeper intention in the work. What's at stake is not simply the use of "elemental conditions" or "invisible" materials as the basis for design, but rather *how* their use allows for the construction of an alternative type of space, an "im-mediate" space (Décosterd and Rahm 2002, 320) of bio-physical inter-action and physiological stimulation. The space of the Hormonorium as described above has been calibrated not just to simulate the high-altitude environment but to *actually* physiologically make it and therefore *actually* foster the corresponding bio-physical effects within inhabitants, as if they really were trekking at 3,000 meters.

> The Hormonorium is an alpine-like climate, but it is also an assemblage of physiological devices acting on the endocrine and neurovegetative systems. It can be viewed as a sort of physiological representation of an alpine environment, to be ingested, through respiration, through the retina and the dermis.
>
> *(Décosterd and Rahm 2002, 321)*

These assembled "physiological devices" are expressed in multiple ways. The intensity of bright white reflected light emanating from below at "between 5,000 and 10,000 lux stimulates the retina, which transmits information to the pineal gland that causes a decrease in melatonin secretion" (Décosterd and Rahm 2002, 321). This results in lowering fatigue, and a probable increase in sexual desire and mood regulation, while the UV-B rays help to increase the synthesis of vitamin D (Décosterd and Rahm 2002, 321). The effects of such an oxygen-depleted space also potentially cause a slight hypoxia, characterized by states of confusion, disorientation or erratic behavior and also possibly slight euphoria due to increased endorphin production (Décosterd and Rahm 2002,

321) (Figure 7.8). The potential of such a space is not to adopt any one purpose, but rather provide opportunities for many different activities, freedom and exploration depending on one's individual needs or even biology.

> The Hormonorium will therefore be a climate that stimulates the body physiologically, while simultaneously offering a new model for a decontextualized, degeographized public space. A physiochemical place, a partial displacement of a climate from higher elevations to the seaside, for well-being, for health, to enhance the body's equilibrium through regulation of the neurovegetative system. Moreover, it will be a place of potential transformation of our physical performance, through stimulation, through the physiological modification of human nature.
>
> *(Décosterd and Rahm 2002, 322)*

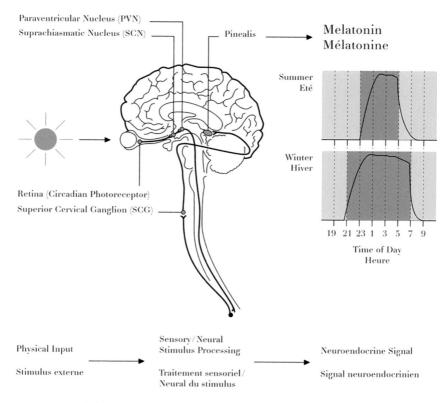

FIGURE 7.8 Philippe Rahm and Jean-Gilles Décosterd, *Hormonorium*, diagram of the neuro-physiological impact of inhabiting the installation at the 8th Biennale of Architecture, Swiss Pavilion, Venice, Italy, 2002. Image courtesy of Philippe Rahm & Jean-Gilles Décosterd.

The potential of this approach is to design and construct more healthful, more physiologically beneficial environments of habitation capable of "transformation" offering a profound possibility for remaking a "Terrestrial" *architectural* "dwelling place" as one of adaptation for human-beings, and through a deeper more expansive sense of self, even possibly the total collective "being-with." Despite the potential adaptive and altruistic benefit of such an approach, especially in the face of the necessary "catastrophic changes" we're facing in our relationship to the world, there is another possibility, one resulting in a significant loss of induvial autonomy which cannot be overlooked or disregarded. Décosterd and Rahm describe this possibility in the following way: "The Hormonorium is a physiologically stimulating space where humanistic free will does not exist, thus associating itself with modern uneasiness regarding the current evolution of human nature, between biological determinism, therapeutic hope and the ontological death of the individual" (Décosterd and Rahm 2002, 321). The significance of these words cannot be overstated in the context of the bio-physical project of inter-action, physiological stimulation and the possibility for a beyond sustainable model of design. To avoid the possibility of an unsolicited inter-action instigated through a bio-physical design approach intent on creating predetermined effects, then the constructed environments we inhabit must offer changeability and variation. Or rather the "physiologically stimulating space" must be conceived itself as a "landscape" of change, an "evolving environmental habitation," not unlike Banham's argument for the "freedom and variability" produced by the campfire (Banham 1965, 75).

In an interview response to a question Javier García-Germán more recently posed regarding the need to develop a theory of environmental aesthetics connecting atmospheric effects to specific psycho-subjective affects, Philippe Rahm answered in the following way concerning the impact on "free will" and the responsibility of the architect.

> Psychology is a subjective matter and a very precious personal propriety. I really don't want an architect designing my psychology. As an architect, you don't have to interfere with personal psychology, with a person's free will. My work is to create open spaces with some physical or thermal qualities which inhabitants are free to interpret freely. This is also the reason why I always want to propose variety of spaces, with different qualities, some more comfortable whilst other not. This means that an inhabitant has always to keep his free will and I an architect should not decide for him. I conceive architecture like a background where you can invent your own story. It is similar to a natural landscape where you are free to go either under the shadow of the forest or to an open meadow under the sun. It depends on individual choice. I want to do the same: offer an open background.
>
> *(García-Germán 2017, 64)*

This conception concerning the role and responsibility of the architect provides both an opportunity to design variable and evolving *architectural environments* of habitation that may contribute to the bio-physical stimulation of co-productive and/or adaptive possibilities, while also maintaining an individual's freedom. This understanding combined with a life-affirming architectural ethical approach grounded in a "Terrestrial" and transpersonal conception of the self may then provide opportunities for inhabitants of all kinds, human and non-human alike, to *cope* and *adapt* within the radical changes already underway in the world.

★ ★ ★

As discussed at the start of this chapter, American paleontologist George Gaylord Simpson, writing in his book *The Meaning of Evolution,* proposed what he called "the new evolution," dependent not on the direct transmission of genetic characters, but rather upon the accumulation, preservation and transference of knowledge developed over an individual's lifespan and more broadly over many generations within a community group. Though greatly influential and quick moving, this knowledge fundamentally reflects a specific and potentially more fleeting cultural intelligence tied to a specific social context and history, as opposed to the more deeply embedded adaptive phenotypic expressions held within the genome. Architecture has often been exclusively regarded as a segment of this cultural knowledge, both as a form of technology capable of mediating the external environment toward greater survival and comfortability, but also as an art form capable of expressing specific cultural meanings and messages. However, within the architectural project of co-productive bio-physical inter-action and physiological stimulation, there exists a different potential that maintains the possibility for it, as an evolving environmental context we inhabit, to act directly on human physiology and psychology.

Supposing that the necessary life-affirming[7] architectural ethics are in place, several important questions arise: what is the potential for these temporarily stimulated bio-physical responses to be sustained *outside* the constructed environment of habitation that fostered them? If possible, could this sustainment lead toward more permanent genetic adaptive change? And what are the biological and evolutionary mechanisms at work that could support this process of genetic fixation? We have seen in the previous discussion of the *Reaktionsnorm* (Norms of Reaction) that there is an inherent potential within the genetic material of organisms to innately provide varying phenotypic responses toward different types of environmental potentials (phenotypic plasticity). However, linking this potential to long-term evolutionary changes harkens a dubious corollary to a neo-Lamarkian understanding of evolution; an argument for the inheritance of acquired characteristics that was rejected initially by the neo-Darwinists and

Beyond the Prosthesis **235**

definitively put to rest by the modern synthesis.[8] Despite these clear refutations over the last 125 years, there have been a number of concepts put forth that maintain the tenets of the synthetic theory and the predominance of natural selection, while offering an explanation for how some beneficial phenotypic responses to immediate environmental stimuli could be maintained genetically even after the initial environmental stimuli has been removed.

The first concept to consider incorporates the complementary ideas of "organic selection" and "orthoplasy" as articulated by the American psychologist James Mark Baldwin in an 1896 paper titled "A New Factor in Evolution." Today, this concept is known as the Baldwin effect (Crispo 2007, 2470), a name coined by George Gaylord Simpson in an essay published in 1953 of the same name to describe Baldwin's "new factor" in the adaptation of organisms. Simpson notes that the concept, attributed first to Baldwin and henceforth given his name, was independently and almost simultaneously developed by two other scientists at that time, C. Lloyd Morgan in a book titled *Habit and Instinct* (1896) and H. F. Osborn in a paper titled "A mode of evolution requiring neither natural selection nor the inheritance of acquired characters" (1896). Simpson suggested that the development of such an idea was likely an inevitable result of the "intellectual atmosphere of the time…at the height of the neo-Darwinian *versus* neo-Lamarkain controversy and shortly before the rediscovery of Mendelism gave a radically different turn to biological thought" (Simpson 1953, 110). In a way, the Baldwin effect provides a kind of reconciliation between neo-Darwinism and neo-Lamarckism, seemingly describing a mechanism capable of facilitating the genetic fixation of environmentally instigated phenotypic characters (Simpson 1953, 110).

In his initial 1896 paper as well as his more expansive 1902 book that addressed the subject *Development and Evolution*, James Mark Baldwin provided an explanation for how these responsive phenotypic characters could become heritable. The primary concept was what he called "organic selection," which he defined as: "The process of individual accommodation considered as keeping single organisms alive, and so, by also securing the accumulation of variations, determining evolution in subsequent generations" (Baldwin 1902, 119). As Simpson clarifies, Baldwin's use of the term "accommodation" was intended to refer to characteristics that were not yet heritable, while his use of the word "variation" referred to those characters that were already genetically defined (Simpson 1953, 111). In this sense, those phenotypic qualities brought about temporally through bio-physical inter-action may over time be "secured" and eventually replaced by corresponding genetic determinants through the process of natural selection. The other aspect of his "new factor" and its broader implications for the course of evolution Baldwin called "orthoplasy" defining it as:

> All the influences which work to assist the animal to make adjustments or accommodations will unite to give directive determination to the course

of evolution. These influences we may call "orthoplastic" or directive influences. And the general fact that evolution has a directive determination through organic selection we may call "Orthoplasy".

(Baldwin 1902, 142)

In this way according to Baldwin evolution as a process is influenced, or to be more precise, it is readily provided options more likely to be successful, through "organic selection" and the accumulation of "orthoplastic" responses – plastic variations. Evolutionary ecologist Erika Crispo writes a succinct synopsis of the Baldwin effect as follows:

> [Baldwin] thus proposed that plasticity would be a positive driving force in evolution, setting the stage for further neo-Darwinian evolution increasing the survival of those who display a plastic response. Over time, standing genetic variation can be selected upon so that evolution can proceed in the direction of the induced plastic response. He referred to the ability of plasticity to increase survival as "organic selection," and the directional influence of organic selection on evolution as "orthoplasy."

(Crispo 2007, 2470)

And so, while the end result of the Baldwin effect is the genetic fixation of an adaptive phenotypic characteristic occurring during an individual's lifetime, natural selection is still acting as the final actualizing agent of the process[9] – as Crispo remarks, plasticity is "setting the stage" for eventual selection and eventual genetic adaptation. Simpson, while skeptical that the Baldwin effect provided a primary role in evolution,[10] also clearly stated that it is "both possible and probable" (Simpson 1953, 115). He also recognizes its consistency with the synthetic theory of evolution, and that "It is simply one way in which natural selection may sometimes affect populations, and clearly it is not a factor either contradictory or additional to natural selection" (Simpson 1953, 115). In *Development and Evolution*, Baldwin describes the productive effect of natural selection applied to both basic and additional utility provided by plastic responses of accommodation.

> natural selection may seize upon any utility, additional to that already springing from any functions which animals may perform, no matter how they perform them. Many functions may be passably performed through accommodation, supplementing congenital characters, which would be better performed were the congenital characters strengthened. Congenital variation would in these cases be seizing upon this additional utility, carry evolution on farther than it had gone before.

(Baldwin 1902, 209–210)

Beyond the Prosthesis **237**

In this sense, Baldwin argues that natural selection is indiscriminate in its process, operating upon the additional utility provided through the Baldwin effect (organic selection and orthoplasy), and in a certain sense acting more deliberately because of them as an agent of greater adaptive performance.

Developmental cell biologists Marc Kirschner and John Gerhart, writing about the history and implications of the Baldwin effect in their 2005 co-authored book *The Plausibility of Life*, maintain that it did not contradict the principles of Darwinian selection but did give prominence to the adaptive potential of an individual's phenotypic plasticity. "Without that preexisting adaptability, the new selective conditions might extinguish the organism before it had a chance to adapt genetically" (Kirschner and Gerhart 2005, 77). For Kirschner and Gerhart, the most meaningful implication of the Baldwin effect may be in recognizing how the underlying genetic potentialities of an organism, its *Reaktionsnorm*, provide the ability for plastic phenotypic responses to variable environmental conditions, a critical aspect for more easily allowing an environmentally instigated adaptive trait of great long-term value to become genetically fixed.

> The main implication is that complex phenotypic variation is not created from nothing, but rather from preexisting processes and components of the organism's somatically adaptable phenotype, whereas mutations merely stabilize and extend what is already there. Thus, the mutations need not be creative and numerous, a proposal that of course greatly reduces the difficulty in generating phenotypic change.
>
> *(Kirschner and Gerhart 2005, 77)*

Simpson makes a related observation on the Baldwin effect concerning an individual's phenotypic "reaction range" of accommodating characters initiated by a particular environmental context. He points out that while the range of responses may be plastic, it is not stable, and may become broader or narrower depending on the changes to the underlying genetic system (Simpson 1953, 116). As plastic responses to particular stimuli get selected, the range effectively becomes narrower and those responses if adaptable become the dominant developmental outcome and thus fixed. "Then the Baldwin effect may occur: a response formerly dependent on a combination of genetic and environmental variables may become relatively or even absolutely invariable" (Simpson 1953, 116). In this sense, it is not a simple dichotomy between inherited and acquired characteristics, but rather a more dynamic and fluid process of increasing or decreasing the likelihood that a particular phenotypic trait will develop within a particular environment and from a particular individual's genetic system. And like the description provided by Kirschner and Gerhart above, Simpson maintains that "The ability to 'acquire' a character has, in itself, a genetical basis" (Simpson 1953, 116), meaning in a sense that the forces of selection are really only acting on the genetic system indirectly through the phenotype, effectively

238 Bio-Physical Inter-Action

selecting for the "ability" to obtain particular adaptive traits. This was a position also taken by the eminent British developmental biologist, geneticist and philosopher of science Conrad H. Waddington, who regarded the phenotype as a product of genotype-environment interaction and the immediate focus of selection. This led him to conclude that "all natural selection is in fact a selection for the ability of the organism to adapt itself to (that is, to develop into a fit form in) the environment in which it finds itself" (Waddington 1957, 104).

Waddington, like Baldwin, provided an explanation for the stabilization of plastic phenotypic responses induced by an environment, and further described the environment's more general role in the developmental process. He discusses these ideas in a paper delivered to the Institute of Animal Genetics in Edinburgh in 1952 titled "Genetic Assimilation of an Acquired Character," describing in detail an experiment conducted on "a strain of *Drosophila melanogaster* [selected] for its ability to form a phenocopy in response to some definite environmental stimulus" (Waddington 1952, 118). The experiment sought to test for the occurrence of a mechanism that "would provide a means by which an 'acquired character' in the conventional sense [in this case crossveinless wings] could be 'assimilated' by the genotype, and eventually appear comparatively independent of any specific environmental influence" (Waddington 1953, 118). The results were clear; those selected for crossveinless wings and subsequently selected "upward," bred with one another over multiple generations, when removed from the inducing environmental stimuli of abnormally high temperature continued to maintain the trait of crossveinless wings. In conclusion to this paper, Waddington provides the following summation to his hypothesis which he calls "genetic assimilation."

> The hypothesis which was put forward suggested that if an animal subjected to unusual environmental conditions develops some abnormal phenotype which is advantageous under those circumstances, selection will not merely increase the frequency with which this favorable result occurs, but will also tend to stabilize the formation of it, and the new development may become so strongly canalised that it continues to occur even when the environment returns to normal.
>
> *(Waddington 1953, 125)*

While there are similarities between Waddington's concept of genetic assimilation and the Baldwin effect, the primary difference is the way in which those "advantageous" plastic phenotypic responses induced by the environment become fixed into the genetic system. Waddington's primary criticism of the Baldwin effect is that it provides no real connection between the occurrence of particular plastic phenotypic characters and their eventual genetic fixation – in the end, it relies on "random mutations" to arise that match the instigated character and that they then be independently selected through natural selection (Waddington 1957, 164). Describing the results of his crossveinless

Drosophila melanogaster experiment, Waddington is emphatic that his results are not the product of random mutation.

> This has certainly not happened solely through the selection of a chance mutation which happens to mimic the original acquired character. The genetic basis which is eventually built up for crossveinlessness differs from the genotype of the foundation stock in several genes. There is evidence of polygenic segregation even in crosses between the high and low lines, both derived from the upward selected stock, and there are still more gene differences between the high lines and the downward selected stock.
>
> *(Waddington 1953, 123–124)*

The resultant differences between the upwardly and downwardly selected stocks as well as their crosses, reinforced the idea for Waddington that the genetic assimilation for crossveinlessness was not a single random change arising out of happenstance, but rather that multiple genes were being affected by the assimilation process and therefore likely played a part in producing the selected trait – polygenic inheritance. For Waddington this also reinforced his ideas about how individual organisms develop over time; how environmental conditions alongside genetic and other "internal" factors play an integral part in the definition of developmental pathways, specific phenotypic expression and the genetic fixation of adaptive instigated characters embodied in their genome. This developmental construct of possible pathways of expression was what Waddington symbolically represented in the concept of the "epigenetic landscape" (Waddington 1940, 91–93).

The idea of the epigenetic landscape was first illustrated in a drawing by John Piper placed as the frontispiece to Waddington's 1940 book *Organisers and Genes*. It depicted a valley with a river flowing down it toward the sea from the mountains, as it flows passing a "hanging valley" and other "branch valleys" with one side of the valley being significantly steeper than the other. Waddington described this developmental field of possibility as follows:

> The system of developmental paths has been symbolised in two dimensions as a set of branching lines. Perhaps a fuller picture would be given by a system of valleys diverging down an inclined plane. The inclined plane symbolises the tendency for a developing piece of tissue to move towards a more adult state.
>
> *(Waddington 1940, 92)*

And

> The symbolic representation of developmental processes can be spoken of as the "epigenetic landscape." It would be difficult to find a similar

240 Bio-Physical Inter-Action

configuration in any actual piece of country. As one goes downhill, the valley which was originally wide and gently sloping, branches into more and more subdivisions, some of which (representing tracks realised only under the influence or special genes or environmental conditions) may be hanging valleys whose floors disembouch up the side, above the main valley bottom.

(Waddington 1940, 93)

The terrain was meant to represent the continuous developmental pathways of *possible* phenotypic expression as a result of specific environmental stimuli and the underlying genetic system. The river flowing through the terrain represented the specific individual developmental process as it related to a particular trait, or the whole organism. Architectural theorist and historian Matthew Allen has recounted that the concept and image of the epigenetic landscape draws on several familiar ideas of the time: "Epigenesis was a common concept from eighteenth-century biology, and biologists in the mid-twentieth-century would also have known Sewall Wright's adaptive landscape, which explained adaptation as a genetic drift up and down humps and pits on a topological surface" (Allen 2015, 124). However, it has been Waddington's further developed illustrations of the epigenetic landscape included in his later publications that have become widely known and referenced.[11]

Waddington referred to this type of illustration as a "three-dimensional diagram" (Waddington 1957, 168). It is precisely the non-linearity of "genotype-environment interaction" and the corresponding phenotypic expression that was fundamental to Waddington's understanding of development and the genetic assimilation of so-called "acquired characters." In this sense, the diagram actually operates beyond three dimensions as its visualization of the sloped and undulating surface of the epigenetic landscape reflects the development of an individual over a period of time as well as the respective likelihood of particular formalizations.

The most developed of these illustrations were included in Waddington's 1957 book *The Strategy of the Genes*; these versions include a ball poised at the top of the landscape composed of undulating peaks and valleys set to roll down the landscape along the line of least resistance (Figure 7.9). Waddington surmises how different factors related to an individual's underlying genetic system as well as particular environmental factors or stimuli may reshape the landscape as the ball begins to roll down, resulting in alterations to its initially projected trajectories. The ball's final destination at the opposite end of the sloped surface of possibilities depends upon the continuous (re)shaping of the surface, which makes certain destinations more or less likely to be actualized depending upon the specific slopes. Selection acts over time to "deepen" specific valleys that are most beneficial, making them stronger in terms of the ball's destined trajectory and thus resulting in a more permanent and predictable phenotypic outcome,

Beyond the Prosthesis **241**

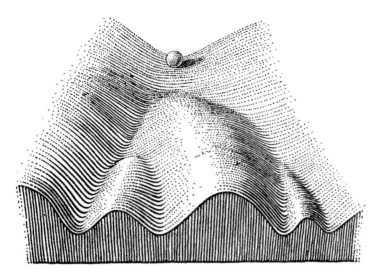

FIGURE 7.9 Conrad H. Waddington, part of an epigenetic landscape, 1957. © 2015 From The strategy of the genes: A discussion of some aspects of theoretical biology by Conrad H. Waddington, p. 29, fig. 4. Reprodcued by permission of Taylor and Francis, a division of Informa plc.

even with future genetic or environmental perturbances. Waddington called this phenomenon "buffering" or "canalisation."

In his critique of the Baldwin effect, Waddington argued that it was "based on the over-simplification of forgetting that the environment is one of the determinants of the phenotype" (Waddington 1957, 166). For Waddington, environmental conditions played a part in phenotypic development, not just as stimuli instigating particular phenotypic responses, but also in the broader sense of how the underlying genetic system informs numerous "chemical forces" that together specifically shape the landscape "above," which, in turn, impacts developmental pathways (Waddington 1957, 35–36) (Figure 7.10). It is therefore the "remodeling" of the epigenetic landscape that leads to the genetic fixation of environmentally induced traits. In this sense, what is ultimately being selected for is the genetic system most capable of providing a variety of possible adaptive phenotypic outcomes in response to changing environmental stimuli, while still preserving the necessary base characteristics fundamental to an organism's overall functioning.

> It is more realistic to envisage these phenomena as the selection, not of genes whose effects, though not modified by the environment, happen to be parallel to the direct adaptations, but rather of factors which control the capacity for response to the environment...If the selection is for the capacity to respond adaptively to the environment, it will mould the epigenetic landscape into a new form, in which the response is facilitated

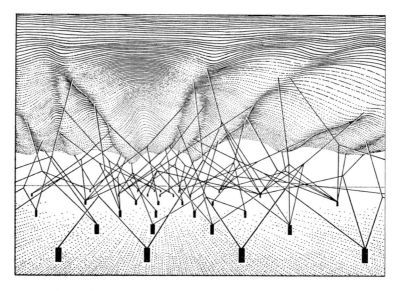

FIGURE 7.10 Conrad H. Waddington, the complex system of interactions underlying the epigenetic landscape, 1957. © 2015 From The strategy of the genes: A discussion of some aspects of theoretical biology by Conrad H. Waddington, p. 36, fig. 5. Reprodcued by permission of Taylor and Francis, a division of Informa plc.

and perhaps adjusted so as to reach the most favourable end-result. There will then be two ways in which genetic fixation of the originally acquired adaptive character may take place. Either a gene-mutation occurs which suffices to direct development into the channel which has been prepared for it; or the remodeling of the epigenetic landscape goes so far that what was initially the side-valley, reached over a threshold, becomes the most easy path of change, so that one cannot point to any particular genes as being responsible for switching development into it.

The more thorough the remodeling of the landscape, the more likely will it be that some random gene-mutation will be able to take over the switching function of the original environmental stimulus.

(Waddington 1957, 166–167)

Through this conception, Waddington provides additional means for an environmentally instigated character of adaptive value to be stabilized, through a remodeling of the epigenetic landscape rather than only a specific random mutation as in Baldwin's scenario. In *The Strategy of the Genes*, Waddington provides a comparative illustration of all these specific scenarios, each depicting modified versions of a portion of the epigenetic landscape (Figure 7.11) and how it's adjustment, depending upon the particular activation of the underlying

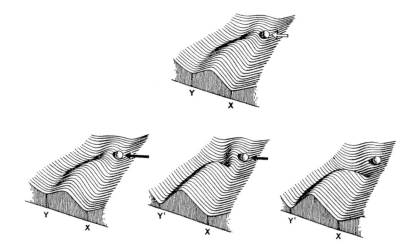

FIGURE 7.11 Conrad H. Waddington, organic selection (the Baldwin effect) and genetic assimilation, 1957. "The three diagrams [above] show ways in which the 'acquired character' Y might become incorporated into the genotype. On the left, the original environmental stimulus is replaced by a mutant allele (dark arrow) which happens to turn up; this is 'organic selection.' On the right are two modes of 'genetic assimilation.' In the central one, the threshold protecting the wild type is lowered to some extent, but there is an identifiable major gene which helps push the developing tissues into the Y path. On the right, the genotype as a whole causes the threshold to disappear and there is no identifiable 'switch gene.'" © 2015 From The strategy of the genes: A discussion of some aspects of theoretical biology by Conrad H. Waddington, p. 167, fig. 30. Reprodcued by permission of Taylor and Francis, a division of Informa plc.

genetic system, may decrease the threshold of expression for the actualization of certain characters, effectively increasing their frequency within a given population (Crispo 2007, 2473).

An additional point of advancement from Baldwin and Waddington comes from Marc Kirschner and John Gerhart in their recognition of how the innate potentiality held within an individual's genetic system (its *Reaktionsnorm*) is regulated through the function of what they call "conserved core processes"[12] that are integral to an organism's development and formation, while still maintaining an ability to respond and ultimately adapt to changing environmental stimuli. They point out the somewhat counterintuitive idea that these "conserved core processes" (the deepest and steepest valleys of Waddington's epigenetic landscape) effectively buffer out the variations of the environment (i.e. canalisation), but also simultaneously serve as primary vehicles for creating the variation necessary for evolution (Kirschner and Gerhart 2005, 107), what they refer to as "facilitated variation"

244 Bio-Physical Inter-Action

(Kirschner and Gerhart 2005, 219-243). They claim that "evolution can build on physiology by acting on highly poised, switch-like systems, which themselves are highly constrained and conserved" (Kirschner and Gerhart 2005, 105). It is the *poised* nature of these systems that make them so readily capable of providing variation and increasing the potential for adaptive responses toward environmental changes. This assumes those responses are demonstrably higher performing and that the necessary genetic change required to fixate them is also much less as compared to a more rigid developmental system.

A further development of these ideas is expressed in the concept of modularity, which provides a common compartmentalized or modular organizational framework for the organism, a developmental map. Kirschner and Gerhart refer to this map as an organism's "compartment map,"[13] which underlies the developmental process of specific groups of advanced multi-cellular organisms with diverse anatomies and traits. Modularity as a developmental idea describes the overall genotype-phenotype "map" that can be broken down into smaller independent modules or localized integrated compartments, a kind of "invisible anatomy because the compartments are only identifiable if one can establish which genes are expressed there...The actual differentiation of the organism will depend not only on the compartments but also on the interactions of cells of one compartment with signals from other compartments" (Kirschner and Gerhart 2005, 183). In this way, these modular maps are spatial constructs imposing a loose or "extensible" organization upon the developing organism, providing similar cell types located in different compartments to maintain similar structure and activity, while also allowing for variations in other aspects of their functional potential.

> The result is a platform for local differentiation and for use by the genome in many different ways. Stated in terms of the conserved core processes, the compartment map makes possible the use of different combinations of processes at different places in the body. In fact, it provides those places. The map makes possible the use of different combinations of genes in different locations.
>
> *(Kirschner and Gerhart 2005, 183)*

The extreme example of modularity would be an idealized model of the genome where the locus of each gene produces one specific phenotypic trait. The converse example of extreme non-modularity would be a genome where every individual gene has an effect on every other phenotypic outcome, effectively a total integration of genotype-phenotype interaction and uniform universal pleiotropy (Altenberg 2005, 99).

As both ends of this modular spectrum define highly restrictive models of development and adaptive potential, theoretical biologist Lee Altenberg has stated: "Real organisms, one could argue, have genotype-phenotype maps that range somewhere in between these extremes" (Altenberg 2005, 99). Existing somewhere in the middle of the modular spectrum allows for producing modular organizations of development that are both flexible, yet decidedly structured through the integration of these specific localized regions. These spatialized maps may then be independently altered through selection or mutation without necessarily destroying the organism's overall organizational structure. In the production of more highly complex organisms, modularity provides a means to locally produce specificity of character while maintaining the possibility of adaptive responses as well as an overall relative stability of form. They constantly maintain the balance between hierarchical and flexible organizational relationships, between parts and whole. If the modular system is too rigid requiring highly coordinated changes across many distinct loci, then the space for adaptation will be so small that the selective pathway or combination of random mutational events necessary couldn't ever possibly arise. Yet, if the system is too flaccid, then complex form is simply not possible at all, as it will never be able to maintain the necessary organizational qualities.

Altenberg further describes the benefits of modularity this way:

> It may seem intuitively obvious why modularity in the genotype-phenotype map should benefit evolution: if genetic changes tend to map to changes in a small number of phenotypic traits, then the genome can respond to selection on those traits alone, independently of the rest of the phenotype, with a minimum of deleterious pleiotropic side effects. Hence modularity would enhance the ability of the genetic system to generate adaptive variants, which one can refer to as it "evolvability."
>
> *(Altenberg 2005, 99)*

The concept of "evolvability"[14] could be understood as a more targeted and intentioned conceptualization of the *Reaktionsnorm*, a reflection of the total range of phenotypic expressions possible within an individual's genome – its virtual potentiality – that is, the capacity of a system to adapt. In contrast to specialized linear systems of development, modularity initiates a method favorable to the creation of complexity that is capable, and even primed, for further evolutionary development, while more effectively absorbing the potentially lethal effects of random variants.

In this sense, what may be exceedingly relevant to architects and designers living with a newly mutated relationship to the changing world is not the possibility for them to act as an outside authority selecting specific characters for a specific environment through design, but rather the awareness of an organism's *ability* to produce a variety of different responses to variable environmental stimuli. This reflects an embodied capacity *to evolve* (evolvability), and the possibility of a movement beyond the conceptualization of an architectural surround as a prosthesis only for sustainment and toward one of bio-physical inter-action capable of helping us cope and adapt in this "new" world. What's required is the making of a constructed environment full of "freedom and variability," of inhabitant and

246 Bio-Physical Inter-Action

community participation. In assuming a design methodology based upon a concept of evolvability, alongside an architectural ethics that seeks to affirm life, then cultivating a human-architecture-environment of co-productive inter-actions may provide one possible means for confronting change. Architects and designers may adopt new parameters based upon inter-active physiological potentials and the possibility of sustaining meaningful bio-physical responses, which have the potential, as discussed through the work of Baldwin, Waddington, Kirschner and Gerhart to be genetically fixed over time. This approach would aim to cultivate a co-relational concept between the constructed environment and a greater collective of inhabitants, able to generate local specificity while maintaining an overall adaptability in the face of current issues and future change.

Notes

1 For a more extensive overview of the historical development and conceptual potential of the *Reaktionsnorm* (Norms of Reaction) as it relates to architectural design, see Ryan Ludwig, "Formation and Variation: Woltereck's Concept of Reaktionsnorm and the Potentials of Environment," *Thresholds* 42 (2014): 134–147.
2 See Chapter 1 "In Pursuit of Comfort" and Reyner Banham, "A Home is Not a House," *Art in America* 2 (1965): 75.
3 "Architecture is a social art. It becomes an instrument of human fate because it not only caters to requirement but also shapes and conditions our responses. It can be called reflective because it mirrors a program of conduct and living. At the same time this art of a planned environment does more, it also programs our daily conduct and our entire civilized life. It modifies and often breaks earlier established habit"; see Neutra (1954, 314).
4 The term "underbelly" was used by Darden as a way of referencing the "shadow," the unknown, of architecture and suggested a means "to explore the substratum of unnamed emotions in a pit of our stomach that forced us to seek shelter in the first place"; see "Part 1: Pointing to the Underbelly," *Douglas Darden: Looking After the Underbelly*, DVD, directed by Douglas Darden and Robert Miller (1992); found in the Douglas Darden papers and drawings, 1979-1996, Series IV: Professional Papers, Box 10: Folder 03, Documentary, 1992, Avery Architectural & Fine Arts Library, Columbia University.
5 According to Ben Ledbetter, a friend and collaborator of Douglas Darden, this term originated in a conversation they had while attending the Graduate School of Design at Harvard University over the idea of using the concept of layered histories as an originary point for design. Ledbetter referred to them as "archaeologies" while Darden called them "genealogies" and later "discontinuous genealogies"; see Ben Ledbetter, "Digital Darden: Resisting the Rhinoceros," http://www.benledbetter.com/blog/2015/5/18/digital-darden-resisting-the-rhinoceros (accessed September 30, 2019).
6 As previously described in Chapter 1 by Reyner Banham.
7 See Chapter 3 "Of Life and Death" for a more extensive examination of life-affirming architectural ethics.
8 The synthetic theory of evolution, first described by Theodosius Dobzhansky in his 1937 book *Genetics and the Origin of Species*, was a concept of species formation that integrated Charles Darwin's fundamental idea of natural selection and gradual change with Mendelian genetics. The period directly preceding Dobzhansky's book, as more contributions to the theory were made by others, became known as the "modern synthesis." The other primary contributors to the theory

were Ernst Mayr, Julian Huxley, George Gaylord Simpson and George Ledyard Stebbins.

9 Baldwin also makes this same point in his text *Development and Evolution* when he says:

> We come to view, therefore, that evolution from generation to generation has probably proceeded by the operation of natural selection upon variations with the assistance of the organic selection of coincident (*i.e.*, those which produce congenitally what coincides with the acquisitions of the individuals) or correlated variations.
>
> (Baldwin 1902, 142)

10 "It probably has occurred, but there is singularly little concrete ground for the view that it is a frequent and important element in adaptation"; see Simpson (1953, 115).

11 Within architectural discourse these diagrams were brought to light by Sanford Kwinter in his essay "Landscapes of Change: Boccioni's 'Stati d'animo' as General Theory of Models," *Assemblage* 19 (1992): 50–65 and more recently in a lecture titled *What Is Life?* presented at the Graduate School of Design at Harvard University – as well as at other institutions – on April 29th 2008.

12 These conserved core processes are the equivalent of Waddington's deepening of the valley to maintain certain developmental paths that are fundamental to a particular organism, but also on an even deeper level for advanced life of any form. In the glossary of their book *The Plausibility of Life*, Marc Kirschner and John Gerhart define these processes as:

> The processes that generate the anatomy, physiology, and behavior of the organism in the course of its development (several hundred in number) and comprise the organism's phenotype. The various traits are generated by different combinations of the processes operating in different parts of their adaptive ranges of performance. Some of these processes have been unchanged (conserved) for hundreds of millions or even billions of years.
>
> (Kirschner and Gerhart 2005, 277)

Examples of some of these core processes are DNA, proteins, metabolism, structures of the nucleus, organelles, cytoskeleton, sexual reproduction, signaling, matrix, junctions, epithelia, compartments, anteroposterior and dorsoventral axes, among many others; see Kirschner and Gerhart (2005, 49).

13 Of these compartment maps Kirschner and Gerhart state: "It was a map of cells, some of which produced localized signals for localized responses including cell differentiation and tissue anatomy. It was also a map of cell groups that were spatially differentiated in their response to those signals. It was a map of partially overlapping spatial domains in the embryo that effectively divided the embryo into different compartments, each distinguishable from the others by a few genes expressed within it. The map has no anatomical counterpart, and the borders of compartments often crossed anatomical boundaries, just as political boundaries sometimes cross mountain ranges"; see Kirschner and Gerhart (2005, 181–182).

14 See Marc Kirschner and John Gerhart, "Evolvability," *Proceedings of the National Academy of Sciences of the United States of America* 95, (July 1998): 8420–8427.

References

Allen, Matthew. 2015. Compelled by the diagram: Thinking through C. H. Waddington's Epigenetic Landscape. In *Contemporaneity* 4, no. 1: 120–141.

Altenberg, Lee. 2005. Modularity in evolution: Some low-level questions. In *Modularity: Understanding the Development and Evolution of Natural Complex Systems*, eds. Werner Callebaut and Diego Rasskin-Gutman, 99–128. Cambridge, MA: The MIT Press.

Baldwin, James Mark. 1896. A new factor in evolution. Reprint in *Diacronia* 7 (April 27): 1–13.

———. 1902. *Development and evolution. Including psychological evolution, evolution by orthoplasy, and the theory of genetic modes*. Repr. Selected works of James Mark Baldwin: Developmental psychology and evolutionary epistemology, vol. 3. Bristol: Thoemmes Press, 2001.

Bosari, Giovanna. 2006. Between nature and environment: "In truth, man is hard to accommodate." In *Environ(ne)ment: Approaches for tomorrow*, trans. Marie Aquilino, Guillemette Morel Journel, John Tittensor and Alice Winkler, 35–49. Milan: Canadian Centre for Architecture/Skira.

Crispo, Erika. 2007. The Baldwin Effect and genetic assimilation: Revisiting two mechanisms of evolutionary change mediated by phenotypic plasticity. *Evolution* 61 (November): 2469–2479.

Décosterd, Jean-Gilles and Philippe Rahm. 2002. *Physiological architecture: Published for the exhibition at Swiss pavilion as part of the 8th International Architecture Exhibition at Venice 2002*. Basel: Birkhäuser.

Douglas Darden papers and drawings. 1979–1996a. Series I: Condemned Building, Subseries 10: Oxygen House, Box 04: Folder 04, Condemned Building, Oxygen House, Research Material, c.1980s–1993. Department of Drawings & Archives, Avery Architectural and Fine Arts Library, Columbia University.

———. 1979–1996b. Series I: Condemned Building, Subseries 10: Oxygen House, Box 04: Folder 05, Condemned Building, Oxygen House, Generative Material, c.1980s–1993. Department of Drawings & Archives, Avery Architectural and Fine Arts Library, Columbia University.

Darden, Douglas. 1993. *Condemned building: An architect's pre-text*. New York: Princeton Architectural Press.

García-Germán, Javier. 2017. *Thermodynamic interactions: An architectural exploration into physiological, material, territorial atmospheres*. New York: Actar Publishers.

Griffiths, Paul E. 2006. The fearless vampire conservator: Philip Kitcher, genetic determinism, and informational code. In *Genes in development: Re-reading the Molecular Paradigm*, eds. Eva Neumann-Held and Christoph Rehmann-Sutter, 175–198. Durham, NC: Duke University Press.

Harmon, Darell Boyd and American Seating Co. 1951. *The co-ordinated classroom*. Grand Rapids, MI: American Seating Company.

Kirschner, Marc W. and John C. Gerhart. 2005. *The plausibility of life: Resolving Darwin's dilemma*. New Haven, CT: Yale University Press.

LaMarche, Jean. 1998. The life and work of Douglas Darden: A brief encomium. *Utopian Studies* 9, no.1 (Winter): 162–172.

Levins, Richard and Richard Lewontin. 1985. *The dialectical biologist*. Cambridge, MA: The Harvard University Press.

Lewontin, Richard C. 1974. The analysis of variance and the analysis of causes. *American Journal of Human Genetics* 26: 400–411.

Neutra, Richard. 1954. *Survival through design*. New York: Oxford University Press.

Philippe Rahm architectes. Description of the Hormonorium installation. http://www.philipperahm.com/data/projects/hormonorium/index.html.

Simpson, George Gaylord. 1953. The Baldwin effect. In *Evolution* 7, no. 2 (June): 110–117.

———. 1967. *The meaning of evolution*. New Haven, CT: Yale University Press.

Tortosa, Guy. 2002. Décosterd & Rahm associés, the sense(s) in the senses. In *Physiological architecture: Published for the exhibition at Swiss pavilion as part of the 8th International Architecture Exhibition at Venice 2002*, 56–64. Basel: Birkhäuser.

Waddington, Conrad H. 1940. *Organisers and genes*. Cambridge Biological Studies. Cambridge: University Press.

———. 1953. Genetic assimilation of an acquired character. *Evolution* 7, no. 2 (June): 118–126.

———. 1957. The strategy of the genes: A discussion of some aspects of theoretical biology. London: George Allen & Unwin Ltd.

Whitman, Walt. 1899. *Leaves of grass: Including sands at seventy, good bye my fancy, old age echoes, and a backward glance o'er travel'd roads*. Boston, MA: Small, Maynard & Company.

8

THE BIO-PHYSICAL DWELLING

Shūsaku Arakawa and Madeline Gins's Bioscleave House (Lifespan Extending Villa)

> A prescriptive supposition, the Closely Argued Built-Discourse Hypothesis presents architecture as the supreme context for the examined life, a stage set for body-wide thought experiments. With architectural procedures prodding the body to know all that it is capable of, this becomes an intrusive and active stage set. The body must either escape or "reenter" habitual patterns of action – habitual actions that have customized life into only a few standard patterns. Upon the body's mastering new patterns of action, bioscleave emerges reconfigured.
>
> (Gins and Arakawa 2002, 62)

The "intrusive and active stage set" articulated above by the artists Shūsaku Arakawa and Madeline Gins suggests that the constructed *architectural environments* we design and inhabit are not passive backdrops, scenography within which things happen, but rather participatory actors compelled to provoke human actions in daily life. Throughout the years they spent focused on considering the unique possibilities which architecture provided to affect human inhabitants, they developed a whole vocabulary to better describe their approach. The idea of the constructed environment as a participatory actor is what they called an *architectural surround*, encompassing the "boundaries and all objects and persons within it" (Gins and Arakawa 2002, 39), the collection of elements with which one continuously engages – innkeeping with the concept of the "Terrestrial" *architectural* "dwelling place." In this sense, it's not a predetermined or static context but rather an active ongoing series of interactions, an "evolving matrix" (Gins and Arakawa 2002, 40) made possible through a person's continual dispersal of what they call *landing sites* – a person's "fielding" of his/her surroundings. This is the process of receiving external stimuli (information), synthesizing it and then apportioning[1] that understanding outward to form specific territories that together construct an

The Bio-Physical Dwelling **251**

FIGURE 8.1   Arakawa and Madeline Gins, *Landing Site Study*, digital rendering, 1994. © 1997 Estate of Madeline Gins. Reproduced with permission of the Estate of Madeline Gins. Image courtesy of Reversible Destiny Foundation.

environment constantly in flux. The specific territory formed through this process is a *landing site*; when several are linked together, they elicit a "characteristic series of ubiquitous sitings or landing-site configurations" (Gins and Arakawa 2002, 9) (Figure 8.1). Together these changing and adjusting collections of "landing-site configurations" are understood by an organism as its specific world, a concept very similar to Jakob von Uexküll's idea of "self-worlds" or *Umwelt* (see Chapter 6). Consequently, they also help to define the organism itself; "Through landing-site configurations, organism-person-environment takes hold and holds forth" (Gins and Arakawa 2002, 9). In a 1994 essay, "Architecture: Sites of Reversible Destiny" accompanying their first architectural monograph, Arakawa and Gins write the following axiom concerning a person's constructing of their world: "The universe as caught by perception is the world" (Arakawa and Gins 1994, 18). Its definition is defined by an individual's abilities to perceive it, and therefore construct it, yet its complexity is all but limitless.

> It would obviously be a mistake, when constructing a site of a person, to have this site be ground-oriented in the manner of all architectural sites; after all, the site of a person does not begin and end on that piece of ground on which a person stands nor with the piece of furniture on which she sits, nor even, for that matter, with the many points of contact

her body progressively makes with the water through which she swims. How complex the site of a person is remains to be seen...

The fabric of the world equals all a person presently perceives plus all she believes she perceives or believes herself to have ever perceived plus all she feels she might perceive. Each instance of perception lands as a site. The fabric of the world consists of a multitude, a plentitude, of sites.

(Arakawa and Gins 1994, 19)

This construction of world through the sensorial and cognitive systems of an individual has broad implications for Arakawa and Gins, and most importantly provides an opportunity for architecture, if reconceived with this understanding in mind, to take an even more integral role in life and in life reconfiguration. It has the potential to achieve this through the creation of provocations and ultimately actions, fostered by various *procedures* embedded within the construction of the architectural surround, collectively and continuously, "recasting or reconfiguring" life.[2]

A person's variable construction and engagement with their environment, their surroundings, through the dispersal of landing sites, evolves as one changes location and their relative intake of stimuli. In this way, landing sites are continuously reconfigured and thus "architectural surrounds stand as elaborately structured pretexts for action" as "atmospheric conditioners" (Gins and Arakawa 2002, 41), their features effecting, but also effected by, one's actions. "Sets of landing sites form contexts for each other, and this happens more within the *here* of the body than anywhere else in the world" (Arakawa and Gins 1994, 21). In this way, all human action is dependent upon, but also influenced by, the formation of landing sites – and the consequent construction of world – which themselves are dynamically configured relative to the sensing, perceiving and thinking individual, but also indirectly by all other individuals participating within them. So even while the continuous (re)creating, (re)configuring and (re)sequencing of landing sites is personal, the architectural surround as an "intrusive and active stage set" claims an indispensable role in the formation of the individual human-being and vice versa. Person (body) and architecture (surround) are inextricably connected, enmeshed with and within one another.

Bodily movements that take place within and happen in relation to works of architecture, architectural surrounds, are to some extent formative of them. Those living within and reading and making what they can of and architectural surround are instrumental in and crucial to its *tentative constructing toward a holding place.* We do not mean to suggest that architecture exists only for the one who beholds or inhabits it, but rather that the body-in-action and the architectural surround should not be defined apart from each other, or apart from biocleave.

(Gins and Arakawa 2002, 50)

The Bio-Physical Dwelling **253**

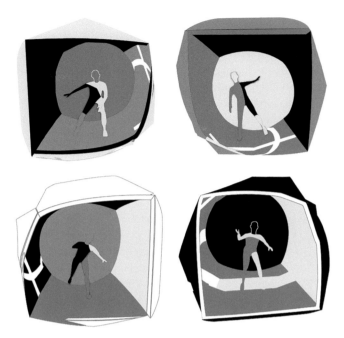

FIGURE 8.2 Arakawa and Madeline Gins, *Body Proper + Architectural Surround = ARCHITECTURAL BODY*, digital rendering, 1997. © 1997 Estate of Madeline Gins. Reproduced with permission of the Estate of Madeline Gins. Image courtesy of Reversible Destiny Foundation.

This intensive relationship between an individual human inhabitant, what they refer to as an "organism the persons," and the architectural surround becomes the "basic unit of study" for their conceptualization of their architectural project: *procedural architecture*. The name they give this unit is the *architectural body*, held together in "a tentative constructing towards a holding place" (Gins and Arakawa 2002, 51) (Figure 8.2).

This idea of "holding" is critical as it reflects an unstable-stability, one that is open to change, to reconfigurations of landing sites, in relationship to the changing of the conditions around its holding. Architects Jesse Reiser and Nanako Umemoto have made similar observations in their book *Atlas of Novel Tectonics* concerning their approach to design referring to this relationship as a state of "dynamic poise" (Reiser and Umemoto 2006, 96). They poignantly sum up this idea in the last sentence of the introduction to the book: "We hold to the idea that architecture is not simply reducible to the container and the contained but that there exists a dynamic exchange between the life of matter and the matter of our lives" (Reiser and Umemoto 2006, 34). For Arakawa and Gins, this type of inter-active collaborative and collective agency, can be extended not just between inhabitants and the *architectural environments* they occupy, but also to the greater surrounding environmental context of living and non-living beings with which they inter-act concurrently. The total of all inhabitant-environment constructs is what they call *biocleave*, a term specifically adopted as an alternative to the more conventional idea of biosphere. Their interest is in emphasizing the inter-active potential of the space between all environmental constructs and the actions of all kinds of living-beings. In her own words, quoted from the 2012 documentary film *We* directed by Nobu Yamaoka, Madeline Gins defines biocleave as "the place that allows life to happen" (Yamaoka and Gins 2012, 17: 36–38), and describes her and Arakawa's interest in using the term in the following way: "we changed biosphere to biocleave because 'scleave' is attaching-separating, attaching-separating, it is the dynamics that underly our possibility" (Yamaoka and Gins 2012, 17:48–18:00).

Biocleave is also the name Arakawa and Gins gave to their first-built architectural work in the United States and perhaps the most ambitious built manifestation of their procedural theory of architecture. The Biocleave House (Lifespan Extending Villa) is located in East Hampton, New York, commissioned in 1998 and completed in 2008. It was originally conceived and designed as an addition to an existing 1964 A-frame summer residence of Ms. Angela Gallman, the longtime partner of artist Vincenzo Agnetti, who had died in 1981, but with whom Arakawa and Madeline were friends (Bernstein 2008). While Ms. Gallman ended up abandoning the project during construction with costs well exceeding the initial construction budgets, and the obtainment of a building department certificate of occupancy remaining elusive, the property was bought by a group of "professors" (Professors Group, LLC), committing an additional $1 million or so to see the project completed (Bernstein 2008). While the full identity of the ownership group is not clear, according to project documents they brought in a new architect of record, Lawrence Marek, and a new general contractor to finish the construction (Figure 8.3). With the exception of one significant design element, the flooring surface which will be discussed shortly, as the project stands its construction methodology and finishes are fairly typical being composed of a stepped concrete foundation, CMU block, wood and steel framing, translucent polycarbonate panels, cement board, recycled cotton blue jean and blown-in cellulose insulation, concrete tiles, marmoleum and low voc paint.[3] Earlier design development drawings and images of the project show a much broader pallet of interior wall finishes, like copper, cedar siding, felt, rubber, faux stone panels, adobe, cork, rammed earth and wallpaper – all varying in color and textural qualities, to further intensify the multi-sensory interior experience (Figure 8.4). As built, this material diversity was replaced with a more cost-effective approach relying primarily on paint color variations, of which there are approximately 40 used on both the interior and exterior surfaces of the house.[4] Despite the use of fairly normative construction methodologies, the design logic and composition of the house – following the concepts of *procedural architectural* described above – is anything but typical.

FIGURE 8.3 Arakawa and Madeline Gins, *Bioscleave House (Lifespan Extending Villa)*, photo of exterior, East Hampton, New York, completed 2008. Photograph by Eric Striffler. Reproduced by permission from Eric Striffler Photography.

The house is organized as a series of four rectangular volumes, or "shape defining elements," each containing a different programmatic function (master bedroom, bathroom, guest bedroom and study), all of which are dispersed around an open free-flowing living space enclosed by walls spanning between the primary volumes, these intermediate walls are constructed of wood studs and translucent polycarbonate panels. The rectangular volumes are primarily solid, with punched windows inset along the top of the side walls as a kind of clearstory or at the base of the wall directly along the floor. The wall surfaces at the back of each volume are partially constructed using translucent polycarbonate panels and also incorporating more typical double hung windows of varying sizes inset somewhat randomly, but often allowing a view out to the surrounding vegetation. The lighting effect created by such window/wall compositions is continuously varying – sometimes direct through the transparent glazing, often ambient through the translucent polycarbonate, and because all of the window frames have been painted different colors, there is a continuously changing glow of colored light coming in from the clearstory or bouncing up from the floor (Figure 8.5).

The area at the very center of the house, like the hearth at the center of an early human shelter, is the kitchen and off to one side, the built-in dining table. Both spaces are recessed into the floor a little more than three feet from the surrounding area, but over six feet, from the level at which one enters the central space. This significant difference in elevation is a result of the dwelling's most

FIGURE 8.4 Arakawa and Madeline Gins, *Bioscleave House (Lifespan Extending Villa)*, view to the south, digital rendering, 2004. © 2008 Estate of Madeline Gins. Reproduced with permission of the Estate of Madeline Gins. Image courtesy of Reversible Destiny Foundation.

radical design element, the floor surface; it surrounds the kitchen, extends down to become a seat for the dining table and extends up to become the floor of the two-bedroom volumes. This floor surface has not been conceived like a flat surface, but rather more like an undulating terrain of ebbs and flows, peaks and valleys, beginnings and endings (Figure 8.6). The floor surface is also not smooth; it's textured with small bumps like dimples in reverse that provide localized anchor points, momentarily providing a footing as one traverses across the space. These bumps are repetitive, in the sense that they cover the entirety of the central floor terrain, but their size, frequency, overall composition and exact shape varies (Figure 8.7). The consequence of this variation, in conjunction with the varying geometry of the floor surface and light qualities created from the different types of fenestration, results in the constant shifting of one's perception of the terrain itself – its form, slope and pattern – as well as the overall space of the central void.

The Bio-Physical Dwelling **257**

FIGURE 8.5 Arakawa and Madeline Gins, *Bioscleave House (Lifespan Extending Villa)*, photo of interior window wall within one of the volumes, East Hampton, New York, completed 2008. Photographs by author.

FIGURE 8.6 Arakawa and Madeline Gins, *Bioscleave House (Lifespan Extending Villa)*, photo of interior, East Hampton, New York, completed 2008. Photographs by author.

Although the terrain is physically continuous, when moving about you are forced to constantly revaluate where you're going, what trajectory you might travel and how to physically move your body to follow it – you are obligated to participate in various procedures of dwelling.

258 Bio-Physical Inter-Action

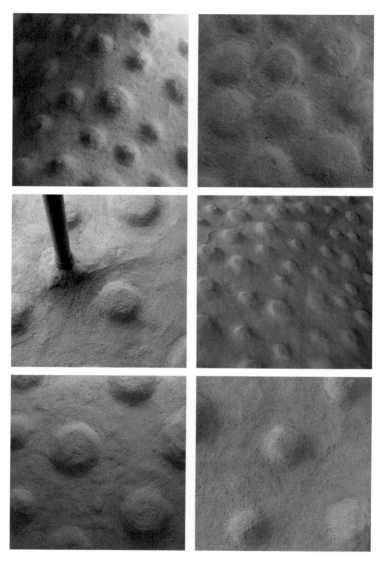

FIGURE 8.7 Arakawa and Madeline Gins, *Biocleave House (Lifespan Extending Villa)*, photos of variations of the interior floor surface, East Hampton, New York, completed 2008. Photographs by author.

The floor terrain is materially constructed as a traditional Japanese earthen floor called *tataki*, a mixture of cement and clay that has been molded on top of the stepped concrete foundation and a sculpted subfloor of stacked extruded polystyrene sheets. In addition to the undulating floor terrain, there are a number of floor-to-ceiling poles painted a variety of colors and placed throughout the central space, though not adhering to any obvious frequency or pattern. While they provide helpful points of stability from which one can navigate the undulating floor terrain, they also serve as elements with which one can begin to mark out relative distance and perception of the space, and therefore how to proprioceptively navigate the terrain.

The conceptual and procedural importance of the undulating floor terrain cannot be overstated as a means for achieving the dynamic and inter-active type of habitation Arakawa and Gins were fundamentally trying to achieve. As a point of contrast, during the approximately ten years of time that the Bioscleave House was being designed and constructed, Arakawa and Gins designed and built a house prototype located in Nagoya City, Japan, in accordance with the 2005 international, *Ai-chikyūhaku* (愛・地球博) "Love the Earth Expo" (ARAKAWA+GINS Tokyo Office). The house is called the External Genome House – Shidami, and is designed as a kind of multi-level townhouse that could be replicated and aggregated into larger multi-unit organizations. Though only one unit was constructed as a model home for the Expo, there were proposals to build whole neighborhoods of similarly designed units. The prototype house is designed with a similar organizational strategy as the Bioscleave House and another contemporaneous residential project, the Reversible Destiny Lofts – Mitaka, constructed outside Tokyo in 2005 (Figure 8.8). They both adopted a similar layout as the Bioscleave House with an open centralized

FIGURE 8.8 Arakawa and Madeline Gins, *Reversible Destiny Lofts – Mitaka (In Memory of Helen Keller)*, digital rendering, Mitaka, Tokyo, Japan, 2001. © 2019 Estate of Madeline Gins. Reproduced with permission of the Estate of Madeline Gins. Image courtesy of Reversible Destiny Foundation.

living space, central sunken kitchen and a series of rooms dispersed around the perimeter, each containing a different programmatic function. While the elevation of the floor across the entirety of the central space of the External Genome House does change significantly, there's a critical difference between it and the central floor terrain of the Biocleave House and Mitaka Lofts. Instead of the *tataki* mixture of cement and clay molded into a continuously undulating surface from one side of the house to the other, its central floor is constructed as a series of wooden steps and platforms. While some of the shapes and overall configuration of the stepped areas are non-standard, their application and detailing are traditional, made of simple wood planking, integral nosing and base molding where they meet the surrounding vertical surfaces (Figures 8.9 and 8.10). Other significant differences in the design of the External Genome House are its overall more compact layout and more consistent interior materiality of surfaces, mostly white walls with accents of red, green, yellow and pink on the window frames, columns or ceiling. These accenting colors are not as extreme as the discord of paint colors, let alone the rotated electrical wall outlets, switches and colored marmoleum and concrete tiles of the Bioscleave House. These differences in the actualization of the External Genome House result in a radically different interior expression and experience from the

FIGURE 8.9 Arakawa and Madeline Gins, *External Genome House – Shidami*, photo of exterior, total ground area 21,528 sq. ft. (2,000 m^2); total building area 4,098 sq. ft. (380.68 m2); total floor area 6,275 sq. ft. (582.98 m^2), Shidami, Nagoya, Japan, 2005. © 2019 Estate of Madeline Gins. Reproduced with permission of the Estate of Madeline Gins. Photo courtesy of Nagoya City Housing Supply Corporation.

FIGURE 8.10 Arakawa and Madeline Gins, *External Genome House – Shidami*, photo of interior, total ground area 21,528 sq. ft. (2,000 m^2); total building area 4,098 sq. ft. (380.68 m2); total floor area 6,275 sq. ft. (582.98 m^2), Shidami, Nagoya, Japan, 2005. © 2019 Estate of Madeline Gins. Reproduced with permission of the Estate of Madeline Gins. Photo courtesy of Nagoya City Housing Supply Corporation.

Bioscleave House, one that's more stable, predictable and normative, ultimately less capable of producing the tentative holding of *architectural body* so critical to the *procedural architectural* project.[5]

For Arakawa and Gins, the primary intent of inhabiting the Bioscleave House was to cultivate a state of tentative holding whereby the "organism that persons," the architectural surround and elements of the larger external context are all in constant communication – reconfiguration. This was not intended to be a singular event, but rather the experience of living within a procedural work of architecture was considered "daily research" (Gins and Arakawa 2002, 95–96). The house was specifically conceived as an "interactive laboratory of everyday life" (Arakawa and Gins 2004), a test ground for bettering your mental and physical health. They wrote a manual for how to live in the house which they called "Directions for Use," a more general version of which was compiled into a custom-designed letterpress book/box printed from hand-processed photopolymer plates and hand-set type, designed by Inge Bruggman/INK-A! Press. On the back of each page is a partial image of the Bioscleave House plan that when each page is removed and folded out, they can be put together to reconstruct a complete architectural plan of the house (Bruggeman 2003) (Figure 8.11). The text of the manual describes the various procedures one might undertake while living in a construction of *procedural*

FIGURE 8.11 Inge Bruggeman, *A Crisis Ethicists' Directions for Use – or How to be at Home in a Residence-cum-Laboratory*, a limited-edition artist's book project, 2003. Image courtesy of Inge Bruggeman.

architecture in order to better oneself and achieve the full potential of the *architectural body*. This requires an inhabitant's full commitment to living as an extension of the architecture and vice versa. "As you step into this house fully believe you are walking into your own immune system."[6] Madeline explained this experience of daily living, with and within the house, further through the concept of "bio-topology," the name she and Arakawa gave to their "new science" of *procedural architecture* and the *architectural body*.

> Bio-topology asks that you take into consideration as many different scales of action as you can, all at the same time, and it's not easy to do that. You can not do that yourself. You can not remember it all. You can not be aware of all that you need to be aware of, but what if your house is helping you? Your house is, "oh, I'm here. I'm your friend. I'm your physician. I'm your ally. I will help you remember this scale of action, and that scale of action. This is necessary for you to do. Don't forget you need to do this. This has to happen also." There are just so many ways it can be done. We have to really tear open ignorance.
> (Nobu and Gins 2012, 21:00–21:38)

In this sense, the Bioscleave House maintains its own agency, it speaks to, and with, inhabitants throughout their daily lives and provides them with insights and information they might otherwise not readily retain. The philosopher of art and performance Jondi Keane, who has spent an extended amount of time in the Bioscleave House as a "daily researcher," has described this inter-active state as being between what he refers to as the "noetic" and the "somatic," as a kind of "body-wide processing passing through the conceptual organisation" of the house (Keane 2005, 2). He provides three specific examples of how the architectural construction instigates this awareness through the repetition of various references to the house's overall plan within numerous spaces.

> The table in the sunken dining room is the plan of the house turned 90°. The ceiling of the bathroom has a plan of the house. The [proposed] labyrinth in the garden is the floor plan of the house in smaller scale.
>
> *(Keane 2005, 2–3)*

There are also a number of other instances within the house that we can include on this list like the stainless steel home automation control pad wall plates in the shape of the house's plan; the study has a plan of the house centered within the floor tiles and the shape of the central skylight over the kitchen is also a plan of the house. Concerning the relationship between the body's physical experience and the cognitive awareness created through these scalar shifts referencing the plan of the house, Keane states the following:

> One's bodily position to the plan and to the house requires a transposition and correlation making it evident to the resident researcher which mode of sensing or memory is deployed. Dining becomes an exercise in memory and transposition. Bathing becomes an exercise in imaging and dimensional sing and walking in the garden an exercise in muscle memory and orientation.
>
> *(Keane 2005, 3)*

Similarly, to Keane's observations and assessment concerning the repetition of the plan figure throughout the house, another tactic of *procedural architecture* that Arakawa and Gins deploy is to purposefully create "contradictory" prompts of the body (Figure 8.12). The specific example they've often cited in their early writings is the incorporation of a multilayer "labyrinth," which consists of a series of mazes compressed, differently scaled and overlaid on top of one another to create superimposed and contradictory paths of movement within spaces.

> As a person walked through the multilevel labyrinth with its distinctly different segments stacked one on top of the other, she might be receiving instructions to follow a path of one kind from the labyrinth at, say, her knees, and indications of quite another shape and direction for a path to be taken from a labyrinth at her waist or chest. To follow multiple and contradictory paths, the body would have to enlist far more than the usual number of landing sites. Due to unexpected blockages on one labyrinth level or another, the passage as a whole would be one through which the body would have to twist, bend, shove, squeeze and propel itself.
>
> *(Arakawa and Gins 1994, 21–22)*

264 Bio-Physical Inter-Action

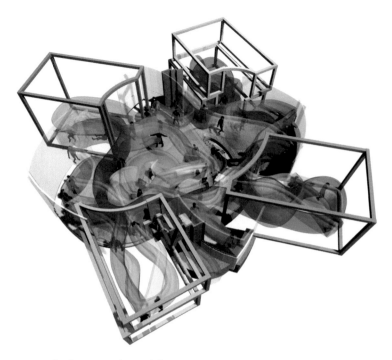

FIGURE 8.12 Arakawa and Madeline Gins, *Bioscleave House (Lifespan Extending Villa)*, digital rendering study, 2002. © 2019 Estate of Madeline Gins. Reproduced with permission of the Estate of Madeline Gins. Image courtesy of Reversible Destiny Foundation.

The Bioscleave House has some evidence of this tactic in the design of the two perimeter volumes that contain the bedrooms. Each has been "cut" about halfway up the wall and shifted out to create a horizontal split in space as well as a cove for concealing light fixtures and a shelf on the other side. Within the other two volumes, the bathroom and the study, it was proposed but never built that each would have an elevated diagonal wall that moved across the space from one corner to the other producing a multilayered experience. These layering moments in the Bioscleave House are modest compared to earlier multilayer "labyrinth" proposals, such as the Reversible Destiny House I, Reversible Destiny House II (the Critical Resemblance House), the Trench House, Cleaving Wave House, Modular Labyrinth House and studies for public housing (Figure 8.13). These proposals are extreme and quite literal in their incorporation and layering of the labyrinth as a device for impacting the body and forcing contradictory actions. In these projects, the architectural surround is responsible for altering our "shape of awareness" (Gins and Arakawa 2002, 85) and hopefully our perpetual reshaping and biological reconfiguration.

Arakawa and Gins's approach of challenging the human body, destabilizing it and instigating contradictory actions through the design of a constructed

The Bio-Physical Dwelling   **265**

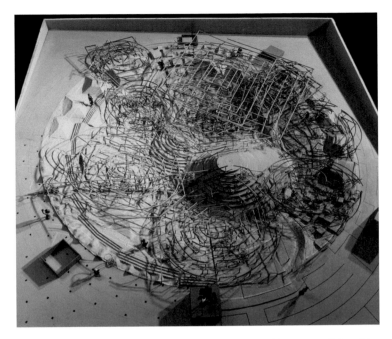

FIGURE 8.13   Arakawa and Madeline Gins, *Site of Reversible Destiny IV*, architectural model, 7 × 37 × 72 in, 1981–1993. © 2019 Estate of Madeline Gins. Reproduced with permission of the Estate of Madeline Gins. Image courtesy of Reversible Destiny Foundation.

environment was briefly explored earlier in the twentieth century by Austrian architect Günther Feuerstein. Generally motivated by a critique of the prevailing functionalist utilitarian approach of many European postwar architects and urbanists, he submitted proposals in 1960 to the German section of the Situationist International, *Spur* no. 5, a special issue devoted to "unitary" urbanism, proposing what he called "impractical flats"[7] (McDonough 2009, 20–23). The proposals were a kind of inversion of modern convenience to instead actively work against what he perceived as an antiseptic, detached approach of functionalism that provided no real feeling and no real understanding of living or being. Writing in reference to Feuerstein's proposed "impractical flats" in his book *The Situationist City*, Simon Sadler described them in the following way:

> By declining labor-saving devices, devising tortuous routes through his apartment, and fitting it with noisy doors and useless locks, Feuerstein refused to allow his own home to become another cog in the mechanized world. It would no longer protect him from the environment nor the sensations of his own body: ripping out his air conditioning and throwing open his windows, he could swelter, shiver, and struggle to hear himself think above the roar of the city; later he might bump and hurt himself

against one of the myriad sharp corners in his flat, and sit at his wobbly table and on his uncomfortable sofa. Or he might unwind by throwing paint against the walls and drilling holes through them, filling out his flat with traces of his own ideas and history.

(Sadler 1998, 7–8)

The "impractical flats" not in spite of, but because of their conception as a series of tortuous obstacles to be endured, moved away from a functionalist utilitarian approach; "The creative, the spiritual, the emotional qualities have no longer any place" (Feuerstein 1964–1965, 33) and toward an architecture of radical experience and challenge. While his conception did away with the mechanized comforts of modern life, or even inverted them, it provided the inhabitant new agency to act, to participate, to engage and even create his/her *architectural* "dwelling place." This type of active participation and construction was fundamental to a contemporaneous Austrian architect and fellow critic of the post-war functionalist utilitarian approach, Friedensreich Hundertwasser. In his 1958 recitation of his essay "Mould Manifesto against Rationalism in Architecture," Hundertwasser argues like Feuerstein that a functionalist utilitarian approach was a mistaken approach, "a wrong road," and that it cannot be overcome until architecture first becomes "impractical, unusable, and finally uninhabitable" (Hundertwasser 1970, 158) and "covered in mould" (Hundertwasser 1970, 160). It is only at this point of complete uninhabitability that architecture and the human-being can be reborn. And according to Hundertwasser, this rebirth can only effectively be carried out by inhabitants themselves.

Only when architect, bricklayer and occupant are a unity, i.e. one and the same person, can one speak of architecture. Everything else is not architecture but the physical incarnation of a criminal act...

If the unity architect-bricklayer-occupant is lost there is no architecture...Man must regain his critical-creative function, which he has lost and without which he ceases to exist as a human being.

(Hundertwasser 1970, 159)

Feuerstein makes a similar point concerning the value of what he calls the "emotional recall" related to things we make ourselves when he says, "The ideal would be for everyone to build his own house – and this of course would make the architect superfluous" (Feuerstein 1964–1965, 35). In this sense, the Bioscleave House, having been conceived of and designed by two conceptual artists not trained as professional architects, may have made its inception as an environment of critical-creativity and inter-action possible. Perhaps the house was even a space Arakawa and Madeline imagined living in themselves,[8] a house that by its very nature becomes a part of any inhabitant who steps inside and spends time within its surround, formulating an *architectural body.*

In his short 1958 essay "Theses on Unpremeditated Architecture," Feuerstein argues that practicality is equivalent to the pursuit of the "superperfect" house.

> The ideal, then, would be the superperfect house so smooth in functioning that one ceases to be aware of it…A dwelling of this sort would be described as "comfortable" or "practical"; one has no further contact with it. We grow quickly accustomed to whatever is practical or pleasant; the experience of "dwelling," of living in a place, is no longer real, because there have ceased to be surfaces of friction.[9]
>
> *(Feuerstein 1964–1965, 34)*

Friction, correspondence, communication are exactly what Arakawa and Gins seek through their concept of *procedural architecture* and the formation of the *architectural body*. In comparison to what he calls "contemporary classical architecture," Feuerstein makes a similar claim that "Unpremeditated architecture, on the contrary, allows of change, allows of history, invites such changes" (Feuerstein 1964–1965, 36), and that over time "*because* of the aging process the building acquires an increasingly intense historicity and sensitivity" (Feuerstein 1964–1965, 37). While Feuerstein is speaking predominantly about the physical elements of architecture, the registration of time in the transformation of its materials, he is also indirectly referring to the positive emotional and psychological effects on the experiences of inhabitants he claims are a result of an unpremeditated architecture's collecting of "patina."

Taking Feuerstein's proposals for "impractical flats" alongside his larger critique of a functionalist utilitarian architectural approach and the proposition of "unpremeditated architecture," his architectural conceptualization, much like Arakawa and Gins, is both physically demanding as well as mentally and emotionally engaging. Within the short introduction to Feuerstein's essay as it was first published in the German journal *Spur* no. 5, the editors characterized his approach in the following way: "Feuerstein's incidental architecture is absolutely *zersetzend* – starting from micro-areas, coincidences, processes, emotions, human behaviors, intimacy, new units of measurement, new material concepts, etc"[10] (Prem et al. 1961, para. 1). The use of the term "zersetzend" is very interesting as its root (zersetzen) can literally be translated as "to decompose" or "to corrode"; but it has a secondary meaning that comes from its use in psychological warfare of the East German state as a covert technique for repressing political opponents and dissidents.[11] As it was used here by the editors of *Spur* in reference to Feuerstein's concept of "unpremeditated architecture," Tom McDonough has translated it to mean "absolutely subversive" (McDonough 2009, 20). To the architect intent on designing spaces of comfort and accommodation, the architectural design approach articulated by Arakawa and Gins maintains a similarly subversive approach of co-production. Their architecture aims to facilitate the continuous creation of new experiences that challenge the *architectural body*, in all its forms and configurations, to act differently, to reconfigure.

268 Bio-Physical Inter-Action

The point is to construct that which will elicit landing site configurations that will exceed all expectations or that will offer new levels of expectations.

Fundamental change will not be brought about by chance meetings with unusual landings site configurations; instead what is required is constant contact with configurations capable of spinning one about in one's tracks.

(Arakawa and Gins 1994, 22)

Arakawa and Gins conceive a tentative constructing of the organism-person-architecture-environment as a collective being, a constructing in and of bioscleave (Figure 8.14). "An architectural work that will serve the body well will maximize its chances of drawing on and blending with bioscleave, positioning the body in such a way that it can best coordinate itself within its surroundings" (Gins and Arakawa 2002, 49). Living in the Bioscleave House is living with and within bioscleave itself, as part of the total collective "being-with." It is the fulfillment and consequence of this tentative engagement between inhabitant and habitation that provides the underlying ambition for Arakawa and Gins's most ambitious goal of subversion, to reverse our mandated destiny, to reverse mortality altogether – what they refer to as "reversible destiny." Although a seemingly naïve or fantastical aspiration, they approached the idea as an intensely serious proposition,

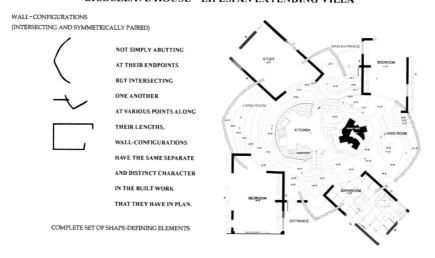

FIGURE 8.14 Arakawa and Madeline Gins, *Bioscleave House (Lifespan Extending Villa)*, set of Shape Defining Elements digital rendering plan, 2006. © 2010 Estate of Madeline Gins. Reproduced with permission of the Estate of Madeline Gins. Image courtesy of Reversible Destiny Foundation.

developing the notion for the better part of their 45-year artistic collaboration together (Schonbek 2016). Their first architectural retrospective held at the Guggenheim Museum SoHo in 1997 was even titled "We Have Decided Not to Die." In the 2010 documentary film *Children Who Won't Die*, Arakawa describes his view of humans and their ultimate fate of death in the following way: "The current state of humans around the world is getting worse. At this point in time I wanted to get a grip on evolution. Left to the natural world, once we are born, we are just heading toward death" (Yamaoka and Arakawa 2010, 46:05–46:24). Later on in the film, he goes on to state: "Existing theories of human evolution are laughable" (Yamaoka and Arakawa 2010, 56:26–56:31).

Although both Arakawa and Gins have now passed away – he in 2010 from ALS and she in January of 2014 from metastatic cancer (Schonbek 2016) – the potential of their ideas related to "reversible destiny" remain potent. Their collaborative work started within the medium of conceptual art, most demonstrably through their ambitious, large-scale, multipaneled series, produced over a number of years, titled *The Mechanism of Meaning*, which, writing in the preface to their book of the same name, they describe as a study not of individual phenomena like "images, percepts, or thoughts" but rather concerned with "all given conditions brought together in one place" and even at this early stage claiming that "Death is old-fashioned" (Arakawa and Gins 1979, 4). *The Mechanism of Meaning* canvases were large enough (96 × 68 inches) to be visually and cognitively immersive, taking up most of one's field of vision and putting forth questions and mental exercises to the viewer/participant that would intentionally instigate thought, self-reflection and the questioning of accepted social, cultural and cognitive norms, and even action. Writing about the project in the catalog to their Guggenheim retrospective show, philosopher Fred Leland Rush describes *The Mechanism of Meaning* in terms of reframing meaning relative to a radical reconsideration of contemporary morality.

> Arakawa and Gins seek a fundamental reordering that results in a different conception of what it is to be a morally responsible subject. The reordering aims at creating agents whose subjectivity no longer carries with it the irrational desire to consume nature and a compulsion for mass murder and self-destruction. Such subjects would view themselves as coeval with other beings, all the while recognizing the moral obligations that flow from the fact that we are creatures that influence our environment by our conceptions. Such a moral bearing involves nothing less than organizing our interactions in the world so as not to implicitly transfer to others the authority latent in our having this or that concept of the world as a whole. For while what counts as a world for us may have very much to do with our conception of it, no one conception of it (or even the fact that it can only be a world for us under some conception or another) should be

taken as authority to make the world just that way....We must continually remake ourselves in as inclusive a manner as possible at any given time.

(Lush 1997, 52)

Rush's reading of intent behind *The Mechanism Meaning* carries an interesting corollary to the ideas of Arne Naess's personal approach to deep ecology, *Ecosophy T*, and might also be applied to Arakawa and Gins's architectural projects (and perhaps most potently to their urban proposals). Madeline herself has claimed: "Everything that we are doing now in our procedural architecture, everything, comes from *The Mechanism of Meaning*" (Yamaoka and Gins 2012, 6:58–7:03). After completing the vast majority of *The Mechanism of Meaning* cycle in 1973,[12] their collaborative work began to evolve toward more overtly spatial propositions, becoming full-scale physically immersive proposals and constructions[13] – *Bridge of Reversible Destiny / The Process in Question* (1973–1979), *Rubber Labyrinth, Critical Resemblances* (1979–1991), *Truncated Cone, Critical Resemblances* (1979–1991) and *Paintings for Closed Eyes* (1989–1990) – ultimately leading to a full-fledged realization and commitment to architecture as the medium most capable of advancing their effort toward the moral imperative of creating "reversible destiny." Speaking about the aim of their work to more directly engage with people and create a dialogue toward opening up and reconfiguration, Gins states, "Once we knew we had to surround them, then we were at architecture" (Yamaoka and Gins 2012, 28:00–28:06).

While the Bioscleave House reflects the most advanced single construction of *procedural architecture* intent on creating reversible destiny in human beings, it is the application of their ideas at an even greater scale of the collective – the village, the city – that Arakawa and Gins spoke of as having the most potential for reversing mortality and instigating more healthful lives: "City planning must become reversible destiny planning" (Arakawa and Gins 1994, 23). In 1994, their entry to the international competition to build a city in Tokyo Bay, tilted "Sensorium City," was awarded first prize. Though never realized, it initiated a number of subsequent large-scale planning and urban design proposals for new settlements of collective *procedural* dwelling.[14] What's important to recognize is that for them, this expansion of scale, from the singular to the collective, did not require a re-thinking of their strategies for designing spaces of habitation, it was quite simply a multiplication of their ideas applied toward a greater territory, becoming a kind of ecological intervention (Figures 8.15). Rather than redefine their concepts of the unitary dwelling, their urban proposals were very much a substantiation of them in general. Their conception of the collective – the village, the city – was simply a more expansive and continuous "Terrestrial" *architectural* "dwelling place."

> To reverse destiny one must first re-enter destiny, re-positioning oneself within the destiny of being slated to live without ever knowing exactly how and why. The re-entering of destiny must be highly calculated. The world

FIGURE 8.15 Arakawa and Madeline Gins, *Isle of Reversible Destiny – Fukuoka*, digital rendering, 2003. © 2016 Estate of Madeline Gins. Reproduced with permission of the Estate of Madeline Gins. Image courtesy of Reversible Destiny Foundation.

and everything in it will have to be transformed into a site of reversible destiny. The site must function not as a museum or a park, but as a dwelling, and not an isolated dwelling, but as a whole complex of dwellings, a city.

(Arakawa and gins 1994, 23)

Within the context of the reversible destiny city as described by Arakawa and Gins, the "Terrestrial" *architectural* "dwelling place" becomes a more collective environment, one expanded beyond the individual domestic spaces of habitation to include the collective experience, the public sphere as well as nature integral to the pursuit of reversible destiny. This expansion out into nature was included in various versions of the Bioscleave House, where process drawing sets and images show the incorporation of an enclosed swimming pool taking the shape and configuration derived from replicating the adjacent geometry of the central portion of the house and offsetting it out toward the side yard. The surrounding exterior area around the house was also proposed as another whole "terrain" of different constructions arrayed around the volumes of the house, sometimes replicating the outline of its plan at various scales through retaining walls, vegetation, manipulation of the ground and the insertion of other materials, even a maze (Figure 8.4). The intention being, as it was with their urban scale proposals, for the inhabitant to always be in some way engaged with the house as a communicating actor, engendering but also challenging one's continued experience of habitation. The pool and the extended landscape surrounding the house were never realized, and their urban planning proposals all met the same fate as well. Despite this, however, Arakawa and

Gins's urban proposals remain radical in their approach, much more derivative of their early ideas concerning the overlapping and multilayered labyrinths of contradictory paths and prompts at the scale of territory rather than adopting a rational exposition of hierarchical planning. These collective living proposals value complexity, layering, irregularity and a kind of controlled chaos that might be described as tangled or jumbled. But these proposals also recognize that the space outside the dwelling proper, the shared public space of the city, is a critical element contributing toward an architectural "project" capable of moving beyond the sustainable and toward one of actively participating in the advancement of human lives – and in their moral construct toward reversible destiny. The public spaces of Arakawa and Gins are almost always inclusive of other various ecological elements and activities – shared green roofs, gardens of anti-aging and self-invention, healing parks, recreational parks, playgrounds, farmer's markets, communal activity areas and undulating terrains of trees, grass and other plant life.[15]

Considering the architectural work of Arakawa and Gins as a "Terrestrial" *architectural* "dwelling place" aimed at cultivating a dynamically engaged inhabitant, one capable of collaborating with his/her architectural surround, instigating exploration and providing the possibility to actively take control of your person, suggests another reading of their work that is profoundly political. Architect, writer, social critic and former collaborator of the Reversible Destiny Design office Léopold Lambert elaborates on the political nature of their architectural work in an article titled "Towards an Architecture That Does Not Know What the Body is." He articulates how their conception of architecture accepts a reality of not fully knowing, understanding or defining a "normative" human body for whom architects are supposed to design; instead, they take an opposite position focusing on what architecture "embraces to ignore" (Lambert n.d., para. 2). In this sense, there is no pretense for control or for standardization, unlike, as he points out, in the Modernist project whose effects still impact design today through disciplinary and industry standards toward the human body[16] (Figures 8.16 and 8.17). The effects of such standardization, though helpful to industry, produce what Lambert calls an "essentializing" of the body and its traits, resulting in marginalization. Lambert argues these kinds of standardizing systems set the stage for forms of "corporeal violence," discrimination against those who do not fall within what is determined to be normal.

> It appears more and more to me that all forms of corporeal violence (racism, misogyny, transphobia, homophobia, etc.) can be said to be built upon a complete knowledge of what a body is. In other words, essentializing a race or a gender, whether to value it or denigrating it – it is ultimately the same thing – would constitute in saying "I know what a body is."
>
> *(Lambert n.d., para. 2)*

FIGURE 8.16 Arakawa and Madeline Gins, *Bioscleave House (Lifespan Extending Villa)*, photo of wall detail showing the placement of switches, lighting and HVAC controls, East Hampton, New York, completed 2008. Photograph by author.

FIGURE 8.17 Arakawa and Madeline Gins, *Bioscleave House (Lifespan Extending Villa)*, photo of interior, East Hampton, New York, completed 2008. Photograph by Eric Striffler. Reproduced by permission from Eric Striffler Photography.

And

> Not thinking of any particular body while designing architecture can prove difficult if not impossible; yet, we can consider socially marginalized bodies in an effort to redistribute violence in a given society, or more precisely embrace our ignorance for what a body is. Arakawa and Gins did both…interested in denying any incarnated category altogether to favor an acknowledgement for our profound ignorance of what makes a body.
>
> *(Lambert n.d., para. 3)*

Arakawa and Gins's architectural project suggests an alternative approach that considers and accepts all bodies as they are, challenging them, stimulating them, but providing possibility and ultimately a form of self-determinism. It is in this sense that their work might be regarded as political, while not the only contributing factor toward greater "freedom and variability"; [17] in fact, Lambert specifically rejects an architecture of liberation,[18] but acknowledges that it "embodies the way bodies are organized in space within a given society and, for this reason, influences the way the latter operates politically" (Lambert n.d., para. 5). To reconceive the individual not in terms of accepted norms or standards, but rather as a unique individual within and along what Harvard psychologist Ellen Langer refers to as a "continuum" of life, reflects a new-found agency for inhabiting the constructed environments we create, as individuals, but also humanity, and the total collective "being with." This inter-action which is at the core of Arakawa and Gins's conception of *procedural architecture* and all its potentials provides an alternative way forward that is not about reducing the impact of environment on our bodies toward the pursuit of ideal comfort, but rather intends to provide an evolving environment of habitation with and within which to interact and "corelate" – it becomes *more* present, *more* active in the lives of human-beings.

The cerebral potential of this inter-action to foster meaningful collaborations between architecture and the human-being helps to establish what Langer calls "mindful health," cultivated by a conscious awareness of the variability in one's everyday environment through observation, discovery, interaction and mindfulness.[19] Regarding variability in her book *Counterclockwise*,[20] she says: "With attention to variability comes an increase in perceived control, which in turn will make us pay more attention to the situation; an increase in mindfulness will increase health and increase our control over symptoms" (Langer 2009, 92). Actively engaging this variability of environment cultivates an individual responsibility, an awareness, not really possible when we give over control to various personal and home automation technologies (see Chapter 1). According to Langer, the potential is for a collaborative understanding of the relationship between the body, mind and environment – not a cartesian dualism of separation between body and mind, nor a kind of early behaviorism describing life "without reference to mental events" and only as "physical stimuli and physical responses" (Langer 1989, 173). The possibility is for a conception of health and well-being influenced by an integrated conception of thought and emotion as understood through a perceived *context*. Langer's view of context and its related influence on our health is not simply as an external stimulus projected and received, but rather includes our learned interpretation of these influences through personal, social and cultural experiences. In this way learned context is a form of mediation (Langer 1989, 175–177).

> Any stimulus can be seen as simultaneously many stimuli. Our perceptions and interpretations influence the way our bodies respond. *When the "mind" is in a context, the "body" is necessarily also in that context.* To achieve

The Bio-Physical Dwelling **275**

a different physiological state, sometimes what we need to do is to place the mind in another context.

(Langer 1989, 177)

Understood through this lens, architecture, as an integral element of the human being's "Terrestrial" *architectural* "dwelling place," for which the Bioscleave House provides one possibility of its design and formulation, has the potential to productively challenge and stimulate people, providing greater "freedom and variability" of individual and collective experience. And it reflects a conception of the individual not as static predetermined human-being but as a continuously changing human-becoming.[21] In this sense, the architect is provided an opportunity but also a responsibility to consider foremost how the constructed environments he/she creates may provide opportunities for co-productive stimulation of bio-physical actions and, on a more expansive scale, the collective human experience, and how we might now choose to live-in-the-world-ecology. It is through this understanding that the work of Arakawa and Gins fosters a deeply political dimension, requiring architects and designers who shape our constructed environments of habitation to consider its potential to impact and effect positive change with and within the total collective "being-with." Concerning the reversible destiny aspiration of the Bioscleave House, and the work of Arakawa and Gins more generally, Madeline Gins sums up this potential in an interview with Léopold Lambert in the following way:

> Thus far architects have ignored, or given scant thought to, the fact that each species has its niche and unfortunately have not sought to design that niche that could greatly prolong human life, the best of all niches that would maximally provide members of our species with a heroic means for survival. To repeat: Think of a work of Procedural Architecture (aka *Reversible Destiny* Architecture) as a new scientific device (a new art-scientific device?!) that you can use for reconfiguring yourself so that you can come to grasp what goes on and learn how to stay alive ongoingly.
>
> *(Lambert 2014, 45)*

Notes

1 Apportion is the word Arakawa and Gins often used to describe the cognizant recognition of information taken in from the environment and then dispersed out to form specific areas that together form a person's world.
2 Within the preface of their book *Architectural Body*, they describe the selection of the book's title, having rejected the title "Constructing Life" because "the work has

276 Bio-Physical Inter-Action

more to do with recasting or reconfiguring life than with and out-and-out constructing of it"; see Gins and Arakawa (2002, ix).

3 See document, "Bioscleave House Fact Sheet," n.d., digital file, Reversible Destiny Foundation Archive, New York.

4 Ibid.

5 The External Genome House – Shidami was Arakawa and Madeline's first-built residential project, and because of its perceived deficiencies seems to have been somewhat eclipsed in the office after its completion by focus on the construction of the Reversible Destiny Lofts – Mitaka and the Bioscleave House.

6 This point comes from a "Directions for Use" document specifically related to the Bioscleave House; see Document, "Bioscleave House: Directions for Use," n.d., digital file, Reversible Destiny Foundation Archive, New York.

7 See Günther Feuerstein, "Thesen über inzidente Architektur," in *Spur*, no. 5, "Spezialnummer über den unitären Urbanismus" (Munich, June 1961).

8 It seems fairly clear, despite the anonymity of the "Professors Group" who purchased the property from the original client midway through construction that Arakawa and Madeline were somehow directly connected to this group, if not the major contributors, and were in large part directly responsible for the house being completed and in fact did have regular access to the house upon its completion.

9 It is worth noting Alexander Klein's 1928 proposal of the "Functional House for Frictionless Living" as an earlier example of the smoothing out Feuerstein is generally references in his essay.

10 Tom McDonough also makes a reference to this *Spur* editorial introduction written in German in note #25 of the introduction to his book *The Situationists and the City* noting that there is a French translation of this passage included in a book by Luc Mercier, *Archives Situationnistes,* vol. 1 (Paris: Contre-Moule and Paralléles, 1997), 53. Translated to English from the German here by Alex Witteman.

11 This tactic was implemented by the Ministry for State Security (Stasi) of the German Democratic Republic and outlined in "Directive no. 1/76 on the Development and Revision of Operational Procedures," section 2.6. https://www. bstu.de/informationen–zur–stasi/quellensammlungen/die–grundsatzdokumente– des–ministeriums–fuer–staatssicherheit/.

12 Two additional panels were produced in 1996 specifically to be included in the 1997 Guggenheim SoHo show. Interestingly, these two panels were intended to be placed together as a kind of diptych and showed a sprawling village-scape of reversible destiny dwellings with the statement "City without graveyards (Reversible Destiny)"; see Michael Govan, *Reversible Destiny: Arakawa Gins: We Have Decided Not to Die* (New York: Guggenheim Museum,/Harry N. Abrams, 1997), 54–111.

13 On this moment of transition towards more overt theoretical architectural explorations see the recent exhibition "Arakawa and Madeline Gins: Eternal Gradient," curated by Irene Sunwoo and installed in the Arthur Ross Architecture Gallery at the Columbia University, Graduate School of Architecture, Planning and Preservation, March 30, 2018 – June 16, 2018.

14 In 1998 the NTT InterCommunication Center (ICC) in Tokyo held an exhibition on these early city planning proposals titled "The City as the Art Form of the Next Millennium ARAKAWA / GINS" from January 24, 1998 – March 29, 1998, which prominently featured a massive physical model of a Reversible Destiny City along with other prints and models of these early urban scale proposals.

15 For instance, see their proposal *Rabbit in the Moon – Longevity Residential Park* (1999) or the *Isle of Reversible Destiny*, Fukuoka (2003) or *Sensorium City*, Tokyo Bay (1994).

16 Also see Lambert's article "A Subversive Approach to the Ideal Normatized Body" https://thefunambulist.net/architectural–projects/architectural–theories–a– subversive–approach–to–the–ideal–normatized–body.

The Bio-Physical Dwelling **277**

17 See Chapter 1 "In Pursuit of Comfort" and Reyner Banham, "A Home is Not a House," *Art in America* 2 (1965): 75.

18 "I remain convinced that architecture cannot be a messianic instrument that would 'liberate' us..."; see Lambert (n.d., para. 5).

19 In general see Langer's books on mindfulness: *Mindfulness* (1991), *The Power of Mindful Learning* (1998), and *Counterclockwise: Mindful Health and the Power of Possibility* (2009).

20 This name is the same as her well-known 1979 experiment which provided evidence of the idea that one's mental and physical environment may be a primary contributing force in one's physical and psychological well-being; see Langer (2009, 5–6, 79–80,164–167).

21 For more on the ideation of "becoming," see Henri Bergson, *Creative Evolution* (1911); Gilles Deleuze Felix Guttari, *A Thousand Plateaus* (1987); Manual De Landa, *A Thousand Years of Nonlinear History* (2000); and Sanford Kwinter, *Architectures of Time* (2001).

References

ARAKAWA+GINS Tokyo Office Web site. 志段味循環型モデル住宅. http://www.architectural-body.com/?p=1260.

Arakawa and Madeline H. Gins. 1979. *The mechanism of meaning: Work in progress (1963–1971, 1978) based on the method of Arakawa.* New York: H. N. Abrams, Inc., Publishers.

———. 1994. *Architecture: Sites of reversible destiny (Architectural experiments after Auschwitz-Hiroshima).* Art and Design Monographs. London: Academy Editions.

———. 2004. *Architecture against dying: Bioscleave house 1999–2004.* Unpublished informational booklet. New York: Reversible Destiny Foundation Archive.

Bernstein, Fred A. 2008. A house not for mere mortals. *New York Times*, April 3. https://www.nytimes.com/2008/04/03/garden/03destiny.html.

Bruggeman, Inge. 2003. A crisis ethicist's directions for use: Or how to be at home in a residence-cum-laboratory. https://www.ingebruggeman.com/A-Crisis-Ethicist-s-Directions-For-Use-or-How-to-be-at-Home-in-a.

Feuerstein, Günther. 1964–1965. Theses on unpremeditated architecture (1958). *Landscape* 14, no. 2 (Winter): 33–37.

Gins, Madeline and Arakawa. 2002. *Architectural body.* Tuscaloosa: The University of Alabama Press.

Hundertwasser, Friedensreich. 1970. Mould manifesto against rationalism in architecture. In *Programs and manifestos on 20th-century architecture*, English ed. Ulrich Conrads, trans. Michael Bullock, 157–160. Cambridge, MA: The MIT Press.

Keane, Jondi. 2005. A bioscleave report: Perceptual learning and the invention of architectural procedures. Paper presented at the International Conference on Arakawa and Gins: Architecture and Philosophy, Paris, France.

Lambert, Léopold. n.d. Toward an architecture that does not know what a body is. *The Funambulist.* https://thefunambulist.net/architectural-projects/arakawagins-towards-an-architecture-that-does-not-know-what-a-body-is.

———. 2014. Architectures of joy: A conversation between two puzzle creatures [Part B]. In *The funambulist pamphlets 8: Arakawa + Madeline Gins*, ed. Léopold Lambert, 41–45. Brooklyn: Punctum Books.

Langer, Ellen J. 1989. Mindfulness. Reading, MA: Addison-Wesley Pub.

———. 2009. *Counterclockwise: Mindful health and the power of possibility.* New York: Ballantine Books.

Lush, Fred Leland. 1997. To think, to invent, to be invented: Reflections on *The Mechanism of Meaning*. In *Reversible Destiny: Arakawa/Gins*, ed. Shūsaku Arakawa, Madekine Gins, Michael Govan and Guggenheim Museum Soho, 43–52. New York: Guggenheim Museum Publications: Hardcover ed. distributed by H.N. Abrams.

Mcdonough, Tom, ed. 2009. *The Situationists and the city*. London: Verso.

Prem, Heimrad, Helmut Sturm, Hans Peter Zimmer, and Lothar Fischer, eds. 1961. Zu Feuersteins inzidenter architektur. *Spur* (München) 5, "Spezialnummer über den unitären Urbanismus" (June).

Reiser, Jesse and Nanako Umemoto. 2006. *Atlas of novel tectonics*. New York: Princeton Architectural Press.

Sadler, Simon. 1998. *The Situationist city*. Cambridge, MA: The MIT Press.

Schonbek, Amelia. 2016. The house where you live forever: The reversible Destiny of Madeline Gins. *The Awl*, August 16. https://www.theawl.com/2016/08/the-house-where-you-live-forever/.

Yamaoka, Nobu and Arakawa. 2010. *Children who won't die*. RTAPIKCAR, Inc. Streaming video, https://vimeo.com/277491410.

Yamaoka, Nobu and Madeline Gins. 2012. *We*. RTAPIKCAR, Inc. Streaming video, https://vimeo.com/278172725.

AFTERWORD

Today, almost two years since I started writing this book and several more since the ideas first began to germinate in my mind, the world has suddenly become a very different place. The onset of the COVID-19 global pandemic precipitously arose in a matter of weeks, forcing us to dramatically and radically alter our everyday actions of living, instigating profound effects on how we inhabit our constructed environments. Our dwelling spaces, our homes, have become more present, taking on a deeper significance in ways previously unfelt or unrecognized. Time itself has become more fluid as the previously felt markers of the traditional workweek have melted away into the unbroken virtual spaces of our many shared screens.

The completion of this manuscript was realized in relative isolation under a "stay at home" order issued by the Ohio Governor on March 22, 2020. The everyday social exchanges of handshakes, hugs, elevator small talk, glances from a coffee shop window at people rushing about, the awkward press of riding a crowded subway car, the collective laughter in a movie theater or the fanatical cheering attending a sporting event are, at this moment, no longer possible, no longer safe. While these necessary measures of isolation have undoubtedly saved an untold number of lives, it has not been easy. We as human-beings, as *Homosapiens*, have in so many ways evolved precisely through our ability to effectively communicate, to inter-act, to socialize, to converse, to exchange and share complex ideas. While we are in no way alone in this ability – many species across the spectrum of life have developed advanced forms of collective communication – humans have no doubt most radically leveraged these abilities toward furthering our inhabitation of the earth, formulating complex societies, technics and arts well beyond any other species. Within this self-imposed collective isolation, we have leveraged our technological advancements and

280 Afterword

creativity to be able to "virtually" connect. However, in the ways that matter most, these "virtual" connections have failed as a substitute for "real" inter-actions with family, friends, colleagues and the everyday social exchanges we had no idea meant so much to daily life.

Over the last number of weeks, the US has largely decided "it's time to open up," to get back to work, to get the economy back up and running. And, as the pandemic continues seemingly unabated, or with another wave coming around the corner all are asking the same question: "When can we just get back to normal?" A reasonable reflection of our collective desire for "real" social inter-action and a tribute to the value of daily life once taken for granted. I too have asked this question to myself many times, hoping to reschedule cancelled events, reestablish new timelines for goals, visit with friends, to simply get on with life, but in finishing this manuscript I have also come to acknowledge a much deeper, somewhat subconscious question that has been waiting in the wings now ready to take center stage: "What does it actually *mean* to get back to normal?" The near total shutdown of daily life and vast segments of the global economy, while creating historic economic and personal devastations for many human-beings, has had no less remarkable contrary effects on the planet and those other "-beings" with whom we share the ecosphere. In a few months of lockdown, there have been radical reductions in CO_2, NO_2 and other atmospheric emissions in many places (Figure 9.1) – the skies over LA, Beijing, Delhi and many global metropolises have turned blue again! Sources of pollution to water and land have been dramatically reduced, and wildlife has begun to reclaim habitat lost through human intervention and development. What has been a deadly pandemic for human-beings has seemed to be an elixir for the health of the ecosphere.

So, "What does it *mean* to get back to normal?" Normal means many things; it means the embrace of the "real" social inter-actions of daily life, but it also means reinforcing a way of living on the planet that is fundamentally destruc-tive and degrading to the majority of "other-beings" inhabiting the world. In the time it's taken to write this manuscript, there have been many significant instances of death and destruction in the ecosphere, undoubtedly rooted in, or exacerbated greatly by, global temperature increases and climate disruption brought about by "normal" human actions. Getting back to normal means eradicating half a billion animals in Australian wildfires triggered by a pro-longed heat wave derived from increasing annual temperatures, its effects surely hastening the extinction process for many animals on the only continent where they exist. Getting back to normal means a continued rise in the intensity, strength and impact of hurricanes (and probably an increase in the rate of their occurrence) due to warming ocean temperatures and higher sea levels. Storms like Hurricane Harvey that hit Texas and Louisiana in August 2017 dropped 40 inches of rain in four days, causing unprecedented catastrophic flooding and $125 billion in damages. Hurricane Maria devastated the island of Puerto Rico

Afterword **281**

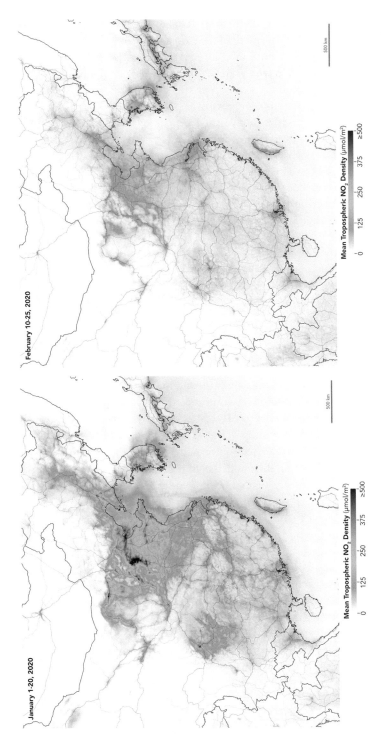

FIGURE 9.1 Comparative maps showing the concentrations of nitrogen dioxide and other pollutive emissions over China before and then during the quarantine, January and February of 2020. Image courtesy of the NASA Earth Observatory.

282 Afterword

in September 2017, causing $90 billion in damages and estimates of up to 4,600 deaths in the catastrophic aftermath of the storm. Getting back to normal means greater intensity and occurrence of wildfires in the western states of California, Oregon and Washington as well as in British Columbia, Canada, due to higher temperatures drying out more vegetation and soil, a reduced rainy season and shifting global wind patterns. A report issued by Governor Gavin Newsom in April of 2019 titled "Wildfires and Climate Change" states that "Fifteen of the 20 most destructive wildfires in the state's history have occurred since 2000; ten of the most destructive fires have occurred since 2015." In 2019, unfathomable fires also raged in the Amazon rainforest in Brazil due to drought but also likely human-made slash-and-burn methods used for clearing land intended for agriculture, livestock, logging and mining operations. It's been estimated that these fires resulted in a loss of over 906,000 hectares of rainforest, directly contributing to the release of CO_2 and CO in the atmosphere through combustion and indirectly through the loss of the forest as a natural carbon sink. There has been an extended heat wave and record temperatures, even reaching above 100 degrees Fahrenheit in June 2020 in the Siberian Tundra, helping to fuel a massive rash of wildfires and accelerating permafrost thawing. Getting back to normal means increased heat waves and droughts worldwide, like the South African drought of 2018–2019 which was the worst in 1,000 years, and heat waves throughout Europe and Northeast Asia in the summers of 2018 and 2019 that killed thousands. Getting back to normal means that the Great Barrier Reef, alongside other major coral reefs throughout the oceans, bastions of oceanic biological diversity, could see worldwide die-offs of 70%–90% in the next several decades. The Great Barrier Reef has already seen a 30% die-off event in 2016, a 20% die-off event in 2017 and in 2020 is undergoing another die-off that is ongoing. And, getting back to normal means the persistence of systemic racial injustice, police brutality and the indiscriminate murder of black and brown bodies. The murder of George Floyd at the knee of the Minneapolis police, among so many others, has rightly sparked immense pain, outrage, the demand for equality and the abolishment of police brutality, requiring us more than ever to physically come together in-the-world, arms locked tightly together in-the-streets. Questioning what normal *means*, questioning how we *choose* to live-in-the-world today, is a matter of life and death – a fact black and brown Americans and many other minority groups in the US and around the globe have felt for generations.

If the COVID-19 pandemic is a wave that's knocked us down, forcing us to hold our breath while simultaneously exposing the many failures in our systems of public health readiness, proactive planning, effective federal governmental leadership, strategic mobilization of resources, general agility to effectively deal with a quickly emerging crisis, systemic inequity and racism, then the megatsunami already spotted on the horizon spurned by global warming and radical climate change may simply be the last thing we ever see – its impending approach a direct result of our "normal" way of how we have chosen and continue to choose to live-in-the-world. Though social inter-action and connection are fundamental requirements of living a healthy life, the devastating events outlined above, as well as countless others that have likely taken place since this book's publication, make clear that returning to "normal" is a choice with "real" consequences not just for humanity but for the entire ecosphere. The COVID-19 pandemic has only revealed how ill prepared we are to effectively deal with a sudden global crisis for which we have no immediate control. While humanity will in all likelihood arrive at a vaccine to effectively deal with COVID-19, there is no such remedy to be discovered for the destabilization of the climate and earth-system already underway. While our future actions may still impact this trajectory, whether to amplify adverse effects through a "business as usual" approach or temper them through focused collective and conscious changes in how we *choose* to live, there really is no going back. If we are to face the coming waves, we must hold our breath and swim; we must *cope*; we must *adapt*; and we must grow gills and webbed feet, and move our bodies with the changing current and learn how to navigate its flows.

This book reflects only a humble attempt to challenge how we have, and how we might in the near future, *choose* to live-in-the-world through the constructed environments we design and ultimately inhabit. It considers architecture a fundamental aspect of this choice and how we might continue to evolve to the changing conditions of the earth-system. While I have tried to position the ideas of this book from a place of acceptance, emerging from the reality now clearly facing us, my hope is that its message is not taken as doomsday prophecy or nihilistic resignation, but rather as a call toward awakening a shared consciousness concerning "Our" relationship to the constructed environments of habitation we design, and those we might imagine. This book does not put forth technical solutions to such questions, there are others much more qualified than I who may make such suggestions; rather, its aim has been to help reconsider how we define our architectural "dwelling place" in the world, thereby changing our relationship to it, from one of control and dominance toward one of identification and engenderment. In the Preface to the 1960 second edition of Le Corbusier's book *Précisions sur un état présent de l'architecture et de l'urbanisme (Precisions on the Present State of Architecture and City Planning)* he writes a simple statement concerning what he views as the principle issue facing architects: "Our problem is this: men [and women] live on the earth." I believe this simple fact has never been more fundamental as we reconsider how we might collectively dwell with and within in its spaces.

R. L. Cincinnati, Ohio
June 2020

INDEX

Note: *Page numbers in italics refer to figures and tables.*

Abraham, Burnden 223–226
abundance, designing for 131
acquired characters 234–235,
  237–240, 247n9
Adam (of Eden) 43, *43*
adaptation 2, 6, 12, 23n2, 55, 141, 181, 185,
  222, 228, 233, 234, 235–246, 247n10
Addington, Michelle 195–198, 201
Adler & Sullivan Architects 61
aeration ponctuelle see under Corbusier, Le
After Geo-engineering (Buck) 24n9, 178n14
Agamben, Giorgio 193–194
Agnetti, Vincenzo 254
agriculture 64, 147, 150, 151–152, 198
air-conditioning *see* HVAC systems
  (heating, ventilating, air conditioning)
Alberti, Leon-Batista 5, 41–43, 50, 56n8;
  fundamental elements of architecture
  41–42, 43; lineaments 41, 42, 43; *On
  the Art of Building* 41–43; structure
  41–42
Allen, Matthew 240
*Almanach de l'Architecture modern (Almanac
  of Modern Architecture)* (Le Corbusier) 62
Altenberg, Lee 244, 245
Amateur's Greenhouse and Conservatory
  (Hibbard) 110n5
Amazon rainforest 282
America: approach to building 52–53
American Blower Corporation 74

animal: as site to inhabit 40–41; as
  sustenance 40; world of 193–195, *194*
Animal Liberation Front (ALF) 178n28
Anthropocene 3, 20, 30, 113, 116, 160, 171
Anthropocene or Capitalocene (Moore) 23n6
Ape to Man 2, 23n3
apocalyptic future *see* collapse, civilization
Appetite (journal) 215n19
Apple (company) 143n15
apportion 250, 275n1
Arakawa and Gins 250–275, 275–276n1–2,
  276n5, 276n8; "A Crisis Ethicists'
  Directions for Use – or How to
  be at Home in a Residence-cum-
  Laboratory" (text) 261–262; *Architectural
  Body* (text) 275–276n2; *architectural body*
  (concept) 253, *253*, 261–262, 266–267;
  architectural surround 7, 250, 252–253,
  253, 261; "Architecture: Sites of
  Reversible Destiny" 251; biocleave 252,
  254, 268; bio-topology 262; "City as
  the Art Form of the Next Millennium
  ARAKAWA / GINS" (exhibit) 276n14;
  configure 200, 251, 252–253, 267–268;
  daily research 261–262; directions for
  use 261–262, 276n6; landing sites 250–
  253, *251*, 268; *Mechanism of Meaning*
  (paining) 269–270, 276n12; *Mechanism
  of Meaning* (text) 270; political potential
  272–273, 275; *procedural architecture*

7, 252, 253–254, 261–263, 267, 270, 274–275; reversible destiny 7, 268–269, 270–272, 275; tentative constructing towards holding 7, 252–253, 261, 268; use of paint 254, *255, 257,* 260; "We Have Decided Not to Die" (exhibition) 269

Arakawa and Gins, architectural works of: Bioscleave House (Lifespan Extending Villa) 6, 254–264, *255–258, 264,* 266–268, *268, 270–271, 273,* 275, 276n3–6; Bridge of Reversible Destiny / The Process in Question 270; Cleaving Wave House 264; External Genome House – Shidami 259–260, *260, 261,* 276n5; Isle of Reversible Destiny Fukuoka *271,* 276n15; Modular Labyrinth House 264; Museum of Living Bodies *20;* Paintings for Closed Eyes 270; Rabbit in the Moon – Longevity Residential Park 276n15; Reversible Destiny House I 264; Reversible Destiny House II (the Critical Resemblance House) 264; Reversible Destiny Lofts – Mitaka (In Memory of Helen Keller) 259–260, *259,* 276n5; Rubber Labyrinth, Critical Resemblances 270; Sensorium City 270, 276n15; Site of Reversible Destiny IV *265;* Trench House 264; Truncated Cone, Critical Resemblances 270

Arakawa, Shūsaku. *Children Who Won't Die* (film) 269; *see also* Arakawa and Gins

architectural origin narratives 5, 30, 33–51, 53; instinctual (physical) 30–32, 41, 43, 47, 55; rational (conceptual) 35, 36, 41, 44–47, 55

Architectural Record (magazine) 214n1

architecture: adaptive benefit 2, 4, 14, 19, 20, 170, 173, 181, 183–184, 188–189, 222–226, 228, 232–233, 234, 261, 283; affirmation, amplification of life 86, 100–101, 214, 223–226, 227, 234, 246n7, 252, 272; form of mediation 27, 85, 123, 234; modernist approach to 61–62, 81n1, 81n3, 81n6, 98, 109, 110n7, 184–185, 188–191, 214n3, 214n9, 215n11, 215n21, 272; sensitive image of 123–124, 138; stimulation by 7, 54, 189, 199–200, 201, 213, 219, 221–222, 229, 231–233, 246n3, 250, 263–264, 265–267, 271, 273–275; as technology 2, 19, 138, 234; toward survival (sustainment) 1–3, 14, 27, 30,

41, 45, 86, 124, 181, 189, 223–226, 232, 234; vernacular 31, 32–33, 45–47, *46,* 60, 82n9

Architecture as Measure (Turan) 179n29

Architecture of the Well-tempered Environment (Banham) 52, 81n5

Architectures of Time (Kwinter) 277n21

Are we human? (Colomina and Wigley) 19, 189, 214n9

Art in America (magazine) 246n2, 277n17

Art OMI 38

Assemblage (journal) 247n11

Atlas of Novel Tectonics (Reiser and Umemoto) 253

atmosphere: carbon sequestration 8, 148, 160, 178n14; design of 101, 206, 209, 213, 227–228, 229–232; interior 5, 27, 51, 60, 69–70, 73, 77–78, 83n22, 85, 87, 96, 197, 205–206, 208

atmosphere-environment: *explication* of 5, 101–102, 104, 105–106, 116, 228; interior 5, 27, 54, 81, 85, 87, 91, 94–95, 100, 109, 223–227, 229; toward life affirmation 5, 38, 81, 95, 100–101, 108, 109, 213, 223–227; toward life destruction 5, 81, 103–106, 109

Auschwitz-Birkenau, concentration camp 107–108, *108, 109,* 111n16

Baldwin, James Mark 6, 235–238, 242–243, 246, 247n9; Development and Evolution 235, 236, 247n9; "New Factor in Evolution" 235

Baldwin effect 6, 235–237, 238, 241, *243,* 247n10

Banham, Reyner 5, 27, 52–54, 74, 77, 81n5–6, 82n9, 82n19, 83n29, 85, 94–95, 100–101, 110n7, 233, 246n6, 277n17; *Architecture of the Well-tempered Environment* 52, 81n5; *Concrete Atlantis* 81n6; "Environmentalist" 85, 110n7; freedom and variability 53, 54–55, 208, 214, 215n20, 219, 228, 233, 246, 274, 275; hollow shells 51; "Home is Not a House" 52, 57n20, 246n2, 277n17; mobile living unit 57n20

Banner, Stuart: *Death Penalty* 111n13

Bartlett, Lewis J.: "Robustness Despite Uncertainty" 56n7

Basalla, George 23n5; "Some Persistent Energy Myths" 23n5

Basile, Salvatore: *Cool* 57n18

Baubotanik tower 38

BBC (Britain) 143n14
beautiful acts 6, 171, 172, 174
Beck, Ulrich 25n24
Beek, Johan van de: "Adolf Loos – Patterns of Town Houses" 214n8
Behrens, Peter 66, 81n7
being: ecological 14, 113, 164; physiological 222; understanding of 21, 265
being-with 20–21, 29, 30, 49, 61, 113, 146, 233, 268, 274–275
Bennetts, Helen: *Understanding Sustainable Architecture* 123–124
Benton, Tim 62–63, 78–79, 81n3
Bergson, Henri: *Creative Evolution* 277n21
Bernard, Claude: *Introduction á l'étude de la medicine expérimentale* (*An Introduction to the Study of Experimental Medicine*) 199
Bernini 56n3
Bertalanffy, Ludwig von 133, 144n23; *Modern Theories of Development* 144n23
Beyond Growth (Daly) 178n17
Beyond the Limits (Meadows) *159,* 177n11
biodegradable *see under* material
biofuel: energy (*see under* energy: renewable)
biological 6, 12, 13, 14, 15, 19, 23n2, 55, 137, 170, 176, 181, 192, 201, 234, 235; determinism 233
bio-physical: stimulation 14, 109, 200, 201, 213–214, 221–223, 231, 233–234, 235, 239–241, 245, 275; inter-action 4, 6, 181, 200, 208, 221–223, 231, 233, 234, 235, 245, 275; needs 193–194, 204–205; sustainment 223–227, 245
Biopolitics and the Emergence of Modern Architecture (Wallenstein) 215n21
bio-power 214, 215n21
bioscleave *see under* Arakawa and Gins
biotechnique *see under* Kiesler, Frederick
Birth of Biopolitics (Foucault) 215n21
Bjørn, Anders: "Absolute versus relative environmental sustainability" 143n17; "Cradle to Cradle Concept" 143n19
body (human) 20, 119, 142n3, 170, 185, 188–189, 191, 196, 198–199, 200, 201, 215n15, 222, 227, 232, 244, 251–252, 262–263, 265, 274; actions by 250, 252, 254, 257–259, 262, 264; equilibrium of 199, 208, 213; standardization of 109, 185, 188, 190, 214n9, 272–274
Bogner, David: *Frederick J. Kiesler: Endless Space* 215n14

Bookchin, Murray (Lewis Herber) 24–25n18, 116–118, 122–123, 140, 142n2, 142n7, 178n24; *Crisis in Our Cities* 142n7; critique of modern society 25n19; "Ecology and Revolutionary Thought" 23–24n18; *Our Synthetic Environment* 116, 142n7; "Thinking Ecologically" 25n19, 178n24
Borasi, Giovanna: "Environ(ne)ment" (exhibit) *203–204;* "Environ(ne)ment" (text) 230
botanicals 86, 87, 93, 95, 110n7
Boulding, Kenneth 6, 162–163, 178n19–20; "Economics of the Coming Spaceship Earth" 162–163
Boyle, Gov. Emmet D. 103
Braudel, Fernand 23n4
Braungart, Michael 6, 126–131, 137, 143n18, 161; cherry tree 129–130, 131, 137; *Cradle to Cradle* (text) 127, 143n16; Cradle to Cradle (*see Cradle to Cradle,* approach to design); Designtex 143n18; Ford Truck plant 143n18; NASA Ames Office Building 143n18; Steelcase 143n18; *Upcycle* 130
brazier 87
Brazil 282
BREEAM (Building Research Establishment Environmental Assessment Method) 126
Breuer, Marcel 214n9
Brisbane (Australia) *117*
brise-soleil 83n29
British Columbia (Canada) 282
British New Guiana 95
Brooklyn, New York *52*
Brower, David 151
Brown, Gov. Jerry 160
Bruggman, Inge 261–262, *262;* "A Crisis Ethicists' Directions for Use – or How to be at Home in a Residence-cum-Laboratory" (book design) 261–262
Bruno, Kenny: *Greenwash* 124–125, 142n8
bubble 193–195
Bucharest (Romania) 164
Buck, Holly Jean: *After Geo-engineering* 24n9, 178n14
Bucknell, Erin 208
Buenos Aires 59, 65
Buffalo (New York) 61
building: energy consumption 113, 123–124, 126, 132; as energy flows 132–133,

288 Index

143–144n21; deleterious effects of 122; synthetic materials 120–122, *121, 123*
Burgess, James: "Cross Currents" 142n10
Bushman hut *32*
Business Roundtable press release 177n13

Cahiers d'Art (magazine) 68, 71, 80
California (state) 160–161, 282
Campbell, Joseph 56n6; *Power of Myth* 56n6
campfire 51, 53–55, *54,* 233; thermal differentiation of 53–54
Canadian Center for Architecture (CCA) 203, *203–204,* 230
Cannon, Walter B. 199; *Wisdom of the Body* 199
Capitalism and the Web of Life (Moore) 23n4
capitalist global economic system 3, 6, 15, 16, 22, 23n4, 23n6, 24n17, 113, 123–124, 126–128, 131, 136, 137–138, 144n27, 146, 159–160, 171, 176–177n1, 178n24, 191, 280; growth of 6, 113, 132, 137, 153, 156–158, 162, 178n17
Capitalocene 23n6
capital punishment 103–105, 106, 109, 111n13
carbon capture *see under* atmosphere: carbon sequestration
carbon dioxide (CO_2): global level in the atmosphere 7–8, *9,* 24n14; *see also* emissions, carbon dioxide
carbon footprint *see* emissions, carbon dioxide
Carrier, Willis 77
carrying capacity 150, 177n6
Carson, Rachel 115–120, *120,* 125, 129, 141–142n1, 165–166; *Silent Spring* 115, 116, 119, 125, 142n4; total environment 116
Caus, Salomon de *86*
Cesariano, Cesare *49*
Chadwick, George 95, 100; *Works of Sir Joseph Paxton* 95
Charlson, Robert J.: *Earth System Science* 56n1
Chatsko, Maxx: "Big Oil is Investing Billions in Renewable Energy" 142n9
chemicals, toxic 115–116, 120, 142n2–3; impacting humans 115–116, 119, 142n6
Chicago (Illinois) 61, *130, 174*
Children Who Won't Die (Yamaoka and Arakawa) 269

chimney 57n17
China 142n5, 280, *281*
Christianson, Scott 106
Clear Lake (California) 118
climate 87, 209, 232; actions 13–14; agreeable 42, 56n8; artificial 86, 87, 90, 101, 110n4, 208; engineering of (*see* geoengineering); equilibrium sensitivity of 8, 11; feedback loops in 11; global instability 14, 29–30, 161, 283; interior 86, 94, 110n7, 197, 201, 203, 204–208; micro 209, 213
climate change 13, 48, 113, 120, 161, 171, 177n12, 178n16, 282; activism concerning 7; adapt to 4, 5, 6, 13–15, 17, 22, 109, 113, 160, 174–175, 181, 195, 234, 283; anthropogenic cause of 7–8, 12, 17, 148; cope to 4, 5, 6, 13–15, 17, 22, 109, 113, 160, 174–175, 181, 195, 234, 283; deniers of 3; refugees of 12; tipping points 8, 10
Climates (Graham) 179n29
climax state 135–136, *136, 137,* 147, 177n2
Club of Rome 152
Cohen, Jean-Louis 66, 70, 73, 82n16–17, 83n24
Cohen, Jeffrey Jerome: *Prismatic Ecology* 125
collaboration, collaborative 20, 30, 40, 53, 61, 175, 185, 221, 223, 253
Collapse (Diamond) 24n12
collapse, civilization 24n12, *137,* 147, 150, 153, 156, 159–160, 163, 174, 177n3
Collapse of Complex Societies (Tainter) 147
Collapse of Western Civilization (Conway; Orekes) 24n12
collective, of beings 4, 17, 20, 22, 30, 61, 113, 140, 146, 158, 160, 163, 172, 175, 181, 200, 233, 253, 268, 270–271, 274–275, 279
Colomina, Beatriz 19–20, 187, 189; *Are we human?* 19, 189, 214n9; "Endless Drawing" 188–189; *Privacy and Publicity* 187
Colquhoun, Alan 60; *grands travaux* 60, 81n4; *Modern Architecture* 81n7
Columbia University 191
comfort 3, 27, 49, 51–52, 54–55, 60, 137, 197, 213, 230, 233, 234, 266–267, 274
commerce 15, 16, 126–127, 138, 140, 144n27
compartment map 244, 247n13

Index **289**

concrete (cement) 64, 120, 140, 142n5, reinforced 60, 61, 64, 73, 81n7, 81n8, 120, 214n5
Concrete Atlantis (Banham) 81n6
Condemned Building (Darden) 223
conditions of life *see under* Darwin, Charles
conduction 209
conservation 125, 170
conservative (structure) 52–53
conserved core processes 243–244, 247n12
convection 205–206, 209
convergence 132–133, 142–143n20–21
Conway, Erik M.: *Collapse of Western Civilization* 24n12
cooking 50–51, 147
Cool (Salvatore) 57n18
Cooper, Steven J.: "From Claude Bernard to Walter Cannon. Emergence of the Concept of Homeostasis" 215n19
Cooper Hewitt, Smithsonian Design Museum 200
co-production 4, 5, 6, 19, 20, 22, 48, 113, 170, 176, 181, 185, 189–190, 195, 200–201, 213–214, 219, 223, 228, 234, 245, 267
Corbusier, Le 5, 29, 41, 43–47, 56n12, 59–81, *63, 67–71, 75, 78–79,* 82n18, 83n24, 185, 190, 195, 214n4, 214n6, 283; *aeration ponctuelle* 5, 70–71, *71, 73;* Buenos Aires lectures 59–60, 65, 68, 72, 80, 81n1–2; conditioned air 70, 72–73, 83n22, 83n27; early education of 46, 56n10; *fenêtre en longueur (horizontal strip window)* 62–63, 64, 67–68, 70; four functions *63;* free façade 62; liberation of ground plane 46, 47, 62, 64, 65; lieu de toutes les measures 79–81, modernist conception of architecture 46–47, 59, 60, 66, 185; Modular 188, 214n9; *mur neutralisnat (neutralizing wall)* 5, 70–71, *71,* 73–74, 83n26, 83n29; *pan de verre (window wall)* 5, 61, 62–63, 65–70, *70, 75,* 76–77, *78,* 80; pilotis 62, 63, 64, 65, 82n11; primitive house (temple) 44–47, *44, 46,* 56n10; purity of form (prisms) 5, 45–47, *46,* 56n14, 60, 61, 65–67, 67, *69,* 74, 76–78, 80; regulating lines 45; *respiration exacte* 60, 72, 74, *75,* 76–77, 83n26, 83n29; roof garden 62, 78
Corbusier, Le, architectural works of: Centrosoyus Building 5, 60–62, 64–74, *68, 69,* 76–81, *78, 79,* 81n4, 82n10, 82n16–17, 82n19, 83n25, 83n29; Cité

de Refuge (Salvation Army Building) 62, 76–77, 81n4, 83n26, 83n29; Dom-Ino Houses (L'ossature standard) 62, 81n7; Errázuris House 81n2; Immuebles Villas 81n7; L'Esprit Nouveau Pavilion 73, 82n9; Maison Citrohan 82n9; Maison Cook 60; Maisonsenserie pour artisans 82n9; Maisons La Roche-Jeanneret 60, 82n9; Maison Standarisée 81n7; Mandrot House 81n2; Palais des Nations 45–46, 63–64, 66, 70, 73, 81n4, 82n11; Palais de Soviets 81n4; Pessac Housing (CitéFrugès) 60; Studio Ozenfant 82n9; Swiss Pavilion 62, 82n19; Villa Besnus 82n9; Villa Mongermon 82n9; Villa Savoye 81n2; Villa Schowb 73, 83n23; Villa Stein 60; Weissenhof-Siedlung 60
Corbusier, Le, written works of: *Almanach de l'Architecture modern (Almanac of Modern Architecture)* 62; "Five Points Towards a New Architecture" 62, 64; *L'Esprit Nouveau* 64; *Œuvre Compléte* 76, 82n11; *Précisions sur un étatprésent de l'architecture et de l'urbanisme (Precisions on the Present State of Architecture and City Planning)* 59–60, 62, 79, 81n1, 81n3, 283; *Quand les cathédralesétaient blanches (When the cathedrals were white)* 73, 83n22; *Une maison – un palais (A House – A Palace)* 45–46, 56n10, 60, 63; *VersUne Architecture (Towards a New Architecture)* 29, 44–45, 56n12, 81n8, 214n6; *Urbanisme (City of Tomorrow)* 214n5; *Villa Radieuse (Radiant City)* 72, 74, 76, 77, 214n4
corporeal 201; extra 201; violence 272
correalsim *see under* Kiesler, Frederick
Counterclockwise (Langer) 274, 277n19
COVID-19, global pandemic 279–280, *281,* 282–283
Cradle to Cradle (Braungart and McDonough) 126, 143n16
Cradle to Cradle, approach to design 6, 126–132, 135, 143n16, 143n18, 161
crannog (d'Irlande) 45–47, *46, 47,* 56n13–14, 60
Creative Evolution (Bergson) 277n21
crisis, climatological and ecological 3, 4–5, 24n10, 126, 144n27, 165; anthropogenic cause of 4, 24n10, 163–164, 178n24; beyond 13, 14, 15, 30, 59, 113, 123, 140–141, 160–161, 170, 173, 181, 213; evidence of 7

290 Index

Crisis in Our Cities (Bookchin/Herber) 142n7
Crispo, Erika 236
Critical Zone 30
Cruzten, Paul 3, 23n6
curtain wall *see* enclosure system (of a building)

Dalkeith Palace 90
Daly, Herman 6, 161; *Beyond Growth* 178n17; "Sustainable Growth" 161–163
Darden, Douglas 223–228, 246n4–5; Composite Ideogram 224–225, *226,* 246n5; *Condemned Building* 223–224; *Douglas Darden: Looking After the Underbelly* (film) 246n4; Oxygen House 223–228, *225, 226, 228, 229;* underbelly 223, 246n4
Dark Mountain Project 14, 24n17
Darwin, Charles 246–247n8; conditions of life 17, 19, 25n20, 27; indefinite variability 25n20; *Origin of Species* 25n20
DDD (chlorinated hydrocarbon) 118
DDT (Dichloro-Diphenyl-Trichloroethane) *117,* 118, 141–142n1–2
death penalty *see* capital punishment
Death Penalty (Banner) 111n13
decentralization 123, 164
decomposition 38, 267
Décosterd, Jean-Gilles 201, 205, 229, 233; Hormonorium (installation) 229–233, *229, 230, 232;* "Physiological Architecture" 201
Deep Ecology (Devall and Sessions) 166
Deep Ecology movement 6, 164–172, 176, 178n23–24, 270; concept of morality 170–171; Earth wisdom 165–166; *formal* sense 165–166; *philosophical* sense 166–168; *popular* sense 169–170; questioning more deeply 165–166
Deep Green Resistance (DGR) 178n28
de-growth 162, 178n18
DeLanda, Manuel: "Immanence and Transcendence in the genesis of form" 144n24; *Thousand Years of Nonlinear History* 277n21
Deleuze, Gilles: *Thousand Plateaus* 277n21
design 19–20, 22, 101–103, 140, 144n27, 185, 191, 199, 200, 206, 214–215n10, 219, 221, 228, 231, 233, 272, 275
Detroit (Michigan) 61
Devall, Bill 166; *Deep Ecology* 166

development, process of organismal 213, 219, 237–241, 243–244, 247n12
Diamond, Jared: *Collapse* 24n12
digestive system (digestion) 59
Discipline and Punish (Foucault) 215n21
Dobzhansky, Theodosius 246–247n8; *Genetics and the Origin of Species* 246–247n8
domesticationof space 48
Domus (magazine) 138
downcycling 128
Down to Earth (Latour) 29, 177n5
Dreyfuss, Henry: body dimensional standards 188
Drosophila 221, 238–239
Duke of Devonshire 95, 99
dwelling place 30, 56n2, 166; *architectural* 5, 6, 30, 48, 61, 77, 140, 146, 165, 174, 195, 198, 213, 219, 221, 223, 233, 250, 266, 270–272, 275, 283

Eaarth (McKibben) 24n11
earth 59, 122–123, 148, 169, 279, 283; as a building material (*see* mud); limitations of 6, 152, 156, 161–162, 177n5
Earth First! 178n28
Earth Liberation Army (ELA) 178n28
Earth Liberation Front (ELF) 178n28
Earthmasters (Hamilton) 24n9
earth-system 5, 29, 56n1, 113, 124, 125, 163; transformation of 14, 15, 148, 160–161, 174, 181, 283
Earth System Science (Jacob; Orians; Rodhe) 56n1
Earth System Science (Lenton) 56n1
East Hampton (New York) 254, *255, 257, 258, 273*
ecocentric 163–164
ecocritique 20–21, 125
eco-effective: approach to design 6, 113, 127–129, 131–132, 135, 137, 140, 161
eco-efficient: approach to design 113, 127
ecological environment *see under* environment
ecological: economics 161–163; explication 116–117, 120; restoration 137; self 6, 113, 167–168, 170, 171, 173–174, 175–176; thought (thinking) 125, 129, 164, 173
ecology 56n2, 115, 119, 137, 143n11, 164–165, 168; social 178n24; transpersonal 170, 171, 173–174
Ecology Without Nature (Morton) 17

economy: circular 129, 140; development of 82n13, 123, 144n27, 152, 162–163; as energy hierarchy 135; growth of 82n13, 119, 130–131, 152, 153, 156, 161–163, 177n17; local 138, 140; restorative 137–138, 144n26; steady-state 161–163

eco-philosophy 126, 163–165, 169, 178n24

ecosophy see under Naess, Arne

ecosphere 12, 161, 169, 170, 171

ecosystem 115, 118, 119, 125, 129, 131, 135, *136,* 140, 162, 177n6; toxification of 116, 118–119

Edwardes-Evans, Henry: "Cross Currents" 142n10

egalitarianism 123, 164, 169, 170, 172

Ehrlich, Anne and Paul 6, 151, 156, 161, 177n9; *Population Bomb* 151–152, 178n17; "Population Bomb Revisited" 151; scenarios 151

Eisen, Charles 36, *37*

electrocution *see* execution

elementarization (composition) 60, 66

emergy 148, 150

emissions, carbon 8, *9,* 11, 120, *121,* 123, 140, 148, 280, *281,* 282; business as usual approach to 8, 11, 163–164, 283; current amount of 10, 142n5; reduction of footprint 10, 113, 124, 160; sequestration of (*see under* atmosphere)

emissions, greenhouse gas: global amount of *9,* 10, 24n13, 24n15, *122,* 178n16; reduction of footprint 15, 148, 280, *281*

Empire, State & Building (Moe) 133

enclosure system (of a building) 41–42, 45, 50, 61–62, 71, 73, 77–78, 80–81, 82n19–20, 83n26, 96–97, 195–197, 255–256

Encyclopedia Britannica Online 143n11, 177n7, 215n16, 212n18

End of Nature (McKibben) 24n12

energy: cheap 146; consumption of 15, 113, 123–124, 126, 127, 148, 150, *150,* 177n2, 206, 230; flows of 132–133, *134,* 135–136, 147, 177n2, 206, 208; global system of 11, *121,* 132, 150, 177n4; hierarchy of (transformation) 135, *149;* new forms of 23n5; renewable sources of 14, 125, 132, 144n26, 147–148, 150, 177n4

Engels, Frederick: "Role of Labour in the Transition from Ape to Man" 23n3

England 50, 87, 94, 110n5

envelope (building) *see* enclosure system (of a building)

environment: architectural, built, constructed 14, 15, 30, 80, 106, 113, 122, 123, 127, 133, 135, 140, 143–144n21, 146, 161, 164, 167, 170, 171, 172–173, 175–176, 190–191, 198, 199, 203, 213, 218–219, 221–223, 234, 245–246, 250, 253, 264, 274–275, 279, 283; concept of 15–18, 20, 25n24, 80, 101, 115, 125, 168, 181, 184–185, 193–195, 196, 198, 200–201, 218–219, 233, 245, 274; control of 2, 21, 53, 93, 95, 116, 126, 140–141, 144n27, 173, 213, 218–219, 283; design of 1–2, 18, 19–20, 99, 101, 116, 146, 215n17, 218, 221, 269; ecological 100, 110, 120, 122, 127, 175, 213, 221; equilibrium with 5, 20, 59, 61, 80, 124, 161–163, 164–165, 199, 201, 222, 274; human impact on (degradation of) 12, 15, 23n7, 24n18, 31, 48, 113, 116–120, 122–124, 127, 130, 135, 137, 143–144n21, 147–148, 152, 160–163, 168–169, 170, 171, 172, 174, 177n9; identification with 4, 5, 113, 163, 167–168, 171, 173, 221, 283; impact on human health 119, 122, 142n6, 162–163, 183–184, 199, 214n3, 222, 223–226, 232–233, 261, 274–275; mediation of 5, 27, 30, 40, 43, 46, 47, 51, 60–61, 69, 76, 83n29, 85, 91, 170, 181, 190, 196, 221, 234; potentials of 4–5, 20, 22, 185, 190, 234; relationship with organisms 1, 16, 18, 19, 20, 25n20, 85, 122, 129, 183–185, *184,* 189–192, 193–200, 201, 213–214, 215n17, 219, 221–222, 223–226, 229–234, 235, 237–243, 245, 246n3, 250–252, 250–251, 262, 268, 274; thermal 50, 54, 196–198, 205–208, 213

environmentalism 17

environmentalist 116, 127, 131, 156; approach to architecture 5, 27, 100–101, 109

Environment, Power and Society (Odum) 133; 144n22

epigenetic landscape 6, 239–243, *241, 242,* 247n11

equilibrium state (economy) *see* economy: steady-state

Essai sur l'architecture (Essay on Architecture) (Laugier) 35–36, *37*

Essay on the Principle of Population (Malthus) 151

292 Index

Ethics (Spinoza) 167
evaporation 209, *211–212*
evidence-based design 188, 214–215n10
Evidence-Based Design for Multiple Building Types (Hamilton and Watkins) 214–215n10
evolvability 245
evolution: concept of 218, 246–247n8; influence our 221; mechanism of 234–235; process of 199, 219, 236, 243–245, 247n9, 269
exact breathing *see under* Corbusier, Le: *respiration exacte*
execution: method of electrocution 103–104, 105, 111n13; method of hanging 105; method of lethal gas 103–106, 111n13–16; mobile 105; predictability (lethal gas) 105, 111n14–15
extinction 48, 113, 120, 280

façade 56n3, 62, 63, 66–69, 68, 73–74, 76–77, 82n17, 95–97
facilitated variation 243–244
Facing Gaia (Latour) 3
Feliz, Nerea: Hidden in plain sight *176*
fenêtreen longueur (horizontal strip window) *see under* Corbusier, Le
Fernández-Galiano, Luis 23n2
Feuerstein, Günther 265, 266–267, 276n7, 276n9; impractical flats 265–267; "Theses on Unpremeditated Architecture" 267
Field Notes from a Catastrophe (Kolbert) 24n12
Filarete 5, 43, *43*; *Treatise on Architecture* 43, 56n9
fire (flame) 35, 50–51, 87; discovery of 49–50, *49*; protection of 50–51, 61; tending to 51, 57n16
fireplace 50; flue 87–89, *88*
five year plan 64, 82n13
floor (architectural element) 42, 63, 68, 88–89, 254–260, *254, 255*
Floyd, George 282
forcing (of plants) 86, 110n2; frame (house) *88, 92*
Fordism 188
fossil fuels: coal 11, 51, 89, *90*; concentrated energy 3, 147–148; dependence on 14, 16, 120, 146; twentieth-century use of 3, 120–121, 147–148, 150
Foucault, Michel: *Birth of Biopolitics* 215n21; *Discipline and Punish* 215n21

Foundation Le Corbusier 82n14, 82n17, 83n28
Four Elements of Architecture (Semper) 50
Fowler, Thomas 89
Fox, Warwick 126, 163–164, 165–171, 178n25; *Towards a Transpersonal Ecology* 165, 178n23, 178n26
Frampton, Kenneth 64, 76–77; *Modern Architecture* 81n7
Francis, Pope: encyclical letter on climate and ecological crisis 4, 24n10
Franzen, Jonathan 13–14; "What if we Stopped Pretending?" 13
Frederick J. Kiesler: Endless Space (Bogner and Noever) 215n14
freedom and variability *see under* Banham, Reyner
Friedrich Kiesler: Endless House / Friedrich Kiesler-Zentrum Wien 215n14
fuel: sources of 11, 51, 89, 146–148
Fuller, Buckminster: *Operating Manual for Spaceship Earth* 178n20; Spaceship Earth 178n20; standardized living unit 57n20
functionalist, functionalism 185–187, 188–191, 229–230, 265–267
furnace 51, 89, *90*

Gaia *see under* Lovelock, James
Gallman, Angela 254
Gandhi, Mahatma 167
García-Germán, Javier 233
garden: design of 86–87
Gardener's Chronicle 96, 98, 111n10
gas (toxic): humane use of 103–106, 109; technologies 100, *102,* 103, 105, 106
gas chamber 5, 85, 101, 103–107, *104, 107,* 109, 111n13, 111n15–16
Geddes, Sir Patrick 190–191
gene, genome, genotype 219, *220,* 223, 234–235, 236, 237–242, 247n14; mutation in 115; potentials in 219, 234, 237, 243–244
genetic: assimilation 238–240, *243*; determinism 219; drift 240; fixation 234–236, 238–239, 241–242, 244, 246
Genetics and the Origin of Species (Dobzhansky) 246–247n8
Geneva, Lake 64
Geneva (Switzerland) 45, 82n11
geoengineering 3, 13, 24n9
geometry (mathematical order) 41–42, 43–45, 61, 80, 185, 188, 196

Gerhart, John 237, 243–244, 247n12–14; "Evolvability" 247n14; *Plausibility of Life* 237, 247n12

Germanification, re- (resettlement) 107–108

Ghosn, Rania: *Two Cosmograms* 179n29

Gins, Madeline *see* Arakawa and Gins

Gissen, David: "The Architectural Production of Nature, Dendur / New York" 23n1

glass 60, 63, 64, 66–67, 69–72, 74–78, 80, 82n9, 83n27, 87, 89, 92, 105, 110n6

glasshouse 87, 94

glazing (building system) 66–67, 69, 73, 75–76, 89, 92, 96, 185; angle of 90, 91, *91*; double layer of 62, 63, 67, 70, 73–74; ridge and furrow 92–93, *94*, 96–97, 100, 111n11

global warming: above preindustrial times 7–8, 12; actions to limit 10; amplification of 24n13, 160; in pipeline 8; effects of 7, 11, 12, 113, 120, 161, 171, 177n12, 178n16, 280, 282; possible future levels of 8, 10–11, 14; reduction of 10; survival in 14, 160

globalization 30, 177n5

Govan, Michael: *Reversible Destiny: Arakawa and Gins* 276n12

gradient energy 196–198, *197*

Graham, James: *Climates* 179n29

Great Barrier Reef 282

green design 15, 123, 125–126

greenhouse (hothouse) 5, 27, 85–87, 90–101, *90, 91, 93, 94, 97, 98*, 107, 108–109, *108, 109*, 110n5

Green Revolution 151, 177n9

Greenwash (Bruno and Greer) 124–125, 142n8

green-wash 124–125, 160

Greer, Jed: *Greenwash* 124–125, 142n8

Griffis Sculpture Park *172, 173*

Gropius, Walter 61, 81n7, 214n9; Fagus Factory 81n7; model factory (Deutsche Werkbund) 81n7; Tribune skyscraper 81n7

growth 150–152, 153–158, 177n2; sustainable 160–161

Growth Delusion (Pilling) 178n17

Guardian (UK) 23n7, 142n10

Guggenheim Museum SoHo 269

Guttari, Felix: *Thousand Plateaus* 277n21

gutter 89, 96–97

Habit and Instinct (Morgan) 235

Habitations of Man in All Ages (Viollet-le-Duc) 33–35

Haeckel, Ernst 115–116, 143n11

Hamilton, Clive: *Earthmasters* 24n9

Hamilton, D. Kirk: *Evidence-Based Design for Multiple Building Types* 214–215n10

Hansen, James 8

Harmon, D. B. 221–222; "Co-ordinated Classroom" 222

Harvard Gazette 7

Hauschild, Michael Z.: "Absolute versus relative environmental sustainability" 143n17

Hausfather, Zeke 11

Hawken, Paul 137–138, 144n26–27, 156

Hawkins, Waterhouse *2*

Hearn, M. Fil 35

hearth 50–51, 57n17, 255

heating 147, 205; building system 27, 31, 50–51, 54, 70–71, 73–74, 76, 87, 89, 110n6; steam 89, hot water 74, 89, *90*, 100

Heringer, Anna 138–141; "Laufen Manifesto for a Humane Design Culture" 140; METI School 138, *138, 139*, 144n28; Ways of Life house 140–141, *141*

Herrmann, Wolfgang 36

Hibbard, Shirley: *Amateur's Greenhouse and Conservatory* 110n5

Himmler, Heinrich 107–108

Hine, Dougald: *Uncivilization* manifesto 24n17; *see also* Dark Mountain Project

Hitchcok, Henry-Russell: *International Style* (exhibit) 190

Hix, John 88, 92–93, 109n4

Holdren, John 7, 8, 10

home, house 1, 48, 51–52, 54–55, 143n11, 166, 167, 187, 188–190, 195–196, 205, 223–226, 254–255, 259, 262, 265–267, 279

homeostasis 20, 199, 215n19, 222

Homer-Dixson, Thomas 152

Homes Fires Burning (Wright) 50

Hothouses, Greenhouses, and Aquaria etc. (Tod) 99

humanbeings: evolution of 2, 12, 14, 17, 22, 109, 115, 122–123, 147, 161, 181, 185, 188–189, 199, 233, 269, 279; idea of 146, 183, 215n17, 218, 221; primitive shelter *32*, 33, *34*, 35, 40–41, 43–47, 49–50, 56n5, 184, 198, 255, 265;

294 Index

survival of 1–3, 12, 22, 123, 141, 167, 199; thermal needs of 85, 170, 198–201, 208, 213, 232; toxification of 115–118, 142n3, 142n6

humanism 101

humanity 103, 148, 156, 178n24, 274; dominant global force 3; *see also* Anthropocene

humanization of space 47–48, 187–188

human parasitism 24n17

Humboldt, Alexander von 115

Humlebæk (Denmark) 205

Hundertwasser, Friedensreich 266; "Mould Manifesto against Rationalism in Architecture" 266

Huxley, Julian 246–247n8

Huxtable, Ada Louise 31

HVAC systems (heating, ventilating, air conditioning) 27, 31, 51–52, *52*, 54–55, 57n19, 60–61, 69–72, 74, 76–78, 80–81, 83n29, 85, 87, 120, 126, 197–198, 265; digital control of 54–55, 57n20, 274; history of 52, 57n18, 73, 81n5

Hwang, Joyce, (Ants of the Prairie) 172–176, 179n30; Bat Tower *172, 173*; Habitat Wall *174*; habitecture 172–173; Hidden in plain sight *175, 176*; "Living Among Pests" 172–173

Ice age *9, 40*

identification 167–168, 171, 173

IEA (International Energy Agency) 10; World Energy Outlook report 11, 160, 178n15

incorporeal 132–133

indigenous material 138, *138, 139, 140, 141*

Ingels, Margaret: *Willis Haviland Carrier Father of Air Conditioning* 57n18

inosculation 38

Inquiry (journal) 164

insecticide 117–118, 141–142n1–2

Institute of Animal Genetics (Edinburgh) 238

inter-action (interactive) 7, 14, 55, 61, 79, 80, 101, 135, 152, 183, 185, 200, 231, 233, 240, *242,* 245, 269, 274, 279–280, 283; between or with beings 19–20, 30, 48, 119, 131, 132, 167, 181, 193–195; biophysical (*see* biophysical: inter-action); of forces 183, 185; with architecture 188–189, 190–192, 195, 208, 213, 250–252, 253–254, 256–257, 259, 262, 264–266

InterCommunication Center (ICC) 276n14

interior 5, 6, 30, 46, 47, 50, 51, 53–55, 70, 91, 120, 188, 195–196, 199, 254; isolation of (sealed) 27, 55, 60–61, 77, 78, 80, 85, 206, 208

Introduction á l'étude de la medicine expérimentale (*An Introduction to the Study of Experimental Medicine*) (Bernard) 199

Invisible Committee 146

IPCC (Intergovernmental Panel on Climate Change) 7; conservative assessments 8; reports 7, 8, 10, 24n13

iron (building material) 87, *88,* 96; cast 89, *90,* 95, 96, 110n6, 111n10

isomorphies 133, 144n24

Jacob, Michael C.: *Earth System Science* 56n1

Jazairy, El Hadi: *Two Cosmograms* (Ghosn and Jazairy) 179n29

Jeanneret, Pierre 45, 60, 62–64, 67, *68,* 69–71, *69,* 71, 73–74, 77, *78, 79,* 82n17–18; "Five Points Towards a New Architecture" 62, 64

Jenny, William Le Baron 61

Johnson, Philip: *International Style* (exhibit) 190

Journal of Industrial Ecology 143n17

Julliard School of Music 215n13

Kahn, Louis 205

Kant, Immanuel 171

Keane, Jondi 262–263

Ketcham, Christopher: "Fallacy of Endless Economic Growth" 152, 153

Kew Gardens (London) 95

Kewlwy, James 89

Kiesler, Frederick 6, 183–192, *184, 186, 189, 192,* 195, 198, 203, 204, 208, 215n11–13; biotechnique 6, 190–191; correalism, correalist 6, 183–185, 191, 208, 213; endless house 191–192, 215n14; Laboratory of Design Correlation 191; Mobile-Home-Library 191, *192;* poly dimensional design approach 187, 195; psycho-function 188, 195, 208; Space House 190; third environment 183–184, *184;* total environment 184, *184*

Kiesler, Frederick, written works of: "From Architecture to Life" 214n1; "Notes on Architecture" 190; "On Correalism and Biotechnique" 183, 214n1, 215n12;

"Pseudo-Functionalism in Modern Architecture" 185–186; "Space City Architecture" 185
Kingsworth, Paul: *Dark Ecology* manifesto 24n17; *Uncivilization* manifesto 24n17; *see also* Dark Mountain Project
Kirschner, Marc 237, 243–244, 247n12–14; "Evolvability" 247n14; *Plausibility of Life* 237, 247n12
Kjeldsen, Kjeld *207*; "Green Architecture for the Future" 205, *207*
Klein, Alexander: Functional House for Frictionless Living 276n9
Kolbert, Elisabeth 23n7; *Field Notes from a Catastrophe* 24n12; *Sixth Extinction* 23n7
Kostienki (Russia) 40
Kriszat, G. *193, 194*
Kwinter, Sanford 247n11; *Architectures of Time* 277n21; "Landscapes of Change" 247n11

labyrinth 263–264; 272
La Chaux-de-Fonds 46, 62, 73
Lally, Sean, (Weathers) 6, 195–198, 201, 213, 215n15; amplification 198, 199–200; material energies 6, 195, *197,* 198, 199–200, 201, 203, 215n15; SIM House 196, *197*
LaMarche, Jean 223–224
Lambert, Léopold 272–275, 276n16, 277n18; "A Subversive Approach to the Ideal Normatized Body" 276n16; "Towards an Architecture That Does Not Know What the Body is" 272–273
Langer, Ellen 274, 277n19–20; *Counterclockwise* 274, 277n19; *Mindfulness* 277n19; mindful health 274; *Power of Mindful Learning* 277n19
Latour, Bruno 3–4, 15, 18, 20, 22, 24n8, 29–30, 56n2, 113, 177n5; *Down to Earth* 29, 177n5; *Facing Gaia* 3; madness 3–4, 15; mutation in our relation to the world 3–4, 29, 113; *We Have Never Been Modern* 25n23
Laugier, Marc-Antonie 5, 35–37, 38, 56n3, 56n10; *Essai sur l'architecture (Essay on Architecture)* 35–36, *37*; frontispiece 36, *37*; rationalist ideas 36
Lear, Linda 119–120
Leaves of Grass (Whitman) 226
Le Corbusier *see* Corbusier, Le
Le Corbusier – Noble Savage (Vogt) 45
Ledbetter, Ben 246n5; "Digital Darden" 246n5

Ledoux, Claude Nicolas 56n10
LEED (Leadership in Energy and Environmental Design) 126
Lenton, Timothy M. 10, 56n1; "Climate Tipping Points – Too Risky to Bet Against" 10; *Earth System Science* 56n1
Leopold, Aldo 166
l'Eplattenier, Charles 46
Leroi-Gourhan, André 5, 40, 41, 48
L'Esprit Nouveau (Le Corbusier) 64
Levins, Richard 19
Lewontin, Richard 16–19, 219; "Analysis of Variance and the Analysis of Causes" 219
light: as an element of design 27, 31, 42, 52, 62, 69, 92, 185, 200–201, 203–204, 206–208, 214n3, 221–222, 229–230, 255–256
lily, giant water 95, *97,* 98–100
Limits to Growth (Meadows) 6, 152–160, *154–155, 156, 157, 158,* 161
Lindsey, Rebbeca *9*
lineaments *see under* Alberti, Leon Batista
Lipps, Andrea: "Senses" (exhibit) 200
live-in-the-world 5, 6, 21, 22, 23n2, 27, 34, 41, 113, 137, 153, 165, 168, 218, 221; catastrophic change to 15, 22, 61, 140–141; how we choose to 6, 10, 13, 15, 17, 30, 110, 113, 119, 123–124, 126, 135, 146, 152, 158, 161, 164, 169–170, 175, 275, 282–283
locality 42
long sixteenth century 3, 23n4
Loos, Adolf 32–33, 35, 187, 189, 214n8, 215n13; "Architecture" 32–33, 187; conception of culture 33; craftsman 33; draughtsman 33; Moller House 214n8; Müller House 214n8; *Raumplan* 187, 214n8
Los Padres, CA: Forest fire *12*
Loudon, J. C. 87, 89, 90, *91,* 92–93, *93, 94,* 99, 110n3; aquatic house *99*; campanulated house 92, *93*; *Encyclopedia of Gardening* 99; *Remarks on the Construction of Hothouses* 89, 90, 92
Loudon and the Landscape (Sima) 110n3
Louisiana Museum of Modern Art 205, *207*
Lovelock, James 18; Gaia 18
Ludwig, Ferdinand 38
Ludwig, Ryan: "Formation and Variation" 246n1
Lupton, Ellen: "Senses" (exhibit) 200
Lyon, Gustave 70, 71, *71,* 73–74, 83n22

296 Index

Macalister, Terry: "Green Really is the New Black" 142n10
MacArthur, Robert H. *16*
Mackenzie, Sir George 92
macroscopic view 133, 135
Madrid (Spain) 176
Mahayana Buddhism 167
Malthus, Thomas 6, 151, 156, 177n7–8; Essay on the Principle of Population 151
mammoth hut 40
man *see* human-beings
Manhattan (NYC) 133, 190
Mann, Charles C.: "The book that incited a worldwide fear of overpopulation" 177n8
Marek, Lawrence 254
Martin, Reinhold: "Environment, c. 1973" 25n24
Maslow, Abraham 170
Massachusetts Institute of Technology (MIT) 152
mass extinction (sixth) 23n7
Massumi, Brian 132
material: biodegradable 38, 39, 138, 140; flows 132–133, 134, 135
material energies *see* under Lally, Sean (Weathers)
Mauna Loa Observatory 25n14
Mayr, Ernst 246–247n8
McDonough, Tom 267, 276n10; Situationists and the City 276n10
McDonough, William 6, 126–131, 137, 143n18, 161; cherry tree 129–130, 131, 137; Cradle to Cradle (text) 127, 143n16; Cradle to Cradle (*see* Cradle to Cradle, approach to design); Designtex 143n18; Ford Truck plant 143n18; NASA Ames Office Building 143n18; Steelcase 143n18; Upcycle 130
McIntosh, Charles 90
McKibben, Bill: Eaarth 24n11; End of Nature 24n12
McLeod, Mary 81n1
Meadows, Dennis 152, 177n11; Beyond the Limits 159, 177n11; Limits to Growth 6, 152–160, 154–155, 156, 157, 158, 159, 161
Meaning of Evolution (Simpson) 218, 234
mechanical systems *see* HVAC
Medical Society of Allegheny County 103
meeting place 17
megafauna: extinction by humans 41

Mendelism 235, 246–247n8
meteorology 53
Method manufacturing facility 130
Mezhirich (Ukraine) 40
Miasnitskaia Street (Moscow) 65, 67–68, 82n17
Miesvan der Rohe, Ludwig 61, 190; Concrete Office Building 81n7; Friedrichstrasse Glass Skyscrapers 81n7
milieu: internal 199; unlivable 101, 103–104, 163
Miller, Martin 38
Miller, Philip 90
Miller, Robert 227; Douglas Darden: Looking After the Underbelly (film) 246n4
Mindfulness (Langer) 277n19
Ministry for State Security (Stasi) for the German Democratic Republic 276n11
Missouri (state) 105
modern aesthetic 61, 62, 74–75, 79–80, 81n7, 185
Modernage Furniture Company 190
Modern Architecture (Frampton) 81n7, 214n8
Modern Architecture (Colquhoun) 81n7
modern synthesis 234–235, 236, 246–247n8
Modern Theories of Development (Bertalanffy) 144n23
modularity 244–245
Moe, Kiel 132, 143–144n20–21; Convergence 143n20; Empire, State & Building 133
Moholy Nagy, Sibyl 31, 190; Native Genius in Anonymous Architecture 31
monstrous hybrids 127–128
Moore, Jason W. 15, 19, 21, 23n4, 23n5, 176–177n1; Anthropocene or Capitalocene 23n6; Capitalism and the Web of Life 23n4
Moos, Stanislaus von 83n25
Moravian Gap 107
Morgan, C. Lloyd: Habit and Instinct 235
Mori, Stegano 141
Morton, Timothy 17, 20–21, 29; Ecology Without Nature 17
Moscow (USSR) 5, 60, 64–65, 69, 71, 73, 76, 82n17, 83n24, 83n27
Motley Fool 142n9
Moyers, Bill 56n6; Power of Myth 56n6
mud, building material 138, 138, 139, 140

Mumford, Lewis 2, 190, 214n2; Technics and Civilization 2, 214n2; modification of environment 2, 23n2
murneutralisnat *see under* Corbusier, Le
Museum of Modern Art (MoMA) 31, 190
Mustgrave (stove) 88
mutation 3, 4, 29, 113, 115, 237, 238, 239, 242, 245
Myer, Adolf 81n7; Fagus Factory 81n7; model factory (Deutsche Werkbund) 81n7; Tribune skyscraper 81n7

Naess, Arne 6, 164–172, 178n24–27, 270; *ecosophy* 163–165; personal definition of deep ecology (*Ecosophy T*) 164–165, 166–168, 170, 171–172, 178n24, 270; Self-realization! 166–168, 169, 171, 181
Naess, Arne, written works of: "Basics of Deep Ecology" 168; "Equality, Sameness, and Rights" 169; "Self-Realization" 167, 170; "Shallow and the Deep, Long-Range Ecology Movement" 164; "Through Spinoza to Mahayana Buddhism or Through Mahayana Buddhism to Spinoza" 178n25
Nagoya City (Japan) 259, *260, 261*
NASA (National Aeronautics and Space Administration) 8, 195
National Environmental Policy Act (NEPA) 25n24
Native Genius in Anonymous Architecture (Moholy Nagy) 31
natural disasters 7, *12,* 160–161, 280, 282–283
natural resources: consumption of 113, 132, 137, 148, 150, *150, 157,* 158–161; depletion of 152, 153, 156–157, 162–163, 164; extraction of 12, 120, 140, 147
natural selection 235, 236–239, 246–247n8–9
nature 17, 21, 24n17, 25n19, 30, 32, 36, 38, 48, 59, 110n7, 116, 119, 148, 166, 167–168, 170, 171, 181, 191, 223, 233, 271; cheap 146, 176–177n1; control of 48, 92–93, 125–126, 174, 183, 213; elements of 50, 79–80; production of 1–2, 23n1; relation to capitalism 23n6, 138, 144n26, 146, 161, 176–177n1; revolt against 2; rhythm of 48–49
Nature (journal) 10
Nature-Society: dialectic 25n19; dualism 15, 21, 22

Nazis: agricultural estate 107–109; concentration camps 107–109, *108, 109*; mobile gas chamber 105; use of lethal gas 105, 106–107, 109, 111n16
neo-Darwinism 234–235, 236
neo-Lamarkism 234–235
nervous system 19, 59, 201
Neufert, Ernst: body dimensional standards 188
Neutra, Richard 187–188, 214n9, 221–222; design and environment 1, 19, 221–222; *Survival through Design* 1, 221
Nevada (state) 103, 105
new normal 160–161
New York (city) 61
New York (state) 103
New Yorker (magazine) 13
New York Times 31, 55, 103, 153
Newsom, Gov. Gavin: "Wildfires and Climate Change" 282
niche 15–16, *18,* 275; partitioning *16*
Niche Tactics (O'Donnell) 195
NOAA (National Oceanic and Atmospheric Administration) 8, *11,* 24n14; report card 24n13
Noever, Peter: *Frederick J. Kiesler: Endless Space* 215n14
Norms of Reaction *see reactions norm*
North Carolina (state) 105
nutrient cycle: biological 127–129, 161; technological 127–129, 161

obsolescence, built-in, planned, premature 128, 143n14–15
O'Donnell, Caroline 38, 195; *Niche Tactics* 195
Odum, Howard T. 6, 133, 135–136, 144n22, 148, 150, 161, 177n2; *Environment, Power and Society* 133, 144n22
ŒuvreCompléte (Le Corbusier) 76, 82n11
oikos 125, 143n11, 166
Okal, Marianne 82n12, 82n21, 83n30
OMG! (O'Donnell Miller Group): primitive hut 38, *39*
On Adam's House in Paradise (Rykwert) 41
On the Art of Building (Alberti) 41–43
Operating Manual for Spaceship Earth (Fuller) 178n20
orangery *86, 87*
Ord, Tony: *Precipice* 177n3
Oregon (state) 282

298 Index

Orekes, Naomi: *Collapse of Western Civilization* 24n12
organic selection 6, 235–237, *243,* 247n9
Organisers and Genes (Waddington) 239
organism 16, 59, 133, 169, 193–195, 199, 218, 234, 235, 237–241, 243–244, 245, 247n12, 251
Orians, Gordon H.: *Earth System Science* 56n1
Origin of Species (Darwin) 25n20
orthoplasy 235–237
Osborn, H. F.: "A Mode of Evolution Requiring Neither Natural Selection not the Inheritance of Acquired Characters" 235
OSHA (Occupational Safety and Health Administration) 142n6
Oud, J. J. P. 190
Our Synthetic Environment (Bookchin / Herber) 116, 142n7
overpopulation 6, 148, 150–152, 153, 157–158, 177n8

Page-Turner, Sir Gregory 94
Paleolithic 40–41
pan de verre (window wall) see under Corbusier, Le
Paris (city) 62, 64, 73, 77, 82n9, 82n18
Paris Climate accords 10, 24n15
Paxton, Joseph 27, 93–100, *97, 98,* 110–111n7–9; Crystal Palace (Hyde Park and Sydenham Hill) 94, 110n7–8, 111n11; Great Conservatory at Chatsworth 94, 96, 111n11; Victoria Regia House at Chatsworth 94–99, *97, 98,* 110n8, 111n11
Paxton's Magazine of Botany 111n11
Pelt, Robert-Jan: "Machinery of Mass Murder at Auschwitz" 111n16
perception *see* senses, sensation
Perret, Auguste 81n7
pests 173; control of (pesticide) 111n16, 115–118, *116,* 119–120, *120,* 142n2, 165
phenotype 219, *220,* 222, 234–235, 237–241, 244–245, 247n12; plasticity 234, 236, 237–239
Phillips, Stephen 190, 191, 215n12
physiology, physiological 2, 80, 100, 170, 175–176, 183, 188–189, 191–192, 199, 201, *202,* 203–205, 208, 213, 223, 227, 244, 247n12, 274–275; effects of 6, 80–81, 198–199, 204, 213–214, 221–224, 228–232, *232,* 234, 235

Pilling, David: *Growth Delusion* 178n17
Piper, John 239
plan 45, 62, 68, 82n17, 97–98, 185, 187, 205, 263, 271
planetary imaginary 171, 179n29
plants 86–87, 89–91, 93, 108, 148, 172; aquatic 95, 99; exotic 87, 93–95; fruit (citrus) 86–87, 90, 91–92, 209
Plausibility of Life (Kirschner and Gerhart) 237, 247n12
pollution 12, 120, 124, 209, 213; reduction of 113, 160, 164, 280
Population Bomb (Ehrlich) 151–152, 178n16
population growth 132, 140, 148, 150–152, 153, *157,* 158–160, 178n16
posterity 163
Powder River (Oregon) *117*
Powell, Alvin 7–8
power 52, *136,* 144n25, 177n2; applied 53; generation of electrical 51
Power of Mindful Learning (Langer) 277n19
Power of Myth (Campbell) 56n6
Précisions sur un état présent de l'architecture et de l'urbanisme (Precisions on the Present State of Architecture and City Planning) (Le Corbusier) 59–60, 62, 79, 81n1, 81n3
preservation 125, 167, 170
Pressac, Jean-Claude: "Machinery of Mass Murder at Auschwitz" 111n16
primitive hut 1, 30, 34, *35,* 35–36, 38, 44–45, 47, 50
Prismatic Ecology (Cohen) 125
Prometheus 35, 50
proportion 46, 56n14, 65–66
prosthesis 219, 223–226, 245
psychology 13, 100, 163, 170–171, 175, 188–189, 201, 213–214, 222, 233, 267; transpersonal 170–171, 234
pulsing paradigm 135, *136, 137,* 141, 144n25, 177n2

qualitative materials 27
Quand les cathédrales étaient blanches (When the cathedrals were white) (Le Corbusier) 73, 83n22
quietists 24n8

Radford, Antony: *Understanding Sustainable Architecture* 123–124
radical stability 5, 54, 55
Rahm, Philippe 6, *22,* 201–213, 229–233; interior climate 203, *203*; meteorology

203, 205, 208; "Physiological
Architecture" 201
Rahm, Philippe, architectural works of:
Central Park, Meteorological Garden
22, 202, 208–213, *210–212;* Domestic
Astronomy (installation) 205–208, *207;*
Hormonorium (installation) 229–233,
229, 230, 232; Interior Weather
(installation) 203–204, *203, 204;* Mollier
Houses 205, *206*
Ramirez–Balas, C. "Mur Neutralisant as an
active Thermal System" 83n26
Ransome, Ernest L. 61
Rawlings state prison *104*
RCP8.5 scenario 11
Reader's Digest 111n15
reaktionsnorm (Norms of Reaction) 6, 219,
220, 221, 234, 237, 243, 245, 246n1
reciprocity: approach to design 113; with
architecture 14
recycling 128
reductionism 218
regenerative (structure) 52–53
regulated air 70, 73
Reiser, Jesse 253; *Atlas of Novel Tectonics*
253; dynamic poise 253
relative humidity: as an element of design
200, 203, 205, *206,* 207, 213, 230
Remarks on the Construction of Hothouses
(Loudon) 89, 90, 92
Renaissance 86
respiration, respiratory system 59, 72, 198,
223–225, 229, 231
Reuters 143n15
reversible destiny *see under* Arakawa and Gins
ribbon window *see under* Corbusier, Le:
fenêtreen longueur (horizontal strip
window)
ridge and furrow *see under* glazing
Ritchie, Justin 11
Rodhe, Henning: *Earth System Science*
56n1
Rome 86
roof (architectural element) 42, 50, 53,
89, 92, *94,* 95–96, 196, *197;* most basic
protective barrier 42–43, 61; structure
of 36, 38, 40, 87, *90, 91,* 92, *94,* 95–98,
100, 111n11
Roswag, Eike *138, 139*
Rousseau, Jean-Jacques 47, 56n10
Rudofsky, Bernard 5, 31, 33; *Architecture
without Architects* (exhibition) 31; non-
pedigreed architecture 31

Rudrapur (Bangladesh) 138, *138, 139*
rue de Sévres 68, 82n18
Rush, Fred Leland 269–270
Rykwert, Joseph 32–33, 41, 43; *On Adam's
House in Paradise* 41

Sackett & Wilhelms *52*
Sadler, Simon: *Situationist City* 265–266
St. Gervais (church) 56n3
Saint-Gobain 74, 83n26
St. Louis (Missouri) 61
St. Sulpice (church) 56n3
S & P Global Platts Insight 142n10
Schellenberger, Michael: "Why renewables
can't save the planet" 177n4
Schindler, R. M. 214n9
Schomburgk, Sir Robert 95, 99
Sea Shepard Conservation Society 178n28
selective (structure) 53
self-defense 170–171, 178n28
self-realization 113, 168, 170, 187
Self-realization! *see under* Naess, Arne
self-world 175, 193–195, 200, 251
semidome 92
Semper, Gottfried 5, 50, 51; *Four Elements
of Architecture* 50
sensation, senses, sensual (perception) 6,
175, 183, *186,* 187–189, 189–190, *189,*
191–192, 193–200, *193,* 201–203,
205, 208, 209, 213, 215n16, 215n18,
222, 231, 251–252, 254, 256, 259, 265,
274–275
sensorial design 187, 200, 203
Sessions, George 166; *Deep Ecology* 166
Siberian Tundra 282
Sierra Club 151
Silent Spring (Carson) 115, 116, 119, 126,
142n4
Simo, Melanie Louise: *Loudon and the
Landscape* 110n3
Simpson, George Gaylord 218, 221,
234–235, 236, 237, 246–247n8; *Meaning
of Evolution* 218, 234; new evolution
218, 234
Situationist City (Sadler) 265–266
Situationist International 265–266
Situationists and the City (McDonough)
276n10
Sixth Extinction (Kolbert) 23n7
Slawinski, Emma: "Cross Currents"
142n10
Sloterdijk, Peter 2, 5, 101, 105, 228;
explication of environment 101–102,

104, 105–106, 116, 228; *Terror from the Air* 101

smart home 5, 54–55, 57n22, 100, 274

Smithsonian Magazine 177n8

socialization, human 48–50, 54, 55, 57n15

social unrest 29–30, 144n27, 163

Socrates 166

solar: energy (*see under* energy: renewable); exposure, orientation, radiation 59, 61, 70, 85, 87, 89, 91–92, *91, 94,* 110n2, 148

Solutrean village 40

sophos 166

South Atlantic Quarterly (journal) 144n24

Soviet Union (USSR) 5, 60, 64–65, 74, 76, 77, 82n13

Spaceship Earth 162–163, 178n20

speciation 17; types of *18*

Spinoza: *Ethics* 167; conatus 167

spirituality, spiritual 40–41, 54, 80, 163, 165–166, 190, 214

Spur (journal) 265, 267, 276n7, 276n10

SS (Schutzstaffel) 107–108

Stebbins, George Ledyard 247–248n8

steel 59, 61, 64, 68, 120, 214n5

Stempel, Jonathan: "Apple to pay up to $500 million to settle U.S. lawsuit over slow iPhones" 143n15

Stoermer, Eugene F. 3, 23n6

stove 51; as heat source 87, *88, 89*

Strandesen, Maria: "Cradle to Cradle Concept" 143n19

Strategy of the Genes (Waddington) 240, 242

structural system (of a building) 31, 34, 36, 38, 61–62, 73

succession, concept of 135–136, *136, 137,* 147, 148

Sullivan, Louis 204

Sunwoo, Irene: "Arakawa and Madeline Gins: Eternal Gradient" 276n13

Survival through Design (Neutra) 1, 221

sustainability 20–21, 123–125, 127, 136, 143n17, 146, 161, 170; current disciplinary model of 5–6, 15, 21, 113, 123–124, 126, 135–138, 168, 174

Sutich, Anthony 170

synthetic theory *see* modern synthesis

systems theory methodof analysis 6, 133, *134,* 135, *136,* 152, *154–155, 156*

Taichung City (Taiwan) 208–209

Tainter, Joseph: *Collapse of Complex Societies* 147

tataki 258, 260

Taylor, William M. 92

Taylorism 188

Tchéco-Verre 74–75

technics 3, 19, 101, 214n2, 279

Technics and Civilization (Mumford) 2

technological mediation 4, 5, 27, 30, 41, 47, 77, 80, 85, 106, 109, 221

technology, tools: use and advancement of 16, 50–51, 74, 113, 124, 126, 147, 151, 153, 156–158, 161, 163–164, 168, 174, 198, 200, 279; capitalization of 54–55, 57n19; of modern construction 27, 59–61, 64, 73, 81n1, 81n7, 185, 214n5; smart 54–55, 274

temperature: as an element of design 27, 196–197, 200, 203, 205–208, 213, 229–230

temperature, global: anomalies in *11;* increases in (*see* global warming)

Terrestrial 29–30, 40, 49, 56n2, 61, 77, 125, 140, 146, 174, 177n5, 195, 198, 214, 219, 221, 223, 233–234, 250, 270–272, 275

Terror from the Air (Sloterdijk) 101

terrorism 101

thermosiphon 89

Thoreau, Henry David 116

Thousand Plateaus (Deleuze and Guttari) 277n21

Thousand Years of Nonlinear History (DeLanda) 277n21

Thresholds (journal) 246n1

throughput 162, 178n21

tipping points *see under* climate

Tod, G: *Hothouses, Greenhouses, and Aquaria etc.* 99

Tokyo (Japan) 258, *258,* 270, 276n14

tools *see* technology, tools

Tortosa, Guy 231

Towards a Transpersonal Ecology (Fox) 165, 178n23, 178n26

transduction 198

Treatise on Architecture (Filarete) 43, 56n9

Turan, Neyran: *Architecture as Measure* 179n29

Two Cosmograms (Ghosn and Jazairy) 179n29

Uexküll, Jakob von 6, 193–195, 193, 194, 198, 251; carriers of significance 194, 194, 198; functional cycle 193–194, 193; "Streifzugedurch die Umwelten von Tieren und Menschen" (A Stroll

Through the Worlds of Animals and Men") 193

Umemoto, Nanako 253; *Atlas of Novel Tectonics* 253; dynamic poise 253

Umwelt 6, 193–195, *194,* 198, 251

U.N. (United Nations) 12, 123

Understanding Sustainable Architecture (Bennetts, Radford and Williamson) 123

Une maison – un palais (A House – A Palace) (Le Corbusier) 45–46, 56n10, 60, 63

Uninhabitable Earth (Wallace-Wells) 10

United Kingdom 87

United States (US) 103, 106, 280, 282; Army, Signal Corps *102*

Upcycle (Braungart and McDonough) 130

upcycling 6, 130–133, 135, 161

Upper Silesia (Poland) 107

urbanization 122, 143–144n21, 185, 208–209, 214n4

US Bureau of Mines 142n5

US Geological Survey *121,* 142n5

US Green Building Council 143n13

Vassivièreen Limousin (France) 205

Venice Biennale 229, *229, 230, 232*

ventilation 51, 68, 85, 87, 96, 100, 105, 205, 206

Versailles, Chateau de 56n3

Vers Une Architecture (Towards a New Architecture) (Le Corbusier) 29, 44–45, 56n12, 81n8

Victoria regia (Victoria amizonica) 95, 97, 98–100

Villa Radieuse (Radiant City) (Le Corbusier) 72, 74, 76, 77

Viollet-le-Duc, Eugéne-Emmanuel 5, 33–35; Habitations of Man in All Ages 33–36

visceral experience 61, 80–81

visual 105; connection to nature 61, 78, 79–81

Vitruvius 5, 49, 51, 57n15

Vogt, Adolf Max 45–47, 56n10, 56n11, 56n13; Le Corbusier – Noble Savage 45

Waddington, Conrad H. 6, 238–243, 241, 242, 243, 246, 247n12; canalisation 238, 241, 241, 243; "Genetic Assimilation of an Acquired Character" 238; *Organisers and Genes* 239; *Strategy of the Genes* 240, 242

wall: architectural element 42, 43, 55, 61–63, 69–70, 73, *78,* 80, 87–89, 96–98, 185, 190, 196, 255

Wallace-Wells, David 10–11, 13, 24n15, 142n5, 160; *Uninhabitable Earth* 10

Wallenstein, Sven-Olov: *Biopolitics and the Emergence of Modern Architecture* 215n21

Warbler *16*

Washington (state) 282

waste equals food 129, 144n26

Watkins, Davis H.: *Evidence-Based Design for Multiple Building Types* 214–215n10

We (Yamaoka) 254

web of life 15, 17, 22

We Have Never Been Modern (Latour) 25n23

Western spruce budworm *117*

White, Lynn, Jr.: "Historical Roots of Our Ecological Crisis" 163–164

Whitman, Walt 226; *Leaves of Grass* 226; "Song of the Open Road" 226–227

Wigley, Mark 19–20, 189; *Are we human?* 19, 189, 214n9

Wilde, Sir William Robert Willis 46

wildfire *12,* 160–161, 280, 282

William McDonough + Partners *130;* Designtex 143n18; Ford Truck plant 143n18; NASA Ames Office Building 143n18; Steelcase 143n18

Williamson, Terry: *Understanding Sustainable Architecture* 123–124

Willis Haviland Carrier Father of Air Conditioning (Ingels) 57n18

wind: energy (*see under* energy: renewable)

Wisdom of the Body (Cannon) 199

Woltereck, Richard 6, 219

Works of Sir Joseph Paxton (Chadwick) 95

world: changing of 4, 6, 151, 161, 214, 234, 245; concept of 125, 126, 193, 200, 269; construction (remaking) of 17, 47–49, 192–195, 200, 201, 251–252, 270–271; limitations of (*see under* earth); new 11, 13–15, 17, 22, 109, 120, 160, 181, 195, 200, 219, 228; our place within the 17, 126, 140, 160, 163, 165, 169–170, 171, 174

World3 152, 178n19

World Bank 161

world-ecology 21, 22, 49, 113, 116, 123, 126, 130–133, 135, 148, 160, 162, 168, 170, 200, 214, 233

World Commission of Environment and Development 123; "Our Common Future" 123

302 Index

World Future Research Conference 164
World Green Building Council 120
world system 151–152, *154–155*, 153; feedback loops in 152, *156*; standard model of 153, *157*; stable model of 156–157, *158, 159,* 160; steady state relationship to 157–160
World War I: gas attacks *102,* 103, 106
World War II 106, 107
Wright, Lawrence 50–51, 57n16; *Homes Fires Burning* 50

Wright, Sewall: adaptive landscape 240
Wyoming (state) *104*

Yamaoka, Nobu: *Children Who Won't Die* (film) 269; *We* (film) 254
Ypres Salient 100

Zardini, Mirko: "Environ(ne)ment" (exhibit) *203, 204*
zersetzend 267
Zykon B 111n16